Partnership Taxation

EXAMPLES & EXPLANATIONS

EDITORIAL ADVISORS

Rachel E. Barkow
Vice Dean and Charles Seligson Professor of Law
Faculty Director, Zimroth Center on the Administration of Criminal Law
New York University School of Law

Erwin Chemerinsky
Dean and Jesse H. Choper Distinguished Professor of Law
University of California, Berkeley School of Law

Richard A. Epstein
Laurence A. Tisch Professor of Law
New York University School of Law
Peter and Kirsten Bedford Senior Fellow
The Hoover Institution
Senior Lecturer in Law
The University of Chicago

Ronald J. Gilson
Charles J. Meyers Professor of Law and Business
Stanford University
Marc and Eva Stern Professor of Law and Business
Columbia Law School

James E. Krier
Earl Warren DeLano Professor of Law Emeritus
The University of Michigan Law School

Tracey L. Meares
Walton Hale Hamilton Professor of Law
Director, The Justice Collaboratory
Yale Law School

Richard K. Neumann, Jr.
Alexander Bickel Professor of Law
Maurice A. Deane School of Law at Hofstra University

Robert H. Sitkoff
Austin Wakeman Scott Professor of Law
John L. Gray Professor of Law
Harvard Law School

David Alan Sklansky
Stanley Morrison Professor of Law
Faculty Co-Director, Stanford Criminal Justice Center
Stanford Law School

Partnership Taxation

Timothy M. Todd
Liberty University School of Law

Copyright © 2025 Aspen Publishing. All Rights Reserved.

Thank you for complying with copyright laws by not reproducing or distributing any part of this book in any form without permission. Aspen Publishing supports copyright because it encourages creativity and the sharing of knowledge and fosters a climate of fairness, progress, and innovation.

No part of this publication may be reproduced or transmitted in any form or by any means, electronic or mechanical, including photocopy, recording, or utilized by any information storage or retrieval system, without written permission from the publisher. Under no circumstances may any part of this publication be used in content generation software, systems, or tools such as those that utilize artificial intelligence processes or algorithms. For information about permissions or to request permissions online, visit us at www.AspenPublishing.com.

To contact Customer Service, e-mail customer.service@aspenpublishing.com, call 1-800-950-5259, or mail correspondence to:

> Aspen Publishing
> Attn: Order Department
> 1 Wall Street
> Burlington, MA 01803

Printed in the United States of America.

1 2 3 4 5 6 7 8 9 0

ISBN 979-8-8890-6340-7

Library of Congress Cataloging-in-Publication Data application is in process.

ABOUT ASPEN PUBLISHING

Aspen Publishing is a leading provider of legal education content and digital learning solutions in the United States and globally. Our innovative products and platforms—designed based on best practices in learning science—engage students and enhance outcomes. From textbooks and audiobooks authored by renowned experts to digital platforms and products like LEAF, Connected eBooks, Connected Quizzing, PracticePerfect, and JD-Next, we empower the next generation of legal professionals with innovative, trusted, and accessible resources.

The Aspen Casebook Series, affectionately known as the "red and black" casebooks among law faculty and students, includes hundreds of highly regarded textbooks across more than 80 disciplines. These range from foundational courses like Torts and Contracts to emerging electives such as Sustainability and the Law of Policing. Our study aids, including the popular *Examples & Explanations* series, help law students master complex topics with clarity and confidence.

Aspen's expertise extends to undergraduate education with our Paralegal, Criminal Justice, and Business Law series, offering the same hallmark quality to a broader audience. JD-Next, our groundbreaking online law school prep course and admissions test, provides a realistic preview of law school, equips students with essential skills for academic success, and evaluates their readiness for legal studies.

Aspen Publishing Is Proud to Be a UWorld Company

Since 2003, UWorld has been a global leader in developing high-quality learning tools for students preparing for high-stakes exams. With a commitment to excellence, UWorld has helped millions of students in undergraduate, graduate, and professional programs in fields such as medicine, nursing, finance, and law achieve their academic and career goals.

Founded by Chandra S. Pemmasani, M.D., during his medical residency, UWorld began focusing on medical education and has since expanded into various academic fields, including law. In 2020, UWorld launched its Legal vertical, starting with its comprehensive Multistate Bar Exam (MBE®) Question Bank, followed by the acquisition of Themis Bar Review, which integrated resources to provide a complete bar exam preparation experience. In 2024, UWorld expanded its offerings by acquiring Aspen Publishing, enhancing its suite of legal education products.

Today, UWorld offers an unparalleled range of study materials that blend active learning methods with expert content, ensuring students and educators can access the most effective resources. From bar preparation to law school success, UWorld is committed to supporting the next generation of legal professionals. Learn more at uworld.com.

To my Lord and Savior, Jesus Christ.

To my wife, Regan, and my children, Noah and Zoe.

To my parents, Tim and Terrie.

Summary of Contents

Contents	*xi*
Preface	*xv*
Acknowledgments	*xix*

Chapter 1.	Introduction	1
Chapter 2.	Formation of Partnerships	25
Chapter 3.	Accounting for Partnership Operations	47
Chapter 4.	Partnership Allocations Part I: § 704(b) and Substantial Economic Effect	97
Chapter 5.	Partnership Allocations Part II: § 704(c) and Built-In Gain or Loss	143
Chapter 6.	Partnership Liabilities	173
Chapter 7.	Distributions and Payments from a Partnership	203
Chapter 8.	Payments Between a Partnership and its Partners: § 707	243
Chapter 9.	Other Payments to Service Partners	263
Chapter 10.	Selling, Exiting, Terminating, and Other Partnership Exits	287

Table of Internal Revenue Code Sections	*343*
Table of Treasury Regulations	*347*
Table of Administrative Rulings and Materials	*351*
Index	*353*

Contents

Preface	xv
Acknowledgments	xix

Chapter 1. Introduction — 1

The Nature of a Partnership	1
Approaches to Partnership Taxation (Asset vs. Entity)	4
Overview of Subchapter K and Partnership Taxation	6
Key Partnership Tax Themes Throughout the Text	10
Choice of Entity and Related Issues	14
Nontax Factors	15
Tax Factors	17
Check-the-Box and Electing the Tax Regime	22

Chapter 2. Formation of Partnerships — 25

Introduction	25
Nonrecognition Framework	28
Basis, Holding Period, and Character	30
Outside Basis	31
Inside Basis	32
Holding Period	37
Character Matters	39
Converting from a Sole Proprietorship	40

Chapter 3. Accounting for Partnership Operations — 47

Introduction	47
Partnership Taxable Income	48
Computing the Partnership's Taxable Income: § 703	49
Separately Stated Items: § 702	51
Partners' Distributive Share	54
Synthesis of Partnership Taxable Income and Partner's Distributive Share	56
Timing Matters	59
The Partnership's Taxable Year	59
Taxable Year of Including a Partner's Distributive Share	60
Taxable Year of the Partnership	61

Partnership Accounting Methods ... 66
Additional Limits on Losses ... 68
   Basis Limitation ... 69
   At-Risk Limitation ... 73
   Passive Losses ... 77
   Applying the Loss Limitations ... 80
Capital Accounts ... 81
   Maintenance of Capital Accounts ... 82

Chapter 4. Partnership Allocations Part I: § 704(b) and Substantial Economic Effect ... 97

Introduction ... 97
Substantial Economic Effect ... 100
   Economic Effect ... 100
      Capital Account Requirement ... 101
      Liquidation Requirement ... 104
      Deficit Restoration Obligation Requirement ... 105
   Synthesis of the Main Test ... 107
   Alternate Test for Economic Effect ... 108
      Qualified Income Offset Provisions ... 111
      Partial Economic Effect ... 116
Economic Equivalence ... 118
Substantiality ... 118
   General Rule for Substantiality ... 119
   Shifting Tax Consequences ... 121
   Transitory Allocations ... 125
   The Concept of Strong Likelihood and the Partnership Agreement ... 126
Partner's Interest in the Partnership ... 128
Items That Cannot Have Economic Effect ... 130

Chapter 5. Partnership Allocations Part II: § 704(c) and Built-In Gain or Loss ... 143

Introduction ... 143
General Matters and Definitions ... 146
The Traditional Method ... 147
Traditional Method with Curative Allocations ... 153
Remedial Allocation Method ... 157

Chapter 6. Partnership Liabilities ... 173

Introduction ... 173
Determining the Partner's Share of Liabilities ... 175
Recourse Liabilities ... 176

	Nonrecourse Liabilities	178
	Partnership Minimum Gain	178
	Nonrecourse Deductions	179
	Partners' Share of Partnership Minimum Gain	180
	Section 704(c) Gain	181
	Partner's Share of Excess Nonrecourse Liabilities	181
	Allocating Nonrecourse Deductions	187

Chapter 7. Distributions and Payments from a Partnership — 203

Introduction	203
Operating Distributions	204
Distributions of Property Other Than Money	208
Liquidating Distributions	216
Character Issues and Holding Period	222
Distributions of "Hot Assets" and § 751(b)	222

Chapter 8. Payments Between a Partnership and its Partners: § 707 — 243

Introduction	243
Partner Acting in a Non-Partner Capacity: § 707(a) Payments	245
Sales of Property Between a Partnership and a Partner Acting in a Non-Partner Capacity	247
Disguised Payments for Services and Sales	248
Disguised Payments for Services	249
Disguised Sales	250
Guaranteed Payments	254
Section 707 Synthesis	256

Chapter 9. Other Payments to Service Partners — 263

Introduction	263
Payment with a Capital Interest in the Partnership	267
Payment with a Profits Interest in the Partnership	271

Chapter 10. Selling, Exiting, Terminating, and Other Partnership Exits — 287

Introduction	287
Sale of a Partnership Interest	287
The Transferor-Partner	290
Additional Look-Through and Collateral Impacts for Transferor-Partner	297

Contents

The Transferee-Partner	300
§ 754 Elections and § 743 Adjustments	303
Life After the § 743(b) Adjustment	312
Liquidating Distributions	314
Death of a Partner	317
Impact of Death or Retirement on the Taxable Year	318
Death of a Partner and Income in Respect of a Decedent	319
Termination of a Partnership	320
Varying and Shifting Partnership Interests	322
Partnership Mergers	327
Partnership Divisions	330
Table of Internal Revenue Code Sections	*343*
Table of Treasury Regulations	*347*
Table of Administrative Rulings and Materials	*351*
Index	*353*

Preface

This book is about the federal income taxation of partnerships. A judge on the United States Tax Court once remarked in a judicial opinion that "[t]he distressingly complex and confusing nature of the provisions of subchapter K present a formidable obstacle to the comprehension of these provisions without the expenditure of a disproportionate amount of time and effort even by one who is sophisticated in tax matters with many years of experience in the tax field."[1] With respect to the partnership tax provision at issue in that case, the judge continued to query "whether it is reasonably comprehensible to the average lawyer or even to the average tax expert who has not given special attention and extended study to the tax problems of partners."[2] The judge concluded this lament by explaining that "its complex provisions may confidently be dealt with by at most only a comparatively small number of specialists who have been initiated into its mysteries."[3]

This text, therefore, serves to start your initiation into the mysteries of partnership taxation. This book covers the main canon of the domestic taxation of partnerships and partners; it uses the partnership's lifecycle to accomplish this by starting with the formation of a partnership, continuing with its operations, and finishing with various ways to exit or terminate the partnership. The book focuses on the tax consequences to the partnership as entity and to the partners. Given that the book generally focuses on domestic tax issues, international tax rules and international tax planning with partnerships are not discussed in this text. Relatedly, this book was primarily written in 2022 and 2023, and the rules and authorities discussed are based on this period. Tax is always changing, which is good for the business of the tax practitioner, but it means that rules change. The author therefore gives the reader a general exhortation to make sure you consult for developments that may have occurred after the writing of this book.[4] The

---

1. Foxman v. Comm'r, 41 T.C. 535, 551 n.9 (1964).
2. Id.
3. Id. The complexity that has plagued partnership tax has not just been noted by Tax Court judges. For example, in recommending reforms to the Tax Code in 1954, the Senate Finance Committee remarked that "[t]he existing tax treatment of partners and partnerships is among the most confused in the entire tax field." S. Rep. No. 1622, 83d Cong., 2d Sess. 89 (1954).
4. Another key practical point that the author wants to convey is that sometimes the administrative state lags primary (statutory) law changes. For example, it is not uncommon for a statute to be changed but the regulations (and the examples in those regulations) to be based on older versions of the statute. Another dimension to be mindful of is to ensure that cross

Preface

text also generally assumes an understanding of fundamental taxation principles, such as the concepts of income, gain, basis, depreciation, annual tax accounting and the like. Nevertheless, some of these concepts are unpacked in-text and in footnotes for completeness.

Although this book discusses the statutory partnership tax rules, as well as key judicial and administrative partnership tax rulings, the main focus—and key feature—of the book is explaining the *why*, *purpose*, and *object* of partnership tax. As we explain throughout the text, a deep understanding of these items makes the mechanics of partnership tax more intuitive and easier to understand. Indeed, by the end of reading and working through this text, we hope that the reader will be able to predict and intuit what the answer to a problem ought to be.

This book includes in-text and end-of-chapter problems (excluding Chapter 1) that support the key feature of explaining the why, purpose, and object of partnership tax. These problems allow for seeing the object in action and to tie the mechanics of the rules to their overarching purpose and aim. As noted, there are two types of examples in text. The first are in-text examples in the chapters. These examples tend to follow the elucidation of a partnership tax rule to show its operation and how its operation comports with the object trying to be achieved. These examples are fully worked out in text. In addition to the in-text examples, the chapter ends with additional *examples and explanations* for the reader to work through and to check his or her answers and understanding. Although both types of examples bear some resemblance to the real world, they are unlike real world problems insofar as they tend to be clean single-issue problems. Another intentional aspect of these problems is that they tend to be based on examples from the Treasury Regulations. Often lawyers must compare, contrast, and distill rules and principles from regulatory or administrative examples and apply them to their particular facts; thus, working through Treasury Regulation-like examples is another skill to be gained from working through this text.

Related to the types of examples used, partnership balance sheets are used throughout the text to demonstrate the before and after consequences to a transaction (and, sometimes, intra-transaction steps). We encourage the reader to follow along with these balance sheets and to construct balance sheets of his or her own while working problems. Creating balance sheets helps visualize the various important relationships between partnerships and partners. As well, some important concepts require this type of approach.

Generally, this text refers to partners as *individuals* (i.e., living, breathing persons), as compared to other entities (like corporations) who, of course,

---

references between statutes and regulations are accurate, as sometimes statutes and regulations are mapped to prior versions, which may have been renumbered or the like.

Preface

can also be partners of a partnership.[5] In addition, some other simplifying conventions are present in the text, such as a general assumption that capital account values reflect fair market values (which is sometimes but not always the case in real life). Many of these simplifying conventions are to reduce clunkiness and to improve tractability of examples. The text also uses a "we" convention, even though it was written by a single author; the use of "we" was intentional to refer to the shared journey that the author and reader are embarking on while you work through this text.

With the conclusion of this preface, the author desires to encourage you as you embark on your study of partnership taxation. Without doubt, challenges may lie ahead—it is a tough subject. But keep going. It is worth it. As you work through the text, the author reminds you of the advice to focus on the *why*, *purpose*, and *object* of partnership tax. If you can appreciate those items (and there are four main themes of partnership tax unpacked in Chapter 1), you will have a firm foundation upon which to build your partnership tax skillset. Indeed, the author believes that embracing these themes will help you see the *beauty* and *elegance* of various partnership tax rules.

Timothy M. Todd
September 2024

---

5. The Code makes this distinction between *individuals* (the term that refers to living, breathing people) as compared to *persons*, which also includes entities. I.R.C. § 7701(a)(1) (defining "person" to include *individuals*, as well as entities such as trusts, estates, and corporations).

Acknowledgments

I would like to thank my colleagues and students at Liberty Law who, over the years, have made me a better teacher, professor, and writer.

I would like to specifically thank Professor F. Philip Manns, Jr., who has been an exemplar mentor, colleague, and friend. I have been blessed beyond measure by his mentorship, instruction, and wisdom—across law and life. Truly, it has been an honor to sit under his tutelage.

I'm also thankful to my loving family who constantly support me; this book and my work generally would not be possible without them. My beautiful wife, Regan, is the epitome of a *Proverbs* 31 wife. My children, Noah and Zoe, have also contributed to this manuscript through their love and support. More poignantly, my family has also contributed to this manuscript through the time that I was not able to spend with them while working on this manuscript. I'm also thankful for my parents, Tim and Terrie, who love me, work hard, and are always there for me.

Above all, I'm thankful for my Lord and Savior, Jesus Christ.

Partnership Taxation

EXAMPLES & EXPLANATIONS

Introduction

THE NATURE OF A PARTNERSHIP

The first preliminary item addressed in this text is the nature of a partnership for both tax and non-tax purposes. We will observe that this fundamental question informs various properties of partnership tax and administration. In addition to the traditional partnership, we must also consider partnership varieties, such as the limited partnership, and more modern innovations, such as the limited liability company (LLC). We will see that the different state law characteristics of these forms of business have direct impact on their taxation.[1]

The partnership is an old form of business.[2] A common form of partnership related to maritime trade, in which one party would supply the capital for a venture, and the other would conduct the operations.[3] This arrangement was mutually beneficial because it allowed those with capital to get a return on that capital without transgressing the canon laws regarding usury, and it also allowed others to access needed capital

---

1. A prime example is that of determining the share of partnership liabilities borne by the partners (see Chapter 6). In a traditional general partnership, for example, all partners bear the economic burden of partnership liabilities; in a limited partnership, however, a limited partner would bear no such risk. Furthermore, in an LLC, it is likely that *no member* would bear any direct legal liability for the entity's debts.
2. WILLIAM MITCHELL, EARLY FORMS OF PARTNERSHIP, IN 3 SELECT ESSAYS IN ANGLO-AMERICAN LEGAL HISTORY 183, 183 (1909).
3. Id.

1. Introduction

and resources.[4] Our modern partnership law traces its lineage to the Law Merchant, which was the law for merchants.[5] Over time, this body of law was integrated into English and American common law.[6]

Today, contemporary partnership law features a combination of statutory rules and common law principles.[7] Statutorily, the Uniform Partnership Act promulgated in 1914 represented the genesis of modern partnership law formulation.[8] Refined over the years (namely in the 1990s), the present formulation of uniform partnership law is the Revised Uniform Partnership Act of 1997.[9] There are two broad types of partnerships. The first and most basic (as well as the easiest to form) partnership is the *general partnership*; unless we note otherwise, our use of the term "partnership" refers to such general partnerships. This type of partnership is governed by state statutes that are generally based on the Uniform Partnership Act or the Revised Uniform Partnership Act. The second type of partnership is a *limited partnership*. This type of partnership is governed by state statutes based on the Uniform Limited Partnership Act (ULPA) or the Revised Uniform Limited Partnership Act.[10]

As we discuss more in Chapter 2, a partnership (to be clear, the general partnership) can be created informally (that is, without any state filing or state process). Indeed, no written agreement is even required to form it; a partnership essentially just requires two or more persons to carry on a business for profit.[11] Once a partnership is formed, state law provides a range of default statutory rules that govern unless displaced by a partnership agreement. Moreover, these default rules for partnerships provide baseline rules that govern various aspects of the partnership and the relationships of its partners, such as rules governing the rights of partners to conduct the affairs of the partnership, to vote on business matters, to share in profits, to be liable for the debts of the partnership, to provide for fiduciary duties, and even how to dissolve the partnership. As you may imagine, partners may not desire these default rules, so the drafting of a thoughtful partnership agreement becomes critical.

---

4. Id.
5. *See, e.g.*, STEPHEN M. BAINBRIDGE, AGENCY, PARTNERSHIPS, & LLCs 121 (3rd ed. 2019).
6. Id.
7. Id.
8. Id.
9. It is also referred to sometimes as the Uniform Partnership Act (1997). *See, e.g.*, BAINBRIDGE, *supra* note 5, at 122.
10. Louisiana, a civil law-based system, stands as a prominent exception to these uniform statutes.
11. *See, e.g.*, Va. Code Ann. § 50-73.88.

I. Introduction

The other main type of partnership is the *limited partnership*. Limited partnerships were designed to allow for profit-sharing by passive investors who would benefit from limited liability.[12] Limited partnerships are not so easily formed. Unlike general partnerships, limited partnerships require a formal state filing. Limited partnerships have two basic classes of partners: general partners and limited partners. The key differences between a general and limited partnership, then, relate to those of limited partners. Unlike a general partner, a *limited* partner is not personally liable for obligations of the partnership.[13] In exchange for this limited liability, a limited partner cannot act for or bind the limited partnership.[14] Historically, this tradeoff was even more acute because the limited partner was not able to participate in the control of the business. With the advent of the other limited liability entities, such as the LLC, the control rule has been relaxed over time.[15]

Although not a partnership for state law purposes, it is helpful here to discuss the *limited liability company* (LLC). The LLC has taken the business world by storm.[16] LLCs are a popular entity choice for new businesses.[17] The birth of the LLC is traced to the tradeoff that was typically required by new businesses—they could choose to be a partnership and have pass-through taxation but unlimited downside liability or they could choose to be a corporation and have limited liability but have double taxation.[18] In short, new businesses had to make a choice between limited liability or limited taxation.

Before the advent of the LLC, several options were provided to bridge this suboptimal choice. The limited partnership was an early option. As noted above, this allowed some limited liability (for the limited partners at least) and pass-through taxation. But due to the need for a general

---

12. *See, e.g.*, BAINBRIDGE, *supra* note 5, at 122.
13. E.g., Va. Code Ann. § 50-73.24; Uniform Limited Partnership Act § 303.
14. E.g., Va. Code Ann. § 50-73.24.
15. *See* Uniform Limited Partnership Act § 303, Comment.
16. *See* Rodney D. Chrisman, *LLCs Are The New King of The Hill: An Empirical Study of The Number of New LLCs, Corporations, and LPs Formed in The United States Between 2004-2007 and How LLCs Were Taxed For Tax Years 2002-2006*, 15 FORDHAM J. CORP. & FIN. L. 459 (2009).
17. *Id.*
18. Although this is unpacked throughout the text, some context may be helpful at this early stage. Corporations are taxed directly, i.e., the entity pays a tax on the income it generates. Then, when those profits are distributed to shareholders, the shareholders pay individual income tax on that distributed income. Thus, corporate profits are subject to what is known, colloquially, as a "double tax"—that is, a tax at the *corporate* level and a tax at the *shareholder* level. Partnerships, however, are not subject to a double tax because the partnership does not pay an entity-level tax; rather, the income "passes through" to the partners, who then pay income taxes on their share of partnership income. Thus, partnership profits are taxed only once at the partner level.

I. Introduction

partner, coupled with the historic restrictions on what limited partners could do vis-à-vis the business operations, this was not a complete solution.[19]

The next patch was the *S corporation*, introduced when Congress enacted Subchapter S of the Internal Revenue Code.[20] Under this statutory regime, eligible corporations could elect to be taxed as a "small business corporation."[21] After this election, the entity enjoys conduit (pass-through) taxation, in which the corporation is not subject to income taxes, but rather items of income, loss, and deduction flow through to the shareholders of the S corporation.[22] Although the S corporation had much promise to usher in the solution to the tradeoff of limited liability and pass-through taxation, Congress put restrictions on the nature of corporations that could elect S corporation status.[23]

Finally, the LLC entered the scene. Commentators hoped that the LLC would provide the best of both worlds—namely, that it would provide limited liability and pass-through taxation.[24] This promise was not realized at first due to the then-existing regulations that governed how LLCs would be taxed, which was uncertain.[25] Eventually, this uncertainty would be resolved, though, with the advent of the "check-the-box" regulations that allow LLCs to choose how to be taxed for federal income taxes—including to be taxed as a partnership.[26] After the resolution of this tax uncertainty, the LLC became ubiquitous.[27] Thus, although this text concerns the taxation of *partnerships*, practically these issues will often arise in the context of a LLC that is taxed as a *partnership* for federal income tax purposes.

APPROACHES TO PARTNERSHIP TAXATION (ASSET VS. ENTITY)

This short section serves to introduce the core doctrinal issue that lurks in the background of all partnership tax rules: Is the partnership an entity

---

19. *See, e.g.*, Chrisman, *supra* note 16, at 465–66.
20. I.R.C. §§ 1361–1379; *see also* Chrisman, *supra* note 16, at 466.
21. I.R.C. §§ 1361, 1362.
22. I.R.C. §§ 1363, 1366.
23. For example, the current restrictions include, *inter alia*, the corporation cannot have more than 100 shareholders (subject to various counting rules), cannot have a nonresident alien as a shareholder, and cannot have more than one class of stock. I.R.C. § 1361(b).
24. Chrisman, *supra* note 16, at 466.
25. *See id.*
26. *Id.* The check-the-box regulations are discussed later in this chapter.
27. *Id.*

I. Introduction

that is separate from its owners or is the partnership an aggregate of assets owned by its owners?[28] These are known as the entity and aggregate views, respectively.[29] Under the entity view, the partnership has a tax existence apart from its partners and should therefore be taxed separately; partners, then, have an interest in the partnership entity, not its underlying assets.[30] On the other hand, under the aggregate view, the partnership represents an "aggregation" of partners who own a direct undivided interest in partnership assets.[31]

Each of these views would result in a different application and operation of partnership tax rules. Indeed, these differences span the entire lifecycle of the partnership from formation, operation, and exit. For example, under a pure entity approach, the taxation of partnerships would closely resemble, if not follow fully, the taxation of corporations.[32] The partnership as entity would be taxed on the results of its operations.[33] Partners, just like shareholders, would not be taxed on partnership operations. Without a nonrecognition provision, transfers of property between the partnership and its partners (e.g., a contribution or distribution) would be taxable.[34] Thus, if the partnership paid a distribution of earnings, the partner would then be taxable on that distribution, just like corporate shareholders are taxed upon a corporate dividend.

In juxtaposition, under a pure aggregate approach, each partner would own a proportionate sliver of partnership assets and would be taxed on a corresponding amount of partnership income.[35] This is akin to being a tenant-in-common of Blackacre and therefore being entitled to a proportionate share of Blackacre's rental income; continuing the analogy, if the partner owned half of Blackacre, the partner would be taxed on half of the rental income. Transfers of property between the partners and the partnership, moreover, would also not trigger any tax unless they changed the underlying proportionate ownership of the assets.[36]

---

28. Note that this doctrinal issue reaches beyond tax considerations, too. Daniel S. Kleinberger, *The Closely Held Business Though the Entity-Aggregate Prism*, 40 WAKE FOREST L. REV. 827, 827 (2005). As well, other aspects of partnership law raise this doctrinal issue, too, such as the nature of partners' ownership of partnership property and the extent of the partners' liability for partnership obligations. Bradley T. Borden, *Aggregate-Plus Theory of Partnership Taxation*, 43 GA. L. REV. 717, 724 (2009).
29. *See, e.g.*, WILLIAM S. MCKEE ET AL., FEDERAL TAXATION OF PARTNERSHIPS ¶ 1.02 (2022); Alfred D. Youngwood & Deborah B. Weiss, *Partners and Partnerships—Aggregate vs. Entity Outside of Subchapter K*, 48 THE TAX LAWYER 39, 39 (1944).
30. MCKEE ET AL., *supra* note 29, ¶ 1.02.
31. *Id.*
32. *Id.* ¶ 1.02[2].
33. *Id.*
34. *Id.*
35. *Id.* ¶ 1.02[1].
36. *Id.*

I. Introduction

Subchapter K does not fully adopt either paradigm, rather it tends to blend these entity and aggregate perspectives in various ways.[37] Although the rules have ebbed and flowed over the years, the present state of affairs between the two can be summarized as follows.[38] Generally, the taxation of partnership income, contributions, and distributions follows the aggregate paradigm.[39] Partners are taxed on their share of partnership income, and contributions and distributions generally benefit from nonrecognition provisions. However, generally transfers of partnership interests follow the entity paradigm,[40] and under it, partners have a basis in their partnership interest that is separate from the basis that the partnership has in its assets.[41]

In sum, current Subchapter K reflects a blending of the aggregate and entity paradigms. Often, we will see this blending designed to achieve a certain policy aim of Subchapter K or to prevent a certain tax abuse (e.g., the shifting of income between partners or the changing of income character). Although the application of these rules can be challenging enough when they are spelled out in black and white, further complexity, ambiguity, and uncertainty is injected when addressing an issue not expressly addressed by the Code, the Treasury regulations, or other guidance.[42] Indeed, whether an entity or aggregate perspective is used may change the tax consequences of a transaction. As noted earlier, sometimes the perspectives are blended in various sections and therefore tax consequences are possible that would not occur otherwise.[43]

OVERVIEW OF SUBCHAPTER K AND PARTNERSHIP TAXATION

The basic rules of partnership taxation can be mapped to its lifecycle, which loosely tracks the organization of Subchapter K. As presently codified, Subchapter K has three parts. The first part (Part I) governs the taxation of partnership operations. The second part (Part II) has four subparts (lettered A through D); each of these subparts governs a particular aspect of the

---

37. See id. ¶ 1.02[3].
38. See id.
39. Id.
40. Id. Subject to a very important aggregate paradigm exception concerning "hot" assets. I.R.C. § 751.
41. McKee et al., supra note 29, ¶ 1.02[3]. But, as we will see, there is a relationship between the partner's basis and the partnerships basis, as well as partnership income, which has an aggregate nature to it. Id.
42. See, e.g., William S. McKee, Partnership Allocations: The Need for an Entity Approach, 66 Va. L. Rev. 1039, 1039 (1980).
43. See id. at 1039–40.

I. Introduction

partnership, like that of contributions or distributions. The last subpart is a single section (§ 761), which is a definitions section.

The lifecycle of a partnership includes (1) the formation and contributions to the partnership, (2) the operation of the partnership, (3) distributions from the partnership, and (4) transfers of partnership interests (i.e., exits). Statutorily, the rules of formation and contributions are found in §§ 721 through 724 (Subpart A of Part II of Subchapter K), the rules of operation are found in §§ 701 through 709 (Part I of Subchapter K), distribution rules are found in §§ 731 through 737 (Subpart B of Part II of Subchapter K), and the rules for transfers of partnership interests are found in §§ 741 through 743 (Subpart C of Part II of Subchapter K). Lastly, Subpart D contains rules that apply for all the subparts.

With that statutory roadmap in mind, we now proceed with a short overview of partnership taxation. Each of these subjects are discussed in more detail in various parts of this text. However, at this juncture, it is important to see the forest from the trees, and for us to appreciate the tension and resolution that the aggregate and entity perspectives have in various taxation contexts. As with this text generally, our overview maps to the lifecycle of a partnership.

The first step in the lifecycle of a partnership is its formation and the capital contributions to it from the partners. Typically, the owners contribute capital and property in exchange for their partnership interests. As we will see, the Code generally treats this as a tax-free exchange, which it accomplishes by preserving the basis that partners had in their exchanged property for their newly acquired partnership interest (thus also preserving the built-in gain or loss that existed).[44]

This tax-free treatment embraces the aggregate aspect of the partnership. Conceptually, if the partnership is an aggregate of assets used in concert to conduct a business, then an owner ought not have a gain (i.e., an accession to wealth) unless he or she somehow receives more assets than he or she started with. Importantly, this treatment makes sense doctrinally so long as the partner contributes *property* that is being aggregated with property from other partners such that the partners' investment is not being "cashed out" but is merely changing forms (say, from Blackacre to Partnership Interest). That reasoning breaks down, however, if the partner contributes *services*. With a provision of services to the partnership in exchange for an interest in the partnership, there is no longer an aggregation of assets, and this looks more like payment for services (i.e., compensation), which is how it is treated.

After the partnership is formed, it then proceeds to operate and conduct its business. It is here that we see an integration of both entity and aggregate approaches. The taxation of partnership income is best described

---

44. I.R.C. §§ 721, 722, 723.

I. Introduction

as a "conduit approach." The partnership itself does not pay income tax but rather income flows through the partnership (like a conduit) to its partners. For example, if a partnership has two equal partners and generates $1,000 in income, each partner reports $500 of income on his or her individual income tax return. Given the required income inclusion for the partner, the partner also benefits from an increase in his or her partnership basis, which tracks how much of his or her capital has been subjected to income tax. From this angle, this embraces the aggregate perspective. This is analogous to the situation in which Blackacre has two equal owners who share its rental income.

The taxation of partnership income, though, does have entity elements to it. For example, the calculation of a partnership's income is done from an entity perspective—that is, items are calculated and characterized at the partnership level.[45] Relatedly, tax elections are made by the partnership as entity.[46] In addition, the partnership has its own taxable year.[47] The partnership also has its own method of accounting.[48] The partnership files an informational tax return as an entity.[49] And, as we'll see, for certain partner-partnership transactions, an entity approach is used to calculate the tax impacts of these transactions.[50]

After that partnership income has been calculated and characterized at the partnership level, it is then allocated to the partners.[51] This is the conduit nature of partnership taxation—the partnership acts as a conduit through which income flows to the partners, who ultimately report that income on their income tax returns. Subchapter K gives the partners tremendous flexibility to decide how they will share items of partnership income, gain, loss, and deduction. That flexibility, moreover, is what gives rise to much of the complexity of Subchapter K. Indeed, some of the toughest aspects of Subchapter K are there to ensure that partners are not abusing this flexibility. In short, the rules require that tax consequences follow the actual economic consequences of the partnership. This is a simple rule to state, but devilishly complex in application as we'll see in Chapter 4.

After a partnership has been operating—and hopefully earning an economic return—it is natural for the partners to desire to receive a distribution from the partnership. Just like with contributions, we also observe an aggregate approach to distributions. Partnership distributions are generally

---

45. I.R.C. § 703.
46. I.R.C. § 703(b).
47. I.R.C. § 706.
48. I.R.C. § 446.
49. I.R.C. § 6031.
50. I.R.C. § 707.
51. Technically, Subchapter K uses the term "distributive share" of partnership income. As we discuss in Chapter 4, however, this is an unfortunate term given what it means. Thus, we prefer the phrase "allocation" when describing how partners share the income of a partnership.

I. Introduction

nonrecognition events, subject to some exceptions.[52] Generally, these exceptions are triggered when we cannot accommodate the nonrecognition treatment due to the amount of basis at play.

It is helpful to appreciate why Subchapter K strives for nonrecognition treatment of distributions. At bottom, it is tied to the aggregate perspective of partnerships, coupled with the nature of basis. Let's revisit the Blackacre example that we used earlier with partnership income. Conceptually, if Blackacre is owned by two equal owners, and it is then subdivided (partitioned) into two equal parts that are given to each owner, there is no economic gain—each owner has just been given their share of Blackacre that they owned before the subdivision. This is like what is going on in a partnership distribution. This is a result of the aggregate perspective. Under the aggregate perspective, each partner is an owner of a proportionate share of partnership assets; to the extent he or she receives those assets in a distribution, the partner hasn't received new economic value.

Now, you may be wondering about any built-in gain or loss that might be inherent in these properties. Well, that's an excellent query, and it demonstrates another elegant feature of Subchapter K (and nonrecognition sections generally). Of course, the Code is generally concerned with gain or loss vanishing, and it goes to great lengths to make this rather impossible.[53] For nonrecognition transactions (like with partnership contributions and distributions), it accomplishes this preservation of built-in gain or loss by way of affecting the basis of the received property. Stated simply, if the partner had a built-in gain of $500 before a distribution, that $500 gain will be preserved in the received property (unless if it was recognized). That is why one of the key exceptions to the nonrecognition rule on distributions is if the partner receives more cash than basis—in this case, the basis can't police the built-in gain, so it must be recognized at that time.[54]

Eventually, a partner desires to exit the partnership. Sometimes, this departure may be involuntary, like the death of a partner. Transfers of partnerships interests adopt an entity perspective—that is, they are treated as the transfer of an interest in the partnership rather than its underlying assets.[55] As well, the transfer of a partnership interest does not affect the basis in the partnership's underlying assets.[56] As with other parts of the lifecycle, though, a pure entity approach could blur the character of the gain. For example, if we treat the partnership interest as one that gives rise to

---

52. I.R.C. §§ 731, 732, 733.
53. In Chapter 2, we analogize this to the law of conservation of energy that states that energy cannot be created or destroyed but only transferred.
54. I.R.C. § 731(a)(1).
55. I.R.C. § 741.
56. This is generally true under I.R.C. § 743. However, this rule may give rise to an imbalance between the aggregate partnership basis in its assets and the aggregate basis in the partnership interests; the partnership can make an election to remedy this distortion.

I. Introduction

capital-gain treatment (i.e., with lower, preferential tax rates), but the underlying partnership assets are ordinary income assets, the entity and aggregate perspectives would result in a different tax bill. Thus, although transfers of partnership interests are generally treated under the entity perspective, that can yield to an aggregate perspective to prevent character shift.[57]

In sum, as we trace the lifecycle of the partnership (from cradle to grave), we see instances in which the Code adopts an entity perspective and instances in which it adopts an aggregate perspective. As we explain more in the next section, generally these changes in perspectives are to prevent various abuses or tax shenanigans in light of the tremendous flexibility that partners and partnerships have in arranging their economic affairs.

KEY PARTNERSHIP TAX THEMES THROUGHOUT THE TEXT

In the preceding sections, we introduced the aggregate and entity perspectives to partnership tax and then surveyed the tax lifecycle of a partnership. As we dive deeper into each of these areas throughout this text, some themes will be ever-present, and we want to raise them now so that you will appreciate these themes when you see them. As well, this comports with the pedagogical approach to this text, namely, to focus on the *why*, *purpose*, and *object* of partnership tax, which makes the mechanics more intuitive and easier to understand. The themes broached in this section include (a) tracking and preserving basis, (b) ensuring tax consequences follow economic consequences, (c) preventing income shifting, and (d) preventing character changes. If you can keep these four themes in the fore while you read this text and learn partnership tax, it will make the mechanics of the rules easier to understand and even allow you to predict their results.

One of the most important things that Subchapter K strives to do is to preserve and track *basis*. Indeed, many Subchapter K rules are ultimately about basis (e.g., contributions, distributions, impact of debt, etc.). Basis is an incredibly important concept in taxation. In short, basis represents amounts that have already been subject to tax (i.e., basis equals already taxed capital). This is inherent in the definition of *income*, which includes accessions to wealth — meaning *increases* in wealth.[58] Basis therefore distinguishes *increases* of wealth and *returns* of wealth. For example, if you purchase

---

57. *See* I.R.C. § 751.
58. *See, e.g.*, Comm'r v. Glenshaw Glass Co., 348 U.S. 426, 431 (1955) (explaining that income constitutes "undeniable accessions to wealth, clearly realized, and over which the taxpayers have complete dominion").

I. Introduction

Blackacre for $500, the Code gives you a $500 basis in Blackacre.[59] If you were to later sell Blackacre for $500, you do not have an *increase* in wealth, you are merely *returned* your wealth; thus, there is no gain (and income) on that transaction.[60] If, on the other hand, you sell Blackacre for $750, your wealth has *increased* by $250, which represents the gain (and income) from the transaction.[61]

Tracking basis, therefore, is a critical element of Subchapter K, and it must track basis across several dimensions, including property contributions, property distributions, and partnership operations. Here again we see the import of the aggregate versus entity perspectives. Let's consider a simple example using a property contribution and later distribution. Assume that Darius contributes $1,000 of cash to a partnership. As we will learn, Darius now has a $1,000 basis in his partnership interest. What if, a few years later, the partnership distributes $500 to Darius (when he still has a $1,000 basis in his partnership interest) — what does that $500 represent? Does it represent *new* money to Darius or a return of his *old* money (i.e., the money he earlier contributed to the partnership)? If we assume that it represents first a return of his earlier contributed money, then Darius does not have an *increase* (accession) to wealth — his money is just being returned to him. Therefore, he has not been made economically better off, and there should not be any income resulting from this distribution.

The need to track basis is even more acute when we factor in the conduit nature of partnership taxation. The conduit nature of partnership taxation embraces the aggregate theory of taxation, meaning that partners are taxed directly on their share of partnership income (and the partnership, as an entity, is not taxed on its income). We now must add to our basis tracking the amount of income that a partner has included in income from partnership operations. Going back to the Darius example above, assume that in Year 1, Darius's share of partnership income is $200, which he includes on his individual tax return. To prevent the double taxation of that $200 in income (when it is later distributed), we must add that amount to the basis of Darius's partnership interest. Thus, at the end Year 1, Darius has a basis of $1,200 in his partnership interest. This $1,200 represents the $1,000 that he contributed initially plus the $200 of flow-through income. In other words, the $1,200 represents his already taxed capital inherent in the partnership. We can now better appreciate how this notion informs partnership distributions: To the extent Darius receives $1,200 from the partnership, that represents capital that he has already paid tax on, and it therefore does not represent an *increase* in wealth.

---

59. I.R.C. §§ 1011, 1012.
60. I.R.C. § 1001.
61. I.R.C. §§ 1001, 61.

I. Introduction

A key state law feature of partnerships is their flexibility, which is rooted in the idea of freedom of contract. Contractually, partners can decide how to share profits, share losses, and share the obligation to pay debts, among other economic consequences. Importantly, they need not share these things in the same way. For example, they can share items of profit and loss differently. For tax purposes, the Code generally wants to accommodate this flexibility. With this flexibility, though, is the concern that the tax consequences will not follow the true economic consequences of the partnership. As well, another concern is that partners will use the flexibility of the partnership tax rules to either avoid or shift tax consequences. Thus, much of the complication inherent in Subchapter K is the interaction between the ability for flexibility and the concern to prevent these shenanigans, some of which we raise briefly below, and are covered in more depth at appropriate times later in the text.

Related to the theme of ensuring that tax consequences follow economic consequences is the treatment of debt within a partnership. As you may recall from your study of income taxation, the Code generally allows basis for property that is debt-financed. The underlying reasoning here is that the debtor will need to repay the debt, so the debt reflects a future economic cost and payment. Indeed, you may also recall the flip side of this coin that debt forgiven or released needs to be included in the amount realized on the sale of the underlying property. This is rooted in symmetry and preventing leakage: Because the taxpayer received a basis credit for the debt-financed portion of the property (and did not recognize income upon the receipt of the debt-financed funds), if the taxpayer does not fully repay the debt, then the basis does not truly reflect the economic cost of the asset to the taxpayer.[62]

To illustrate, consider the following example. Tom purchases Blackacre for $1,000, using $400 of his own funds and borrowing $600 from Big Bank. Because of the repayment obligation, Tom does not have an income inclusion upon receipt of the borrowed funds.[63] Moreover, Tom's basis in Blackacre under § 1012 is $1,000 — that is, he receives a "basis credit" for the borrowed funds. This makes sense conceptually because the property did "cost" Tom $1,000 — it cost him $400 of his own funds and then the $600 repayment obligation to Big Bank. What if Big Bank, though, releases Tom of his repayment obligation? To the extent of the release, Tom now has basis in Blackacre that was never actually subject to income tax — and recall that the entire purpose of basis is to reflect the *already taxed* investment in the asset. This creates an asymmetry unless Tom must include the debt release

---

62. This is the reasoning also supporting cancellation of debt income.
63. That is, he does not have an *accession* to wealth — the repayment obligation offsets his receipt of the $600.

I. Introduction

in his income, which the Code requires him to do.[64] The same asymmetry applies if, instead of being released of the debt from Big Bank, the later purchaser of Blackacre assumes Tom's debt. In this case, Tom will have to include the amount of his debt assumed by the purchaser as part of his amount realized, which ensures that it is captured by the income tax base.

The interaction between debt and basis arises regularly in partnership tax. As we just saw in the simple Blackacre example, the Code allowed a basis credit under the assumption that the taxpayer would later repay the debt. If that was not true, the Code strives to remedy the problem. This manifests the theme that tax consequences should follow economic consequences; that is, you should benefit taxwise from the debt only if you are economically liable for the debt. As we will see when we turn to partnership liabilities, a key question that will be asked is who, if any, of the partners are economically liable to repay the debt—the answer to this question will inform how we treat the debt for tax purposes.

Another concern implicit in the Subchapter K rules is that of income shifting. Income shifting refers to the situation in which a partner has income that he tries to shift to another partner. This typically arises with contributed property. For example, consider a partner who owns Blackacre with a value of $500 and a tax basis of $100—the partner has a $400 gain inherent in the property (colloquially described as *built-in gain*). If the partner contributes Blackacre to the partnership, he should not be allowed to avoid that built-in gain inherent in Blackacre. If the partnership later sells Blackacre, the contributing partner should have to recognize the first $400 of gain from Blackacre. Indeed, § 704(c) does exactly that and prevents the partner from shedding this built-in gain when contributing Blackacre to the partnership. This example with Blackacre is relatively straightforward, but the concern can arise in more subtle ways. For example, if instead of selling Blackacre the partnership *distributes* Blackacre to another partner, that could also effectuate an income shift due to how the distribution rules work (recall the earlier summary that distributions can benefit from nonrecognition treatment).[65] Thus, as we'll see, we also must be concerned with income shifting when we have partnership distributions.

In addition to concerns about income shifting, partnership tax is also concerned with *character change*—that is, where the partners try to effectuate a change in the nature (i.e., character) of the income. The quintessential example is trying to change *ordinary* gains into *capital* gains. The Code generally taxes long-term capital gains at lower rates compared to ordinary gains; thus, partners are incentivized to change things from ordinary gains to capital gains, trying to benefit from the lower tax rate that will be applied. Thus, if the Code was just concerned about magnitude protection, the Treasury

---

64. *See* I.R.C. § 61(a)(11), which is subject to some exceptions, *see* I.R.C. § 108.
65. This gives rise to the "mixing bowl" rules, which are also present in § 704(c).

I. Introduction

could still lose out if partners were able to change the rate of tax applied against those amounts.

A simple example illustrates this concern. Alfred and Bob form a partnership. Alfred contributes $1,000 in cash, and Bob contributes $1,000 of accounts receivable with a $0 tax basis. The accounts receivable is not a capital asset to either Bob or the partnership, thus it will generate ordinary income upon its realization. For reasons that we unpack in the next chapter, Bob will also have a $0 basis in his partnership interest. Assume that Bob sells his partnership interest to Charlie for $1,000. With the $0 basis, this generates a gain of $1,000.[66] This is an example of magnitude protection — the Code is preserving the built-in gain and the status quo ante. We saw in our summary of partnership tax that the Code treats this under the entity perspective, meaning Bob's partnership interest is separate from the underlying assets. As well, the partnership interest is likely a capital asset to Bob, meaning his $1,000 gain from selling his partnership interest generates capital gain. Doctrinally, that can't be the right answer! If that were the right answer, Bob would have effectuated a *character change* merely by dropping property into a partnership — transforming the $1,000 of ordinary income inherent in his accounts receivable to a $1,000 capital gain inherent in his partnership interest. The actual rule in this case is that Subchapter K will make Bob recognize the underlying ordinary income here (not capital gain).[67] Thus, Subchapter K must be vigilant to protect both against *income shifting* and *character changes*.

CHOICE OF ENTITY AND RELATED ISSUES

The last part of this opening chapter is dedicated to a short overview of choice of entity planning and related issues. Choice of entity planning refers to planning thoughtfully about the type of entity that a business enterprise should adopt. In this analysis, there are considerations steeped in tax and nontax factors. Common nontax factors include duration and continuity, limited liability, management structure, and transferability. Common tax factors include double tax versus single tax, loss limitations, impact of § 199A, tax flexibility, and exit tax planning. We provide a brief overview of these factors and how they arise in popular forms of business.[68] At the

---

66. Under § 1001, gain is defined as the amount realized (here, $1,000) less adjusted basis (here, $0), resulting in a gain of $1,000.
67. *See* I.R.C. §§ 741, 751.
68. Importantly, a full choice of entity analysis is beyond the scope of this text. This section highlights some of the issues so that readers can better understand the broader business planning context incorporating tax and nontax factors.

I. Introduction

outset, it is important to emphasize between state law entity selection and then how that entity is taxed for federal income tax purposes. A prime example of this is the corporation. After a corporation is formed from a state law perspective, it may qualify for S corporation status, which is a separate federal income tax election. Another example is that of the limited liability company. After a limited liability company is formed, it may have several tax options available to it (e.g., to be taxed as a sole proprietorship, as a partnership, or as a corporation—or even as an S corporation). Realizing this distinction is particularly important in this text because many entities that are taxed as partnerships are not partnerships under state law—rather, they are formed as limited liability companies that are taxed as partnerships (under the check-the-box regulations explained later).

Nontax Factors

Duration and continuity, limited liability, management structure, and transferability are common state law considerations to consider when selecting a new business entity. We will explore these factors across sole proprietorships, corporations, general partnerships, and limited liability companies. The first factor is duration, which refers to how long the company lasts and whether it survives the death of its owners. Sole proprietorships necessarily end with the death of the owner—this is because the law does not differentiate between the business and the owner, i.e., they are one in the same.[69] Other types of businesses, like the corporation or limited liability company, are entities that have a legal existence separate from their owners; therefore, the entity survives the death of the owners. Traditionally, the death or other dissociation of a partner would cause a dissolution of the partnership, but it is possible to draft around this in a partnership agreement.

Limited liability is an important factor to consider. Historically, this was one of the main constraints in the decision-making process. In a multiple-owner business, the business could decide to be a corporation or a partnership. A major nontax difference between those choices was the availability of limited liability for doing business in the corporate form. Partners in a general partnership, on the other hand, are liable for the debts of the partnership.[70] The corporate limited liability, however, came at the expense of double taxation (i.e., corporate taxation). Despite that historical vintage,

---

69. Nettlesome planning issues arise with the deathtime planning for the owner of a single member LLC. See F. Philip Manns Jr. & Timothy M. Todd, *Issues Arising Upon the Death of the Sole Member of a Single-Member LLC*, 99 Marquette L. Rev. 725 (2016); see also F. Philip Manns Jr. & Timothy M. Todd, *The Tax Lifecycle of a Single-Member LLC*, 36 Va. Tax Rev. 323 (2017).

70. This also explained the reasoning behind the evolution of other forms of partnerships, like limited partnerships and limited liability partnerships.

I. Introduction

limited liability is easy to achieve today given the advent of the LLC. Indeed, as explained in the tax section below, a multi-member LLC can have both state law limited liability and the flexibility of flow-through taxation as a partnership for federal income tax purposes. For sole proprietors there is no limited liability because there is no entity—again, the proprietor is the business, so if the business incurs a liability, the proprietor incurs the liability personally.

Management structure is another factor that differentiated the business forms at state law. Management structure refers to how the business is controlled and how decisions are made. A sole proprietor has the simplest structure, namely there is a single owner who has total control and gets to make all the decisions. Corporations, on the other hand, have the most complex form. Corporations are owned by shareholders, and shareholders delegate their decision making to the board of directors.[71] Boards of directors, in turn, typically delegate day-to-day decision making to various corporate officers (like the chief executive officer).[72] Although this is how this division of control is typically done in large corporations, smaller corporations may have simpler structures, but the basics remain the same (i.e., shareholders delegate decision making to a board of directors). Corporations can issue different types of shares that differ on voting and dividend rights. Thus, there is some flexibility inherent in the capital structure and resulting control structure at the shareholder level.

The default rule is that partnerships and limited liability companies are managed by their members. Partnerships and limited liability companies have tremendous flexibility on how to allocate control and management. This is inherent in the freedom of contract that doctrinally underpins these forms of business. Consequently, a partnership or LLC management structure can range from simple (e.g., all partners have control and voting rights on all matters) to more complex structures that resemble that of a corporation (e.g., various committees and groups of partners that vote on certain things). LLCs can also have a manager-managed structure meaning that the day-to-day affairs of the entity are managed by managers (who may or may not be owners).

The last state law factor we will examine is the transferability of interests, i.e., how we transfer the ownership of the business. For a sole proprietorship, the business can be transferred by transferring all the assets of the business. Depending on the number of assets at play, this can be very

---

71. *See, e.g.*, Del. Code Ann. tit. 8, § 141.
72. *See, e.g.*, Del. Code Ann. tit. 8, § 142.

I. Introduction

tedious—particularly considering, by comparison, how easy it is to transfer the shares of a corporation. For a general partnership, a partner can assign his or her interest in the partnership to another; however, this interest is only the financial interest, meaning the partner's interest in profits, losses, and distributions.[73] A partner's interest in the partnership is treated as personal property.[74] If the transferee is to be admitted as a partner (i.e., to gain management rights), that is determined by the partnership agreement or applicable state law. The rules for LLCs are like that for partnerships, i.e., LLC interests are transferable, but consist only of economic rights,[75] and that admission as a member will depend on the operating agreement or state law.[76] As a default matter, shares in a corporation are freely transferable, but such transfer may be restricted by an agreement between the shareholders.[77]

Tax Factors

There are many tax factors that can influence the choice-of-entity analysis. Some major tax factors include formation taxation, the taxation of operations, employment and fringe benefit taxation, taxation of distributions, exit taxation, and other special considerations, like the impact of § 199A. The tax choice-of-entity decision involves selecting the tax regime to use for a business, which may be limited due to the number of owners (e.g., a sole proprietor cannot be taxed as a partnership) or state law entity (e.g., a corporation cannot be taxed like a partnership). Some of these mechanics and default rules are discussed in the next section about the check-the-box regulations. In this section, we discuss these factors across sole proprietorship taxation, corporation taxation, S corporation taxation, and partnership taxation.

We will start with probably the major factor, which is to decide between double taxation or pass-through taxation for the taxation of business operations. As an entity, a corporation pays its own taxes on the taxable income it generates.[78] This is the first level of taxation. When the corporation distributes its earnings, the shareholders then must include those distributions in income, which generates a second level of taxation. A dollar in corporate income, therefore, is exposed to two levels of taxation before it can be enjoyed by its shareholder-owner. Naturally, business owners prefer less tax

---

73. E.g., Va. Code Ann. § 50-73.106; Uniform Partnership Act § 502.
74. E.g., Va. Code Ann. § 50-73.106.
75. See, e.g., Va. Code Ann. § 13.1-1038; Uniform Limited Liability Company Act (2006) § 502.
76. See, e.g., Va. Code Ann. § 13.1-1038.1; Uniform Limited Liability Company Act (2006) § 401.
77. E.g., Va. Code Ann. § 13.1-649; Model Business Corporation Act § 6.27.
78. I.R.C. § 11.

1. Introduction

to more tax, so another option is to consider an S corporation election or partnership taxation.

An S corporation election is an election that can be made by a "small business corporation" that allows it to benefit from pass-through taxation under Subchapter S.[79] In other words, if a corporation elects S corporation status, its earnings will pass through the entity (like the conduit nature of partnership taxation) and will be taxed to the individual shareholders. To qualify as a small business corporation, the entity must be (i) a domestic corporation, (ii) not have more than 100 shareholders, (iii) not have an ineligible shareholder, and (iv) not have more than one class of stock.[80] Thus, not all corporations necessarily qualify for S corporation status. Moreover, corporations that desire S corporation status must qualify for it, must properly elect it, and must ensure that it does not later disqualify itself from S corporation status. A salient issue to note here is the one class of stock requirement. This essentially means that all shares must confer identical rights to distribution and liquidation proceeds.[81] In other words, you lose some of the economic flexibility that you have with partnerships to specially allocate certain tax items.

The historical tax advantage to partnerships (over their corporate counterparts) was pass-through taxation. The partnership does not pay taxes as an entity. Rather, the taxable income of the partnership flows through the partnership to the partners who then report their share of partnership income. Although this advantage has somewhat ebbed because of the advent of the S corporation, partnerships enjoy tremendous flexibility to custom tailor how partners share those tax items, something that, by definition, cannot be done with an S corporation. A sole proprietorship also does not have double taxation; the operations of the business are taxed to the individual on his or her tax return.

Related to whether the business profits are exposed to one or two levels of taxation is the impact of § 199A, which was passed as part of the law colloquially known as the Tax Cuts and Jobs Act (TCJA). Prior to the TCJA, the highest marginal corporate income tax rate was 35%, which the TCJA lowered to 21% as part of corporate tax reform. Because Congress provided corporate tax relief, it was pressured to give relief to non-corporate businesses too. It accomplished this relief by way of § 199A.[82] The full scope and operation of § 199A is complex, and it is not unpacked here; importantly, like with other changes ushered in by the TCJA, it is presently set to expire

---

79. I.R.C. § 1363.
80. I.R.C. § 1363(b). The exact contours and application of these requirements are outside the scope of this text. However, it is important to note that various exceptions and conventions apply to these rules (e.g., special counting rules for family members). E.g., I.R.C. § 1361(c).
81. Treas. Reg. § 1.1361-1(l).
82. I.R.C. § 199A.

I. Introduction

at the end of 2025. Briefly, § 199A allows non-corporate taxpayers—which include partners—a deduction equal to 20% of their "qualified business income" from a "qualified trade or business."[83] The TCJA's corporate rate reduction, the new § 199A deduction, and other changes has dramatically impacted the historical tax choice-of-entity analysis for income tax planning.[84]

Whether business income is subject to two levels of tax or benefits from § 199A both presuppose that the business does, in fact, generate income. Some businesses, though, generate losses, particularly in the start-up phase. Thus, a critical issue in tax choice-of-entity analysis is how the losses are handled. The main issue here is whether losses are "trapped" in the entity. The losses of a corporation are trapped inside it. That is, the owner will not get to benefit personally taxwise from a corporation's generated loss. For pass-through entities, though, the loss will flow-through to the owners.[85] Similarly, sole proprietors also get to benefit personally from losses of the enterprise by deducting the losses on their individual tax returns.

Another factor to consider in tax choice-of-entity analysis is the impact of employment taxes and fringe benefits. A full explication of the various planning opportunities and pitfalls here is beyond the scope of this text; however, a summary is still helpful. Employment taxes, such those relating to Social Security under the Federal Insurance Contributions Act (FICA)[86] and unemployment taxes (such as those under the Federal Unemployment Tax Act),[87] are levied on "wages." FICA taxes are levied on the employer and the employee. FICA taxes have two parts: first, the Old-Age and Survivors Insurance and Disability Insurance ("OASDI," also known as Social Security), and second, the Hospital Insurance (also known as Medicare). The OASDI portion is levied on wages up to a certain wage limit each year; the Medicare portion is levied on all wages with no cap. At time of this writing, the Social Security levy is 6.2% and the Medicare levy is 1.45%, both of which are levied on the employer and employee—so, in total, the combined levy is 15.3%. In an S corporation, if a shareholder is also employed, the portion of the wages paid to the shareholder-owner are subject to FICA.[88]

In addition to employment taxes, there is also the self-employment tax. The Self-Employed Contributions Act (SECA) mimics the FICA taxes on

---

83. I.R.C. § 199A(a), (b).
84. For some additional materials on the impact of § 199A on choice-of-entity planning, *see* MCKEE ET AL., *supra* note 29, ¶ 9.02 and John Cunningham, *What Every Business Lawyer Should Know About New IRC Section 199A*, 64 No. 4 PRACTICAL LAWYER 57 (Aug. 2018).
85. As we discuss in a later chapter, those losses may be subject to further restrictions, though.
86. *See* I.R.C. §§ 3101–3128.
87. *See* I.R.C. §§ 3301–3311.
88. In both corporations and S corporations, the wages paid are also deductible as an ordinary business expense. I.R.C. § 162. The wages are also included as income by the shareholder-owner. I.R.C. § 61.

I. Introduction

self-employment income; the SECA levy is 15.3%, which mimics the total employer-employee FICA rate discussed above.[89] At a policy level, therefore, we see a congressional desire to levy a similar tax on "wage" income, whether that be wages paid by an employer or income earned by a self-employed person (whose self-employment income serves as a proxy for wages). Thus, in a sole proprietorship, the net earnings from the business are subject to self-employment taxes.[90]

A critical issue in employment tax planning is whether partners can be employees; the quick answer is in the negative—partners cannot be employees.[91] This has been expressly confirmed in relation to employment taxes too.[92] Although partners cannot be employees, SECA prevents leakage from the employment tax base. The definition of net earnings from self-employment includes a partner's distributive share of partnership income from a trade or business.[93]

Although Congress has tried to match these taxes at the policy level, opportunities for tax planning exists. The main area for tax planning here surrounds the definition of self-employment earnings, which does not include the distributive share of an S corporation. The quintessential planning device, then, is to have an S corporation that pays its owner-employees a "reasonable salary," which exposes those amounts to FICA, but then the rest of the earnings (which would be the S corporation pass-through income) is excluded from wage taxes (FICA or SECA).[94]

The status of being an employee is important for other reasons too. One salient reason is the tax impact of other fringe benefits. The Code generally allows employers to provide various fringe benefits—like cafeteria plans—to its employees.[95] The tax benefits associated with various fringe benefits require them to be paid to "employees." Self-employed persons and partners, therefore, are not eligible generally for these tax

---

89. I.R.C. §§ 1401–1403.
90. This is a simplified explanation of the scope of the SECA levy.
91. *See, e.g.*, Comm'r v. Robinson, 273 F.2d 503, 505 (3d Cir. 1959) ("A partnership is not an employer of the partners.").
92. Rev. Rul. 69-124, 1969-1 C.B. 256 ("Bona fide members of a partnership are not employees of the partnership within the meaning of the Federal Insurance Contributions Act, the Federal Unemployment Tax Act, and the Collection of Income Tax at Source on Wages (chapters 21, 23, and 24, respectively, subtitle C, Internal Revenue Code of 1954).").
93. I.R.C. § 1402(a). A noteworthy exception is that for limited partners. The scope and contours of the limited partner exception is controversial; probing it is beyond this text. Indeed, Congress once even passed a law to prevent the Treasury from implementing further regulations on this point. *See, e.g.*, Renkemeyer, Campbell & Weaver, LLP v. Comm'r, 136 T.C. 137, 148 (2011).
94. *See, e.g.*, Timothy M. Todd, *Multiple-Entity Planning to Reduce Self-Employment Taxes: Recent Cases Demonstrate the Pitfalls and How to Avoid Them*, 13 JOURNAL OF TAX PRACTICE & PROCEDURE 31 (2011).
95. I.R.C. § 125.

I. Introduction

preferences.[96] We saw above that S corporation shareholders can also be employees, but a specific rule applies here, namely that, for certain purposes, the S corporation is treated as a partnership and any 2-percent shareholder is treated as a partner of such partnership.[97] Consequently, this also makes these owner-shareholders ineligible for many of the tax preferences for fringe benefits.

The last two factors consider the formation and exit of the enterprise. The tax consequences of business formation are broadly the same across business form, namely, that formations generally benefit from nonrecognition sections. The Code provides for nonrecognition treatment (meaning no gain or loss) for contributions of property to either a corporation or partnership.[98] Contributions of services, though, for an interest in the entity (whether it be a corporation or a partnership) may result in the recognition of income.[99] For a sole proprietorship, there is no transfer of property or services to an entity, obviating any particular formation tax issues.

Getting funds out of the entity, though, differs greatly between corporations, S corporations, and partnerships. Corporate dividends are taxable.[100] S corporation shareholders and partners can receive funds generally income-tax free to the extent of their basis in their interest[101] because the Code treats distributions first as a return of capital. Another dimension to consider is not just withdrawing funds from the entity, but also selling the entity interest. Given the entity approach to corporate taxation, selling corporate shares triggers a gain or loss based on the amount realized and the basis of the shares in the hands of the seller.[102] Selling an interest in a partnership similarly uses an entity approach, but then also uses an aggregate approach to prevent character shift.[103] For a sole proprietorship, there is no entity to sell, so the business is transferred by selling the underlying assets, each of which triggers a gain or loss calculation. In addition to straight sales, depending on the nature of the transaction, other provisions might operate. For example, corporations can benefit from various mergers and related transactions that can be tax deferred.[104] As well, special sections, such as

---

96. Although, they may be treated as employees for some benefits. E.g., Treas. Reg. § 1.132-1(b)(1), (2) (including in the definition of "employee" for purposes of a no-additional-cost-services fringe and working condition fringe a partner who performs services for the partnership).
97. I.R.C. § 1372.
98. See I.R.C. § 351 (providing nonrecognition treatment for contributions of property to a contributions) and § 721 (providing nonrecognition treatment for contributions of property to a partnership). Granted, the contours differ for a corporation and partnership; some of these differences are highlighted in Chapter 2.
99. This may be tempered by the application of § 83.
100. I.R.C. § 61.
101. See I.R.C. § 1368 (for S corporations) and § 731 (for partnerships).
102. I.R.C. §§ 61, 1001.
103. I.R.C. §§ 741, 751.
104. I.R.C. §§ 368 et seq.

I. Introduction

§ 1202—which allows an exclusion from income from the sale of qualified small business stock—are also important to consider in a choice-of-entity exit planning analysis.

Check-the-Box and Electing the Tax Regime

In the prior section, we briefly surveyed some of the relevant tax and nontax factors in a choice-of-entity analysis. As we saw, federal income taxes recognize the corporate, S corporation, partnership, and sole proprietor forms of business taxation. Historically, the federal taxation of the entity followed from its state law classification because the definitions were coterminous. So, a partnership under state law was taxed as a partnership (under Subchapter K) for federal income tax purposes. With the advent of hybrid-type entities, though, like the LLC—which share characteristics of both a partnership and a corporation—the Code wrestled with how these entities ought to be classified for federal income tax purposes.[105]

Before the advent of the "check-the-box" regulations, the taxation of LLCs were determined under the "Kintner Regulations."[106] These regulations were issued after *United States v. Kintner*, in which the Ninth Circuit held that an unincorporated group of physicians was taxable as a corporation even though corporations were not allowed to practice medicine.[107] The Kintner Regulations identified six characteristics to determine whether an entity looked more like a corporation or a partnership, which would determine its status for federal income tax purposes. Those characteristics included carrying on a business and dividing the gains, continuity of life, centralization of management, and limited liability.[108] Under these regulations, therefore, LLCs were forced to analyze these factors to determine whether they looked more like a corporation or a partnership.

In Revenue Ruling 88-76,[109] the IRS analyzed a Wyoming LLC under the Kintner factors and concluded that the LLC looked more like a partnership and should be taxed as such for federal tax purposes. Despite this ruling that advanced that LLCs could be taxed as partnerships, taxpayers and the government had to navigate continually this "classification morass."[110] Eventually, the IRS conceded in Notice 95-14 that the factor-based system was largely unworkable.[111] In 1996, the Service proposed (and later finalized)

---

105. *See, e.g.*, F. Philip Manns Jr. & Timothy M. Todd, *The Tax Lifecycle of the Single-Member LLC*, 36 VA. TAX REV. 323, 326–27 (2017).
106. *See id.*
107. 216 F.2d 418 (9th Cir. 1954).
108. Treas. Reg. § 301.7701-2(a)(1) (1993).
109. 1988-2 C.B. 360.
110. Manns & Todd, *supra* note 105, at 328.
111. *See id.*

1. Introduction

regulations that are colloquially known as the "check-the-box" regulations because the entity can simply check a box to elect its tax classification.

The regulations recognize three tax classifications for entities: (1) entities that are disregarded, (2) entities that are taxed as corporations, and (3) entities that are taxed as partnerships.[112] The regulations provide a default classification for a business entity. If a business entity is organized under a statute that refers to the entity as "incorporated," then it is a corporation for tax purposes.[113] An entity that is not a corporation but has two or more owners is classified as a partnership.[114] An entity that is not a corporation but has only one owner is treated as "disregarded,"[115] meaning it is treated as a sole proprietorship.

In addition to the default classifications, an entity that has two or more owners that is not a corporation can elect (i.e., check-the-box) to be taxed as a corporation or a partnership. Thus, as a default matter, a three-member LLC is a partnership for tax purposes; however, it can elect under the check-the-box regulations to be taxed as a corporation.[116] On the other hand, a LLC with only one member is a disregarded entity as a default matter, but it can elect to be taxed as a corporation.[117] Based on its number of owners, it cannot elect to be a partnership. The check-the-box election is made on IRS Form 8832 "Entity Classification Election."

---

112. *See* Treas. Reg. § 301.7701-3 (1996); Manns & Todd, *supra* note 105, at 329.
113. Treas. Reg. § 301.7701-3(a), § 301.7701-2(b)(1).
114. Treas. Reg. § 301.7701-3(b)(1)(i).
115. Treas. Reg. § 301.7701-3(b)(1)(ii).
116. It is more likely that the LLC desires to be taxed as an S corporation; conceptually, then, the election to be taxed as a corporation is a necessary intermediate step.
117. As above, it likely desires to be an S corporation and the corporate election is an intermediate step.

Formation of Partnerships

INTRODUCTION

In this chapter, we discuss the formation of a partnership. A partnership can receive capital in three ways: (1) from its owners (partners), (2) from creditors (i.e., debt), and (3) from operations. This chapter focuses exclusively on the first source, namely the partners making contributions of money or property to the partnership. As part of that discussion, we analyze the tax consequences to the partners and to the partnership as an entity. These tax consequences require the consideration of the need to recognize gain or loss on the contribution, the basis to the partners in their partnership interests, the basis to the partnership in the property it receives, and the holding period of both the contributed property and the partnership interests received. As we will observe, the Code generally strives for nonrecognition treatment (i.e., no gain or loss) on the contribution of property to a partnership in exchange for an interest in the partnership. This nonrecognition treatment is noteworthy because generally a taxpayer must recognize a gain or loss when he or she exchanges one piece of property for another.[1] The tradeoff for this nonrecognition treatment is the preservation of gain or loss in the contributed property. Although this chapter discusses the contribution of property to a partnership, the discussion here is focused on property

---

1. I.R.C. § 1001.

2. Formation of Partnerships

that is not subject to a liability. We turn to the impact of liabilities and debt in Chapter 6.

When forming any business, tax and nontax considerations need to be considered. This text, of course, focuses on the tax considerations in such decisions. However, it is important at the outset to be mindful that, although tax considerations are a driving factor in many of these decisions, they are not the only factors to consider.

Partnerships can be formed intentionally and, unlike their corporate and LLC counterparts, unintentionally as well. The state law issues incident to formation are normally examined as part of your Business Associations or Business Organizations course. But a quick overview is helpful for completeness and context. Let's start with the latter, as it probably piqued your interest.

A partnership is generally defined as two or more persons who carry on a business together under state law,[2] and this partnership can be formed intentionally or unintentionally.[3] In these informal partnerships, the various state partnership statutes provide a partnership agreement by default. For example, partners share equally in partnership profits and losses,[4] each partner has equal rights in the management of the partnership,[5] each partner is an agent for carrying on the partnership's business,[6] and the partners owe fiduciary duties to each other and the partnership.[7]

Partnerships can also be formed intentionally. Ideally, when partnerships are formed by design, they will be accompanied by a well-drafted partnership agreement. From a state law perspective, partnership agreements can modify many of the default rules provided by the state partnership statute.[8] The importance of a well-drafted partnership agreement—for both tax and nontax considerations—cannot be overstated. Indeed, as we will see throughout our study of partnership tax, the partnership agreement plays a central role in analyzing the tax consequences of many transactions. Moreover, tax provisions are often the most complicated part of a partnership agreement.[9]

---

2. *See, e.g.*, Va. Code Ann. § 50-73.79; Revised Uniform Partnership Act (RUPA) § 101(6).
3. *See, e.g.*, Va. Code Ann. § 50-73.88(A); Revised Uniform Partnership Act § 202(a).
4. E.g., Va. Code Ann. § 50-73.99.
5. Id.
6. Va. Code Ann. § 50-73.91.
7. Va. Code Ann. § 50-73.102.
8. Va. Code Ann. § 50-73.81.
9. In the LLC context, this is known as an "operating agreement."

2. Formation of Partnerships

So far, this discussion has implicitly regarded the formation of "general partnerships." However, intentionally created general partnerships are rare today.[10] Rather, partnerships with limited liability, such as the limited partnership, or the even more popular limited liability company (LLC) are used regularly. Indeed, the LLC is the darling of contemporary business practice. The tax formation discussion that follows is the same for entities *taxed as a partnership* regardless of their underlying state law classification.[11]

When analyzing any partnership tax issue, including formation issues, it is important to analyze the consequences to both the contributing partner and the entity.[12] The tax dimensions to consider are the same for each: (1) the magnitude of any gain or loss recognized in the property contributed, (2) the tax character of that gain or loss, (3) the basis in the new property received, and (4) the holding period in the property received. For the contributing partner, the focus is on the property contributed to the partnership and the partnership interest that was received in exchange; for the partnership, the focus is on the partnership interest given to the contributing partner in exchange for the contributed property and the received property.

Before we turn to more specifics of the formation of a partnership and its general nonrecognition framework, let's discuss a key theme in this chapter, which will help us see the forest from the trees. We will observe below that the main theme of partnership formation is that of nonrecognition—that is, contributions of property to a partnership are not taxable events. The underlying theory here is that the partners have not "cashed out" of their investment in the underlying contributed property, but rather they changed the form of the investment. Indeed, this is a theme common to all nonrecognition provisions, such as § 1031 (like-kind exchanges).[13] As a preview of things to come later in this text, we will also see this nonrecognition treatment occur in certain partnership exits. Thus, we see a symmetry in entering and exiting a partnership: the Code desires nonrecognition to the fullest extent possible.

---

10. This is due to the unlimited liability borne by all partners in a general partnership.
11. See the discussion in Chapter 1 about the check-the-box regulations.
12. Indeed, students tend to omit discussing entity-perspective considerations. In corporate tax scenarios, this is even more acute because the entity may have its own tax liability to pay; although partnerships don't pay taxes directly, for completeness it is still important to state that with the relevant statutory authority as appropriate.
13. The regulations, for example, state the rationale as "[t]he underlying assumption of these exceptions is that the new property is substantially a continuation of the old investment still unliquidated. . . ." Treas. Reg. § 1.1002-1(c) (note that I.R.C. § 1002 has been repealed).

2. Formation of Partnerships

NONRECOGNITION FRAMEWORK

The main tax sections that govern partnership formations are §§ 721, 722, and 723. Together, these sections provide a generally easy-to-apply nonrecognition framework for the partner and the partnership: No gain or loss is recognized in the case of contribution of property to the partnership in exchange for a partnership interest, and any gain or loss inherent in the contributed property is preserved by way of an exchanged basis in the partnership interest and a transferred basis for the partnership.[14] Each of these sections will be discussed in turn.

Section 721(a) provides that "[n]o gain or loss shall be recognized to a partnership or to any of its partners in the case of a contribution of property to the partnership in exchange for an interest in the partnership."[15] Although this rule is short, its impact is profound. Moreover, this nonrecognition rule applies both at initial formation *and* for partnerships that are already operating.[16] Let's unpack this rule in more detail.

First, note that the rule provides that no gain or loss shall be *recognized*. This brings to the fore the difference between *realized* gains and *recognized* gains. Indeed, this is the familiar § 1001 framework. Under § 1001, gain is defined as the excess of the amount realized over the adjusted basis (AR minus AB), and loss is the excess of the adjusted basis over amount realized (AB minus AR).[17] Section 1001(c) provides the general rule that, when a gain or loss is *realized*, it must also be *recognized*. In this context, to be recognized means to be reported on a tax return. Thus, when you get the economic benefit of a gain (i.e., *realize* it), you must report it for tax purposes (i.e., *recognize* it); colloquially, realization is married to nonrecognition. Nonrecognition provisions, however, separate in time the realization event and the recognition event.[18]

---

14. See I.R.C. § 7701(a)(43) & (44) for the definitions of transferred basis property and exchanged basis property, respectively.
15. I.R.C. § 721(a).
16. See Treas. Reg. § 1.721-1(a). By contrast, the nonrecognition rule for corporate shareholders, § 351, has a "control" requirement, which is absent in § 721.
17. The statutory text uses the word "over" to convey a subtraction operation. For example, $100 over $25 is the same as $100 less [minus] $25.
18. You may have covered other nonrecognition provisions in previous tax courses. For example, § 1031 is a commonly used nonrecognition provision for the exchange of like-kind property. And, if you have studied corporate tax, you have undoubtedly examined § 351, which is the analogue nonrecognition provision for corporate formations. It is imprecise (and incorrect) to refer to these as "tax-free" provisions. This nomenclature is unfortunate. As we will see, the gain or loss does not vanish or go away, it merely gets transferred (by way of the basis provisions).

2. Formation of Partnerships

Second, note that § 721 applies only to contributions of *property*.[19] The term property is not defined in § 721 or the accompanying regulations. The closest analogue is the use of the word "property" in § 351,[20] which is the nonrecognition provision for shareholders in corporate formations. Some common items of property contributed to a partnership under § 721 include cash, investment assets, equipment, real or personal property, and installment obligations. Regardless of the exact contours of "property" for § 721 purposes, some items are clearly beyond its ambit. For example, services are not property.[21] As well, the regulations make a distinction between a contribution of property and transferring a right that allows the partnership to use the property.[22]

The contribution of personal notes (i.e., notes in which the partner is the debtor) presents thorny issues. Although commentators note that personal notes can be property for § 721 purposes,[23] there are collateral issues that inject ambiguity into the analysis. For example, the calculation of the note's basis — which will have consequences to the basis for the partnership that will now hold it, as well as the partner's interest in his or her partnership interest — becomes salient. Alas, this same issue arises in corporate formations, too. One of the more noteworthy cases in the corporate context is *Perracchi v. Commissioner*.[24] In *Perracchi*, the Ninth Circuit held that a shareholder had a basis equal to the face value of a contributed personal note.[25] In that case, however, the court expressly disclaimed applying its holding in the S corporation or partnership tax context because of flow-through of losses and the potential for mischief.[26]

Rest assured, we will revisit this potential mischief in later sections. In sum, the regulations note that "the substance of the transaction will govern, rather than its form."[27] Thus, the theme for ascertaining "property" for § 721 is to identify whether the partner is giving up something of value in exchange for the partnership interest.[28]

Third, it is important to note the exceptions to § 721. Section 721(b) provides an express exception in the statutory text: "Subsection (a) shall not apply to gain realized on a transfer of property to a partnership which would be treated as an investment company (within the meaning of section 351) if the partnership were incorporated."[29] An investment company

---

19. In later chapters, we discuss the tax consequences to a partner that contributes or provides *services* in exchange for a partnership interest.
20. WILLIAM S. MCKEE ET AL., FEDERAL TAXATION OF PARTNERSHIPS ¶ 4.02 (2022).
21. Indeed, contribution of services for partnerships interests are covered in Chapter 9.
22. Treas. Reg. § 1.721-1(a); *see also* MCKEE ET AL., *supra* note 20, ¶ 4.02.
23. E.g., MCKEE ET AL., *supra* note 20, ¶ 4.02.
24. 143 F.3d 487 (9th Cir. 1998).
25. Id. at 496.
26. Id. at 494 & n.16.
27. Treas. Reg. § 1.721-1(a).
28. MCKEE ET AL., *supra* note 20, ¶ 4.02.
29. I.R.C. § 721(b).

2. Formation of Partnerships

is defined specifically in Treas. Reg. § 1.351-1(c)(1). An investment company for these purposes is a regulated investment company, a real estate investment trust, or a corporation in which more than 80% of its assets are held for investment and consists of certain property (e.g., readily marketable securities).[30]

Other exceptions to § 721 are provided by regulation, which is intimated by § 721(c). Although a deep dive of § 721(c) is beyond the scope of this text, in brief, § 721(c) applies to partnerships in which there is a contribution of property with a built-in gain and, after the contribution, a related foreign person is a direct or indirect partner.[31] In short, the concern and mischief that § 721(c) and its accompanying regulations are designed to patch is the ability of a U.S. taxpayer to shift items of gain to a foreign partner.[32]

Lastly, it is important to realize that § 721 does not act in isolation. In other words, although § 721 provides generally that no gain or loss is recognized upon a contribution of property to a partnership, there are other sections that interact with § 721—namely §§ 731 and 752, which regard the treatment of liabilities. In short, when considered jointly, these sections can result in the recognition of gain even though § 721 is operating. Importantly, though, the gain emanates not from any built-in gain inherent in the contributed property (due to § 721), but rather from a deemed distribution of cash (under §§ 752 and 731). We will revisit these concepts after we unpack the impact of liabilities on basis.

BASIS, HOLDING PERIOD, AND CHARACTER

On its face, § 721 appears to be a windfall: avoiding the recognition of built-in gain inherent in property contributed to a partnership. However, as noted earlier, nonrecognition sections only *defer* gain, they do not *destroy* gain. Indeed, this is the "magic" behind nonrecognition sections. Whether it is §§ 1031 (like-kind exchanges), 351 (corporate formations), or 721 (partnership formations), nonrecognition sections work by transferring unrealized gain from the contributed property to the received property.

---

30. Treas. Reg. § 1.351-1(c)(1). A similar disallowance rule applies in corporate formation, too. *See* I.R.C. § 351(e). Note, however, that the two disallowance sections are not identical. Section 351(e) prevents the nonrecognition of either gain or loss (as the *section* does not apply), whereas § 721(b) provides that nonrecognition shall not apply to *gain*.
31. As a general disclaimer, as noted in the prefatory pages, this book does not cover international aspects of partnership tax.
32. E.g., H.R. Conf. Rep. No. 220, 105th Cong., 1st Sess. 629 (1997) (noting that "regulatory authority is granted to provide for gain recognition on a transfer of appreciated property to a partnership in cases where such gain otherwise would be transferred to a foreign partner").

2. Formation of Partnerships

Think of this like a tax version of thermodynamics: energy (gain) can't be created or destroyed; it can only be transferred. Similarly, in our nonrecognition sections, the gain inherent in the system (property) before the transaction, will be equal to the gain accounted for after the transaction—either reported on a tax return or inherent in the new property.[33] The Code ensures this result by its basis rules. Relatedly, this equilibrium helps you check your answers: test the gain before the transaction and after—has it all been accounted for? If not, you have an error in your calculations or analysis. The Code does not generally allow for gain leakage—the gain either needs to be inherent in other property or reported on an income tax return.[34]

There are two types of basis in our study of partnership tax. First is the basis of a partner in his partnership interest, which is known as "outside basis."[35] Second is the basis of the partnership (as entity) in the assets it owns, which is known as "inside basis."[36] Together, these concepts ensure that gain does not leak out of the system.

Before we dive into the operation of these sections, it is helpful to recall what basis is conceptually. Basis represents capital (or investment) that has already been subject to income taxation. It is this reason why § 1001 allows you to subtract out the basis in calculating gain: the basis in a piece of property has already been exposed to income tax, it ought not be exposed again. In a simple example, assume a taxpayer earns $100 in wages. Those wages are subject to income tax under § 61. Thus, if the taxpayer takes the after-tax wages and uses them to purchase Blackacre, §§ 1011 and 1012 allow the taxpayer a "cost basis" in the property (as that capital was already taxed). When the taxpayer later sells Blackacre, he or she subtracts out the previously taxed capital (the basis) to determine the gain; therefore, think of the gain as the "new capital" that has not yet been exposed to income tax. Although a simple example, it animates why tracking capital is so important in partnership tax: we are trying to track the capital that has and has not been taxed. The need to do this accurately becomes particularly acute in the partnership context because of the entity versus aggregate distinction.

Outside Basis

The basis of a partner in his partnership interest is governed by § 722. Section 722 provides, in full, that "[t]he basis of an interest in a partnership acquired by a contribution of property, including money, to the partnership

---

33. In other words, tax is the physics of law!
34. Note, on the other hand, the Code has no problem with loss disappearing into the ether. *See, e.g.*, I.R.C. §§ 267, 1015.
35. The Code does not use this language, but it is used colloquially among tax practitioners.
36. *See supra* note 35.

shall be the amount of such money and the adjusted basis of such property to the contributing partner at the time of the contribution increased by the amount (if any) of gain recognized under section 721(b) to the contributing partner at such time."[37] Thus, a simple formula results:[38]

$$\text{Outside Basis} = \text{Money Contributed} + \Sigma\,AB \text{ of property contributed} + \S 721(b) \text{ gain}.$$

In most cases, the last part—§ 721(b) gain—will be equal to $0 (recall that § 721(b) refers to transfers to transfers to investment companies). Practically, then, the formula simplifies to the (beginning) outside basis for a partner is the total of the money contributed plus the sum of all the adjusted bases of property contributed by the partner. The modifier "beginning" was added because, as we'll see, outside basis is not static—it is dynamic and constantly changing due to the results of partnership operations and other transactions.[39]

Inside Basis

The partnership's basis in partnership property is governed by § 723. Section 723 provides, in full, "[t]he basis of property contributed to a partnership by a partner shall be the adjusted basis of such property to the contributing partner at the time of the contribution increased by the amount (if any) of gain recognized under section 721(b) to the contributing partner at such time."[40] Similarly, then, the following formula results:

$$\text{Inside Basis} = \Sigma\,AB \text{ of property contributed} + \S 721(b) \text{ gain}.$$

Noticeably, the inclusion of money is absent in the formula, unlike in § 722. However, it is *implicitly* there, as the partnership must have a basis in the money it received from a partner.

Now that we have the basic operations of §§ 721, 722, and 723, an example can illustrate both the mechanics and the reasoning (the why) behind the rules. Consider Alvin and Barry who each contribute cash and a piece of real property to form the AB Partnership. Alvin contributes $10,000 cash and real property, Blackacre, which has a fair market value of $40,000

---

37. I.R.C. § 722.
38. Σ is the "sigma" operator, representing "sum up."
39. For example, due to a change in partnership liabilities (debt). This is akin to a shareholder's stock basis in his or her S corporation, which similarly ebbs and flows, and in contradistinction to a shareholder's stock basis in a C corporation, which generally does not change due to corporate operations or distributions.
40. I.R.C. § 723.

2. Formation of Partnerships

and a basis of $25,000. Barry contributes $25,000 in cash and real property, Redacre, which has a fair market value of $25,000 and a basis of $20,000.

Consider the status quo ante—the tax characteristics of Alvin and Barry before partnership formation:[41]

Alvin	Barry
Cash FMV: $10,000 AB: $10,000 Built-in Gain: $0	*Cash* FMV: $25,000 AB: $25,000 Built-in Gain: $0
Blackacre FMV: $40:000 AB: $25,000 Built-in Gain: $15,000	*Redacre* FMV: $25,000 AB: $20,000 Built-in Gain: $5,000
Total Built-in Gain: $15,000	Total Built-in Gain: $5,000
"System" Built-in Gain: $20,000	

Take note that Alvin and Barry have built-in gains inherent in their property of $15,000 and $5,000, respectively. In other words, if either of them engaged in a taxable transaction with their real property, that built-in gain would be realized and recognized.[42] Combined, the "system" has a built-in gain of $20,000.

Before we even analyze the operation of §§ 721, 722, and 723, we should be able to intuit the net conclusion based on the rationale supporting nonrecognition provisions. If no gain is recognized (reported), each partner should still have his or her built-in gain after the nonrecognition transaction (i.e., § 721), and the system gain should be preserved: the gain present before should be accounted for after (either still built-in or reported on a tax return). Colloquially, there should not be gain leakage.

Let's work through the Code sections now. Under § 721, both Alvin and Barry have no gain (or loss) recognized for contributing their property in

---

41. In many contexts, the adjusted basis and fair market value of money (cash) is not listed separately; it is instead listed at its face value. However, early in this text, such distinction is used here for completeness and transparency. As an aside, many take for granted that cash tends to have a basis equal to its face value (the underlying reasoning being that generally the cash was included in income when it was received). Though generally true, that isn't *always* true, however. For example, conceptually, if a deductible Individual Retirement Account consisted fully of deductible contributions, and assume only cash was in the account, that cash effectively has a $0 basis (as none of it has been exposed to income taxation). See I.R.C. §§ 408, 72.

42. Assuming, of course, that the property is sold at its fair market value.

2. Formation of Partnerships

exchange for their partnership interest. As well, under § 721, the partnership has no gain or loss upon transferring an interest to the partners. Under § 722, Alvin takes a basis of $35,000 (outside basis) in his newly acquired partnership interest ($10,000 [money contributed] + $25,000 [AB of contributed property] = $35,000); Barry takes a $45,000 basis in his partnership interest ($25,000 [money contributed] + $20,000 [AB of contributed property] = $45,000). Lastly, under § 723, the partnership has an inside basis of $25,000 in Blackacre and $20,000 in Redacre (and, implicitly, a $35,000 basis in the cash).

Consider, now, the tax characteristics of the parties:

Alvin	Barry	AB Partnership	
Cash	Cash	Cash	
$0	$0	FMV: $35,000	
		AB: $35,000	
		Built-in Gain: $0	
Partnership Interest	Partnership Interest	Blackacre	Redacre
FMV: $50,000	FMV: $50,000	FMV: $40,000	FMV: $25,000
AB: $35,000	AB: $45,000	AB: $25,000	AB: $20,000
Built-in Gain: $15,000	Built-in Gain: $5,000	Built-in Gain: $15,000	Built-in Gain: $5,000
Total Built-in Gain: $15,000	Total Built-in Gain: $5,000	Total Built-in Gain: $20,000	
"System" Built-in Gain: $20,000		"System" Built-in Gain: $20,000	

This is an elegant result. Observe that Alvin and Barry each still have their built-in gain (of $15,000 and $5,000, respectively), but it has been transferred from their real property to their partnership interest.[43] The partnership also has $20,000 of built-in gain inherent in the assets *inside* the partnership (hence the colloquialism *inside* basis).

At first blush, you may be concerned about a potential double tax here—that is, there is $20,000 in each system (the individual and entity systems).[44] However, the beauty of partnership tax is that, over time, it equalizes the systems (as we will see in the next chapter). As a preview, say the partnership sells Blackacre for $40,000 and realizes that $15,000 gain.

---

43. The partnership has total assets of $100,000; as such, their 50% interests are worth $50,000 each.
44. The double tax on formation does occur with C corporations and is a reason that taxpayers may prefer partnerships or S corporation taxation.

2. Formation of Partnerships

It will need to allocate that gain to Alvin, who will then report that $15,000 on his individual tax return.[45] Consequently, Alvin will get to increase the basis in his partnership interest by $15,000, obviating the double counting of the gain.[46]

Now, let's see what happens when, instead of built-in gain, there is a built-in loss. Take the same facts with Alvin and Barry, but let's flip Alvin's built-in gain of $15,000 to a built-in loss of $15,000 — that is, the property still has a value of $40,000 but it now has a tax basis of $55,000. Thus, the status quo ante before formation:

Alvin	Barry
Cash	*Cash*
FMV: $10,000	FMV: $25,000
AB: $10,000	AB: $25,000
Built-in Gain: $0	Built-in Gain: $0
Blackacre	*Redacre*
FMV: $40,000	FMV: $25,000
AB: $55,000	AB: $20,000
Built-in Loss: $15,000	Built-in Gain: $5,000
Total Built-in Loss: $15,000	Total Built-in Gain: $5,000
"System" Built-in Gain: $5,000; Built-in Loss: $15,000	

Given the nonrecognition framework, let's predict the result here: The gain should not be able to leak out, so Barry should still have a $5,000 built-in gain after the formation dust settles. But, what about Alvin? Well, there's two potential outcomes here. Perhaps the Code should preserve the built-in loss (harkening back to our energy analogy). On the other hand, perhaps the Code treats losses differently than gains, and it has no problem with the loss evaporating into the ether.[47] Let's examine the statutory result.

---

45. I.R.C. § 704(c).
46. I.R.C. § 705.
47. You may be asking, why does the Code perhaps not care as much about losses evaporating. Well, recall what a loss pragmatically represents: a reduction in income (assuming the loss is deductible). A reduction in income means, everything else being equal, a reduction in taxes owed, and thus less money to the government. Consequently, losses that evaporate (disappear) do not cost the government any money. On the other hand, gains that leak out are anathema — a gain leakage means that the government has lost out on money due to the leakage (by way of the reduction in income). As well, the Code is concerned about the ability of related parties to shift losses to each other to lower taxable income. *See, e.g.*, I.R.C. §§ 267 (disallowing losses between related parties), 1015 (disallowing the transfer of a loss in transfers that constitute a gift).

2. Formation of Partnerships

Let's start first with Barry. Under § 721, Barry has no gain recognized for contributing his property in exchange for his partnership interest. Under § 722, Barry takes a basis of $45,000 in his partnership interest ($25,000 [money contributed] + $20,000 [AB of Redacre] = $45,000). Now, let's consider Alvin. Section 721 provides that *neither gain nor loss* shall be recognized to the partnership or the partner. Consequently, Alvin does not recognize the loss inherent in Blackacre. Under § 722, Alvin will take a basis in his partnership interest of $65,000 ($10,000 [money contributed] + $55,000 [AB of Blackacre] = $65,000). Like before, under § 721, the partnership has no gain or loss upon transferring an interest to the partners. Finally, under § 723, the partnership will have a basis of $55,000 and $20,000 in Blackacre and Redacre, respectively (and an implicit basis of $35,000 in the cash).

After the dust settles in this example, the following results:

Alvin	Barry	AB Partnership	
Cash	Cash	Cash	
$0	$0	AB: $35,000	
		FMV: $35,000	
		Built-in Gain: $0	
Partnership Interest	Partnership Interest	Blackacre	Redacre
FMV: $50,000	FMV: $50,000	FMV: $40,000	FMV: $25,000
AB: $65,000	AB: $45,000	AB: $55,000	AB: $20,000
Built-in Loss: $15,000	Built-in Gain: $5,000	Built-in Loss: $15,000	Built-in Gain: $5,000
Total Built-in Loss: $15,000	Total Built-in Gain: $5,000	Total Built-in Gain: $5,000; Built-in Loss: $15,000	
"System" Built-in Gain: $5,000; Built-in Loss: $15,000		"System" Built-in Gain: $5,000; Built-in Loss: $15,000	

As you can see, the elegant result continues. The status quo ante—the tax characteristics that existed before partnership formation—exists after partnership formation, even in the cases of built-in loss. Just like in the prior example, as a preview of things to come, if the partnership were to recognize that loss in a property transaction (e.g., selling Blackacre), it would need to allocate that loss to Alvin, whose outside basis would concomitantly decrease, thus preventing him from having the loss twice (on the sale of Blackacre and later on the sale of his partnership interest).[48]

---

48. I.R.C. § 704(c).

2. Formation of Partnerships

Holding Period

The next item to consider in the formation analysis is the holding period of property—both with respect to the individual partners (in their partnership interest), which is governed by § 1223(1) and referred to as "exchanged basis," and the partnership (in its newly acquired property), which is governed by § 1223(2) and is referred to as "transferred basis." The holding period of an asset refers to the measurement of time for which the property is to be considered owned by the taxpayer. Holding period becomes primarily important when you calculate the gain or loss on an asset disposition because short-term and long-term capital gains and losses can be treated differently. Generally, long-term capital gains are treated preferentially.[49] Thus, when one property is exchanged for another—like we have in the § 721 context—the issue arises of whether the replacement property can "tack on" to the holding period of the exchanged asset.

Section 1223 provides the rules for determining the holding periods of property. This section provides that the replacement property can tack onto (i.e., include) the holding period of the exchanged property if two elements are satisfied. First, the replacement property must have an exchanged basis—in other words, the replacement property's basis is determined in whole or in part by the exchanged property. In § 721 transactions, that criterion is readily satisfied (recall the operation of § 722). Second—and this is the part with more transactional friction—the exchanged property must have been either a capital asset (under § 1221) or § 1231 property.

Let's briefly discuss § 1221 and § 1231. Capital assets are defined in § 1221. This section works by exclusion; that is, an asset is a capital asset *unless* it is listed in § 1221. Notable examples of items listed in § 1221—and therefore not capital assets—are inventory, depreciable business property, certain intellectual property assets (depending on how they were created), and certain notes and receivables (depending on how they were acquired).

Section 1231, for its part, is opaquer. Section 1231 regards gains and losses on "property used in the trade or business."[50] That term, moreover, is also defined in the section as, generally, "property used in the trade or business, of a character which is subject to the allowance for depreciation provided in section 167, held for more than 1 year, and real property used in the trade or business, held for more than a year. . . ."[51] Certain property is then expressly removed from this definition, including inventory, property held primarily for sale to customers, and certain intellectual property assets.[52]

---

49. E.g., I.R.C. § 1(h) (providing a preferential tax calculation for *net capital gain*).
50. I.R.C. § 1231(a)(3)(A), (B).
51. I.R.C. § 1231(b).
52. I.R.C. § 1231(b)(1)(A), (B), (C).

2. Formation of Partnerships

Synthesizing these sections together, then, certain property is not eligible for a tacked holding period. A key example of such property is inventory because it is not a capital asset, and it is expressly excluded from the definition of § 1231 property. Another *potential* example is depreciable business property. Although depreciable business property is not a capital asset (§ 1221(a)(2)), it becomes § 1231 property if (and only if) it is held for *more* than one year. The last key asset that prevents tacked holding periods is cash.

Consider the earlier Alvin and Barry situation in which they each contribute a piece of real property (Blackacre and Redacre). Whether the parcels of real property are capital assets or § 1231 property depends on their use in the hands of Alvin and Barry. For example, if Alvin was a real estate developer, Blackacre could be inventory or property held for sale to customers. Let's assume that the parcels were just investment property in the hands of Alvin and Barry, and that neither Alvin nor Barry are in the trade or business of real estate investing. Consequently, the properties would be capital assets; if those properties were contributed in exchange for their partnership interests, the holding period of their newly acquired partnership interests would include their holding periods of Blackacre and Redacre.

There is one more wrinkle to discuss with respect to holding period (and it's a big one). Typically, partnership interests are considered "unitary," meaning they are treated like a singular unit or thing, especially with respect to basis.[53] But consider the situation, which can easily and readily occur, if a partner contributes property in exchange for a partnership interest of property that does and does not tack. For example, consider a partner who contributes cash and depreciable business property held for more than one year. In this situation, some property has been contributed that offers no tacking (the cash) and some property that offers tacking (the depreciable property, which is § 1231 property). In these situations, divided holding periods are required.

Treas. Reg. § 1.1223-3 controls in these situations. It provides that, generally, partners do "not have a divided holding period in an interest in a partnership."[54] Two exceptions apply. First, if the partner acquires the partnership interest at different times. Second, if "partner acquired portions of the partnership interest in exchange for property transferred at the same time but resulting in different holding periods."[55] The regulations prescribe a fraction-based method for determining the applicable holding periods. Consider the following simple example from the regulation:

---

53. E.g., Rev. Rul. 84-53, 1984-1 C.B. 159 (1984) ("Consistent with the provisions of Subchapter K of the Code, a partner has a single basis in a partnership interest....").
54. Treas. Reg. § 1.1223-3(a).
55. Id.

2. Formation of Partnerships

A contributes $5,000 of cash and a nondepreciable capital asset A has held for two years to a partnership (PRS) for a 50 percent interest in PRS. A's basis in the capital asset is $5,000, and the fair market value of the asset is $10,000. After the exchange, A's basis in A's interest in PRS is $10,000, and the fair market value of the interest is $15,000. A received one-third of the interest in PRS for a cash payment of $5,000 ($5,000/$15,000). Therefore, A's holding period in one-third of the interest received (attributable to the contribution of money to the partnership) begins on the day after the contribution. A received two-thirds of the interest in PRS in exchange for the capital asset ($10,000/$15,000). Accordingly, pursuant to section 1223(1), A has a two-year holding period in two-thirds of the interest received in PRS.[56]

In conclusion, this section reviewed the general nonrecognition framework for contribution of property in exchange for a partnership interest. The main operating sections are 721, 722, 723, and 1223. Section 721 provides the general nonrecognition rule, i.e., no gain or loss is *recognized*. Section 722 provides the rule for *outside basis*, i.e., the basis of a partner in his or her partnership interest. Outside basis is generally the sum of money contributed and the adjusted bases of contributed property. Section 723 provides the rule for *inside basis*, i.e., the basis of the partnership in the contributed (received) assets. That rule is generally the partnership takes the basis in the property that the contributing partner had. Lastly, § 1223 provided the rules for holding period; holding period can be "tacked" depending on the underlying nature of the assets. Under § 1223(2), for the property contributed by the partners, the partnership tacks the holding period.

Character Matters

In addition to holding period, another matter to consider is the character of the built-in gain or loss inherent in the property received by the partnership. Indeed, one of the themes of partnership tax is to prevent a taxpayer's ability to change the character of a tax item (e.g., to change ordinary income into a capital gain, which may benefit from lower tax rates). Section 724 provides three rules that prevent certain character changes.[57] The first rule is that if a partner contributes an "unrealized receivable,"[58] any gain or loss recognized by the partnership will be ordinary income or loss.[59] The second rule is that if a partner contributes an "inventory item,"[60] any gain or loss recognized

---

56. Treas. Reg. § 1.223-3(f) Example 1.
57. On the distribution side, § 735 provides similar rules concerning property received in a partnership distribution. These rules are discussed in Chapter 7.
58. I.R.C. § 724(d)(1).
59. I.R.C. § 724(a).
60. I.R.C. § 724(d)(2).

2. Formation of Partnerships

by the partnership will be ordinary income or loss if disposed of within five years.[61] The third rule is that if a partner contributes a capital asset, any loss recognized by the partnership within five years will be treated as a capital loss to the extent that such loss existed at the date of contribution.[62]

CONVERTING FROM A SOLE PROPRIETORSHIP

In the earlier section, we had "clean" examples. In other words, two (or more) partners were starting fresh with the partnership, and each was contributing property to that "new" partnership. However, in the real world, partnerships are formed sometimes when someone who has been operating the business solely brings on a new owner. Bringing on the new owner converts the sole proprietorship into a partnership.[63]

Although there are myriad state law considerations to analyze in such a conversion (e.g., how to structure the buy-in, what state law entity to use, updating [or drafting] entity operating documents, etc.), we will focus here on the tax consequences. The framework for these conversions is provided by Revenue Ruling 99-5.[64] In particular, the revenue ruling deals with the "federal income tax consequences when a single member limited liability company that is disregarded as an entity separate from its owner... becomes an entity with more than one owner that is classified as a partnership for federal tax purposes."[65]

There are two ways to structure these buy-ins. First, the new partner ("member" in LLC terms) buys the membership interest from the current single member. Second, the new partner contributes (e.g., cash or property) to the entity in exchange for the membership interest. The same the non-recognition framework under § 721 discussed in the last section applies in these situations too.

Let's first consider the situation in which the new partner buys the LLC interest from the current single member. When the new member buys that interest, the entity is converted to a partnership for tax purposes.[66] Under the revenue ruling, moreover, the purchase of the entity interest is treated as a purchase of a proportionate share of each underlying asset of the entity.[67] So, for example, if the new member is buying a 50% interest, it is like he

---

61. I.R.C. § 724(b).
62. I.R.C. § 724(c).
63. In Chapter 10, we consider an example of the reverse situation, that is, converting from a partnership to a non-partnership (like incorporating an active partnership).
64. 1999-6 I.R.B. 8.
65. Id.
66. Rev. Rul. 99-5, 1999-1 C.B. 434.
67. Id.

2. Formation of Partnerships

purchased 50% of each asset of the entity. Immediately after that deemed purchase of underlying assets, the two members are treated as if they contributed their property to a partnership in exchange for ownership interests in the partnership.[68]

In other words, there are basically two transactions here. First, the single member is deemed to sell a percentage of each asset, which triggers gain or loss under § 1001 for him or her. Second, the two partners then make a § 721 contribution to the partnership. Consider the following example, in which A is the single member of Entity, LLC with the following balance sheet:

Entity, LLC
Cash
FMV: $10,000
AB: $10,000
Blackacre
FMV: $20,000
AB: $10,000

B is going to purchase a 50% interest in Entity, LLC from A for $15,000. The first step of the transaction under the revenue ruling, therefore, consists of a proportionate asset sale from A to B. Thus, it is like A sells $5,000 of cash and $10,000 of Blackacre to B in exchange for $15,000. Personally, A must calculate gain and loss on that transaction under § 1001. There is no gain or loss in the cash, but A would recognize a gain on the deemed sale of Blackacre; that is calculated as the amount realized (here, $10,000 [50% of the FMV]) less the proportionate adjusted basis (here, $5,000 [50% of the AB]) resulting in a gain of $5,000. That gain would be long- or short-term and capital or ordinary depending on the nature and holding period of Blackacre to A. After this deemed sale, the balance sheets of A and B look thusly:

A	B
Cash	Cash
FMV: $5,000	FMV: $5,000
AB: $5,000	AB: $5,000
Blackacre	Blackacre
FMV: $10,000	FMV: $10,000
AB: $5,000	AB: $10,000

---

68. Id.

2. Formation of Partnerships

Now, A and B contribute that property (the cash and Blackacre) to the AB partnership in exchange for their partnership interest under § 721; that analysis is now the same as in the prior section, such that, after the contribution, the balance sheet looks thusly:

A	B	AB Partnership
Cash	Cash	Cash
0	0	AB: $10,000
		FMV: $10,000
Partnership Interest	Partnership Interest	Blackacre
FMV: $15,000	FMV: $15,000	FMV: $20,000
AB: $10,000	AB: $15,000	AB: $15,000

The holding period analysis is governed by § 1223. Note that this example is more complicated than the underlying revenue ruling because cash and property are contributed. Let's assume first if just property (Blackacre) was contributed. In that case, if Blackacre was a capital asset in A's hands,[69] then A's holding period for the partnership interest is tacked (i.e., includes the holding period of Blackacre). B's holding period, on the other hand, begins on the date after the purchase of the LLC interest.[70] For the entity, its holding period in Blackacre includes that of A and B under § 1223(2).

However, the above example, as written, includes a contribution of cash and property. Consequently, we need to use the fractional approach to holding period discussed earlier. Recall that, under § 1223(1), tacked holding period can apply only to capital assets and § 1231 assets; cash, however, is neither of those. Thus, under Treas. Reg. § 1.1223-3(b), the fractional approach must be used. Under that approach, the numerator is equal to the FMV of the portion of the partnership interest received in the transaction (to which the holding period relates) and the denominator is the FMV of the entire partnership interest. In this example, then, the following fraction results for A:

For the portion allocable to Blackacre (a capital asset):

$$\frac{\$10,000\,[\text{the FMV of the partnership interest allocable to Blackacre}]}{\$15,000\,[\text{the FMV of the entire partnership interest}]} = \frac{2}{3}$$

---

[69]. Also, Blackacre could not be a § 1231 asset in A's (or anyone else's) hands because land is not depreciable.
[70]. *See* Rev. Rul. 99-5, 1999-1 C.B. 434; Rev. Rul. 66-7, 1966-1 C.B. 188.

2. Formation of Partnerships

Thus, A's holding period in 2/3 of the partnership interest includes the prior holding period of Blackacre (in which A owned it). So, if A had held Blackacre for 3 years, for example, A's holding period in 2/3 of the partnership interest is 3 years.

For the portion allocable to the cash (neither a capital asset nor a § 1231 asset):

$$\frac{\$5,000 \;[\text{the FMV of the partnership interest allocable to the cash}]}{\$15,000 \;[\text{the FMV of the entire partnership interest}]} = \frac{1}{3}$$

Thus, A's holding period in 1/3 of the partnership interest begins on the day after the contribution. B's holding period, however, begins on the day following the date of his purchasing the LLC interest.[71]

We also need to consider the tax consequences to the newly formed partnership. Fortunately, the typical rules apply because the transaction has been recast as a partnership formation. In other words, under § 723, the partnership has a basis (inside basis) in the contributed property equal to the adjusted bases of the property of the contributing partner (increased by any § 721(b) gain). With respect to holding period, under § 1223(2), the partnership's holding period includes A's and B's holding period for contributed assets.

Consider now the second situation described in Revenue Ruling 99-5, in which B now contributes cash directly to the LLC in exchange for the membership interest. In this case, the LLC is converted to a partnership when B makes the contribution. Therefore, B is treated as making a contribution in exchange for the partnership interest; so, the typical § 721 framework applies to B's contribution. Moreover, A is treated as contributing all the LLC's existing assets (i.e., the cash and Blackacre in our example) in exchange for A's partnership interest; so, the typical § 721 framework applies to A's contribution too. Thus, in the second situation, A has no gain because there is no deemed asset sale prior to the partnership formation. Regarding holding periods, like before, A would be able to tack his or her holding period in the partnership interest under regulation § 1.1223-3(b), and B's holding period would begin on the day following the contribution.

Like before, we also need to analyze the tax consequences to the newly formed partnership. Again, this is now a typical § 721 transaction. Consequently, under § 723, the partnership's inside basis in the contributed property is equal to the bases of the contributing partners. With respect to holding period, under § 1223(2), the partnership's holding period in Blackacre includes A's holding period, and there is no tacking for the cash.

---

71. Rev. Rul. 99-5, 1999-1 C.B. 434; Rev. Rul. 66-7, 1966-1 C.B. 188.

2. Formation of Partnerships

Examples

1. Alfred, Bernard, and Charlie are starting a new business. They make the following contributions of property in exchange for their partnership interests. Alfred contributes $25,000 in cash; Bernard contributes Redacre, which has a basis of $5,000 and a FMV of $25,000; and Charlie contributes Greenacre, which has a basis of $30,000 and a FMV of $25,000. Assume that the assets have been held long-term and were capital assets in the individuals' hands before the formation. What are the tax consequences to the partners and the partnership upon this formation?

2. Diego and Elizabeth are starting a new business. They make the following contributions of property in exchange for their partnership interests. Diego contributes inventory worth $20,000 that has a basis of $10,000, and Blackacre that is worth $30,000 and has a basis of $15,000. Blackacre is a capital asset that Diego has held for several years. Elizabeth contributes $50,000 in cash. What are the tax consequences to the partners and the partnership upon this formation?

3. Assume the facts in Example 2 (Diego and Elizabeth). Thirteen months later, Diego and Elizabeth each contribute an additional $10,000 to the partnership. If the FMV of partnership property and of the partnership interests were unchanged before the new contribution of capital, how does the additional cash contribution affect the outside basis and holding period for Diego and Elizabeth?

Explanations

1. This transaction is governed by § 721 because the partners are contributing property in exchange for their partnership interest. Because there is no difference between the cash's basis and its value, Alfred does not realize a gain or loss. Under § 1001, Bernard has a realized gain of $20,000 ($25,000 less $5,000). Similarly, Charlie has a realized loss of $5,000 (the basis of $30,000 less the amount realized of $25,000). Despite the realized gains and losses, under § 721, no gain or loss is *recognized* upon a contribution of property in exchange for a partnership interest.

    Under § 722, the partners have an outside basis in their partnership interests equal to the amount of money contributed and the bases of assets contributed. Therefore, Alfred has a basis in his partnership (i.e., outside basis) of $25,000; Bernard has an outside basis of $5,000; and Charlie has an outside basis of $30,000. Note that this preserves the built-in gain and built-in loss for Bernard and Charlie, respectively, that was inherent in their contributed property. Under § 1223(1), moreover, Bernard can tack his holding period in his partnership interest because Redacre was a capital asset. Charlie can tack his holding period because

2. Formation of Partnerships

Greenacre was a capital asset. Alfred, however, is not able to tack his holding period because cash is neither a capital nor a § 1231 asset; thus, his holding period in the partnership interest starts the day after the exchange.[72]

Under § 721, the ABC Partnership does not recognize a gain or a loss on the receipt of property in exchange for the partnership interests. Under § 723, the partnership takes an inside basis of the assets equal to the basis of the contributing partner increased by any § 721(b) gain, of which there was none. Thus, the partnership has a basis of $5,000 in Redacre and $30,000 in Greenacre. It is also helpful to use a similar approach for the cash (the cash has a basis of $25,000 and a FMV of $25,000). Under § 1223(2), the partnership takes a tacked holding period in Redacre and Greenacre because "such property has, for the purpose of determining gain or loss from a sale or exchange, the same basis in whole or in part in his hands as it would have in the hands of such other person."[73] Cash does not have a holding period.

2. The formation analyses for Diego and Elizabeth are like the prior example. Under § 721, neither the partners nor the partnership recognizes gain or loss on the transaction. Under § 723, Diego will take a basis of $25,000 in his partnership interest, which represents the sum of the bases of the inventory and Blackacre. Elizabeth will have an inside basis of $50,000. The partnership takes an inside basis of $10,000 and $15,000 in the inventory and Blackacre, respectively. Under § 1223(2), the partnership tacks the holding period for both assets.

What is different, though, is the holding period analysis for Diego. Here, he has contributed property that can be tacked (Blackacre) and property that cannot be tacked (the inventory). The inventory cannot be tacked because it is neither a capital asset nor a § 1231 asset; inventory is specifically excluded from each group.[74] Under the § 1223 regulations, we must apportion the holding period based on a fraction of the property contributed that can and cannot tack:

$$\text{Tacked Holding Period} = \frac{\text{FMV of partnership interest allocable to tacked assets}}{\text{FMV of entire partnership interest}}$$

$$\text{Nontacked Holding Period} = \frac{\text{FMV of partnership interest allocable to nontacked assets}}{\text{FMV of entire partnership interest}}$$

---

72. *See* Rev. Rul. 66-7, 1966-1 C.B. 188.
73. I.R.C. § 1222(2).
74. I.R.C. §§ 1221(a)(1), 1231(b)(1).

2. Formation of Partnerships

As applied here, the portion of Diego's holding period that tacks is equal to ($30,000 / $50,000) × $25,000 = $15,000, and the portion that cannot tack is equal to ($20,000 / $50,000) × $25,000 = $10,000.

3. Before the contribution, the FMV of Diego and Elizabeth's partnership interests were unchanged from the amounts calculated in Example 2; thus, they were each worth $50,000. The additional contribution of $10,000 each increased their respective interests to $60,000. The additional cash contribution results in an increase to their outside bases under § 722. Diego's outside basis is now $35,000 (his beginning basis of $25,000 plus the $10,000 of newly contributed cash), and Elizabeth's outside basis is now $60,000 (her beginning basis of $50,000 plus the $10,000 of newly contributed cash).

The real purpose of this example is to demonstrate the impact on holding period. We need to create a new portion of the holding period for this contribution using the same fraction set forth above. In other words, "each partner has a new holding period in the portion of the partner's interest in [the partnership] that is attributable to the contribution."[75] For Diego, then, his fraction on this contribution is ($10,000 / $60,000) × $35,000 = $5,833.33. This amount represents the portion of his basis that is not considered to have been held long-term. Note that the balance of his holding period is now long-term, as it has been more than 12 months since he has received his partnership interest. For Elizabeth, the fraction for this contribution is ($10,000 / $60,000) × $60,000 = $10,000, which represents her portion that is presently not considered long-term.

---

75. Treas. Reg. § 1.1223-3(f)(4).

Accounting for Partnership Operations

INTRODUCTION

In the last chapter, we covered the typical formation of a partnership in which the partners contributed property (e.g., assets or cash) in exchange for a partnership interest. Now that we have an existing partnership, we turn to accounting for the operations of that partnership. There are four key concepts discussed in this chapter. The first is the calculation of partnership taxable income. The second is other accounting issues such as the partnership taxable year and accounting methods. The third is potential limits on deducting partnership losses. The fourth and last concept is that of capital accounts, which sets up the discussion that follows in the next chapter.

The theme of partnership accounting, as this chapter demonstrates, is how the partnership acts as a conduit through which the income generated from the entity's operations flow through to its partners, who bear the tax responsibility for that income. It is here, therefore, that we address the conduit nature of the partnership. As part of that discussion, we must ensure that conduit nature itself does not blur or muddy the tax consequences of various items that the partnership's operations may generate; thus, we discuss tax items that can be combined together and tax items that must be reported separately. This is another manifestation of the aggregate versus entity distinction that shapes many of our partnership tax rules.

After the discussion of magnitude issues, we turn to timing issues. As an accounting entity, the partnership must have a beginning and ending of its tax year—however, the selection of this year should not be a device to

3. Accounting for Partnership Operations

defer income too far out into the future. We then turn to accounting limitations on the deductibility of losses that the partnership may generate. Lastly, we end the chapter with another balance sheet concept, namely the critical concept of capital accounts, which will play a focal role throughout the rest of this text.

PARTNERSHIP TAXABLE INCOME

In this section, we cover two distinct but related concepts. First is the concept and calculation of partnership taxable income. Second is how that partnership income gets distributed to individual partners (known as the "distributive share"). This framework follows statutorily from §§ 701 to 704 (and § 706 instructs us about the partnership's taxable year). We unpack the statutory mechanics below, but it's helpful to understand the general framework before diving into the thicket. A partnership, as an entity, does not pay income tax (unlike, say, a corporation). Thus, partnership income "flows-through" the partnership to the individual partners. In other words, the partnership acts as a conduit through which partnership income and loss flows to the partners.

First, § 701 provides that "[a] partnership as such shall not be subject to the income tax imposed by this chapter. Persons carrying on business as partners shall be liable for income tax only in their separate or individual capacities."[1] Thus, this section provides that the partnership, as an entity, does not itself pay income taxes; rather, each partner is liable for the income taxation related to the partnership. Second, § 702 provides that each partner shall "take into account separately his *distributive share*"[2] of various items of partnership gain, loss, income, and deduction. Third, § 703 provides that a partnership calculates its taxable income in a manner similar to that of an individual (with certain exceptions). Fourth, § 704 provides that the partnership agreement (the contract between the partners) can determine how income, gain, loss, deduction, or credit is allocated between the partners. Lastly, § 706 provides rules for determining the partnership's taxable year.

Before we dive into the mechanics of those sections, let's appreciate what the statutory framework is trying to accomplish. At the outset, we need to appreciate the aggregate versus entity concept, which was introduced as a central theme in Chapter 1. Indeed, here you see both those concepts at play. A critical point here is that the partnership, as an entity, does not pay income tax; this results from the nature of a partnership as an aggregate of assets and operations of the individual partners. That's why the partners, as individuals,

---
1. I.R.C. § 701.
2. I.R.C. § 702(a) (emphasis added).

3. Accounting for Partnership Operations

need to pay tax on their allocable share of partnership income, again reflecting an aggregate approach. However, we need a method to calculate that allocable share, more formally known as the *distributive share*. This process is mainly spelled out in § 702. Here, you see the partnership is essentially acting as a conduit, in which items "flow through" from the partnership to the partners, who then include those items on their individual tax returns.

Some instances of entity-like concepts are present in these sections, too. For example, § 703 requires the partnership, as an entity, to compute its taxable income. Moreover, under § 706, the partnership has its own taxable year. And, procedurally, under § 6031 the partnership, as entity, files a tax return—which is described colloquially as an "information return" because that return provides information to the IRS and the partners about the operations of the partnership. Let's now get into the specific mechanics, in which you will see how this "conduit" works.

Computing the Partnership's Taxable Income: § 703

Section 703 provides that, with some exceptions, the "taxable income of a partnership shall be computed in the same manner as in the case of an individual."[3] This taxable income, moreover, is reported by the partnership on its information return, known as the Form 1065, "U.S. Return of Partnership Income." Although § 703 states that partnership taxable income is to be computed just like an individual, there are exceptions provided for in the section; those exceptions are:

(1) the items described in section 702(a) shall be separately stated, and
(2) the following deductions shall not be allowed to the partnership:
   (A) the deductions for personal exemptions provided in section 151,
   (B) the deduction for taxes provided in section 164(a) with respect to taxes, described in section 901, paid or accrued to foreign countries and to possessions of the United States,
   (C) the deduction for charitable contributions provided in section 170,
   (D) the net operating loss deduction provided in section 172,
   (E) the additional itemized deductions for individuals provided in part VII of subchapter B (sec. 211 and following), and
   (F) the deduction for depletion under section 611 with respect to oil and gas wells.[4]

Let's start with the first exception—the items that are separately stated under § 702(a). Although we unpack this more specifically below, a brief explanation fits here. There are certain items that the ultimate tax

---

3. I.R.C. § 703(a).
4. Id.

3. Accounting for Partnership Operations

treatment of the item depends on the taxpayer. A quintessential example is capital gain transactions, e.g., short-term and long-term capital gains and losses. How those items are taxed—for instance, at the preferential § 1(h) rate—depends on the taxpayer's specific tax circumstances, as those items are netted together. Thus, depending on who the taxpayer is, those items may be netted out or taxed at a different rate. In other words, for some tax items that a partnership may generate, how that item is ultimately taxed depends on other tax facts specific to the partner. In effect, then, § 702(a) requires those items whose tax treatment may depend on the unique tax circumstances of the taxpayer to be separately stated and not aggregated at the partnership level. In sum, the requirement to be separately stated is to prevent unintended magnitude shifts or character changes that may occur if the items were aggregated at the partnership level.

The other exceptions in § 703, although not obvious on its face perhaps, are present to prevent a double deduction. The clearest example is the first exception—the personal exemption under § 151. Section 703 disallows a partnership-specific individual exemption because the individual partners are allowed a personal exemption on their individual tax return.[5] Thus, if the partnership itself took a personal exemption in calculating its § 703 taxable income, and then the partners receive a personal exemption on their own tax return when they report their share of that § 703 income, the personal exemption has been counted twice: first at the partnership level and second at the individual level, resulting in a "double dip." Consequently, to prevent this double dip, § 703 disallows a personal exemption in the partnership's calculation.

The other exceptions share a similar concern. The second exception—for various taxes paid—are separately stated under § 702, meaning that the partners will report those items directly. Just like above with respect to the personal exemption, the partnership, as entity under § 703, does not take those items into account in calculating taxable income. The same is true for the charitable deduction under § 170; if a partnership makes a charitable contribution, it does not get a deduction under § 703 because the partners will report that item directly and take the deduction on their individual tax returns. The same rationale applies for the itemized deductions noted in § 703(a)(2)(E) and the oil and gas well depletion; those items are reported directly by the partners. A partnership is not allowed a loss deduction because losses are ultimately passed through to the individual partners, who then may be able to deduct partnership losses on their individual returns.

---

5. Importantly, the personal exemption is, at the time of this writing, presently at $0 due to the Tax Cuts and Jobs Act.

3. Accounting for Partnership Operations

Separately Stated Items: § 702

As just described above, § 703 states to calculate the taxable income of a partnership like an individual, but with some exceptions. That first exception carved out the items listed in § 702(a); these items must be accounted for separately.[6] Those items are provided for in § 702(a)(1) to (7):

(1) gains and losses from sales or exchanges of capital assets held for not more than 1 year,
(2) gains and losses from sales or exchanges of capital assets held for more than 1 year,
(3) gains and losses from sales or exchanges of property described in section 1231 (relating to certain property used in a trade or business and involuntary conversions),
(4) charitable contributions (as defined in section 170(c)),
(5) dividends with respect to which section 1(h)(11) or part VIII of subchapter B applies,
(6) taxes, described in section 901, paid or accrued to foreign countries and to possessions of the United States,
(7) other items of income, gain, loss, deduction, or credit, to the extent provided by regulations prescribed by the Secretary . . .[7]

What is the common denominator or theme of the above items? Like intimated in our § 703 discussion above, these items in § 702(a) need to be accounted for separately—that is, apart from the partnership's taxable income—because we are trying to preserve their character. In other words, we don't want the partnership form to distort how these items are taxed.

This tension is readily observable with the capital gains transactions provided for in § 702(a)(1) and (2). To appreciate the issue, a brief review of capital gains taxation is discussed. In brief, long-term capital gains are taxed at preferential (i.e., lower) rates; this is effectuated in § 1(h), which creates a statutory system to ensure that "net capital gain" is exposed to the lower preferential rates.[8] Net capital gain is defined as "the excess of the net long-term capital gain for the taxable year over the net short-term capital loss for such year."[9] Those two terms—net long-term capital gain and net short-term capital loss—are also defined. Net long-term capital gain means "the excess of long-term capital gains for the taxable year over the long-term capital losses for such year."[10] Net short-term capital loss means "the

---

6. *See also* Treas. Reg. § 1.702-1.
7. I.R.C. § 702(a).
8. Wading through the specific mechanics of § 1(h) is not presented here.
9. I.R.C. § 1222(11).
10. I.R.C. § 1222(7).

3. Accounting for Partnership Operations

excess of short-term capital losses for the taxable year over the short-term capital gains for such year."[11] Putting that together, we get the following equation:

$$Net\,Capital\,Gain\,[NCG] =$$

$$Net\,Long\,Term\,Capital\,Gains\,[NLTCG] - Net\,Short\,Term\,Capital\,Loss\,[NSTCL],$$

which can be expressed as its constituent parts as

$$NCG = [LTCG - LTCL] - [STCL - STCG]$$

As implicated by the above equation, whether a taxpayer has a net capital gain — and thus gets the benefit of the lower preferential tax rates — depends on their specific combination of long-term capital gain, long-term capital loss, short-term capital loss, and short-term capital gain.

Consider now this application in the partnership context. Assume that a partnership generates $10,000 in long-term capital gain, $4,000 in long-term capital loss, and $4,000 in short-term capital loss, and $3,000 in short-term capital gain, and it has two equal partners, A and B. Therefore, under § 702, A and B will each receive $5,000 of long-term capital gain, $2,000 of long-term capital loss, $2,000 short-term capital loss, and $1,500 in short-term capital gain from the partnership. How those items are ultimately taxed depends on the partners' unique tax situation.

For example, if A has none of the other types of capital gain or loss in the net capital gain formula other than what he receives from the partnership, he will have a net capital gain of $2,500. That is, A's net capital gain is calculated as follows:

$$A's\,NCG = [\$5,000 - \$2,000] - [\$2,000 - \$1,500] = \$2,500$$

Now, assume that B has an additional $1,000 long-term capital loss, $2,000 short-term capital loss and a $4,000 short-term capital gain from transactions unrelated to the partnership. We must combine B's partnership flow-through items and his unrelated capital asset transactions, resulting in a long-term capital gain of $5,000, a long-term capital loss of $3,000, a short-term capital loss of $4,000, and short-term capital gain of $5,500. Thus, B's net capital gain is calculated as follows:

---

11. I.R.C. § 1222(6).

3. Accounting for Partnership Operations

$$B's\,NCG = [\$5{,}000 - \$3{,}000] - [\$4{,}000 - \$5{,}500] = \$2{,}000$$

Note that the second terms goes to zero (not negative). If we were to combine these items at the partnership level, it could blur the detail needed for these partner-level calculations. As well, the partners need this detailed information (such as the magnitude and character of these capital gains transactions) to complete their individual tax returns. This is exactly why § 702 wants certain items (here, the capital gains transactions) stated separately and not netted at the partnership level—because the ultimate taxation of these partnership items *depends* on other items in the partner's tax situation.

The other items listed in § 702(a) share the same nature insofar as the ultimate tax consequence of the items depends on other items in the partner's individual tax circumstances. For example, § 1231 gains and losses share a similar netting concern that was just illustrated with capital gains transactions. The deduction of a charitable contribution under § 170, moreover, depends on whether the taxpayer has sufficient contribution base to take the deduction.[12] Dividend income needs to be separately stated because of the potential for it being treated as qualified dividend income, which allows it to be subject to the preferential rates under § 1(h). Foreign taxes need to be separately stated because of the partner-taxpayer's option to treat them as either a deduction (under § 164) or a credit (under § 901).

Importantly, § 702(a)(7) allows the Secretary to prescribe by regulation additional items that need to be separately stated. Treas. Reg. § 1.702-1(a)(8)(i) provides that the following items also need to be separately stated:

1. Recoveries of bad debt, prior taxes, and delinquency amounts (§ 111);
2. Gains and losses from wagering transactions (§ 165(d));
3. Soil and water conservation expenditures (§ 175);
4. Nonbusiness expenses (§ 212);
5. Medical and dental expenses (§ 213);
6. Dependent care expenses (§ 214);
7. Alimony payments (§ 215);
8. Taxes and interest paid to cooperative housing corporations (§ 216);
9. Intangible drilling and development costs (§ 263(c));
10. Pre-1970 exploration expenditures (§ 615);
11. Certain mining exploration expenditures (§ 617);
12. § 751(b) income, gain, or loss; and

---

12. I.R.C. § 170(b).

3. Accounting for Partnership Operations

13. "any items of income, gain, loss, deduction, or credit subject to a special allocation under the partnership agreement which differs from the allocation of partnership taxable income or loss generally."[13]

In addition to the above list, the regulations also provide that "[e]ach partner must also take into account separately the partner's distributive share of any partnership item which, if separately taken into account by any partner, would result in an income tax liability for that partner, or for any other person, different from that which would result if that partner did not take the item into account separately."[14] In illustrating this instruction, the regulation notes that various international tax items are applicable here—for instance, gross subpart F income (for controlled foreign corporations).[15]

It's worth emphasizing to pay particular attention to § 702(a)(7) that provides that additional separately stated items can be prescribed by regulation. Although we have some items that are expressly provided for in the accompanying § 702 regulations, that is not always the case. In other words, the instruction to separately state an item may be present in a regulation other than the § 702 regulations. For example, the regulations that accompany § 55 (the alternative minimum tax (AMT)) prescribe that the items of tax preference under the AMT are separately stated items.[16]

In sum, § 702 and its accompanying regulation require an item to be separately stated if the item's character or tax treatment depends on the tax circumstances and other tax items of the individual partner. Thus, you must be always cognizant of this requirement and appreciate its import as you analyze partnership tax issues.

Partners' Distributive Share

The preceding section illustrated how we calculate taxable income at the partnership level. Next, we need to unpack how the partnership operates as a *conduit* by flowing that taxable income through to individual partners. Recall that § 701 provides that partners, not partnerships, are liable for income tax due to partnership operations. To determine the partners' respective income tax burden flowing from partnership operations, two sections operate: § 702 and § 704. We already saw that § 702(a)(1) to (7) demarcates the

---

13. Treas. Reg. § 1.702-1(a)(8)(i).
14. Treas. Reg. § 1.702-1(a)(8)(ii).
15. Id. Rest assured that the intricacies of controlled foreign corporations, subpart F income, and international taxation generally are beyond the scope of this text. Nevertheless, this underlines the importance of reading the entire regulatory scheme.
16. Treas. Reg. § 1.58-2(b).

3. Accounting for Partnership Operations

items that need to be separately stated to a partner (reiterating that such separate statements are generally to preserve character classifications because the ultimate tax consequences depend on collateral tax attributes unique to the partner). There is one more part to § 702(a), however, and that is subsection (a)(8), which provides: "taxable income or loss, exclusive of items requiring separate computation under other paragraphs of this subsection."[17] In other words, (a)(8) provides a catch-all for all other items that are not separately stated. Therefore, the flow-through income (the "distributive share") for a particular partner consists of (1) an itemization of the separately stated items (arising from § 702(a)(1) to (7)) and (2) a generic "catch-all" partnership income or loss (arising from § 702(a)(8)).[18]

Section 704 provides more context for the partner's distributive share. Section 704(a) provides that "[a] partner's distributive share of income, gain, loss, deduction, or credit shall, except as otherwise provided in this chapter, be determined by the partnership agreement."[19] Although the import of this provision may not be readily apparent now, its weight and gravity will solidify in later chapters. In a nutshell, though, it essentially provides that partners can contractually arrange the economic affairs of the partnership. Stated more simply, partners can contract (in the partnership agreement) for who gets what items of income, gain, loss, deduction, etc. Such flexibility is both a blessing and a curse. It is a blessing because it allows the partners tremendous freedom of contract in arranging their economic affairs, which underlies the flexible nature of partnerships at state law. The curse, however, is that such flexibility gives rise to potential abuses—namely, the tax consequences of an item are divorced from its economic consequences. As a result, we have a complicated labyrinth of rules to prevent these abuses, which we turn to in Chapter 4. As a default rule, if the partnership agreement does not provide for the allocation of a particular item, then § 704(b) provides that such item will be allocated "in accordance with the partner's interest in the partnership," a concept that we cover in Chapter 4.

Before we move on, there is one key aspect to state clearly and emphatically here. Although § 704 speaks to a "distributive share," that *does not mean* that actual *cash* or other *property* is *distributed* to the partners. Alas, it is a poor choice of words here in the statute given the natural and intuitive understanding that a "distributive share" should involve an actual distribution of something tangible (like cash or property). Rather, the distributive share is all about *allocation* of tax items (perhaps, then, the "allocative share" would have been a better statutory phrase). Importantly,

---

17. I.R.C. § 702(a)(8).
18. For those familiar with S corporation taxation, you will notice this is like the process of separately stating certain items and aggregating others in allocating S corporation income under § 1366.
19. I.R.C. § 704(a).

3. Accounting for Partnership Operations

an allocation of partnership income (for tax purposes under § 704) does not mean, necessarily, that the partner actually received any cash! Thus, it is totally possible (and often happens with poor planning or drafting) that a partner has flow-through income but no cash with which to pay the actual taxes due on that flow-through income. This phenomenon is known as "phantom income," which is a tax colloquialism to refer to situations in which there is an income inclusion with no real asset (or cash) presently accompanying the inclusion. In sum, don't confuse a partner's *distributive share* with a *distribution* of partnership assets (like cash); they are two entirely different concepts.

SYNTHESIS OF PARTNERSHIP TAXABLE INCOME AND PARTNER'S DISTRIBUTIVE SHARE

We have examined how the partnership calculates its taxable income, which is essentially an accounting exercise. In doing so, the partnership separately accounts for some items, and for items that are not required to be separately stated, it aggregates them together in determining a generic taxable income or loss. After figuring those amounts—the separately stated items and the non-separately stated income or loss—the partnership then acts as a conduit and "flows" those items to the individual partners. This flow-through is allocated to the partners either in accordance with their partnership agreement or the partner's interest in the partnership. This is known as a partner's distributive share, which the partner then reports on his or her individual tax return.

As a summary, therefore, there are four basic steps to this process.

1. The partnership calculates its separately stated items (§ 702(a)(1) to (7)).
2. The partnership calculates its non-separately stated items (§ 702(a)(8)).
3. Those items calculated in Steps 1 and 2 are allocated to the partners under § 704 (the "distributive share").
4. The partner includes on his or her income tax return the "distributive share" determined in Step 3.

Now that we have the basic statutory framework in place to determine partnership taxable income, let's try a few examples. We'll start with a basic and simple example. The GHI Partnership has three partners, G, H, and I. In the taxable year, the GHI Partnership had the following results from partnership operations:

3. Accounting for Partnership Operations

GHI Partnership	
Item	Amount
Service revenue	$300,000
Salaries expense	$175,000
Office rent	$25,000

At the outset, recall that, under § 701, the GHI Partnership does not pay income tax as an entity; rather, each individual partner (G, H, and I) will be liable for income taxes. Next, we turn to § 703, which provides that we calculate the taxable income of a partnership just like an individual but with the stated exceptions. Section 703 requires us to separately state the § 702(a) items and account for the exceptions in § 703(a)(2). In this first example, no separately stated § 702(a) items are present. Moreover, none of the items in § 703(a)(2) items are present either. Consequently, partnership taxable income would be computed as follows, which contains only § 702(a)(8) items:

GHI Partnership	
Items of Income	
Service revenue (§ 61)	$300,000
Items of Deduction	
Salaries expense (§ 162)	$175,000
Office rent (§ 162)	$25,000
Taxable Income	$100,000

The $100,000 of partnership taxable income will need to be split amongst the partners. We have not covered the detailed mechanics of this yet, but we will shortly. For the moment, let's assume that G, H, and I share partnership items equally. Therefore, their distributive shares are $33,333 each; under §§ 701 and 702, they will each report their $33,333 on their individual tax returns.

Consider the JK Partnership, which has the following because of partnership operations:

JK Partnership	
Item	Amount
Service revenue	$250,000
Salaries expense	$135,000
Office rent	$15,000
Gain on sale of real property (LTCG)	$15,000
Charitable contribution	$5,000

3. Accounting for Partnership Operations

Take note that JK has items that need to be separately stated under § 702 (the property gain, which was long-term capital gain, and the charitable contribution) and that no charitable deduction is allowed under § 703. Consequently, JK's taxable income would be calculated as follows:

JK Partnership	
Items of Income	Amount
Service revenue (§ 61)	$250,000
Items of Deduction	
Salaries expense (§ 162)	$135,000
Office rent (§ 162)	$15,000
(a)(8) Non-Separate Income	$100,000
(a)(1)-(7) Separately Stated Items	
Long-term capital gain	$15,000
Charitable contribution	$5,000

The JK Partnership has $100,000 of § 702(a)(8) partnership taxable income to allocate to its partners and two separately stated items that also need to be allocated to its partners. If we assume that J and K share items equally, they will each be allocated $50,000 of the § 702(a)(8) income, $7,500 of the LTCG, and $2,500 of the charitable contribution.

For our last example, consider the LM Partnership, which has the following because of partnership operations:

LM Partnership	
Item	Amount
Service revenue	$95,000
Salaries expense	$75,000
Office rent	$36,000
Gain on sale of Blackacre	$5,000
Charitable contribution	$15,000
Loss on the sale of equipment	$10,000
Loss on sale of Redacre	$2,500

In this example, let's assume that (i) the gain on Blackacre is long-term capital gain, (ii) the loss on the equipment relates to § 1231 property, and (iii) the loss on Redacre is short-term capital loss. Consequently, LM's taxable income would be calculated as follows:

3. Accounting for Partnership Operations

LM Partnership	
Items of Gross Income	Amount
Service revenue (§ 61)	$95,000
Deductions	
Salaries expense (§ 162)	$75,000
Office rent (§ 162)	$36,000
(a)(8) Taxable Income (Loss)	($16,000)
(a)(1)-(7) Separately Stated Items	
Long-term capital gain	$5,000
Short-term capital loss	$2,500
§ 1231 Loss	$10,000
Charitable contribution	$15,000

Note here that the LM Partnership now has a § 702(a)(8) taxable *loss* from operations. That loss, just like the taxable income in the prior examples, will need to be allocated to the partners. However, as an initial matter, the Code is more concerned with potential abuses that arise with flow-through losses than with flow-through gains. Therefore, we have additional rules that regard the flow-through of losses, which we cover shortly. As before, the separately stated items will be allocated to the partners, and the tax treatment of those items will ultimately depend on the other tax items on the partners tax return (e.g., the netting of capital gain or loss transactions).

Now that we have analyzed what happened at the partnership level, it's natural to question more fully what happens next at the partner level. That is, *how* do we *allocate* the items calculated above to the individual partners, particularly given the flexibility we noted inherent in § 704. Before we turn squarely to that, though, let's first consider the *when* question. That is, the determination of the partnership's taxable year, which we turn to next.

TIMING MATTERS

The Partnership's Taxable Year

Just like any other entity, a partnership has a tax year, even though it does not pay income taxes itself. For any taxpayer, tax years can either be a calendar year (January 1 to December 31) or a fiscal year, which is any year

3. Accounting for Partnership Operations

other than a calendar year. Individuals are typically on a calendar year.[20] The rules governing the tax year of a partnership are found in § 706. Section 706 actually informs us of two timing considerations. First, § 706(a) tells us the specific year that partners are required to include their flow-through partnership items. Second, § 706(b) provides for the taxable year of the partnership. Let's consider them in order—first, the taxable year of inclusion for a partner, and second, the taxable year of the partnership.

Taxable Year of Including a Partner's Distributive Share

Section 706(a) states that "[i]n computing the taxable income of a partner for a taxable year, the inclusions required by section 702 and section 707(c) with respect to a partnership shall be based on the income, gain, loss, deduction, or credit of the partnership for any taxable year of the partnership ending within or with the taxable year of the partner."[21] This rule is straightforward. Three examples illustrate the ways this rule operates.

Assume that our partner is an individual (compared to, say, an entity with a fiscal year). Thus, his tax year spans from January 1 to December 31. In this first example, let's say that the partnership tax year ends on September 30, Year 1 (i.e., it has a fiscal year). Under § 706(a), therefore, our individual partner will include his partnership items on his Year 1 tax return (which he files by April 15, Year 2). In other words, September 30, Year 1, ends within the Year 1 calendar year of the partner (between January 1, Y1 to December 31, Y1).

In the second example, assume now that the partnership has a calendar year too. Thus, the partnership's tax year starts on January 1 and goes through December 31. In this case, for Year 1, our partner still includes the partnership items on his Year 1 tax return (due in April of Year 2), because the partnership calendar year ends with the partner's tax year (both ending on December 31, Year 1).

In our last example, for completeness, let's now assume that the partnership's tax year is a fiscal year that ends on January 31. In other words, it spans from February 1, Year 1 to January 31, Year 2. In this case, the partnership items will be included on our individual partner's Year 2 tax return (that is due in April of Year 3) because the partnership's taxable year ends within the Year 2 tax year of our individual partner.

---

20. *See* I.R.C. §§ 441, 441(g).
21. I.R.C. § 706(a).

3. Accounting for Partnership Operations

Taxable Year of the Partnership

There are more rules for determining the taxable year of the partnership than you may anticipate. Before we unpack the rules, understanding the reason for the rules will be helpful. To understand these rules, let's examine natural incentives that arise in the absence of any timing rules. As with any taxpayer, due to the time value of money, generally tax deferral is preferred.[22] Stated more simply, someone would rather pay a dollar in tax at some time in the future rather than today. The reason for this, if it isn't clear, can be illustrated with a brief example. Let's assume that you need to pay someone exactly one dollar in the future, say, a year from today. Let's further assume that savings accounts are yielding 10% per year.[23] So, to satisfy your obligation of one dollar a year from now, you can deposit *something less than a dollar today* to satisfy that future obligation—specifically, you need to deposit about 91 cents.[24] That is, if you deposit your 91 cents today, you will have one dollar a year from now (given the initial deposit of 91 cents plus the accrued interest of 9 cents). So, your one-dollar obligation in future dollar terms "costs" only 91 cents in today's dollar terms. Now, we can just play with those variables to make that distinction even more marked; for example, if the one-dollar obligation were due in two years, then the "cost" today would be only 83 cents because there is more time to build up (i.e., compound) the interest.

This incentive to defer taxes is ever-present in tax planning. Given this incentive, how might partners and partnerships arrange their affairs to optimize this deferral given the general rule in § 706(a) that partners need to include their distributive share in their taxable year in which the partnership's taxable year ends? The natural incentive looks something like this: The partnership ends its taxable year in January, say January 31. So, for its first year, the partnership tax year goes from February 1, Year 1 to January 31, Year 2. In this case, the calendar-year partner's tax year ends on December 31 each year. Thus, for the distributive share arising from the February 1, Year 1 to January 31, Year 2 tax year, the partner would include that on his or her Year 2 tax return (because the partnership year ends during the partner's Year 2 tax year), which isn't due until Year 3 (in April of Year 3)! In this case, then, there are taxable items arising as early as February of Year 1 that aren't being reported on a tax return until April of Year 3! To prevent this elongated deferral, there exists specific rules for determining the taxable year of a partnership.

---

22. This assumes, of course, other factors are constant, such as tax rates and the like.
23. We can wish!
24. This is found by a simple time-value of money calculation in which (i) the future value is $1, (ii) the interest rate is 10%, (iii) and there is one period of compounding; solving for the present value equals 91 cents.

3. Accounting for Partnership Operations

The rules for determining the taxable year of a partnership are found in § 706(b). Preliminarily, § 706(b)(1)(A) provides that we determine the tax year for the partnership as if it were a taxpayer. In other words, it needs a tax year. The actual rules come next in subparagraphs (B) and (C). Subparagraph (B) pegs the partnership's tax year based on the various aspects of the partners' tax years; subparagraph (C) provides that the partnership can have a tax year, other than one described in subparagraph (B), if it is for business purposes.

There are three main rules found in subparagraph (B), which apply in descending order of preference. The first and principal rule is that the partnership's tax year is the "majority interest taxable year." The majority interest taxable year is defined in subparagraph (4) as the "taxable year (if any) which, on each testing day, constituted the taxable year of 1 or more partners having (on such day) an aggregate interest in partnership profits and capital of more than 50 percent."[25] Testing days, moreover, are defined as "(I) the 1st day of the partnership taxable year (determined without regard to clause (i)), or (II) the days during such representative period as the Secretary may prescribe."[26] In essence, the majority interest taxable year desires the partnership to use the taxable year that pairs with the majority of the partners.

The second rule—which applies in the absence of a majority interest taxable year—is the "taxable year of all the principal partners of the partnership."[27] A principal partner is defined in subparagraph (3) as "a partner having an interest of 5 percent or more in partnership profits or capital."[28] The third rule—which applies in the absence of a majority interest taxable year or a principal partner tax year—is a calendar year (i.e., January 1 to December 31) or a year prescribed by the regulations.

Lastly, notwithstanding the above rules, § 706(b)(1)(C) provides that "[a] partnership may have a taxable year not described in subparagraph (B) if it establishes, to the satisfaction of the Secretary, a business purpose therefor."[29] Importantly, it further provides that "any deferral of income to partners shall not be treated as a business purpose."[30]

Let's try some examples of these statutory rules before we dive into additional rules that are present in the regulations. The MNO Partnership is formed on January 1, and it has three equal partners, M, N, and O, who are all individuals with calendar-year tax years. This is a clean and straightforward example. Under § 706, our first rule is to see if there is a majority

---

25. I.R.C. § 706(b)(4)(A)(i).
26. I.R.C. § 706(b)(4)(A)(ii).
27. I.R.C. § 706(b)(1)(B).
28. I.R.C. § 706(b)(3).
29. I.R.C. § 706(b)(1)(C).
30. Id.

3. Accounting for Partnership Operations

interest taxable year. The majority interest taxable year is the tax year, on the "testing day," of the partner (or partners) having interests in partnership profits and capital of more than 50%. The testing day is the first day of the partnership taxable year, here January 1 (date of formation). Partners M, N, and O all have the same tax year (the calendar year), and they constitute more than 50% of the profits and capital of the partnership. Thus, the MNO Partnership has a calendar-year tax year.

Now we need to make this next example a little more complicated to illustrate the next rule. Consider the Alpha Partnership, which has (i) 24 2% individual partners with calendar-year tax years, (ii) a 4% corporate partner with a fiscal year ending March 31, and (iii) a 48% corporate partner with a fiscal year ending September 30. In this case, there is not a majority interest taxable year: there is not an aggregation of more than 50% of the partnership interests that share the same tax year. The individual partners aggregate to only 48% and the other partners can't be aggregated because they don't share the same tax year. The next rule in the sequence is § 706(b)(1)(B)(ii), which is the taxable year of *all* the principal partners. A principal partner is a partner that has "an interest of 5 percent or more in partnership profits or capital."[31] Fortunately there is only one principal partner here: the corporate partner with a September 30 fiscal tax year. Therefore, under the principal-partner rule, the Alpha Partnership will have a September 30 fiscal tax year.

Well, what if there is not a majority interest taxable year or a tax year that all the principal partners share? That comes up regularly. For example, consider this next example. Consider the STU Partnership, in which S is an 10% individual partner with a calendar-year tax year, T is a 40% corporate partner with a fiscal year that ends on March 31, and U is a 40% corporate partner with a fiscal year that ends on May 31. In this case, there is *not* a majority interest taxable year: there is not an aggregation of more than 50% of the partnership interests that share the same tax year. Similarly, the principal partners—here, all of them!—do not share the same tax year. And, at this time in the discussion, we are ignoring the possibility of a business-purpose tax year. So, what does that leave us with? We need to turn to the regulations as required by § 706(b)(1)(B)(iii).

The regulations provide that if there is no majority interest taxable year or a common taxable year of all the principal partners, then the partnership must adopt the taxable year "that produces the least aggregate deferral of income."[32] This regulation puts the rationale for a prescribed tax year front and center: the desire to minimize the opportunity for strategic deferral.

---

31. I.R.C. § 706(b)(1)(3).
32. Treas. Reg. § 1.706-1(b)(2)(i)(C).

3. Accounting for Partnership Operations

Although the rationale is easy to state (and understand), its operation is complicated.[33]

The regulation defines aggregate deferral for a particular year as "equal to the sum of the products determined by multiplying the month(s) of deferral for each partner that would be generated by that year and each partner's interest in partnership profits for that year."[34] It then provides, "[t]he partner's taxable year that produces the lowest sum when compared to the other partner's taxable years is the taxable year that results in the least aggregate deferral of income to the partners."[35]

Let's consider a simple example. The PQ Partnership has two partners, P and Q, which are each fiscal-year taxpayers, with a February 28 and October 31 year end, respectively. Let's calculate the aggregate deferral for each potential year end. If the February year end is used, then P has the following: 0 months deferral × 50% = 0; Q has the following: 8 months deferral [i.e., March to Oct.] × 50% = 4.0. Here, the aggregate deferral is 4.0 with a February year end. Now, if the October year end is used, then P has the following: 4 months deferral [Nov. to Feb.] × 50% = 2; Q has the following: 0 months deferral × 50% = 0. Here, the aggregate deferral is 2.0. Therefore, the *least* aggregate deferral is 2.0, which results from an October year end; consequently, the partnership has a fiscal year with an October 31 year-end.

Let's consider a twist in calculating the least aggregate deferral. Now we have the RS Partnership, in which R is a 50% partner with a calendar year, and S is a 50% partner with a fiscal year ending June 30. Calculating the aggregate deferral for a calendar year end (December 31) results in the following: R has 0 months of deferral × 50% = 0; S has 6 months of deferral × 50% = 3.0. Combined resulting in 3.0 of deferral. Calculating the aggregate deferral for a June 30 year end results in the following: R has 6 months of deferral × 50% = 3.0; S has 0 months of deferral × 50% = 0. Combined resulting in 3.0 of deferral. That is, either tax year produces the same amount of aggregate deferral. Which one to pick? The regulations provide "[i]f the calculation results in more than one taxable year qualifying as the taxable year with the least aggregate deferral, the partnership may select any one of those taxable years as its taxable year."[36]

There is yet another rule for selecting the taxable year for a partnership we need to discuss. Section 706(b)(1)(C) provides "[a] partnership may have a taxable year not described in subparagraph (B) if it establishes, to the satisfaction of the Secretary, a business purpose therefor."[37] In other words,

---

33. Alas, this is a constant theme in tax: easy to understand rationale, but cumbersome rules to effectuate that goal.
34. Treas. Reg. § 1.706-1(b)(3)(i).
35. Id.
36. Id.
37. I.R.C. § 706(b)(1)(C).

3. Accounting for Partnership Operations

even if there is a majority interest taxable year, a principal partner taxable year, or a taxable year that results in the least aggregate deferral, the partnership can have some other tax year for *a good business reason*. Despite the detailed regulations in calculating the majority interest taxable year and the least aggregate deferral methods, there is, surprisingly, no statutory or regulatory elucidation on what constitutes a business purpose. Fortunately, though, the legislative history is helpful here.

In particular, the legislative history to the Tax Reform Act of 1986 expressly notes four nontax factors that are ordinarily not valid business purposes. They are (1) the "use of a particular year for regulatory or financial accounting purposes," (2) "hiring patterns of a particular business, e.g., the fact that a firm typically hires staff during certain times of the year," (3) "administrative purposes, such as the admission or retirement of partners or shareholders, promotion of staff, and compensation or retirement arrangements with staff, partners, or shareholders," and (4) "the fact that a particular business involves the use of price lists, model year, or other items that change on an annual basis."[38]

Administrative material is illuminating here. For example, in Revenue Ruling 87-57, the Service shed additional light on valid business purposes. The revenue ruling explains that "[b]oth tax factors and nontax factors must be considered for purposes of determining whether a taxpayer has established a business purpose for the requested tax year."[39] It further explains that the four rejected purposes in the legislative history "all involve issues of convenience for the taxpayer."[40] Consequently, "if a requested tax year creates deferral or distortion, the taxpayer's nontax factors must demonstrate compelling reasons for the requested tax year."[41]

The revenue ruling then proceeds to analyze eight different situations. The Service determined that four of the situations were not valid business purposes, which included (1) use of the fiscal year used for financial accounting purposes suggested by accounting material for that type of business generally [Situation 1]; (2) by using particular tax year, the taxpayer would receive a discount on accounting fees [Situation 2]; (3) the taxpayer has always used a particular year and to change would cause a hardship in changing the records [Situation 3]; and (4) the taxpayer desires to use a particular year to facilitate the timely sending of information returns (e.g., Schedules K-1) to its owners [Situation 4]. In Situation 1, for example, the Service noted that the desired year was not based on the taxpayer's individual facts and circumstances. And, in Situations 2 through 4, the desired year was rooted in convenience (e.g., reduced accounting fees).

---

38. H.R. Rep. No. 841, 99th Cong., 2d Sess. II-319 (1986).
39. Rev. Rul. 87-57, 1987-2 C.B. 117.
40. Id.
41. Id.

3. Accounting for Partnership Operations

On the other hand, the Service found that four other reasons were valid business purposes. In Situation 5, the Service noted that the taxpayer established a natural business year.[42] In Situation 6, although the taxpayer did not have a technical natural business year, the taxpayer explained that failing the 25% test was due to unusual gross receipt figures (traceable to a labor strike). In Situation 7, the taxpayer wanted to use a fiscal year on the basis that, due to weather conditions, the business was only open certain months during the year (i.e., was a seasonal business). Lastly, in Situation 8, the Service dove more deeply into the requirements of Rev. Proc. 87-32's natural business year and changes of accounting methods. The common denominator in these situations is establishing a "natural business year" (Situations 5, 6, 8) or a seasonal business (Situation 7).

PARTNERSHIP ACCOUNTING METHODS

In the last section, we covered the timing of the partners' and the partnership's taxable year. Another accounting issue to consider is accounting method. The rules to determine the method of accounting are found in § 446. Under § 446, there are generally two methods available: (1) the "cash receipts and disbursements method" (often just referred to as the "cash method"), and (2) the accrual method.[43] Just like the discussion above with respect to accounting periods, a partner and a partnership each have their own accounting method, and they can be different (e.g., a partner can be on the cash method and the partnership on the accrual method).

Before we dive into the selection rules, let's briefly review the two main accounting methods. The cash method provides that "all items which constitute gross income (whether in the form of cash, property, or services) are to be included for the taxable year in which actually or constructively received."[44] Thus, for income inclusions, it focuses on receipt (actual or constructive). For deductions, the cash method provides that "[e]xpenditures are to be deducted for the taxable year in which actually made."[45] That is, when the expenses are actually paid.

The accrual method provides that "income is to be included for the taxable year when all the events have occurred that fix the right to receive the income and the amount of the income can be determined with reasonable

---

42. A "natural business year" was defined in Rev. Proc. 87-32 and focused on, basically, whether 25% of the gross receipts were in the last two months of the desired year. *See also* Rev. Proc. 2002-38, 2002-22 I.R.B. 1037; Rev. Proc. 2006-46, 2006-45 I.R.B. 859.
43. I.R.C. § 446(c).
44. Treas. Reg. § 1.446-1.
45. Id.

3. Accounting for Partnership Operations

accuracy."[46] Deductions are a tad more involved; the regulations provide that deductions are taken "in the taxable year in which all the events have occurred that establish the fact of the liability, the amount of the liability can be determined with reasonable accuracy, and economic performance has occurred with respect to the liability."[47] The regulations clarify, moreover, that the term "liability" here "includes any item allowable as a deduction, cost, or expense for Federal income tax purposes."[48]

Section 446(a) provides that "[t]axable income shall be computed under the method of accounting on the basis of which the taxpayer regularly computes his income in keeping his books."[49] Subsection (b) further provides that "[i]f no method of accounting has been regularly used by the taxpayer, or if the method used does not clearly reflect income, the computation of taxable income shall be made under such method as, in the opinion of the Secretary, does clearly reflect income."[50] Consequently, the critical principle espoused is that the accounting method must clearly reflect income, which is reiterated in the regulations as well: "No method of accounting is acceptable unless, in the opinion of the Commissioner, it clearly reflects income."[51]

Although § 446(c) provides that a partnership can pick its method of accounting (just like any taxpayer), other sections limit that discretion. For example, § 448 limits who can use the cash method of accounting. As applied to partnerships, there are two relevant limitations in § 448. The first is that § 448(a) expressly provides that, unless an exception applies, a partnership that has a C corporation partner cannot use the cash method. There are three exceptions to this prohibition. The first exception is for a "farming business."[52] The second exception is for qualified personal service corporations.[53] The third exception is for corporations that pass the "gross receipts test,"[54] which examines whether the corporation had average annual gross receipts that do not exceed $25,000,000 for the last three tax years.

---

46. Treas. Reg. § 1.446-1(c)(1)(ii).
47. Treas. Reg. § 1.446-1(c)(1)(ii)(A).
48. Treas. Reg. § 1.446-1(c)(1)(ii)(B).
49. I.R.C. § 446(a).
50. I.R.C. § 446(b).
51. Treas. Reg. § 1.446-1(c)(ii)(C).
52. I.R.C. § 448(b)(1); I.R.C. § 448(d)(1). A farming business is defined by reference to § 263A(e)(4), which defines a farming business as "the trade or business of farming," and it also includes "operating a nursery or sod farm," and "raising or harvesting of trees bearing fruit, nuts, or other crops, or ornamental trees." I.R.C. § 263A(e)(4).
53. I.R.C. § 448(b)(2), (d)(2). A qualified personal service corporation is defined as, essentially, a corporation that "substantially all of the activities of which involve the performance of services in the fields of health, law, engineering, architecture, accounting, actuarial science, performing arts, or consulting" and the stock thereof is owned by the service-providing employees. I.R.C. § 448(d)(2).
54. I.R.C. § 448(b)(3); I.R.C. § 448(c).

3. Accounting for Partnership Operations

The second limitation in § 448 with respect to the cash method is that if the partnership is a "tax shelter," it cannot use the cash method. A tax shelter is defined by reference to § 461(i)(3). Section 461 defines a tax shelter in three ways. The first includes "any enterprise (other than a C corporation) if at any time interests in such enterprise have been offered for sale in any offering required to be registered with any Federal or State agency having the authority to regulate the offering of securities for sale."[55] The second is "any syndicate," which is defined by reference to § 1256(e)(3)(B).[56] A syndicate is defined as "any partnership or other entity (other than a corporation which is not an S corporation) if more than 35 percent of the losses of such entity during the taxable year are allocable to limited partners or limited entrepreneurs (within the meaning of section 461(k)(4))."[57] The third is for "any tax shelter," defined by reference to § 6662(d)(2)(C)(ii);[58] this definition is broad and includes any entity (including partnerships) "if a significant purpose of such partnership, entity, plan, or arrangement is the avoidance or evasion of Federal income tax."[59]

ADDITIONAL LIMITS ON LOSSES

We have already seen how the partnership essentially works as a conduit that channels income to the partners. This is manifested in § 702(a), which provides that, in calculating their own income tax obligations, partners include and "take into account" their distributive share of partnership gains, losses, and income. Thus, we've seen that, if a partner's distributive share of partnership income is, say, $10,000, that partner will include that $10,000 on her individual Federal 1040 (individual tax return form). But what happens in the case of partnership flow-through losses? On its face, § 702 (in isolation) would provide the same result—that is, the partner includes a $10,000 loss on her tax return. However, there are more sections to consider when losses are at play.

For a partner to take advantage of a partnership flow-through loss, there are three additional sections that need to be considered: §§ 704(d), 465, and 469, which are the rules concerning the basis limitation on losses, the at-risk limitation on losses, and the passive activity loss rules, respectively. We will consider these in turn. As we will see, these rules operate as tightening

---

55. I.R.C. § 461(i)(3)(A). Note that this is incredibly broad, and it may include many offerings that are not tax motivated.
56. I.R.C. § 461(i)(3)(B).
57. I.R.C. § 1256(e)(3)(B).
58. I.R.C. § 461(i)(3)(C).
59. I.R.C. § 6662(d)(2)(C)(ii).

3. Accounting for Partnership Operations

concentric circles, and that for a partner to presently benefit from a partnership flow-through loss, that loss must fit through each of these circles.

Basis Limitation

Section 704(d)(1) provides that "[a] partner's distributive share of partnership loss (including capital loss) shall be allowed only to the extent of the adjusted basis of such partner's interest in the partnership at the end of the partnership year in which such loss occurred."[60] A simple example demonstrates this rule. Consider the AB Partnership, in which A shares in 50% of the items of partnership income and loss. At the beginning of the year, assume that A has a $15,000 outside basis in her partnership interest. For simplicity, in the tax year, the AB Partnership generates a single item of loss, which is a $50,000 loss; this results in a $25,000 flow-through loss to A. However, of that $25,000, A may only deduct $15,000 of the loss because she runs up against the § 704(d) basis limitation.

What about the $10,000 of the loss that exceeds A's outside basis? Section 704(d)(2) provides a carryover rule: "Any excess of such loss over such basis shall be allowed as a deduction at the end of the partnership year in which such excess is repaid to the partnership."[61] The term "repaid" is a tad strange in the context, but the rule as clarified by the regulations operates as you might suspect; that is, the regulations allow the deduction of the suspended loss once the partner has positive adjusted basis in a later tax year.[62]

Let's do another example of the basic rule.[63] At the end of the partnership taxable year (Year 1), the AB Partnership has a loss of $20,000. Partner A's distributive share of this loss is $10,000. A's outside basis (before taking into account his distributive share of the loss) is $6,000. Consequently, under § 704(d), A's distributive share of partnership loss is allowed to him for this taxable year only to the extent of his outside basis of $6,000. The $6,000 loss decreases A's outside basis to zero. Assume that, at the end of the next taxable year (Year 2), A's share of partnership income has increased his outside basis to $3,000 (not taking into account the $4,000 loss disallowed in the prior year). Of the $4,000 loss disallowed from Year 1, $3,000 is allowed to A for Year 2, which again decreases his outside basis to zero. If, at the end of the next taxable year (i.e., Year 3), A has an adjusted basis of

---

60. I.R.C. § 704(d)(1).
61. Id.
62. Treas. Reg. § 1.704-1(d)(1) ("A partner's share of loss in excess of his adjusted basis at the end of the partnership taxable year will not be allowed for that year. However, any loss so disallowed shall be allowed as a deduction at the end of the first succeeding partnership taxable year, and subsequent partnership taxable years, to the extent that the partner's adjusted basis for his partnership interest at the end of any such year exceeds zero (before reduction by such loss for such year).").
63. This example is modeled after Example 1 in the regulation.

3. Accounting for Partnership Operations

his interest of at least $1,000 (not taking into account the disallowed loss of $1,000), he will be allowed the $1,000 loss previously disallowed.

Although not present on the face of § 704(d), the basis limitation rule has more complexity, however, which is manifested in the regulations. Treas. Reg. § 1.704-1(d)(1) provides:

> A partner's distributive share of partnership loss will be allowed only to the extent of the adjusted basis (before reduction by current year's losses) of such partner's interest in the partnership at the end of the partnership taxable year in which such loss occurred. A partner's share of loss in excess of his adjusted basis at the end of the partnership taxable year will not be allowed for that year. However, any loss so disallowed shall be allowed as a deduction at the end of the first succeeding partnership taxable year, and subsequent partnership taxable years, to the extent that the partner's adjusted basis for his partnership interest at the end of any such year exceeds zero (before reduction by such loss for such year).[64]

This subsection largely restates the rule apparent on the face of § 704(d), namely, that losses are limited to outside basis, and that disallowed losses are carried forward until there is positive basis in a later tax year.

Subsection (d)(2), however, provides an important ordering and adjustment rule. It provides:

> In computing the adjusted basis of a partner's interest for the purpose of ascertaining the extent to which a partner's distributive share of partnership loss shall be allowed as a deduction for the taxable year, the basis shall first be increased under section 705(a)(1) and decreased under section 705(a)(2), except for losses of the taxable year and losses previously disallowed. If the partner's distributive share of the aggregate of items of loss specified in section 702(a)(1), (2), (3), (8), and (9) exceeds the basis of the partner's interest computed under the preceding sentence, the limitation on losses under section 704(d) must be allocated to his distributive share of each such loss. This allocation shall be determined by taking the proportion that each loss bears to the total of all such losses. For purposes of the preceding sentence, the total losses for the taxable year shall be the sum of his distributive share of losses for the current year and his losses disallowed and carried forward from prior years.[65]

This subsection is incredibly important. It tells us that, before applying the basis limitation, we first need to adjust the outside basis for various items. There are two items. The first is the increases to basis under § 705(a)(1), which includes partnership taxable income, tax-exempt income, and excess depletion deduction. Be mindful, moreover, that partnership taxable income is incorporating the concepts we discussed from § 702. The second

---

64. Treas. Reg. § 1.704-1(d)(1).
65. Treas. Reg. § 1.704-1(d)(2).

3. Accounting for Partnership Operations

is the decreases to basis under § 705(a)(2), which includes two items: (1) partnership distributions (under § 733) and (2) "expenditures of the partnership not deductible in computing its taxable income and not properly chargeable to capital account."[66] Note that partnership losses are not subtracted here! Indeed, in calculating the adjustments requiring a decrease under § 705, the regulation expressly states, "except for the losses of the taxable year and losses previously disallowed."[67] This should make intuitive sense: We need to determine the outside basis before we see how much in partnership flow-through losses can be absorbed for the tax year.[68]

What if, even after applying the adjustment and ordering rule, there are more losses than basis? As quoted above, the regulation provides that "the limitation on losses under section 704(d) must be allocated to his distributive share of each such loss"[69] and that "[t]his allocation shall be determined by taking the proportion that each loss bears to the total of all such losses."[70] Let's consider an example that demonstrates the adjustments, ordering, and proportionality rules of the regulations.

Consider the CD Partnership.[71] At the end of Year 1, C has the following distributive share of partnership items described in section 702(a):

C's Items	
§ 702(a) Items	Amount
Short-term capital loss [§ 702(a)(1)]	$2,000
Long-term capital loss [§ 702(a)(2)]	$4,000
Partnership taxable income [§ 702(a)(8)]	$4,000

Assume also that C's outside basis at the end of Year 1, before adjustment for any of the above items, is $1,000. Applying the regulation, we first apply the increases to basis under § 705(a)(1). Here, that is the partnership taxable income, which results in adjusting C's outside basis from $1,000 to $5,000. It's important to note that, in this example, there are not any decreases to basis we need to make; that is, there are no partnership distributions and no nondeductible expenditures. In this example, then, C's total share of partnership loss is $6,000 (the STCL of $2,000 and the LTCL of $4,000). But C has an outside basis of only $5,000, so C runs up against the basis limitation. We thus need to proportionally limit each loss. Therefore, C is

---

66. I.R.C. § 705(a)(2)(B).
67. Treas. Reg. § 1.704-1(d)(2).
68. In other words, excluding partnership losses from this calculation removes the circularity that would be present if we tried to include losses in the calculation to see how much in loss is deductible.
69. Treas. Reg. § 1.704-1(d)(2).
70. Id.
71. This is based on Example 3 of Treas. Reg. § 1.704-1(d).

3. Accounting for Partnership Operations

allowed only $5,000/$6,000 of each loss; that is, $3,333 of the long-term capital loss, and $1,667 of the short-term capital loss. C will carry forward to the succeeding tax years $667 as a long-term capital loss and $333 as a short-term capital loss.

We have covered (d)(1) and (d)(2), which provide that losses are limited to basis and losses in excess of basis carryover, respectively; however, (d)(3) provides "special rules." Let's review the statutory language:

> (3) Special rules.—
> (A) In general.—In determining the amount of any loss under paragraph (1), there shall be taken into account the partner's distributive share of amounts described in paragraphs (4) and (6) of section 702(a).
> (B) Exception.—In the case of a charitable contribution of property whose fair market value exceeds its adjusted basis, subparagraph (A) shall not apply to the extent of the partner's distributive share of such excess.[72]

Section 702(a), of course, provides for how partners take into account various items of partnership income. Paragraph (4) is charitable contributions and paragraph (6) is foreign taxes. So why are these special rules here? Some historical context is important.

Section 704(d)(3) was added by the Tax Cuts and Jobs Act of 2017.[73] Recall that, under § 703(a)(2)(C), charitable contributions are not part of calculating the taxable income of a partnership. Thus, before amending § 703(d), such charitable contributions were not subject to the § 703(d) basis limitation. In effect, then, a partner with an outside basis of $0 could take advantage of a charitable contribution deduction without any concomitant decrease in basis.[74] The IRS even issued a ruling to this effect. In Private Letter Ruling 8405084, the Service noted that § 704(d) "refers to losses and not charitable contributions,"[75] and thus the § 704(d) basis limitation did not apply to charitable contributions.[76]

The new amendments to § 704(d), however, now require the partner to take into account his or her share of partnership charitable contributions in applying the § 704(d) limitation. Unfortunately, as of this writing, there have not been regulations implementing this statutory change. The legislative history on the desired purpose is helpful—it provides that "the amount of the basis limitation on partner losses is decreased to reflect [charitable contributions, among other things]."[77]

---

72. I.R.C. § 704(d)(3).
73. Pub. L. No. 115-97, § 13503, 131 Stat. 2054 (Dec. 22, 2017).
74. *See* H.R. Rep No. 466, 115th Cong., 1st Sess., "Conference Report to Accompany HR 1," at 514.
75. I.R.S. Priv. Ltr. Rul. 8405084 (Nov. 3, 1983).
76. Id.
77. H.R. Rep No. 466, 115th Cong., 1st Sess., "Conference Report to Accompany HR 1," at 514.

3. Accounting for Partnership Operations

There is yet another wrinkle for this new special rule for charitable contributions present in § 704(d)(3). Subparagraph (B) provides that, "[i]n the case of a charitable contribution of property whose fair market value exceeds its adjusted basis, subparagraph (A) shall not apply to the extent of the partner's distributive share of such excess."[78] This concerns when the partnership makes a charitable contribution of *property* (i.e., not cash). Thus, under this rule, the excess of the fair market value over adjusted basis, is not taken into account for the § 704(d) limitation.

Although the past few paragraphs have been talking about these special rules for § 704(d) and charitable contributions, as a closing note, it is important to note that § 704(d)(3)'s rules apply also to foreign taxes under § 901.

At-Risk Limitation

The next limit to consider is provided in § 465 and is known as the at-risk limitation. The policy rationale of § 465 is evident—the Code should allow tax losses only for losses in which the taxpayer has real economic skin in the game (i.e., an amount "at risk"). Section 465 was enacted in the 1970s to combat against tax shelters.[79] The legislative history notes the following rationale:

> When an investor is solicited for a tax shelter activity, it has become common practice to promise the prospective investor substantial tax losses which can be used to decrease the tax on his income from other sources. The committee believes that it is not equitable to allow these individual investors to defer tax on income from other sources through losses generated by tax sheltering activities, to the extent the losses exceed the amount of actual investment the taxpayer has placed at risk in the transaction.[80]

Indeed, § 465 is not a partnership-specific provision, but it applies generally to individuals and certain C corporations.[81] Therefore, if a partner is an individual, the at-risk limitation applies.

Section 465(a) provides:

> (a) Limitation to amount at risk.—
> (1) In general.—In the case of—
> (A) an individual, and

---

78. I.R.C. § 704(d)(3)(B).
79. E.g., S. Rep. No. 94-938, at 47 (1976), 1976 U.S.C.C.A.N. 3438.
80. Id.
81. Though, it is important to note that, in the legislative history, limited partnerships are common in "the typical tax shelter." Id.

3. Accounting for Partnership Operations

>   (B) a C corporation with respect to which the stock ownership requirement of paragraph (2) of section 542(a) is met,
>
>   engaged in an activity to which this section applies, any loss from such activity for the taxable year shall be allowed only to the extent of the aggregate amount with respect to which the taxpayer is at risk (within the meaning of subsection (b)) for such activity at the close of the taxable year.[82]

Stated more simply, then, an individual taxpayer may deduct losses from activities only to the extent that they are "at risk" with respect to that activity as of the end of the tax year. Naturally, this gives rise to the need to define "activity" and how we define how a taxpayer is "at risk."

Let's first consider the definition of activities to which this section applies. Section 465(c)(1) provides that this section applies to:

> (A) holding, producing, or distributing motion picture films or video tapes,
> (B) farming (as defined in section 464(e)),
> (C) leasing any section 1245 property (as defined in section 1245(a)(3)),
> (D) exploring for, or exploiting, oil and gas resources, or
> (E) exploring for, or exploiting, geothermal deposits (as defined in section 613(e)(2))
>
> as a trade or business or for the production of income.[83]

It may be tempting to read that section and conclude that § 465 applies to only a limited and targeted set of circumstances—but that would be incorrect. We need to dive deeper into the subsections. Section 465(c)(3) provides that the at-risk limitations apply also to each activity "(i) engaged in by the taxpayer in carrying on a trade or business or for the production of income, and (ii) which is not described in paragraph (1)."[84] In other words, any trade-or-business or profit-seeking partnership and partner has § 465 implications.

Let's now turn to defining how much is "at risk." Section 465(b) provides that a taxpayer is considered at risk for an activity with respect to "(A) the amount of money and the adjusted basis of other property contributed by the taxpayer to the activity, and (B) amounts borrowed with respect to such activity (as determined under paragraph (2))."[85] Elaborating on the latter part, paragraph (2) notes that amounts borrowed are considered at risk if the individual is either "personally liable for the repayment of such amounts" or "has pledged property, other than property used in such

---

82. I.R.C. § 465(a).
83. I.R.C. § 465(c)(1).
84. I.R.C. § 465(c)(3).
85. I.R.C. § 465(b)(1).

3. Accounting for Partnership Operations

activity, as security for such borrowed amount (to the extent of the net fair market value of the taxpayer's interest in such property)."[86]

Portending potential shenanigans with debt (a theme we see continually in the study of partnership taxation), § 465 also excludes certain debt and borrowed amounts from the at-risk calculation. In short, § 465(c)(3) provides that if the lender has an interest in the activity or is related to a person with an interest in the activity, such borrowed amounts are not considered at-risk.

Before we look at more complicated aspects of § 465, let's review a few basic examples. The EF Partnership has two partners, E and F, who have each contributed $50,000 cash to the partnership, and who each have an outside basis of $50,000. The EF Partnership is in the trade or business of producing movies (and, for reasons discussed later, let's assume it produces a single movie); in the current taxable year, the EF Partnership generates a tax loss of $40,000, which is shared equally between E and F. In this example, E and F each have an at-risk amount in the activity of $50,000 due to their cash contribution to the partnership. Consequently, the at-risk limitation of § 465 does not bar their ability to deduct their respective losses (note, too, that they have sufficient outside basis to absorb the losses).

Now, let's tweak the example slightly. Assume that they had each contributed only $15,000 in cash at the beginning of the partnership. Let's also assume, however, that their outside bases at the beginning of the taxable year was $30,000.[87] And, like before, the partnership generates a $40,000 tax loss that is shared equally between E and F. Thus, in this example, they each have sufficient outside basis ($30,000 each) to absorb the loss under § 704. However, they do not have a sufficient at-risk amount. Under § 465, therefore, of the $20,000 loss that is allocated to each of them, they may only deduct $15,000 each—which is their amounts at-risk under § 465.

Thus, you can see how these sections—704 and 465—act as constricting circles to limit the deductibility of losses. We will add yet another constricting circle shortly in the section below, but before we do so, we need to further unpack the intricacies of § 465. As intimated by the above explanation, the at-risk limitation is not applied to the partnership as an entity, but rather on a partner-by-partner basis.[88] Thus, each partner has their own individual at-risk calculations. Because § 465 applies only to individuals

---

86. I.R.C. § 465(c)(2).
87. You may be wondering how a partner can have an outside basis greater than the amount of property that she contributed. That occurs because, as later discussed, she includes her share of money borrowed by the partnership in her outside basis.
88. This is implicated by the statutory text in § 465 that it applies to individuals (and some corporations, who can also be partners). The partner-by-partner approach is also implicated in the legislative history. See S. Rep. No. 94-938 at 49.

3. Accounting for Partnership Operations

(and some corporations), it is possible that some, none, or all the partners will have § 465 consequences.

In addition to the limitation applying on a partner-by-partner basis, it also applies on an activity-by-activity basis. So, if a partnership has several "activities," a partner's at-risk amount may vary by activity within each partnership. This requires us then to consider is it possible to "aggregate" activities together (e.g., to treat them as the same activity)? Section 465(c)(2)(A) provides an aggregation rule. It provides that:

> Except as provided in subparagraph (B), a taxpayer's activity with respect to each—
> (i) film or video tape,
> (ii) section 1245 property which is leased or held for leasing,
> (iii) farm,
> (iv) oil and gas property (as defined under section 614), or
> (v) geothermal property (as defined under section 614),
> shall be treated as a separate activity.[89]

Continuing the movie example, then, if a movie studio organized as a partnership and has 10 film projects, each of those films constitutes a *separate* activity, and a partner's at-risk amounts need to be determined for each of those films (activities).[90]

What about activities though that are not mentioned in § 465(c)(2)(A)? These types of activities (trade or business activities) can be aggregated to a *single* activity if "the taxpayer actively participates in the management of the trade or business" or "such trade or business is carried on by a partnership or an S corporation and 65 percent or more of the losses for the taxable year is allocable to persons who actively participate in the management of the trade or business."[91] Note, however, that on its face, this aggregation applies only to "trade or business" activities (not production of income activities); the statute contemplates regulations to be issued to handle aggregation issues here, but no such regulations have been issued presently.

There is one more wrinkle in § 465 worth mentioning here. Recall that for purposes of determining the at-risk amount, there is included (i) cash and the adjusted basis of contributed property and (ii) borrowed amounts—and that these borrowed amounts essentially require that the person be personally liable (or have pledged property).[92] The general rule

---

89. I.R.C. § 465(c)(2)(A).

90. Think of these aggregation and separation rules like the structure of the Titanic. There, the ship was divided into watertight compartments, with the belief that flooding in one compartment would not spill over to another compartment. These at-risk separation/aggregation rules operate similarly. In other words, Congress does not want surplus at-risk capital in one activity spilling over to another activity in which there is not enough at-risk capital.

91. I.R.C. § 465(c)(3)(B).

92. I.R.C. § 465(b)(1), (2).

3. Accounting for Partnership Operations

for borrowed amounts thus requires personal liability (or other skin in the game by way of the pledged collateral). There is a noteworthy exception, however, for "qualified nonrecourse financing."[93]

Under this exception, if the activity consists of holding real property, a taxpayer is considered at-risk for qualified nonrecourse financing that is secured by that real property used in the activity.[94] The following are the elements to be qualified nonrecourse financing:

> (i) which is borrowed by the taxpayer with respect to the activity of holding real property,
> (ii) which is borrowed by the taxpayer from a qualified person or represents a loan from any Federal, State, or local government or instrumentality thereof, or is guaranteed by any Federal, State, or local government,
> (iii) except to the extent provided in regulations, with respect to which no person is personally liable for repayment, and
> (iv) which is not convertible debt.[95]

A qualified person, moreover, is defined under § 49(a)(1)(D)(iv), meaning essentially someone who is engaged in the business of lending money but is not related to the taxpayer.[96] Yet another wrinkle is present here. Even if the lender is *related*, the lender can still be a qualified person if the financing is "commercially reasonable and on substantially the same terms as loans involving unrelated persons."[97] Although we have not yet covered how to allocate partnership liabilities, § 465 provides that, "[i]n the case of a partnership, a partner's share of any qualified nonrecourse financing of such partnership shall be determined on the basis of the partner's share of liabilities of such partnership incurred in connection with such financing (within the meaning of section 752)."[98]

Passive Losses

The last limitation to deducting partnership losses are the passive loss rules, which are found in § 469. Like the at-risk limitation, the passive loss rules do not apply to partnerships as entities, but rather to certain types of taxpayers. Taxpayers that are individuals, estates, trusts, closely held C corporations,

---

93. I.R.C. § 465(b)(6).
94. I.R.C. § 465(b)(6)(A).
95. I.R.C. § 465(b)(6)(B).
96. The other exceptions to a qualified person include the person from whom taxpayer acquired the property and a person who receives a fee for the taxpayer's investment in the property. I.R.C. § 49(a)(1)(D)(iv).
97. I.R.C. § 465(b)(6)(D)(ii).
98. Allocating liabilities — recourse and nonrecourse — is covered in Chapter 6.

3. Accounting for Partnership Operations

and personal service corporations are subject to these rules.[99] In short, the passive loss rules—like the operation of the at-risk limitation—provide that a taxpayer cannot deduct passive losses in excess of passive income. Thus, if a taxpayer has $10,000 of passive losses, but only $4,000 of passive income, those losses may be deducted only to the extent of $4,000.

Specifically, § 469 denies a deduction for a "passive activity loss."[100] Passive activity loss is defined as the amount by which all losses from passive activities exceed all income from passive activities for the taxable year.[101] The passive losses from past years that were suspended and carried forward, moreover, are included in this calculation as well, i.e., they are treated as passive losses for the current year.[102] If the taxpayer has multiple passive activities and has more aggregate passive losses than passive income, moreover, the passive loss limitation needs to be allocated among the passive activities.[103]

The regulations further define the term passive activity loss as the amount by which the passive activity deductions exceed the passive activity gross income for the taxable year.[104] This regulation is important, moreover, because it *excludes* items of "portfolio income" from the definition of passive activity gross income.[105] Portfolio income includes items such as interest, annuities, royalties, and dividends, among others.[106]

Passive activities are determined by material participation; that is, any activity which involves the conduct of a trade or business in which the taxpayer *does not materially participate* constitutes a passive activity.[107] There are also some per se passive activities, such as rental activities (subject to a critical exception, discussed later). Subject to regulations, moreover, production of income activities (that don't rise to the level of trade or business) can also be passive activities.[108] Some activities, though, are not passive, such as certain "working" interests in oil and gas property.[109]

Under § 469(h), a taxpayer materially participates if he is "involved in the operations of the activity on a basis of which is ... regular ... continuous ... and substantial."[110] The regulations provide additional bright-line rules for material participation. For example, material participation is

---

99. I.R.C. § 469(a)(2).
100. I.R.C. § 469(a)(1)(A). It also applies to the "passive activity credit," which is not discussed here.
101. I.R.C. § 469(d).
102. I.R.C. § 469(b).
103. Treas. Reg. § 1.469-1T(f)(2).
104. Treas. Reg. § 1.469-2T(b).
105. Treas. Reg. § 1.469-2T(c)(3).
106. Id.
107. I.R.C. § 469(c).
108. I.R.C. § 469(c)(6).
109. I.R.C. § 469(c)(3).
110. I.R.C. § 469(h).

3. Accounting for Partnership Operations

satisfied if the individual participates more than 500 hours in the activity or the individual's participation constitutes substantially all the participation of the year across all individuals in the activity.[111]

Importantly as applied to partners, moreover, "[e]xcept as provided in regulations, no interest in a limited partnership as a limited partner shall be treated as an interest with respect to which a taxpayer materially participates."[112] The regulations define a limited partner by two tests. The first test is if the partnership agreement or state certificate designates the interest as a limited partnership interest. The second test is if "[t]he liability of the holder of such interest for obligations of the partnership is limited, under the law of the State in which the partnership is organized, to a determinable fixed amount (for example, the sum of the holder's capital contributions to the partnership and contractual obligations to make additional capital contributions to the partnership)."[113]

On its face, this second test would appear to capture members in an LLC because, under state law, LLC members are typically limited in their liabilities for the obligations of the entity. However, the regulations also provide that if the individual is a general partner in the partnership, they will not be considered to have a limited partnership interest.[114] Court decisions have thus held that even though LLC interest have limited liability, they fit within the general partner exception because LLC members can participate in the operations of the business.[115]

In addition to the general partner exception, there are three noteworthy exceptions provided in the regulations to the limited partner rule. The first exception is if the partner participates for more than 500 hours in the activity; the second is if the partner materially participated for five of the last ten years; and the third is if the activity is a personal service activity and the individual materially participated for three prior years.[116]

As noted above earlier, there is a critical exception for certain taxpayers involved a real estate business, which is found in § 469(c)(7). This exception provides that if more than one-half of the personal services performed by the taxpayer are in real property businesses, and that the taxpayer provides more than 750 hours of personal services, the rental activities will not be considered a passive activity under the per se rule of § 469(c)(2). Another rental exception is found in § 469(i). This section provides that in

---

111. Treas. Reg. § 1.469-5T(a).
112. I.R.C. § 469(h)(2). You may recall that, under state business organization law, generally a limited partner cannot be involved in the operations of the business—that is the tradeoff for the limited liability.
113. Treas. Reg. § 1.469-5T(e)(3)(i)(B).
114. Treas. Reg. § 1469-5T(e)(3)(ii).
115. *See* Garnett v. Comm'r, 132 T.C. 368 (2009).
116. Treas. Reg. § 1.469-5T(e).

the case of a natural person who actively participates in a rental real estate activity, $25,000 of losses shall not be considered a passive loss; this is subject to phaseout based on adjusted gross income. Active participation is defined with respect to percent ownership—less than 10% ownership (including spousal ownership) is deemed to not be active participation.[117]

To the extent the taxpayer has more passive loss than passive income, the taxpayer may carry the loss forward to the next taxable year.[118] Once a taxpayer disposes of his entire interest in the passive activity in a taxable transaction to an unrelated party, the suspended losses, if any, are no longer considered passive.[119] If, however, the taxpayer dies with a passive activity with suspended losses, those losses are allowed, in effect, to the difference between the date-of-death value of the property and the taxpayer's basis before his death; excess losses are then lost.[120]

The regulations provide rules that are specific to partners. For instance, whether an item is passive is determined on a partner-by-partner basis.[121] These determinations, moreover, are based on the taxable year of the entity, not the partner.[122] The following example, based on the regulation, illustrates these determinations.[123]

A, a calendar year individual, is a partner in a partnership that has a taxable year ending March 31. During its taxable year ending on March 31, Year 2, the partnership engages in a single business activity. From April 1, Year 1, through March 31, Year 2, A does not materially participate in this activity. In A's calendar year tax return for Year 2, A's distributive share of the partnership's gross income and deductions from the activity must be treated as passive activity gross income and passive activity deductions, without regard to A's participation in the activity from April 1, Year 2, through December 31, Year 2.

Applying the Loss Limitations

As earlier sections explained, there are three cumulative limitations on a partner being able to deduct a partnership flow-through loss: (1) the basis limitation, (2) the at-risk limitation, and (3) the passive loss rules; these limits, moreover, need to be applied in this order. This order is provided by the § 469 regulations.[124] That is, the regulations specify that a passive item

---

117. I.R.C. § 469(i)(6).
118. I.R.C. § 469(b).
119. I.R.C. § 469(g).
120. I.R.C. § 469(g)(2).
121. Treas. Reg. § 1.469-2T(e).
122. Id.
123. Treas. Reg. § 1.469-2T(e)(1) Example.
124. See Treas. Reg. § 1.469-2T(d)(6)(i).

3. Accounting for Partnership Operations

that is disallowed by § 704(d) or § 465 is not a passive activity deduction for the year (implying that the §§ 704 and 465 rules are applied before § 469). Additionally, the § 469 regulations also provide that amounts disallowed under § 704(d) are not taken into account for applying § 465.[125] Thus, a partner must first determine if the loss is disallowed by the basis limitation of § 704(d). Second, the partner must determine if the loss is disallowed by the at-risk limitation. And, third, the partner must then consider if the passive activity rules disallow the loss.

These sections—§§ 704(d), 465, and 469—represent the typical rules that further govern the deductibility of losses for partners, and they have been on the books for decades. However, there is a recent addition that we discuss shortly now, which is § 461(l), which was added by the law known as the Tax Cuts and Jobs Act.[126] This newer additional limitation on the deductibility of losses provides that noncorporate taxpayers cannot deduct "excess business loss" for tax years that begin after December 31, 2020, and before January 1, 2026.[127] Essentially this provision prevents deductions attributable to a trade or business in excess of trade or business income plus $250,000 (or $500,000 if married).[128]

CAPITAL ACCOUNTS

The last section of this chapter focuses on the equity portion of the partnership balance sheet and it is therefore included in this chapter about partnership accounting. As well, capital accounts establish key concepts that we turn to in the next chapter about partnership allocations. Capital accounts play a central role in partnership accounting. A capital account is a way to track the partners' claim to partnership assets (i.e., equity). As we saw in Chapter 2, a balance sheet (a traditional financial statement used in financial accounting) is helpful to visualize these relationships. A balance sheet typically presents three types of information: assets, liabilities, and equity. This information stems from the "fundamental accounting equation," which is

$$Assets = Liabilities + Owners'Equity$$

---

125. Treas. Reg. § 1.469-2T(d)(6)(iv).
126. Although frequently and commonly referred to as the "Tax Cuts and Jobs Act," which was its name in prior versions of the bill, the bill that was actually passed and signed by President Trump had its short title removed for parliamentary reasons to comply with the reconciliation process. See Pub. L. No. 115-97, 131 Stat. 2054 (Dec. 22, 2017).
127. As enacted, this limitation would have started for tax years that being after December 31, 2016; this date was changed by the CARES Act. Pub. L. No. 116-136, § 2304, 134 Stat. 281.
128. These amounts are adjusted for inflation.

3. Accounting for Partnership Operations

Although there are technical definitions to these terms in financial accounting,[129] colloquial ideas are helpful here. Assets, for example, are things that you own; those things could be tangible (like cash and property) or even intangible (like a copyright or patent). Liabilities are debts; that is, financial obligations that are owed. Equity is the difference between assets and liabilities; that is, the assets that remain for the owners after all the liabilities have been paid. Another way to think about it is that equity is the accounting amount of what the owners could "walk away" with in a liquidation.[130] A balance sheet, moreover, is captured at a particular date; in other words, it's a snapshot in time of the entity's assets, liabilities, and equity.

The regulations encapsulate an equity-like concept known as a "capital account," which is tracked for each partner. As already noted, and stated again for emphasis, the importance of capital accounts cannot be understated. Although their ubiquity is not quite clear given where we are in this text, by the end of reading this text it will be evident. Right now, however, we introduce the concept initially and describe how capital accounts are maintained.

Maintenance of Capital Accounts

Treas. Reg. § 1.704-1(b)(2)(iv) provides for the maintenance of capital accounts. Maintenance of capital accounts will be a central element of the discussion regarding partnership allocations.[131] The regulation provides seven "basic rules" for determining and maintaining capital accounts; the first three describe when capital accounts are *increased* and the last four describe when capital accounts are *decreased*. The seven "basic" rules are:

Capital accounts are *increased* for:

(1) The amount of money contributed to the partnership by the partner;
(2) The fair market value of property (net of liabilities assumed) contributed by the partner;
(3) Allocations of partnership income and gain (with some caveats).

Capital accounts are *decreased* for:

(4) The amount of money distributed to the partner;
(5) The fair market value of property (net of liabilities assumed) distributed to the partner;

---

129. *See, e.g.,* Financial Accounting Standards Board, *Statement of Financial Accounting Concepts No. 3* (Dec. 1980).
130. Assuming items are sold for their "book" value.
131. *See* Chapter 4.

3. Accounting for Partnership Operations

(6) Allocations of non-capital, nondeductible expenses;
(7) Allocations of items of expenditures, loss, and deduction (with caveats).

The following is a summary table of the capital account rules:

Capital Account "Basic Rules" [§ 1.704-1(b)(2)(iv)(b)]	
Capital Accounts are *Increased* by	Capital Accounts are *Decreased* by
[1] Contributions of money	[4] Distributions of money
[2] Contributions of property(measured by FMV and net of liabilities)	[5] Distributions of property(measured by FMV and net of liabilities)
[3] Allocations of income and gain	[6] Non-capital, nondeductible expenses
	[7] Allocations of loss and deduction

Let's consider a quick (and easy) example. Assume that C and D each contribute $25,000 in cash, and C also contributes $10,000 in equipment. Their respective capital accounts, immediately after formation, would be as follows:

C's Capital Account	D's Capital Account
+ $25,000	+ $25,000
+ $10,000	
= $35,000	= $25,000

Connecting this back to our concept of owners' equity from a financial accounting perspective, C would have $35,000 of owners' equity and D would have $25,000. Moreover, we can now construct an entire balance sheet that represents the accounting state of the partnership (as an entity):

CD Partnership			
Assets		*Liabilities*	
Cash	$50,000	None	$0
Equipment	$10,000		
		"Equity"	
		C's Capital Account	$35,000
		D's Capital Account	$25,000
Total	$60,000	Total	$60,000

As the balance sheet shows, the assets ($60,000) equal the liabilities ($0) plus owners' equity (here, the capital accounts of $60,000). Indeed, a nice way to check your work (and analysis) is to construct a balance

3. Accounting for Partnership Operations

sheet and see if the fundamental accounting equation holds. Now, this is the moment after formation, i.e., there has not been any partnership operations yet (e.g., income or expenses). Moreover, take note that this is a "clean" example insofar as there is no debt present. Fret not, though, we will add those complications as we continue.

Let's reiterate exactly what the capital accounts represent in the above example. If the partnership were to liquidate with the above balance sheet, what would happen? It has two assets: cash and equipment. Let's assume it just distributes those assets. There are no creditors to pay (liabilities are zero), so all the assets inure to the partners. How do they share in those assets? That's exactly what the capital account balances represent! C is entitled to $35,000 in assets and D is entitled to $25,000. Now, practically, how they decide who gets the equipment versus cash (or how they split it) can be more complicated (and depend on the partnership agreement; for example, maybe the partnership sells the equipment and then distributes the cash proceeds). We cover the specifics of this event—known as a liquidating distribution (if a partner is exiting) or a partnership termination (if the partnership is dissolving)—in later chapters.[132]

Before we move on, there's a vocabulary matter to iron out. The § 704 regulations speak about a concept described as "book value," "book purposes," and the like. Think of this concept as the valuation at which the partnership carries (records or reports) an asset. For those with prior accounting coursework, you may be familiar with the "cost" (or "historical cost") principle from financial accounting (i.e., Generally Accepted Accounting Principles or GAAP). Under GAAP accounting, an asset is carried and reflected on the books of a business at its historical cost—that is, the cost at the time the company acquired the asset, and it is *not* adjusted for later events (with some exception). For example, if a company purchased a plot of land for $50,000 in 1950, on its 2022 balance sheet, however, that same piece of land is *still* reported at $50,000. You can readily see that the reported amount of land (the $50,000) may bear very little relation to the property's current fair market value today. (As an important aside, this divergence vividly demonstrates why one cannot simply use a balance sheet to value a business.)

That historical cost—at the time of initial purchase—was likely the asset's then-fair market value.[133] "Book value," for § 704 purposes, is the conceptual equivalent. That is, for partnership tax purposes, we record assets at "book value." Recall that, under our capital account rules, we are going to increase the capital account for the net fair market value of property contributed. Thus, at acquisition, book value will likely be the asset's fair market value minus any liabilities associated with it. But just like with financial

---

132. *See* Chapter 7.
133. Barring any type of part-gift transaction, related-party transaction, and other type of transaction that causes a divergence between purchase prices and a reasonable market price.

3. Accounting for Partnership Operations

accounting, that direct connection may fall apart over time. In other words, an asset's book value for partnership-tax purposes may not be the asset's actual later fair market value at a particular point in time (though, for tractability, this text generally assumes this equivalency). There are instances, however, that the regulations expressly allow us to "revalue" an asset, meaning we can restate (update) the book values to reflect current fair market values.[134] From here out, therefore, we will add the label "book value" to our use of partnership balance sheets. This label becomes even more important when an asset's basis does not equal its book value; that is, we may need to separately track basis. Let's look at an example.

The clearest example is when E contributes property to the partnership in exchange for his partnership interest. Let's say that E contributes Blackacre that has a basis in E's hands of $15,000 and has a current fair market value of $25,000. To keep things simple, let's assume that F (the other partner) contributes $25,000 in cash in exchange for his partnership interest. Before the contribution, the abbreviated balance sheet of E and F looks as follows:

E	F
Blackacre	Cash
FMV: $25,000	FMV: $25,000
Basis: $15,000	Basis: $25,000

After the contribution, the balance sheet of the partnership must reflect the difference in the FMV and the (inside) basis. That is, recall that the basis to the partnership of Blackacre is going to be $15,000. Moreover, now consider that we must track E's capital account, which is going to be increased by $25,000 (not $15,000). Consequently, the partnership balance sheet looks as follows:

EF Partnership							
Assets				*Liabilities*			
	Adj. Basis	Book Value	None		$0		
Cash	$25,000	$25,000					
Blackacre	$15,000	$25,000		*Capital Accounts*			
					Adj. Basis	Book Value	
				E	$15,000	$25,000	
				F	$25,000	$25,000	
Total	$40,000	$50,000		Total	$40,000	$50,000	

---

134. There are other calculations described later in this text that will require us to use the asset's present fair market value, instead of its basis or book values (e.g., § 743 adjustments discussed in Chapter 10).

3. Accounting for Partnership Operations

There are differences in this balance sheet compared to the one introduced earlier, namely that there are now two columns with dollar amounts—the adjusted basis column and the book value column. These columns are tracking two different concepts. Focus first on the asset side. Here, we can now track the inside basis to the partnership of its assets. The term "adjusted" is also present because eventually we will be changing (adjusting) that basis—for example, with depreciation (with §§ 167, 168, and 1016).[135] Moreover, the book value column is tracking the valuation required to comport with the § 704 regulations. Consider now the equity portion, i.e., the capital accounts section. Similarly, you observe both an adjusted basis column and a book value column—indeed, for the same reason as with the asset side. Here, the adjusted basis column here represents the partners outside basis in their partnership interest. The book value column represents the partner's capital account in accordance with the § 704 regulations.

Before we depart this section, let's connect this balance sheet with more fundamental concepts. The basis columns track exactly that: basis. Recall that basis represents already-taxed capital; meaning that to the extent you have dollars in the basis column, those dollars are not taxed again. The book value columns are essentially tracking who is entitled to various economic amounts. For example, on its books, the partnership has $50,000 in economic assets; the book value of the partners' capital accounts reflects how many dollars of those economic assets each partner is entitled.

At the admitted risk of jumping too deep, too early, other concepts we discuss later can be illustrated now, as they are observable given a completed balance sheet. For example, if E sells his partnership interest for $25,000, you can see that E will be getting more economic return than his basis (already-taxed capital); therefore, we need a mechanism to account for that additional economic return, which is *gain*. Similarly, what if the partnership distributes assets to F in excess of his $25,000 inside basis—he, too, will be getting more economic return than his already-taxed capital; therefore, we need a mechanism to account for that gain. On the other hand, what if the partnership distributes $5,000 to E, which is less than his outside basis—perhaps that does not reflect new economic gain but merely return of his already-taxed capital; therefore, we need a mechanism to reflect the relationship between basis and taxed capital that is adjusted regularly. Indeed, we have statutory mechanisms for these, and we discuss them in more detail throughout this text.

---

135. For brevity, in the balance sheets in later examples and chapters, we may omit the term "adjusted."

3. Accounting for Partnership Operations

Examples

1. Aaron, Betty and Camila are forming a new partnership to operate a business. In exchange for their partnership interests, they each contribute the following: Aaron contributes $50,000 in cash; Betty contributes Blackacre, which has a basis of $10,000 and a FMV of $30,000, and Redacre, which has a basis of $35,000 and a value of $20,000; Camila contributes a note receivable with a face value of $25,000, which she received in exchange for providing services in a "side hustle," and inventory that has a basis of $20,000 and a value of $25,000. Complete a partnership balance sheet that depicts the above contributions; be sure to include basis, book value, and capital accounts.

2. The Delta Partnership has four equal partners, Edward, Frank, Grace, and Helen. In the current tax year, Delta has the following items:

Delta Partnership	
Item	Amount
Service revenue	$450,000
Salaries expense	$125,000
Depreciation	$45,000
§ 179 expense	$20,000
§ 1231 gain	$5,000
Short-term capital loss	$10,000
Long-term capital gain	$35,000
Investment interest expense	$4,000

Calculate the partnership's taxable income, consisting of its non-separately stated and separately stated items of income. Assuming the partners share items equally, explain how the partners will account for the calculated items.

3. The Omega Partnership is a newly formed partnership that has four partners, Jake, Karen, Laura, and Mega Co. (a C corporation). They own various amounts of partnership capital and profits as set forth in each of the alternative situations. Except as modified below, the individuals have calendar years and Mega has a fiscal year that ends on September 30. In each situation, determine the required tax year for the Omega Partnership for its first taxable year; the partnership does not have a business purpose year.
   a. Jake, Karen, and Laura each own 20% of partnership profits and capital, and Mega Co. owns the remaining 40%.
   b. Jake, Karen, and Laura each own 10% of partnership profits and capital, and Mega Co. owns the remaining 70%.

3. Accounting for Partnership Operations

c. Jake, Karen, and Laura each own 20% of partnership profits and capital, and Mega Co. owns the remaining 40%, but now Jake has a fiscal year that ends on November 30.

4. Sally is a partner in the STU Partnership. At the end of the current taxable year, Sally has the following distributive share of partnership items: Long-term capital loss, $120,000; short-term capital loss, $60,000, and non-separately stated partnership income of $120,000. Her outside basis before consideration of any of this year's operations is $30,000. For the current year, (i) what is Sally's total distributive share of partnership loss, (ii) how much of the loss is deductible considering the § 704(d) limitation, and (iii) how much loss, if any, carries forward to a later tax year?

5. Tim and Victor form TV, LLC, which is taxed as a partnership. Tim and Victor each contribute $1,000,000 in cash, and they are equal partners. The cash is used to purchase drilling equipment to operate a three oil wells. In addition, the partnership is also engaged in the activity of farming; it operates five farms. The partnership secures its farm equipment using nonrecourse loans. In the current tax year, the partnership incurs losses of $300,000 from its oil exploration activities and $200,000 from its farming activities. Explain how much, if any, of these losses are deductible under § 704(d) and § 465.

Explanations

1. Although not asked for in the problem, this transaction is governed by § 721, and both the partners and partnership recognize no gain or loss on this transaction. Consequently, the bases are preserved under §§ 722 and 723. The capital accounts for the partners are increased for the value of the property they contributed to the partnership. The partnership balance sheet thus looks as follows.

ABC Partnership					
Assets			Liabilities		
	Adj. Basis	Book Value	None		$0
Cash	$50,000	$50,000			
Blackacre	$10,000	$30,000		Capital Accounts	
Redacre	$35,000	$20,000		Adj. Basis	Book Value
Promissory Note	$0	$25,000	A	$50,000	$50,000
Inventory	$20,000	$25,000	B	$45,000	$50,000
			C	$20,000	$50,000
Total	$115,000	$150,000	Total	$115,000	$150,000

3. Accounting for Partnership Operations

The promissory note has a tax basis of $0 because, presumably, as cash-method taxpayer Camila has not yet included the note in her income.[136] On the capital account portion of the balance sheet, observe how each capital account was increased for the value of property contributed under Treas. Reg. § 1.704-1(b)(2)(iv)(b).

2. This question regards the calculation of partnership taxable income under § 703 and as reported under § 702. The first step is to classify the items as separately or non-separately stated. The import of this distinction is to ensure that the impact of items whose tax impact depends on other facts are not lost by being combined with other items. Thus, a separately stated item is an item the ultimate tax treatment of which can vary from partner to partner, depending on the partner's tax situation.

In the example, the following are items that must be separately stated:

(1) *§ 179 expense.* Section 179 expenses are separately stated items because they may be limited under § 179(b).[137] For example, § 179(b)(1) limits the deductible § 179 expenses to $1,000,000 for a taxable year; this limit, moreover, is further limited by § 179(b)(2). Consequently, the impact and treatment of the § 179 expense on the partner's individual tax return depends on collateral tax facts (e.g., does the partner have additional § 179 expenses).

(2) *§ 1231 gain.* Section 1231 gains and losses are separately stated items under § 702(a)(3) and § 1.702-1(a)(3). Section 1231 gains and losses share a similar netting concern that is common to several of the separately stated items. The tax rate applied to a § 1231 item depends on the aggregation and netting of the taxpayer's § 1231 items, which may include items beyond the Delta Partnership.[138]

(3) *Short-term capital loss.* The short-term capital loss is a separately stated item under § 702(a)(1). Its ultimate tax treatment for the partners depends on the netting of their other capital transactions for the tax year.

(4) *Long-term capital gain.* The long-term capital gain is a separately stated item under § 702(a)(2). Like with the short-term capital loss, its ultimate tax treatment for the partners depends on the netting of their other capital transactions for the tax year.

---

136. Generally, a promissory note does not trigger an income inclusion for a cash-method taxpayer because the note — in effect, an "IOU" — does not represent actual payment but merely evidences the obligation to pay.
137. *See* Rev. Rul. 89-7, 1989-1 C.B. 178.
138. As a review, if § 1231 gains for the year exceed § 1231 losses for the year, the gains and losses are treated as long-term capital gains and losses. If, on the other hand, the gains do not exceed losses, they are not treated as capital in nature. I.R.C. § 1231(a)(1), (2).

3. Accounting for Partnership Operations

(5) *Investment interest.* The investment interest is a separately stated item. The deductibility of the investment interest depends on, among other things, whether the partner has sufficient investment income.[139]

Consequently, the non-separately stated items consist of the service revenue, salaries expense, and depreciation. A quick caveat about depreciation; although this example treats it as a non-separately stated item, there are instances in which it may need to be separately stated.[140]

After the classification, we have the following summary:

Delta Partnership	
Non-Separately Stated Items	Amount
Service revenue	$450,000
Salaries expense (subtract)	($125,000)
Depreciation (subtract)	($45,000)
Non-separately stated income	$280,000
Separately Stated Items	
§ 179 expense	$20,000
§ 1231 gain	$5,000
Short-term capital loss	$10,000
Long-term capital gain	$35,000
Investment interest expense	$4,000

If the partners share equally in the items — and how they share (or allocate) partnership items is a topic covered robustly in the next chapter — the partnership will report the following to each partner:

Delta Partnership	
Non-separately stated income	$70,000
Separately Stated Items	
§ 179 expense	$5,000
§ 1231 gain	$1,250
Short-term capital loss	$2,500
Long-term capital gain	$8,750
Investment interest expense	$1,000

---

139. I.R.C. § 163(d)(1); *see* Rev. Rul. 2008-12, 2008-1 C.B. 520; Rev. Rul. 84-131, 1984-2 C.B. 37.
140. *See* WILLIAM S. MCKEE ET AL., FEDERAL TAXATION OF Partnerships ¶ 9.01 (2022); *see also* Rev. Rul. 74-71, 1974-1 C.B. 158.

3. Accounting for Partnership Operations

Observe that the non-separately stated income is $280,000 divided by four, and the amounts for each of the separately stated items are likewise divided by four.

3. Because the partnership does not have a business purpose year, Omega must have a partnership tax year identified in § 706(b)(1)(B). Under that section, the descending order of preference is the (i) majority interest taxable year, (ii) the principal partner tax year, and (iii) the calendar year if no other year is provided under the regulations; although the statute contemplates the backstop of the calendar year, the regulations instead adopt the "the taxable year that produces the least aggregate deferral of income."[141]

   a. In this situation, the partnership has a majority interest taxable year. This is defined as "taxable year (if any) which, on each testing day, constituted the taxable year of 1 or more partners having (on such day) an aggregate interest in partnership profits and capital of more than 50 percent."[142] The testing day is the first day of the taxable year.[143] On the testing day, the individual partners own 60% of the partnership interests and share a calendar tax year. Consequently, the partnership must adopt the calendar year because of the majority interest tax year test.

   b. In this situation, the partnership similarly has a majority interest taxable year. The difference, however, is that the majority interest is now Mega Co., which has a September 30 fiscal year. Consequently, the partnership must adopt the September 30 fiscal year.

   c. In this situation, the partnership *does not* have a majority interest taxable year. That is, no partner or group of partners with over 50% of partnership profits and capitals shares the same tax year. Karen and Laura, with calendar years, own 40%, and Jake and Mega Co., which own the remaining 60% have different fiscal years.

   The second option—the principal partners tax year—likewise cannot apply here. All the partners are principal partners because they have partnership interests that are 5% or greater.[144] Because we have neither a majority interest nor principal partner tax year, we must ascertain "the taxable year that produces the least aggregate deferral of income." That calculation is determined by the following tables, which tests the aggregate deferral under each possible year-end date.[145]

---

141. Treas. Reg. § 1.706-1(b)(2)(i)(C).
142. I.R.C. § 706(b)(4)(A)(i).
143. I.R.C. § 706(b)(4)(A)(ii).
144. I.R.C. § 706(b)(3).
145. These tables are used in the examples of Treas. Reg. § 1.706-1(b)(3)(iv).

3. Accounting for Partnership Operations

Testing 12/31 Year End	Partner Year End	Partnership Interest	Months of Deferral	Interest × Deferral
Jake	11/30	.20	11	2.2
Karen	12/31	.20	0	0
Laura	12/31	.20	0	0
Mega	9/30	.40	9	3.6
Aggregate deferral				5.8

Testing 11/30 Year End	Partner Year End	Partnership Interest	Months of Deferral	Interest × Deferral
Jake	11/30	.20	0	0
Karen	12/31	.20	1	.20
Laura	12/31	.20	1	.20
Mega	9/30	.40	10	4.0
Aggregate deferral				4.4

Testing 9/30 Year End	Partner Year End	Partnership Interest	Months of Deferral	Interest × Deferral
Jake	11/30	.20	2	.40
Karen	12/31	.20	3	.60
Laura	12/31	.20	3	.60
Mega	9/30	.40	0	0
Aggregate deferral				1.6

The tables calculate the aggregate deferral for each possible year end. The months of deferral column represents how many months between the close of the partnership tax year and the year in which the partner would have to include the partnership tax items. For example, in testing the December 31 year, the calendar-year partners would have no deferral, as their years end coincident with that date. Jake's tax year, however, does not end until November 30, of the following year, which is 11 months after the tested partnership year. As the tables demonstrate, the tax year ending September 30 results in the least aggregate deferral amount. Consequently, the partnership must adopt a fiscal year that ends on September 30.

4. Sally's total distributive share of partnership loss is $180,000, which is the aggregate of the long-term and short-term capital losses. Recall that we cannot offset the separately stated items of loss with the non-separately stated items. We must now ascertain how much of that loss can be absorbed under the § 704(d) limitation, which allows a partner's

3. Accounting for Partnership Operations

distributive share of partnership loss "only to the extent of the adjusted basis of such partner's interest in the partnership at the end of the partnership year in which such loss occurred."[146]

The regulations provide that the adjusted basis must first be increased under § 705(a)(1) and then decreased under § 705(a)(2), "except for losses of the taxable year and losses previously disallowed."[147] Consequently, Sally's outside (adjusted) basis is first adjusted upwards to $150,000 (her beginning basis plus her share of the non-separately stated income). Observe now that the amount of distributive loss ($180,000) is still more than her basis (which is now $150,000). Thus, the regulations provide that, in cases like this, "the limitation on losses under section 704(d) must be allocated to his distributive share of each such loss."[148] That allocation is made based on "the proportion that each loss bears to the total of all such losses."[149] Based on these rules, then, Sally is allowed only $150,000/$180,000 of each loss.[150] The calculations are provided in the following table:

Loss	Total	Fraction	Amount Allowed	Carry-Over
Long-term capital loss	$120,000	150/180	$100,000	$20,000
Short-term capital loss	$60,000	150/180	$50,000	$10,000
Total	$180,000		$150,000	$30,000

As shown in the table, Sally is allowed a total loss under § 704(d) of $150,000. For the current year, it consists of a long-term capital loss of $100,000 and a short-term capital loss of $50,000. She also has a $30,000 loss carry-over, consisting of $20,000 and $10,000 of long-term and short-term capital loss, respectively.

Additionally, observe that the approach in the regulation (the tabular method above) is perhaps not the way one may instinctually allocate based on "the proportion that each loss bears to the total of all such losses." You may have thought to allocate in accordance with the following method:

Loss	Total	Fraction	Amount Allowed of $150,000	Carry-Over
Long-term capital loss	$120,000	120/180	$100,000	$20,000
Short-term capital loss	$60,000	60/180	$50,000	$10,000
Total	$180,000		$150,000	$30,000

---

146. I.R.C. § 704(d)(1).
147. Treas. Reg. § 1.704-1(d)(2).
148. Id.
149. Id.
150. See Treas. Reg. § 1.704-1(d)(4) Example 3.

3. Accounting for Partnership Operations

In other words, constructing the fraction as the specific loss bearing to the total of all losses and then multiplying that by the amount of outside basis. Observe that, in either formulation, you arrive at the same destination of allowable and carry-over losses.

5. This example incorporates the loss limitations of § 704(d) and § 465. Section 704(d) presents no obstacle here; the partners each have an outside (adjusted) basis of $1,000,000 from their cash contributions. The partner's distributive share of partnership loss ($250,000 each) does not exceed their adjusted basis. Although § 704(d) presents no obstacle here, § 465 does. Section 465 applies because Tim and Victor are individuals.[151]

   Under § 465, the partnership is engaged in two separate activities: (i) oil exploration and (ii) farming. Each of these are to be treated as separate activities under § 465.[152] The more salient issue is whether *each* well and *each* farm constitutes separate activities unto themselves. Temporary regulations provide that a partner may aggregate these each into a single activity.[153] Consequently, Tim and Victor are engaged in two activities for § 465 purposes: oil exploration (the activity that aggregates their three oil wells) and farming (the activity that aggregates their five farms).

   Now that we have delineated the number and nature of the activities, we must apply the at-risk rules. The at-risk rules provide that losses from at-risk activities may only be allowed to the extent that the taxpayer is "at risk."[154] A taxpayer is at risk for the amount of money and adjusted basis of property contributed to the taxpayer and for amounts borrowed that the taxpayer is personally liable or has pledged property not used in the activity.[155] This at-risk amount needs to be calculated for *each activity*. So, for the oil activity, Tim and Victor are at-risk for $1,000,000 each because the cash they contributed was used in the oil activity. However, they have no amount at risk for the farming activity because they neither contributed cash nor property nor are they personally liable for borrowed amounts in the farming activity (recall the loans were nonrecourse).

   Tim and Victor are each allocated a loss of $250,000, which consists of $150,000 loss from the oil exploration activity and $50,000 from the farming activity. As discussed above, § 704(d) prevents no obstacle here, as they have plenty of outside basis. With respect to the oil exploration

---

151. I.R.C. § 465(a)(1)(A).
152. I.R.C. § 465(c).
153. Treas. Reg. § 1.465-1T(a).
154. I.R.C. § 465(a).
155. I.R.C. § 465(b).

3. Accounting for Partnership Operations

activity, the partners have $1,000,000 at risk each, and therefore § 465 also presents no obstacle to deducting the loss from the oil exploration activity. With respect to the farming activity, however, the partners have no amount at risk, and therefore none of the loss for the farming activity may be deducted by the partners. The entire farming activity loss is disallowed and will be carried over into the next tax year.[156]

---

156. I.R.C. § 465(a)(2).

Partnership Allocations Part I: § 704(b) and Substantial Economic Effect

INTRODUCTION

In this chapter, we discuss § 704(b), which is a labyrinth. Undoubtedly, this will be one of the most complicated items we discuss in this book. Throughout the chapter, though, we will be intentional about trying to distinguish the forest from the trees. Indeed, consistent with the theme of this book, understanding the *why* or the *object* (i.e., purpose) of the § 704(b) rules will help you understand and appreciate the mechanics of the rules.

Under § 701, a partnership, as an entity, does not pay federal income taxes.[1] Rather, partners must include in their personal income taxes their distributive share of partnership items.[2] That distributive share is provided for in § 704, which states that "[a] partner's distributive share of income, gain, loss, deduction, or credit shall, except as otherwise provided in this chapter, be determined by the partnership agreement."[3] Thus, the Code allows tremendous flexibility for the partners to structure the tax affairs of the partnership. This flexibility is reflective of underlying state partnership law that allows partners to structure their rights and obligations vis-à-vis the partnership in any manner that they choose (subject to some minimum

---

1. I.R.C. § 701.
2. I.R.C. § 702.
3. I.R.C. § 704(a).

4. Partnership Allocations Part I: § 704(b) and Substantial Economic Effect

requirements). Consequently, the tax Code mirrors this inherent flexibility, subject to critical limitations that form the labyrinthian special allocation rules that are the subject of this chapter. As used in this chapter, then, the term "special allocation" refers generally to the situation in which partners decide to share a tax item in some way other than in proportion to their ownership percentage (i.e., capital contributions).

Although § 704(a) provides that the partnership agreement can allocate (i.e., determine) the partner's distributive share, guardrails and limits on that discretion are provided for in § 704(b), which provides, in full:

> (b) Determination of distributive share.—A partner's distributive share of income, gain, loss, deduction, or credit (or item thereof) shall be determined in accordance with the partner's interest in the partnership (determined by taking into account all facts and circumstances), if—
>
> (1) the partnership agreement does not provide as to the partner's distributive share of income, gain, loss, deduction, or credit (or item thereof), or
>
> (2) the allocation to a partner under the agreement of income, gain, loss, deduction, or credit (or item thereof) does not have substantial economic effect.[4]

Thus, § 704(b) provides two separate rules. The first rule is a default rule: In the absence of an allocation in the partnership agreement, the partner's distributive share shall be determined in accordance with the "partner's interest in the partnership," which this chapter discusses at the end. The second rule—and the prominent topic of this chapter—is that of the "special allocation." A special allocation is an allocation provided for in the partnership agreement, and it will be respected so long as it has "substantial economic effect."

This chapter primarily deals with understanding and demarcating the contours of *substantial economic effect*. The chapter will also discuss, under the regulations, the other ways in which an allocation will be respected. To be clear, § 704(b) provides that the partners may specially allocate items in their partnership agreement, and, to the extent that agreement does not provide for, or the allocation does not have substantial economic effect, it will be determined "in accordance with the partner's interest in the partnership."[5]

Appreciating the import of the ability to custom tailor allocations of income and loss is made apparent in the following simple example. Consider the AB Partnership, in which A and B are equal partners. Assume further that the partnership generates $100 of taxable pass-through income. If A and B were to split partnership profits equally (which we have been assuming in all our prior examples), each would have to include $50 in income.

---

4. I.R.C. § 704(b).
5. Id.

4. Partnership Allocations Part I: § 704(b) and Substantial Economic Effect

Consider, though, if B has $100 worth of carry-forward loss that needs to be used—perhaps A and B could agree in their partnership agreement for B to be allocated the first $100 of income. In this case, then, A would be allocated $0 in income and B would be allocated all $100 of the income, which would then be absorbed by the carry-forward loss. Together, then, A and B have shielded all the pass-through income by way of this special allocation. This chapter analyzes whether federal income tax rules will allow this allocation.

Let's look at another example to illustrate how special allocations may be used (and potentially abused). C and D enter into a partnership in which C is a 90% partner and D is a 10% partner. Assume that, although D is a minority partner, he has substantial negotiating power in entering this deal, despite his status as a minority partner. Due to the nature of the business, the partnership expects to generate substantial up-front "paper" losses.[6] Moreover, to induce D to enter the partnership, A agrees that they will allocate all the losses to D until he has received two times his initial capital in flow-through losses. (Of course, D desires to use those losses to offset other income.) Does (and should) the Code respect this type of tax structuring? You will be able to answer these questions at the conclusion of this chapter.

To emphasize—as a prefatory matter—the § 704(b) regulations are complex, dense, and long.[7] As mentioned at the beginning, though, understanding the *why* will help with understanding the *mechanics*. In essence, these rules are trying to pair economic benefits and burdens with tax benefits and burdens. In other words, if a partner economically benefits from an item, he or she should bear the tax consequences of that item (i.e., income inclusion). Similarly, if the partner bears the economic loss of an item, he or she should be afforded any tax benefit for that item (i.e., a deduction). Although this mirroring principle is simple to state—in short, it's all about "skin in the game"—the ingenuity of tax lawyers over the years have precipitated the need for complex rules to achieve these goals.

As we start to hike the § 704(b) regulatory mountain, let's add a trail map here at the beginning. Under Treas. Reg. § 1.704-1(b)(1)(i), there are three routes by which an allocation will be respected. The first way is *substantial economic effect*. The second way is that the allocation is in accordance with the *partner's interest in the partnership*. The third way is through a "special rule" (which *deems* the allocation to be in accordance with the partner's interest in the partnership). These rules are found in § 1.704-1(b)(2), (3), and (4), respectively; we will chart each path in turn. Let's start climbing.

---

6. Paper losses refer to the phenomenon that, although the partnership is generating flow-through tax losses, the partnership may not actually be losing "real" cash; that is, the partnership is generating a lot of non-cash deductions (e.g., depreciation) which may be due to debt financing. Indeed, this phenomenon is a prototypical "tax shelter."
7. Indeed, they have their own table of contents!

4. Partnership Allocations Part I: § 704(b) and Substantial Economic Effect

SUBSTANTIAL ECONOMIC EFFECT

The first way for an allocation to be respected is for it to have substantial economic effect under § 1.704-1(b)(2), which has two requirements. The first requirement is that the allocation must have *economic effect*. The second requirement is that the economic effect must be *substantial*. These determinations are "made as of the end of the partnership taxable year to which the allocation relates."[8] Each requirement will be discussed in turn.

Economic Effect

The "fundamental principle" of economic effect is that, "for an allocation to have economic effect, it must be consistent with the underlying economic arrangement of the partners."[9] Thus, as further elucidated by the regulation, "[t]his means that in the event there is an economic benefit or economic burden that corresponds to an allocation, the partner to whom the allocation is made must receive such economic benefit or bear such economic burden."[10]

To operationalize the guiding principle of matching benefits and burdens, there are three requirements for economic effect, which are found in Treas. Reg. § 1.704-1(b)(2)(ii)(b). The first requirement is that the partners' capital accounts must be determined and maintained in accordance with the special rules of the § 704(b) regulations.[11] For shorthand, we will refer to this as the "capital account requirement." The second requirement is that, upon a liquidation (of either the partnership or a partner's interest), liquidating distributions are made in accordance with positive capital account balances.[12] For shorthand, we will refer to this as the "liquidation requirement." The third requirement—which is the implied inverse of the second requirement—is that if, on liquidation, a partner has a deficit capital account balance (i.e., a negative capital account), the partner is unconditionally obligated to restore that deficit (in other words, the partner needs to contribute enough money or property to get rid of the deficit). For shorthand, we will refer to this as the "deficit restoration obligation requirement."[13] It is important to point out that meeting these three requirements is determined by the partnership agreement. A partnership agreement will

---

8. Treas. Reg. § 1.704-1(b)(2)(i).
9. Treas. Reg. § 1.704-1(b)(2)(ii)(a).
10. Id.
11. Treas. Reg. § 1.704-1(b)(2)(ii)(b)(1).
12. Treas. Reg. § 1.704-1(b)(2)(ii)(b)(2).
13. Treas. Reg. § 1.704-1(b)(2)(ii)(b)(3).

4. Partnership Allocations Part I: § 704(b) and Substantial Economic Effect

need to be drafted or examined to determine if these three requirements are satisfied. A summary table is provided below.

Summary of the Economic Effect Test Under § 1.704-1(b)(2)(ii)(b)		
Name	Rule	Pin Cite
Capital account requirement	Capital accounts must be determined and maintained in accordance with § 1.704-1(b)(2)(iv)	§ 1.704-1(b)(2)(ii)(b)(1); § 1.704-1(b)(2)(iv)
Liquidation requirement	Upon a liquidation, "liquidating distributions are required in all cases to be made in accordance with the positive capital account balances of the partners."	§ 1.704-1(b)(2)(ii)(b)(2)
Deficit restoration obligation requirement	If a partner has a deficit (negative) balance following liquidation, the partner "is unconditionally obligated to restore the amount of such deficit balance to the partnership by the end of such taxable year (or, if later, within 90 days after the date of such liquidation)..."	§ 1.704-1(b)(2)(ii)(b)(3)

Capital Account Requirement

In Chapter 3, we introduced the concept of capital accounts. We now see how critical the maintenance of capital accounts is—that is, without properly maintained capital accounts, we will not be able to have special allocations that are respected. As noted, for an allocation to have economic effect, capital accounts must be maintained in accordance with § 1.704-1(b)(2)(iv). These specific capital account regulations will now be unpacked.

The "basic rules" are provided in § 1.704-1(b)(2)(iv)(b), of which there are seven of them. The first rule is that capital accounts are increased by the amount of money contributed by the partner. The second is that capital accounts are increased by the fair market value of property contributed by the partner (net of assumed liabilities). The third is that capital accounts are increased by allocations of income and gain. The fourth is that capital accounts are decreased by the amount of money distributed to the partner. The fifth is that capital accounts are decreased by the fair market value of property distributed to the partner. The sixth is that capital accounts are decreased by the amount of nondeductible expenditures (that are not capital expenses). The seventh is that capital accounts are decreased by allocations of partnership loss and deduction. The rules—with corresponding labels—are summarized in the below table.

4. Partnership Allocations Part I: § 704(b) and Substantial Economic Effect

Capital Account "Basic Rules" [Treas. Reg. § 1.704-1(b)(2)(iv)(b)]	
Capital Accounts are *Increased* by	Capital Accounts are *Decreased* by
[1] Contributions of money	[4] Distributions of money
[2] Contributions of property	[5] Distributions of property
(measured by FMV and net of liabilities)	(measured by FMV and net of liabilities)
[3] Allocations of income and gain	[6] Non-capital, non-deductible expenses
	[7] Allocations of loss and deduction

The regulation continues by providing additional rules in paragraphs (c) through (s)—as you can tell, there are a lot of rules here! Throughout this text, we will refer to some of these rules in more detail as we discuss the applicable subject matter (e.g., treatment of liabilities and certain elections). We discuss some of the main rules here, too.

Although we have not talked directly about partnership liabilities (debt) yet, § 1.704-1(b)(2)(iv)(c) provides two critical rules. The first rule is that, generally, if a partner *assumes* a partnership liability, it is treated as a contribution of money by that partner, which, under the basic rules, results in an increase in his or her capital account. The word *assumes* here is critical because the regulation expressly notes that this deemed-money-contribution rule for capital accounts does not include increases in the "partner's share of partnership liabilities" (see § 752), a topic that we cover in Chapter 6. The second rule is that if the partnership assumes an individual debt of the partner that debt is treated as a distribution of money, which results in a decrease in the partner's capital account (with the same proviso about excluding decreases in the partner's share of partnership liabilities under § 752).[14]

The next important rule to highlight is found in § 1.704-1(b)(2)(iv)(d), which provides that property contributions are measured by "the fair market value of the property contributed to the partnership by such partner on the date of contribution."[15] This regulation also clarifies the treatment of contributed promissory notes for capital account purposes.[16] It provides that "if a promissory note is contributed to a partnership by a partner who is the maker of such note, such partner's capital account will be increased with respect to such note only when there is a taxable disposition of such note by the partnership or when the partner makes principal payments on such note."[17] There is an exception to this rule if the note is readily tradable on an established securities market.[18] Another

---

14. To reiterate, the deemed-money-contribution rule does not increase capital accounts like it does outside basis.
15. Treas. Reg. § 1.704-1(b)(2)(iv)(d)(1).
16. Recall our discussion in Chapter 2 for the treatment of contributed promissory notes for basis purposes (and the divergence with corporate taxation).
17. Treas. Reg. § 1.704-1(b)(2)(iv)(d)(2).
18. Id.

4. Partnership Allocations Part I: § 704(b) and Substantial Economic Effect

important part of this regulatory subparagraph is about how promissory notes affect the deficit restoration obligation, which will be discussed later.

As we saw with the fair market value measurement for contributed property, we see a similar rule for distributed property in § 1.704-1(b)(2)(iv)(e). Importantly, though, the regulation provides that "the capital accounts of the partners first must be adjusted to reflect the manner in which the unrealized income, gain, loss, and deduction inherent in such property (that has not been reflected in the capital accounts previously) would be allocated among the partners if there were a taxable disposition of such property for the fair market value of such property (taking section 7701(g) into account) on the date of distribution."[19] In other words, if the distributed property has unrealized gain inherent in it, that gain must be accounted for across the capital accounts.

Let's take a moment to pause here to explore an example based on the above rules. The AB Partnership is formed by A and B, each of whom contribute $5,000 in cash to the partnership. After the formation, AB purchases $10,000 of property. The balance sheet of AB and the capital accounts of A and B looks as follows:

AB Partnership					
Assets			Liabilities		
	Tax	Book	None		$0
Property	$10,000	$10,000			
			Capital Accounts		
				Tax	Book
			A	$5,000	$5,000
			B	$5,000	$5,000
Total	$10,000	$10,000	Total	$10,000	$10,000

Note that, in the regulations and their examples, "tax" refers to the adjusted basis and "book" refers to the FMV on the appropriate date (typically the contribution date but sometimes the date of revaluation) reduced by book depreciation over time; that convention is adopted here.

Assume that it is now a few years later, and the only change to the above balance sheet is now the property is worth $25,000, and the partnership decides to distribute the property equally to A and B (and that distribution is not one under § 707(a)(2)(B)).[20] The partnership agreement provides that A and B share items of income and gain equally and that capital accounts will be maintained and determined under the § 704(b) regulations.

---

19. Treas. Reg. § 1.704-1(b)(2)(iv)(e)(1).
20. This is based on Example 14(iv) of Treas. Reg. § 1.704-1(b)(5).

Consequently, before distributing the property, the capital accounts must be adjusted to reflect how the taxable gain would have been allocated had the property been sold. Here, there would have been a taxable gain of $15,000, which would be equally shared ($7,500) each to A and B. Thus, the capital accounts of A and B would be determined as follows:

	A	B
Capital account before adjustment	$5,000	$5,000
Deemed sale adjustment	$7,500	$7,500
Less: distribution	($12,500)	($12,500)
Capital account after distribution	0	0

Note that A and B will have received a distribution that exceeds their outside basis. We will consider this in Chapter 7.

There is also a rule for promissory notes on the distribution side, too. The regulations provide that "if a promissory note is distributed to a partner by a partnership that is the maker of such note, such partner's capital account will be decreased with respect to such note only when there is a taxable disposition of such note by the partner or when the partnership makes principal payments on the note."[21] Like before, there is an exception if the note is tradeable on an established securities market.

Subparagraph (h) provides additional rules for determining fair market value, which as you now appreciate is central to the "book" capital account amounts. The regulation provides that the "fair market value assigned to property contributed to a partnership, property distributed by a partnership, or property otherwise revalued by a partnership, will be regarded as correct, provided that (1) such value is reasonably agreed to among the partners in arm's-length negotiations, and (2) the partners have sufficiently adverse interests."[22] To the extent this is not satisfied—and the over- or understatement is by more than an insignificant amount, capital accounts will not be treated as being determined and maintained in accordance with the § 704(b) rules.[23]

Liquidation Requirement

The second of the three main requirements is the liquidation requirement. The regulation, provides, in full:

---

21. Treas. Reg. § 1.704-1(b)(2)(iv)(e)(2).
22. Treas. Reg. § 1.704-1(b)(2)(iv)(h).
23. Id.

4. Partnership Allocations Part I: § 704(b) and Substantial Economic Effect

> Upon liquidation of the partnership (or any partner's interest in the partnership), liquidating distributions are required in all cases to be made in accordance with the positive capital account balances of the partners, as determined after taking into account all capital account adjustments for the partnership taxable year during which such liquidation occurs (other than those made pursuant to this requirement (2) and requirement (3) of this paragraph (b)(2)(ii)(b)), by the end of such taxable year (or, if later, within 90 days after the date of such liquidation).[24]

We cover the liquidation of a partner's interest in our discussion of liquidating distributions and partnership exits in Chapters 7 and 10, respectively. For context here, though, this requirement is about how much money a partner is entitled to at the end of his time as a partner—either because the partnership itself liquidates or the particular partner's interest is liquidated. In this context, "liquidation" refers to paying out the partner's interest. So, this rule requires that upon that event—the partner's interest being paid out—the partner must be entitled to receive his capital account balance (assuming it is positive). Note that this rule also has a timing element—it must be accomplished either at the end of the taxable year of liquidation or 90 days after such date.[25] Now, you may be thinking, "What if the capital account is not positive, i.e., it is negative?" Well, that's the next rule of the main three!

Deficit Restoration Obligation Requirement

We saw above that if the partner has a positive capital account, then, on liquidation, the liquidating distribution must be paid in accordance with that balance. The deficit restoration obligation provides the rule for when a partner has a negative capital account balance. The regulation provides, in full:

> If such partner has a deficit balance in his capital account following the liquidation of his interest in the partnership, as determined after taking into account all capital account adjustments for the partnership taxable year during which such liquidation occurs (other than those made pursuant to this requirement (3)), he is unconditionally obligated to restore the amount of such deficit balance to the partnership by the end of such taxable year (or, if later, within 90 days after the date of such liquidation), which amount shall, upon liquidation of the partnership, be paid to creditors of the partnership or distributed to other partners in accordance with their positive capital account balances (in accordance with requirement (2) of this paragraph (b)(2)(ii)(b)). Notwithstanding the partnership agreement, an obligation to restore a deficit balance in a partner's capital account, including an obligation described in paragraph (b)(2)(ii)(c)(1) of

---

24. Treas. Reg. § 1.704-1(b)(2)(ii)(b)(2).
25. Id.

this section, will not be respected for purposes of this section to the extent the obligation is disregarded under paragraph (b)(2)(ii)(c)(4) of this section.[26]

Like the liquidation requirement, we see a similar timing rule here for deficit restoration obligations, namely it must be accomplished by the end of the taxable year or 90 days after liquidation. Note also to whom the payments must be made, that is either creditors of the partnership or the partners themselves. Finally, note that some types of obligations may be disregarded.[27]

In addition to the main deficit restoration obligation rule above, the § 704(b) regulations provide more elaboration on this specific obligation in § 1.704-1(b)(2)(ii)(c). The primary way a deficit restoration obligation is present is if the partnership agreement expressly provides for it (i.e., the partnership agreement calls for a partner to restore deficit balances in the partner's capital account). However, § 1.704-1(b)(2)(ii)(c) provides two alternative ways that a partner will be treated as having a deficit restoration obligation. The first path is to the extent of "[t]he outstanding principal balance of any promissory note (of which such partner is the maker) contributed to the partnership by such partner. . . ."[28] The second path is to the extent of "[t]he amount of any unconditional obligation of such partner (whether imposed by the partnership agreement or by state or local law) to make subsequent contributions to the partnership (other than pursuant to a promissory note of which such partner is the maker)."[29]

There is a common denominator to these alternative paths: they both require additional capital contributions by the partner—either by way of satisfying an underlying promissory note or by way of some contractual or state-law obligation. However, the regulations also provide a "satisfaction requirement," namely a timeliness requirement that "a promissory note or unconditional obligation is taken into account only if it is required to be satisfied at a time no later than the end of the partnership taxable year in which such partner's interest is liquidated (or, if later, within 90 days after the date of such liquidation)."[30] The complexity doesn't end there, however, as the regulation provides that if the promissory note is negotiable, then the time requirement is satisfied if the partnership agreement provides that the partnership may retain the note (and the partner is required to contribute any principal balance over the note's fair market value).[31]

---

26. Treas. Reg. § 1.704-1(b)(2)(ii)(b)(3).
27. Id.; *see also* Treas. Reg. § 1.704-1(b)(2)(ii)(c)(4).
28. Treas. Reg. § 1.704-1(b)(2)(ii)(c)(1)(A).
29. Treas. Reg. § 1.704-1(b)(2)(ii)(c)(1)(B).
30. Treas. Reg. § 1.704-1(b)(2)(ii)(c)(2).
31. Id.

4. Partnership Allocations Part I: § 704(b) and Substantial Economic Effect

There are some additional caveats to the deficit restoration obligation requirement. The regulations provide that some obligations are not respected; the common theme here is that the purported repayment obligation is an economic nullity (i.e., the likelihood of being called to satisfy the obligation is too remote or attenuated). First, the regulations disregard obligations referred to as a "bottom dollar payment obligation,"[32] which we will unpack when we dive into § 752 (see Chapter 6). In essence, a bottom dollar payment obligation is one in which a partner is liable (e.g., as a guarantor of partnership debt) only to the extent the partnership does not pay the debt. Second, if the obligation is not legally enforceable, it is not considered an obligation to restore a deficit balance.[33] Third, if the "the facts and circumstances otherwise indicate a plan to circumvent or avoid such obligation," then such obligation will not be respected.[34] Here, the regulation provides four nonexclusive factors to consider, such as "[t]he partner is not subject to commercially reasonable provisions for enforcement and collection of the obligation," and "[t]he terms of the obligation are not provided to all the partners in the partnership in a timely manner."[35]

Synthesis of the Main Test

The prior few pages have been spent detailing the main test for economic effect. Let's repeat the purpose (object) behind the test and its elements. The purpose of the economic effect test is to ensure that tax allocations pair with actual economic benefits and burdens. *That is, the tax consequences should follow the economic consequences.* The main test for economic effect thus requires three things. First, that capital accounts be determined and maintained in accordance with prescribed rules. Second, that upon liquidation of the partner's interest, liquidating distributions are in accordance with positive capital account balances. Third, if a partner has a deficit (below $0) capital account balance following liquidation, the partner must restore (i.e., pay back) the deficit.

These rules, although dense, are actually quite elegant. All three rules center around the first; that is, the second and third rules (liquidating distributions in accordance with positive capital account balances and deficit restoration obligations) are how we ensure economic consequences flow from the first rule (respecting capital accounts). Recall that the capital account rules, at bottom, are designed to ensure that contributions, distributions, and

---

32. Treas. Reg. § 1.704-1(b)(2)(ii)(c)(4).
33. Id.
34. Id.
35. Treas. Reg. § 1.704-1(b)(2)(ii)(c)(4)(B).

items of flow-through income and deduction are tracked consistently and comprehensively—that is, they are a closed system. And, we can't have the liquidation (exit) event be a leaky hole, so the second and third rules plug that potential economic leakage. Stated otherwise, capital accounts track the partner's claim to the economic assets of the partnership. As noted, our general theme here is to ensure that tax consequences follow economic consequences. Thus, the second and third rules ensure that the economic entitlement actually binds the partners and is not just an economic nullity.

Alternate Test for Economic Effect

The main test under the regulations for economic effect is the three-part test unpacked above ((1) properly maintaining capital accounts, (2) liquidating distributions made in accordance with positive capital accounts, and (3) an obligation to restore deficit balances in capital accounts). However, the regulations provide an "alternate test for economic effect" under § 1.704-1(b)(2)(ii)(d). In practice, this test is important due to the nature of LLCs, in which by default no member (partner) will have an unconditional obligation to pay the liabilities of the entity.

Essentially, there are three requirements for this alternate test. The first two requirements borrow from the main test and require that (1) capital accounts be properly maintained and (2) liquidating distributions are made in accordance with positive capital account balances. Thus, it is important to underline that, for any special allocation to be respected, you cannot avoid the capital account requirement or the liquidating distribution requirement (as they are required under the main test or the alternate test).

The next part is where the alternate test diverges from the main test. The alternate test provides that if a partner does not have an obligation to restore a deficit balance or is obligated to restore only a limited dollar amount of a deficit, then an allocation can be considered to have economic effect "to the extent such allocation does not cause or increase a deficit balance in such partner's capital account (in excess of any limited dollar amount of such deficit balance that such partner is obligated to restore) as of the end of the partnership taxable year to which such allocation relates," and if the partnership agreement contains a "qualified income offset" (QIO).[36] So, there are two things to note here. First is that the allocation cannot *cause* or *increase* a deficit balance, that is, a negative capital account balance;[37] second is that the partnership agreement must have a QIO provision.

---

36. Treas. Reg. § 1.704-1(b)(2)(ii)(d).
37. This must also factor in the ability for the partner to have a limited deficit restoration obligation, but for simplicity we will generally assume that is not the case unless otherwise noted.

4. Partnership Allocations Part I: § 704(b) and Substantial Economic Effect

The first part's rationale—that the allocation cannot cause or increase a deficit capital account balance—is easy to appreciate. Keep in mind that, under the alternate test, the regulations are concerned about the lack of a deficit restoration obligation. The concern is due to the lack of economic symmetry. In other words, the concern is that if a partner generates a negative capital account balance—which would happen if, say, he's been allocated more items of loss than contributed capital—he may not ever be called to equalize that imbalance. Consider the obviously abusive case if a partner makes a $100 contribution to a partnership, which would generate a starting capital account balance of $100. Let's assume that the partnership then generates a substantial "paper" loss and allocates a $5,000 loss to that partner. The partner's capital account would now be a negative $4,900.[38] Well, what stops the partner from just walking away from the partnership now (and taking his tax loss with him)? The deficit restoration obligation allays the concern of this shenanigan by requiring the partner to contribute more capital—in this example, an obligation to contribute an additional $4,900—which keeps the system closed and prevents leakage.

Without a deficit restoration obligation, though, how does the alternate test prevent the same shenanigan? The alternate test is, in essence, a "no harm, no foul" test. It already requires the maintenance of capital accounts and liquidation in accordance with positive capital account balances. It then says, by way of this third part, that an allocation will be considered to have economic effect if it doesn't create the problem of which we're concerned (i.e., creating or increasing a negative capital account).

Given the concern of the lack of the deficit restoration obligation, moreover, the critical part—that no deficit balance can be created or increased—is further conservatively policed by the regulations providing an additional moat of protection here. That's accomplished by the "reduction" rules and the QIO provisions.

The measuring time for whether an allocation causes or increases a deficit is "as of the end of the partnership taxable year to which such allocation relates."[39] As you might appreciate, though, a partnership can have allocations of many items to consider. The ordering of how these are applied, then, might affect whether a deficit or increased deficit balance is created. Thus, the regulations provide an ordering rule with respect to certain types of allocations, some of which are admittedly niche, that must be applied first before testing

---

38. This same motivation is behind the § 704 basis limitation and the at-risk limitations for deducting losses too. Note that, in this example, under these facts, the §§ 704 and 465 rules would prevent the partner from deducting the loss here because his outside basis and at-risk amounts would both be $100. (Note, moreover, that creative planning with partnership debts may offer strategies on the basis and at-risk regimes, a topic which has been already foreshadowed. We cover, in earnest, partnership liabilities in Chapter 6.)
39. Treas. Reg. § 1.704-1(b)(2)(ii)(d).

whether a special allocation creates the problem of a deficit capital account. The regulations provide three such "reductions" that must occur before seeing if an allocation causes or increases a deficit capital account.

The first type of reduction is in paragraph (4) and is admittedly niche. It applies only to certain depletion allowances for oil and gas properties, which this text generally does not examine.[40] The second type of reduction is in paragraph (5), and it is for "[a]llocations of loss and deduction that, as of the end of such year, reasonably are expected to be made to such partner pursuant to section 704(e)(2), section 706(d), and paragraph (b)(2)(ii) of § 751-1."[41] Nested in here are three different types of deduction or loss. Importantly, the citation to § 704(e)(2) is outdated in the regulation; the proper citation is now § 704(e)(1). The common theme across these three are that they can override the § 704(b) rules. For example, the first—§ 704(e)—provides special rules for family partnerships, in which there may be more incentives for allocations that do not comport with economic reality. Section 706(d) regards allocations for years in which the partner's interest in the partnership changes. For example, § 706(d) regards situations in which a partner may go from a 10% partner to a 60% partner in the same year—thus, there needs to be a way that the allocations of items map to the change in ownership during the year. The last type of these three regards § 751(b), a topic this text covers in more detail in later chapters.

The third type of reduction is in paragraph (6), and it is for reasonably expected distributions. In particular, it provides a reduction for "[d]istributions that, as of the end of such year, reasonably are expected to be made to such partner to the extent they exceed offsetting increases to such partner's capital account that reasonably are expected to occur during (or prior to) the partnership taxable years in which such distributions reasonably are expected to be made...."[42] In effectuating this provision, moreover, the regulation also provides that, "[f]or purposes of determining the amount of expected distributions and expected capital account increases described in (6) above, the rule set out in paragraph (b)(2)(iii)(c) of this section concerning the presumed value of partnership property shall apply."[43] The referenced rule is that "the adjusted tax basis of partnership property (or, if partnership property is properly reflected on the books of the partnership at a book value that

---

40. Treas. Reg. § 1.704-1(b)(2)(ii)(d)(4). For completeness, though, the reasoning for this exception is tied to the fact that § 613A makes the depletion deduction a partner-calculated item, not a partnership item; the concern, then, is that the depletion deduction may bypass other § 704(b) restrictions. *See* WILLIAM S. MCKEE ET AL., FEDERAL TAXATION OF PARTNERSHIPS ¶ 11.02 (2022).
41. Treas. Reg. § 1.704-1(b)(2)(ii)(d)(5).
42. Treas. Reg. § 1.704-1(b)(2)(ii)(d)(6).
43. Treas. Reg. § 1.704-1(b)(2)(ii)(d).

differs from its adjusted tax basis, the book value of such property) will be presumed to be the fair market value of such property...."[44]

Qualified Income Offset Provisions

Now we can unpack qualified income offset (QIO) provisions. Qualified income offset provisions can be opaque to understand initially. Although there is a definition in the regulation for a QIO, it's not as straightforward as it could be. The regulation provides that a QIO exists "if, and only if, [the partnership agreement] provides that a partner who unexpectedly receives an adjustment, allocation, or distribution described in (4), (5), or (6) above, will be allocated items of income and gain (consisting of a pro rata portion of each item of partnership income, including gross income, and gain for such year) in an amount and manner sufficient to eliminate such deficit balance as quickly as possible."[45] This definition thus requires an understanding of the items in paragraphs (4), (5), and (6), which are found in the same regulation and that we discussed above (i.e., the ordering rules to see if a capital account goes negative). For our purposes, the most salient one is going to be paragraph (6), that is, reasonably expected distributions in excess of reasonably expected increases to the capital account.[46]

Let's consider an example of a QIO and the alternate test. Assume that C and D each contribute $100,000 and form the CD Partnership. The partnership agreement does not have a deficit restoration obligation, but it has a QIO and otherwise satisfies the requirements under the alternate test. The partnership then purchases a piece of commercial rental property. The partnership agreement provides that all items will be allocated equally, except that depreciation will be allocated 100% to D. For simplicity, the partnership income equals expenses except for depreciation, which is $15,000. No distributions are made during the current year; none of the special adjustments in paragraphs (4), (5), or (6) are reasonably expected to occur. Consequently, the capital accounts at the end of the first year are calculated as follows:

	Capital Account	
Item	C	D
Contributions of money	$100,000	$100,000
Allocation of net income	0	0
Allocation of depreciation	0	($15,000)
Ending balance	$100,000	$85,000

---

44. Treas. Reg. § 1.704-1(b)(2)(iii)(c).
45. Treas. Reg. § 1.704-1(b)(2)(ii)(d) (flush paragraph).
46. Treas. Reg. § 1.704-1(b)(2)(ii)(d)(3) (flush paragraph).

4. Partnership Allocations Part I: § 704(b) and Substantial Economic Effect

Importantly, because this partnership does not have a deficit restoration obligation, it cannot satisfy the main test for economic effect; this is true regardless of the fact that there not any negative capital account balances. The depreciation deduction does not create or increase a negative capital account balance. Under the alternate test, on the other hand, the allocation of depreciation has economic effect because the partnership agreement (1) requires the maintenance of capital accounts, (2) requires liquidations in accordance with positive capital accounts, and (3) has a QIO (and all the QIO requirements are satisfied).

Alternatively, let's now assume that, at the end of the current year, however, the partnership contemplates a distribution of $100,000 to D and that it is "reasonably expected to be made." Under the rules in paragraph (6), then, this contemplated distribution must be subtracted from D's capital account balance *before* ascertaining whether the depreciation allocation has economic effect (i.e., whether it causes or increases a deficit capital account balance). Consequently, the tentative capital account for D is calculated as follows:

	Capital Account
Item	D
Contributions of money	$100,000
Allocation of net income	0
Paragraph (6) "reasonably expected" distribution	($100,000)
Depreciation deduction	($15,000)
Ending capital account balance	($15,000)

Here, the allocation of depreciation *causes* a negative (deficit) capital account balance after taking into account the adjustments required under the QIO rule, i.e., the "reasonably expected" distribution under paragraph (6). Therefore, the allocation of depreciation to D *does not* have economic effect and must be allocated to C instead.

What if, though, we tweak the facts above such that the distribution is not "reasonably expected" to be made? In that case, we would not need to subtract the potential distribution before the depreciation deduction. Consequently, the capital account of D at the end of Year 1 would be as follows:

	Capital Account
Item	D
Contributions of money	$100,000
Allocation of net income	0
Depreciation deduction	($15,000)
Ending capital account balance	$85,000

4. Partnership Allocations Part I: § 704(b) and Substantial Economic Effect

In this case, the allocation of depreciation to D does not cause or increase a deficit capital account balance and thus passes the alternate test.

Let's change the facts slightly more. Assume the base facts of the CD Partnership above and that, at the end of Year 1, the Year 2 distribution is not reasonably expected. In that case, then, like immediately above, the Year 1 allocation of depreciation has economic effect and let's assume for now that it passes all other requirements for allocations. Thus, D starts Year 2 with a capital account balance of $85,000 and items of income equal items of expense, except for depreciation. Now let's have the distribution *actually* happen. There are three simultaneous results. The first result is that the distribution reduces D's capital account by the distributed amount, which results in a deficit capital account balance of $15,000 ($85,000 − $100,000 = −$15,000). The second result is that because D now has a deficit capital account balance, he *cannot* be allocated the depreciation because it would *increase* a deficit account balance and would violate the QIO rules; thus, the depreciation must be allocated to C.

The third result triggers the actual definition of a QIO. Recall that a provision is a QIO if it "provides that a partner who unexpectedly receives an adjustment, allocation, or distribution described in (4), (5), or (6) above, will be allocated items of income and gain (consisting of a pro rata portion of each item of partnership income, including gross income, and gain for such year) in an amount and manner sufficient to eliminate such deficit balance as quickly as possible."[47]

Here, the partner has unexpectedly received a distribution defined in paragraph (6). In this case, then, D must be allocated items of partnership income until it eliminates the $15,000 deficit balance. In other words, income that would otherwise be allocated to C will need to be allocated to D instead. Practically, we need to add one more complication to this last result. As an implication of the third result, D is going to be allocated income that he "did not sign up for"—that is, not in accord with the economic bargain he entered but one that is required for tax purposes. Thus, a well drafted partnership agreement may also provide that if a QIO allocation is made there will be an "offsetting" provision to "unwind" (or counter) that allocation in a later year (assuming that offsetting allocation itself can have economic effect).

We will do an even more robust example of the alternate test and the application of a QIO provision. Let's start again with the CD Partnership. Recall that the partners start with a capital account balance of $100,000 each, and income and expenses are shared equally except for depreciation, which is allocated exclusively to D. We need to change and add more details than before to illustrate the full operation of the QIO. Assume that the partnership generates

---

47. Treas. Reg. § 1.704-1(b)(2)(ii)(d)(6) (flush language).

4. Partnership Allocations Part I: § 704(b) and Substantial Economic Effect

$30,000 of rental income, $10,000 of interest income, $30,000 of rental expenses, and $20,000 of depreciation expenses annually. At the end of Year 1, the breakdown of C and D's capital accounts can be depicted as follows:

	Capital Account	
Item	C	D
Contributions of money	$100,000	$100,000
Allocation of combined income items	$20,000	$20,000
Allocation of gross expense items	($15,000)	($15,000)
Allocation of depreciation	0	($20,000)
Ending balance	$105,000	$85,000

Further assume that none of the required adjustments are reasonably expected to occur as of the end of Year 1. At the end of Year 1, therefore, there is no economic effect problem because neither capital account is negative.

It is now Year 2 and assume the same facts and figures. In addition, assume that the partners expect the same economic results into Year 3 (that is, items of income and expense will remain the same), but that they expect to pay a distribution of $100,000 to D in Year 3 and that this is "reasonably expected" to occur. Like before, then, we must make an adjustment (i.e., reduce) to the capital accounts for that reasonably expected amount to test the Year 2 special allocation. Recall the language of the regulation, though, which requires these adjustments to be made "to the extent they exceed offsetting increases to such partner's capital account that reasonably are expected to occur during (or prior to) the partnership taxable years in which such distributions reasonably are expected to be made . . . ."[48] In addition to the reasonably expected Year 3 distribution, the partnership also reasonably expects D's capital account to increase in Year 3 by $5,000 (that is, the amount of his expected income items [$20,000] exceed his expected expense items [$15,000]). D's capital account for purposes of testing the allocation of depreciation can be broken down as follows for Year 2:

	Capital Account
Item	D
Starting balance	$85,000
Allocation of Year 2 income items	$20,000
Allocation of Year 2 expense items	($15,000)
Reasonably expected distribution (net of CA increase)	($95,000)
Capital account balance for testing Year 2	($5,000)

---

48. Treas. Reg. § 1.704-1(b)(2)(ii)(d)(6).

4. Partnership Allocations Part I: § 704(b) and Substantial Economic Effect

The $95,000 reduction represents the amount by which the reasonably expected distribution in Year 3 [$100,000] exceeds offsetting increases in the same year of the expected distribution [$20,000 − $15,000 = $5,000]. Consequently, in this case, the Year 2 depreciation deduction must be allocated to C instead because D has a capital account deficit for Year 2 testing purposes.

Let's now turn to Year 3. D's capital account balance starts Year 3 at $90,000 (because he was not allocated the depreciation; he was allocated his income items of $20,000 and expense items of $15,000). As stated, the partnership makes a distribution of $100,000 of D in Year 3. Without factoring in the operation of the QIO (to see the problem), D's capital account balance would be as follows:

	Capital Account
Item	D
Starting balance	$90,000
Allocation of Year 3 income items	$20,000
Allocation of Year 3 expense items	($15,000)
(Actual) distributions	($100,000)
Capital account balance for testing (without a QIO)	($5,000)

The distribution causes a negative capital account balance. D would not be allocated any depreciation; the depreciation would again need to be allocated C. We can now appreciate the QIO: it wants to "fix" the negative capital account balance. In this case, then, the QIO requires *additional* allocations of income to D to fix the deficit balance. Consequently, D's allocation of income needs to be increased by $5,000, which also results in a de facto decrease to C's allocation of income. The QIO allocation must be a pro rata portion of each item of income and gain. In this case, the partnership had rental income of $30,000 and interest income of $10,000. Thus, the QIO allocation would be $5,000, to consist of $3,750 of rental income ($30,000 / 40,000 × $5,000 = $3,750) and $1,250 of interest income ($10,000 / $40,000 × $5,000 = $1,250). After implementation of the QIO, the actual capital account of D would be depicted as follows:

	Capital Account
Item	D
Starting balance	$90,000
Allocation of Year 3 income items	$25,000
Allocation of Year 3 expense items	($15,000)
Distributions	($100,000)
Capital account balance	0

4. Partnership Allocations Part I: § 704(b) and Substantial Economic Effect

This example readily demonstrates how the QIO fixed the problem of the deficit capital account balance by requiring additional income items to be allocated to D.[49]

In closing this section on the alternate test, there are a few things to keep in mind. Practically, the alternate test is common because owners of LLCs, which can be taxed as partnerships, will not have a deficit restoration obligation under state law (as their economic risk is capped to the amount of invested capital, which is the very nature of limited liability) and few, if any, individuals will want to *voluntarily* contract for unlimited liability in the nature of the deficit restoration obligation. Therefore, drafting for the alternate test is extremely common (if not standard) in a well-drafted operating agreement for an LLC taxed as a partnership. Moreover, it should be noted that, even if it is uncommon for a QIO to be *triggered* (as it is triggered by only certain unexpected items), its *presence* is still required under the alternate test.

Under the alternate test for economic effect and its required QIO provision, allocations have economic effect to the extent they do not cause or increase a deficit capital account. Moreover, QIOs are designed to fix *unexpected* items of adjustments, allocations, and distributions because, under the alternate test generally, items that are "reasonably expected" must first reduce the partner's capital account balance. This test occurs at the end of the tax year of the allocation. If, however, these items *unexpectedly* happen *later* and thereby result in a deficit capital account balance, the prior allocation will still be permitted and the QIO requires that items of gross income be allocated to "cure" it as quickly as possible. Further, be mindful that the QIO provision requires the "fix" allocation to be of gross items of income, not net income (this is to speed up the pace with which it can be fixed).

Partial Economic Effect

The alternate test for economic effect also recognizes that an allocation can have partial economic effect. The regulation provides that "[i]f only a portion of an allocation made to a partner with respect to a partnership taxable year has economic effect, both the portion that has economic effect and the portion that is reallocated shall consist of a proportionate share of all items that made up the allocation to such partner for such year."[50]

---

49. Take note that this example could have been even more complicated. For example, the reasonably expected items of income and expense for Year 3 as of the end of Year 2 (the forecasted amounts) could have been different in Year 3 (as realized, which is not unlikely to happen in the real world). Moreover, the testing reduction for distributions is net of increases in the capital account, which we discussed, but the regulation speaks also to the impact of minimum gain chargebacks and nonrecourse liabilities, topics of which we have not tackled yet.

50. Treas. Reg. § 1.704-1(b)(2)(ii)(e).

4. Partnership Allocations Part I: § 704(b) and Substantial Economic Effect

This rule has two implications. The first implication is that it confirms that an allocation can have economic effect in part. A quintessential example, under the alternate test, is that an allocation can be given effect until it causes a deficit in a capital account. Until that threshold is met, the allocation does not cause or increase a deficit and thus satisfies the alternate test. The second implication is the regulation tells us how to treat the items in the allowed and disallowed portions.

The following example, based on Example 15 in the regulation, illustrates partial economic effect.[51] M and N form the MN Partnership. Assume that their capital account balances at the beginning of the year are $2,700 and $300, respectively. In the same year, the partnership generates income of $10,000, operating expenses of $2,000, interest expense of $8,000, and depreciation deductions of $12,000, which sum to a net loss of $12,000 for the year. The partnership agreement allocates the net loss as $10,800 to M and $1,200 to N, i.e., a 90% split of income and expense items. Under the alternate test, the allocation to M is only respected to the extent of $2,700 (otherwise it would cause a deficit capital account balance). The first implication of partial economic effect is that of the $10,800 loss, $2,700 is allowed under the alternate test. That loss, though, consists of the underlying types of expenses, namely the depreciation deductions and expense deductions. The second implication of partial economic effect is now we need to determine of that loss, what parts are allowed and disallowed, which the regulation states to calculate proportionately. Thus, we need to allocate the allocation proportionately, which is shown in the following table for M:

Partial Economic Effect Analysis for Partner M				
Item	Total Amount	Full Economic Effect	Partial Economic Effect (proportionate)	Amount Not Given Effect
Rental income	$10,000	$9,000	$9,000 × ($2,700/ $10,800) = $2,250	$9,000 − $2,250 = $6,750
Operating expenses	$2,000	$1,800	$1,800 × ($2,700/ $10,800) = $450	$1,350
Interest expense	$8,000	$7,200	$7,200 × ($2,700/ $10,800) = $1,800	$5,400
Depreciation	$12,000	$10,800	$10,800 × ($2,700/ $10,800) = $2,700	$8,100
Net income (loss)	($12,000)	($10,800)	($2,700)	($8,100)

---

51. Treas. Reg. § 1.704-1(b)(5).

Let's walk through this table from the left column to the right column. The Total Amount column lists the total amount for each tax item of the partnership. The Full Economic Effect column lists the amount that would be allocated to M if M had a sufficiently positive capital account; here, in the problem, the partnership agreement allocated 90% of each item to M. The Partial Economic Effect column is the one to focus on. Of the purported net loss allocation of $10,800 to M, only $2,700 of it has economic effect under the alternate test (to reduce M's capital account to $0). Thus, only $2,700 of the $10,800 allocation is given effect. That is the fraction to use, then, to determine the proportionate share of each item (i.e., $2,700/$10,800). The final column shows the amount of each item whose allocation is disallowed.

ECONOMIC EQUIVALENCE

In addition to the main and alternate test (including partial economic effect), the regulations also provide for "economic effect equivalence,"[52] which is the last way for a special allocation to pass muster. The regulation provides that, even if an allocation does not have economic effect under the main or alternate test, it will be deemed to have economic effect if a liquidation at the end of the tax year would produce the same result as would occur if the main test had been satisfied.[53]

SUBSTANTIALITY

Under Treas. Reg. § 1.704-1, the substantial economic effect test has two parts. The first part is economic effect, which was discussed above. The second part is that the "economic effect of the allocation must be *substantial*."[54] The regulations provide that "the economic effect of an allocation (or allocations) is substantial if there is a reasonable possibility that the allocation (or allocations) will affect substantially the dollar amounts to be received by the partners from the partnership, independent of tax consequences."[55]

As is not uncommon with tax provisions, the operationalization of this concept works by exclusion; that is, the regulation informs us of what is *not substantial*. The regulations explain three ways that an allocation is not

---

52. Treas. Reg. § 1.704-1(b)(2)(ii)(i).
53. Id.
54. Treas. Reg. § 1.704-1(b)(2)(i) (emphasis added).
55. Treas. Reg. § 1.704-1(b)(2)(iii)(a).

4. Partnership Allocations Part I: § 704(b) and Substantial Economic Effect

substantial. The first path is a general rule. The second path describes allocations that give rise to "shifting tax consequences." The third path describes allocations that give rise to "transitory allocations." Each will be discussed in turn.

General Rule for Substantiality

The regulation provides a general two-part test to see if the economic effect of an allocation is not substantial. The first part is to evaluate whether "the after-tax economic consequences of at least one partner may, in present value terms, be enhanced compared to such consequences if the allocation (or allocations) were not contained in the partnership agreement."[56] The second part provides that "there is a strong likelihood that the after-tax economic consequences of no partner will, in present value terms, be substantially diminished compared to such consequences if the allocation (or allocations) were not contained in the partnership agreement."[57] Importantly, these determinations are made "at the time the allocation becomes part of the partnership agreement."[58]

If we take a step back, we can appreciate the animating principle here. The regulation, in essence, is asking us to evaluate two alternative universes—one with the allocation and one without the allocation. In this evaluation, we examine whether the economics of one partner is made better with the allocation (compared to no allocation) and whether no partner is made worse off (compared to no allocation). In other words, if the allocation makes a partner "better" after the allocation's tax impact, and it makes no partner "worse," then the allocation is just generating a tax differential with no real economic differential. Stated even more simply, think of the substantiality test as whether the allocation is actually affecting a partner's pocketbook (not just his or her tax return). We can refer to this as the "pocketbook test."

The regulations fortunately provide some examples of allocations that are not substantial. Let's consider a simplified version of Example 5.[59] Assume that I and J equally contribute and form a partnership, which then purchases various investments, such as government and corporate bonds. Assume, moreover, that the corporate bonds generate taxable interest income, and the government bonds generate tax-exempt interest income.

---

56. Treas. Reg. § 1.704-1(b)(2)(iii)(a)(1).
57. Treas. Reg. § 1.704-1(b)(2)(iii)(a)(2).
58. Treas. Reg. § 1.704-1(b)(2)(iii)(a).
59. Treas. Reg. § 1.704-1(b)(5).

4. Partnership Allocations Part I: § 704(b) and Substantial Economic Effect

Partner I expects to be in the 50% marginal tax bracket, and J expects to be in the 15% bracket. There is a strong likelihood that, for the next few years, the partnership will realize between $450 and $550 of taxable interest and the same amount of tax-exempt interest. The partnership agreement provides that they will allocate 100% of the taxable interest income to J, but they will allocate the tax-exempt interest 80% to I and 20% to J. Actual cash distributions will follow the tax allocations. Assume also that the partnership agreement provides for all three requirements of the main economic effect test.

In this case, the allocations have "economic effect" because the partnership agreement provides that it will maintain capital accounts, make liquidating distributions in accordance with positive capital account balances, and partners must restore deficits upon liquidation. Even though the income allocations have economic effect, they are *not substantial*. Let's consider why. Recall, in its simplest terms, we are examining whether the allocation actually affects a partner's pocketbook, not just his or her tax return, i.e., the pocketbook test. To do this, we do a what-if analysis—with the allocation and without the allocation.

Consider the economic consequences to the partners if the allocation is respected. For tractability, assume that there is $500 each of taxable and tax-exempt interest. With the allocation, I is allocated $0 of taxable interest, and $400 of tax-exempt interest; J is allocated $500 of taxable interest and $100 of tax-exempt interest. On an *after-tax basis*, I has $400 of cash (as he pays no federal income taxes on the tax-exempt interest); J has $525 (that is, $500 × .15 = $75; $500 − $75 = $425; plus $100 [the tax-exempt interest]). The following table summarizes the "with allocation" scenario:

	With Allocation	
	I (50% bracket)	J (15% bracket)
Tax-exempt interest allocated (and distributed)	$400	$100
Income tax on tax-exempt interest	0	0
Taxable interest allocated (and distributed)	0	$500
Less income tax on taxable interest	0	($75)
Cash, net of federal income taxes	$400	$525

Now consider the scenario if there is no special allocation; in this case, assume that it is proper to allocate and distribute items equally (as they are equal partners). In that case, I and J each receive $250 of tax-exempt interest and $250 of taxable interest. Thus, the table would be as follows:

4. Partnership Allocations Part I: § 704(b) and Substantial Economic Effect

	Without Allocation	
	I (50% bracket)	J (15% bracket)
Tax-exempt interest allocated (and distributed)	$250	$250
Income tax on tax-exempt interest	0	0
Taxable interest allocated (and distributed)	$250	$250
Less income tax on taxable interest	($125)	($37.50)
Cash, net of federal income taxes	$375	$462.50

To make the comparison of the two scenarios easier, consider the following synthesized table:

	I			J		
	With Allocation	Without Allocation	Difference	With Allocation	Without Allocation	Difference
Cash, net of taxes	$400	$375	$25	$525	$462.50	$62.50

The two-part test is to consider is (1) does the allocation make a partner "better off" on an after-tax basis, and (2) the allocation makes no partner "worse off" on an after-tax basis compared to no allocation. In this case, that is readily observable. With the allocation, I's after-tax consequences is "enhanced" by $25, and the allocation does not "diminish" the after-tax consequences of any partner—indeed, they are *both* made better with the allocation. In concluding this example, although the allocation has economic effect, it is *not substantial*. Consequently, the purported allocation of taxable and tax-exempt interest is not respected.

Shifting Tax Consequences

In addition to the general rule of substantiality above, the regulation also describes allocations that can lack substantiality because they give rise to "shifting tax consequences."[60] This is a two-part test. The first part is whether there is a strong likelihood that "[t]he net increases and decreases that will be recorded in the partners' respective capital accounts for such taxable year will not differ substantially from the net increases and decreases that would be recorded in such partners' respective capital accounts for such year if the

---

60. Treas. Reg. § 1.704-1(b)(2)(iii)(b).

4. Partnership Allocations Part I: § 704(b) and Substantial Economic Effect

allocations were not contained in the partnership agreement."[61] The second part is "[t]he total tax liability of the partners (for their respective taxable years in which the allocations will be taken into account) will be less than if the allocations were not contained in the partnership agreement (taking into account tax consequences that result from the interaction of the allocation (or allocations) with partner tax attributes that are unrelated to the partnership)."[62]

The theme here is like the general test, but instead of looking at after-tax economic positions (like net cash, above), we look at (1) capital accounts and (2) total tax liabilities. Thus, this test is just looking at a different dimension of the pocketbook test (recall that capital accounts essentially represent a partner's "equity" in the partnership, i.e., what he or she would be entitled to upon an immediate liquidation). Consider a simplified version of Example 6 from the regulations.[63]

K and L are equal partners in a general partnership that operates § 1231(b) property (e.g., commercial strip malls). The partnership agreement provides for all items required by the main economic effect test. In the current taxable year, the partnership expects to incur a loss on one of its § 1231(b) properties. The partnership agreement is amended allocate the § 1231(b) loss to K (who expects no § 1231(b) gain) and to allocate an equivalent amount of loss (but of a different character) to L, who is expected to have § 1231 gains. Any additional losses will be allocated equally between the partners. The amendment sunsets after the current year, and there is a strong likelihood that the non-§ 1231(b) losses will exceed the § 1231(b) losses.

Like in the earlier example, this allocation has economic effect because the mechanics of the main economic test are present. However, the allocation is not substantial because it gives rise to shifting allocations. Let's consider the capital accounts of the partners with and without the allocation. For tractability, assume the partners' capital accounts start the current year with a balance of $20,000, that items of income equal items of expense, and there is a $5,000 § 1231(b) loss and a non-§ 1231(b) loss of $10,000. As such, their capital accounts can be depicted as follows with the allocation:

---

61. Treas. Reg. § 1.704-1(b)(2)(iii)(b)(1).
62. Treas. Reg. § 1.704-1(b)(2)(iii)(b)(2).
63. Treas. Reg. § 1.704-1(b)(5).

4. Partnership Allocations Part I: § 704(b) and Substantial Economic Effect

	With Allocation Capital Account	
	K	L
Beginning balance	$20,000	$20,000
Allocation of § 1231(b) loss	($5,000)	–
Allocation of other loss equal to § 1231(b) loss	–	($5,000)
Allocation of other excess loss	($2,500)	($2,500)
Ending balance	$12,500	$12,500

Now consider the outcome if there is no special allocation (and, again, assume that the losses would otherwise be allocated equally):

	Without Allocation Capital Account	
	K	L
Beginning balance	$20,000	$20,000
Allocation of § 1231(b) loss	($2,500)	($2,500)
Allocation of other loss	($5,000)	($5,000)
Ending balance	$12,500	$12,500

As shown, the "net increases and decreases" with the allocation (here, a decrease of $7,500) is the same as without the allocation (again, a net decrease of $7,500). Consequently, this satisfies the first part of the shifting tax consequences test.

The second part is that the total tax liability of the partners with the allocation will be less than if there was not an allocation. In this part of the analysis, we also have to "tak[e] into account tax consequences that result from the interaction of the allocation (or allocations) with partner tax attributes that are unrelated to the partnership."[64] This is true in this example, but it is more opaque. Consider in the example that K has no § 1231 gain, which means that after applying § 1231(a)'s netting rule, the loss will not be treated as a capital loss,[65] and it is thus an ordinary loss, which provides a greater tax advantage (as it offsets ordinary income) relative to a capital loss.[66] To illustrate this, assume that K and L each have $100,000 of gross income. All of K's income is ordinary in nature; of L's $100,000 gross income, $10,000 of it is § 1231 gains. We can also make the example

---

64. Treas. Reg. § 1.704-1(b)(2)(iii)(b)(2).
65. See I.R.C. § 1231(a)(2).
66. Both in terms of amount deductible, see §§ 165, 1211, and 1212, which when synthesized provide greater limits on the deductibility of capital losses, and character (assuming that capital gains would otherwise be taxed at a rate lower than ordinary income).

4. Partnership Allocations Part I: § 704(b) and Substantial Economic Effect

agnostic with respect to specific tax rates, so long as net capital gain benefits from a lower, preferential rate. With the loss, K's taxable income is $100,000 less $7,500 = $92,500, all of which is ordinary income.

The driving force behind this allocation was that L had a § 1231 gain, which impacts the tax consequences of § 1231 losses. Under § 1231, if the § 1231 gains exceed the § 1231 losses, then the gains and losses are treated as long-term capital gains and losses.[67] If, however, there are more § 1231 losses than § 1231 gains, then the gains and losses are not treated as capital.

In the example, if the allocation were to stand, the § 1231 gains ($10,000) do exceed the § 1231 losses ($0) for L, meaning that the gain is treated as a long-term capital gain. Thus, L would be taxed on capital gain income of $10,000, and ordinary income of $82,500 [$90,000 − $7,500]. If, on the other hand, there was no special allocation, L's § 1231 loss would need to be netted against the § 1231 gain. Although the § 1231 gains still exceed the losses, there is now net long-term capital gain of $7,500 [$10,000 − $2,500] and ordinary income of $85,000 [$90,000 − $5,000]. A synthesis table follows:

	K			L		
	With Allocation	Without Allocation	Difference	With Allocation	Without Allocation	Difference
Taxable ordinary income	$92,500	$92,500	$0	$82,500	$85,000	($2,500)
Taxable capital gain	$0	$0	$0	$10,000	$7,500	$2,500

In other words, the allocation allows L to treat more of his income as long-term capital gain, which is taxed at a lower, preferential rate compared to ordinary income. Thus, the allocation would result in a *lower* tax bill for L. To fully explicate the example, let's use an effective tax rate on ordinary income of 35% and a net capital gains rate of 15%. In both cases, K's tax bill is $92,750 × .35 = $32,462.50. L's tax liability calculated with the allocation is $10,000 × .15 = $1,500, plus $82,500 × .35 = $28,875, for a liability of $30,375. L's tax liability without the allocation is $7,500 × .15 = $1,125, plus $85,000 × .35 = $29,750, for a liability of $30,875 (i.e., $500 more). Therefore, the second test for shifting allocations is satisfied because total taxes for K and L will be reduced due to the allocation.

---

67. I.R.C. § 1231(a).

4. Partnership Allocations Part I: § 704(b) and Substantial Economic Effect

Transitory Allocations

The next type of allocations that are not substantial are described as "transitory allocations."[68] There are three requirements for a transitory allocation. First, the allocation will be "largely offset" by one or more other allocations. In other words, the "original allocation" (the one being tested) is offset by a later allocation (the "offsetting allocation"). Second, there is a strong likelihood that net increases and decreases that are recorded in the capital account with the allocation do not differ substantially than if the original and offsetting allocations were not in the partnership agreement. Third, the total tax liabilities will be less with the allocation than without the allocation.[69]

The test for transitory allocations is like that of shifting allocations insofar as the analysis focuses on the net increases and decreases to capital accounts along with a reduction of total tax liabilities. The difference in the transitory allocation though is the required time pairing of an original and later offsetting allocation. In other words, shifting tax allocations are contained in the same tax year, whereas transitory allocations happen over multiple tax years. Let's consider an example, which is based on Example 7 in the regulations.[70]

P and O form the PO Partnership, which allocates items equally to P and O and satisfies the requirements for the main economic effect test. The partnership purchases tax-exempt bonds and corporate stock. For the first three tax years, it is expected that P will be in a higher marginal tax bracket than O. Consequently, it is agreed that for these first three years, P will be allocated 90% of the tax-exempt income and 10% of the dividend income; O will be allocated 10% of the tax-exempt income and 90% of the dividend income. Let's assume that the partners start Year 1 with capital account balances each of $100, and that the partnership realizes $100 each of tax-exempt interest and dividend income every year. The following table shows a breakdown of their capital accounts for the three-year period both with and without the allocation.

	With Allocation		Without Allocation	
Capital Account Balances	P	O	P	O
Year 1 beginning balance	$100	$100	$100	$100
Tax-exempt income	$90	$10	$50	$50
Dividend income	$10	$90	$50	$50
Year 1 ending balance	$200	$200	$200	$200

---

68. Treas. Reg. § 1.704-1(b)(2)(iii)(c).
69. Id.
70. Treas. Reg. § 1.704-1(b)(5).

4. Partnership Allocations Part I: § 704(b) and Substantial Economic Effect

	With Allocation		Without Allocation	
Year 2 beginning balance	$200	$200	$200	$200
Tax-exempt income	$90	$10	$50	$50
Dividend income	$10	$90	$50	$50
Year 2 ending balance	$300	$300	$300	$300
Year 3 beginning balance	$300	$300	$300	$300
Tax-exempt income	$90	$10	$50	$50
Dividend income	$10	$90	$50	$50
Year 3 ending balance	$400	$400	$400	$400
Total tax-exempt income	$270	$30	$150	$150
Total dividend income	$30	$270	$150	$150
Total income allocated	$300	$300	$300	$300

As shown, at the time the special allocation is made to the partnership agreement, there is a strong likelihood that the net increases and decreases to the partners' capital accounts are the same with the allocation as they would be without the allocation (e.g., the ending balances after the three-year period are $300 in both scenarios). Moreover, it's readily apparent that P will pay less in taxes with the allocation due to the proportion of tax-exempt interest that is allocated to him with the allocation than without the allocation (and recall that P has a higher marginal tax bracket than O). And, under the transitory test, instead of looking at just one year's worth of allocation (which we do for shifting allocations), we look at several years' worth, which show that this special allocation is not substantial.

The Concept of Strong Likelihood and the Partnership Agreement

A careful reading of the regulations will reveal that the substantiality rules focus on the concept of "strong likelihood." For example, under the general test for substantiality, the analysis queries whether "there is a *strong likelihood* that the after-tax economic consequences of no partner will, in present value terms, be substantially diminished."[71] Similarly, shifting tax consequences require that there be a "strong likelihood" that both the net changes in the capital accounts will not differ substantially and that the total tax liabilities

---

71. Treas. Reg. § 1.704-1(b)(2)(iii)(a)(2) (emphasis added).

4. Partnership Allocations Part I: § 704(b) and Substantial Economic Effect

will be less than without the allocation.[72] The same "strong likelihood" language is also present for the transitory allocation test.[73]

Despite this confidence threshold being a part of all three tests, it is surprisingly not defined expressly in the regulation. However, the regulation does provide two presumptions that apply for shifting and transitory allocations, but curiously not for the general test. Under the shifting allocation test, if a shifting allocation occurs, "it will be presumed that, at the time the allocation (or allocations) became part of such partnership agreement, there was a strong likelihood that these results would occur."[74] Similarly, under the transitory allocation test, in the year an offsetting allocation occurs, "it will be presumed that, at the time the allocations became part of the partnership agreement, there was a strong likelihood that these results would occur."[75] It is important to emphasize that both of these presumptions are retroactive in operation. In both cases, the regulation provides that "[t]his presumption may be overcome by a showing of facts and circumstances that prove otherwise."[76] Further, as indicated above, there is no presumption for the general test.

Although this text does not dive into the tax procedure related to partnerships generally, there is one procedure and administrative wrinkle briefly worth noting here as it concerns substantiality. Section 704 states that allocations can be determined by the "partnership agreement." Under § 761, the partnership agreement "includes any modifications of the partnership agreement made prior to, or at, the time prescribed by law for the filing of the partnership return for the taxable year (not including extensions) which are agreed to by all the partners, or which are adopted in such other manner as may be provided by the partnership agreement."[77] Based on this definition, then, it's possible for the partners to amend their partnership agreement after the close of the tax year but before the partnership tax return is due. You might instinctually see some practical benefit here—for example, to let the partners see what the economics are before they divvy it up or to change the special allocations based on changed tax characteristics of the partner. But you should also appreciate that it is hard (if not impossible) for something to not have a "strong likelihood" after you already know whether it has happened! Indeed, Revenue Ruling 99-43 addresses similar timing concerns.[78]

---

72. Treas. Reg. § 1.704-1(b)(2)(iii)(b).
73. Treas. Reg. § 1.704-1(b)(2)(iii)(c).
74. Treas. Reg. § 1.704-1(b)(2)(iii)(b) (flush paragraph).
75. Treas. Reg. § 1.704-1(b)(2)(iii)(c) (flush paragraph).
76. Treas. Reg. § 1.704-1(b)(2)(iii)(b) (flush paragraph); Treas. Reg. § 1.704 1(b)(2)(iii)(c) (flush paragraph).
77. I.R.C. § 761(c).
78. Rev. Rul. 99-43, 1999-4 C.B. 506.

4. Partnership Allocations Part I: § 704(b) and Substantial Economic Effect

In Revenue Ruling 99-43, the partners amended the partnership agreement to create two allocations that offset each other after the events giving rise to those items had occurred. In holding that the allocations did not have substantiality, the ruling noted that "[t]he substantiality of an allocation, however, is analyzed 'at the time the allocation becomes part of the partnership agreement,' not the time at which the allocation is first effective."[79] Thus, it concluded that, "[p]artnership special allocations lack substantiality when the partners amend the partnership agreement to specially allocate [tax items] after the events creating such items have occurred if the overall economic effect of the special allocations on the partners' capital accounts does not differ substantially from the economic effect of the original allocations in the partnership agreement."[80]

PARTNER'S INTEREST IN THE PARTNERSHIP

We now turn to the analysis concerning the "partner's interest in the partnership."[81] Recall that this standard for allocations is used if (i) the partnership agreement does not speak to a particular allocation (i.e., does not provide for allocation of a specific item) or (ii) a special allocation fails (i.e., does not have substantial economic effect and needs to be reallocated). The regulations provide that a partner's interest in the partnership refers to "the manner in which the partners have agreed to share the economic benefit or burden (if any) corresponding to the income, gain, loss, deduction, or credit (or item thereof) that is allocated."[82]

Instinctually, it's alluring to assume that the sharing arrangement necessarily corresponds to the partner's overall interest in the partnership; for example, that a 50% partner shares in 50% of each item. However, the regulations expressly state that this need not necessarily be true.[83] The regulations provide that "[t]he determination of a partner's interest in a partnership shall be made by taking into account all facts and circumstances relating to the economic arrangement of the partners."[84] The regulations provide four factors to consider:

---

79. Id.
80. Id. The tax items were COD income and a book loss from a revaluation. Id.
81. Treas. Reg. § 1.704-1(b)(3).
82. Treas. Reg. § 1.704-1(b)(3)(i).
83. Id. In particular, the regulation provides, "a partner who has a 50 percent overall interest in the partnership may have a 90 percent interest in a particular item of income or deduction." Id.
84. Id.

4. Partnership Allocations Part I: § 704(b) and Substantial Economic Effect

(a) The partners' relative contributions to the partnership,
(b) The interests of the partners in economic profits and losses (if different than that in taxable income or loss),
(c) The interests of the partners in cash flow and other non-liquidating distributions, and
(d) The rights of the partners to distributions of capital upon liquidation.[85]

The following is an example of determining the partners' interest in the partnership and is based on Example 1 in the regulation.[86] Assume that A and B form a general partnership, and each contributes $50,000. The partnership uses that capital to purchase a piece of depreciable property. The partnership agreement provides that items of income and loss will be shared equally, except depreciation, which will be exclusively allocated to A. Assume that the partnership agreement provides for maintenance of capital accounts, but provides that, upon liquidation, proceeds will be shared equally. Because the liquidating distributions are not made in accordance with positive capital account balances, the allocations do not meet the main test for economic effect, nor can they be sustained under the alternate test.[87] Consequently, the allocations in the partnership agreement—both the stated equal allocations and the exclusive allocation of depreciation—cannot have economic effect. Here, the fact that (i) A and B made equal contributions, (ii) share other items equally, and (iii) will share equally upon liquidation indicates that their economic arrangement is to bear items equally. Therefore, the partners' interest in the partnership are equal and the allocations of items, including depreciation, will be made equally.

As noted above, the general test for determining the partner's interest in the partnership is a factor approach. However, the regulations also provide that, in a certain, specifically defined situation, a different analysis is required.[88] If the partnership agreement provides for the maintenance of capital accounts, liquidation with positive capital account balances, but the special allocation fails in whole or in part because there is not a deficit restoration obligation or the alternate test is not met, then the partner's interest for the year must be determined under a deemed liquidation approach.[89] Under this approach, the partner's interest in the partnership will be determined by comparing distributions and contributions as if the partnership liquidated (sold) all its property at book value for that tax year,

---

85. Treas. Reg. § 1.704-1(b)(3)(ii).
86. Treas. Reg. § 1.704-1(b)(5).
87. Recall that the alternate test also requires liquidations in accordance with positive capital account balances.
88. Treas. Reg. § 1.704-1(b)(3)(iii).
89. Id. (flush language).

4. Partnership Allocations Part I: § 704(b) and Substantial Economic Effect

compared with a similar analysis for the prior taxable year (with some adjustments).[90]

ITEMS THAT CANNOT HAVE ECONOMIC EFFECT

There are certain tax items that a partnership may generate that, definitionally, cannot have economic effect. One prominent example is that of tax credits and tax credit recapture.[91] Because tax credits generally do not give rise to capital account adjustments, they cannot have economic effect.[92] In this case, the regulation provides that "tax credits and tax credit recapture must be allocated in accordance with the partners' interests in the partnership as of the time the tax credit or credit recapture arises."[93] The special rule here is that, other than the investment tax credit,[94] if an expenditure gives rise to a credit also gives rise to a valid allocation of loss or deduction, "then the partners' interests in the partnership with respect to such credit (or the cost giving rise thereto) shall be in the same proportion as such partners' respective distributive shares of such loss or deduction (and adjustments)."[95]

Other specific items are enumerated in § 1.704-1(b)(4) that have special allocation rules. One example is excess percentage depletion, which is generally not covered in this text.[96] In short, the rationale here is the same, i.e., this kind of depletion does not give rise to a capital account adjustment, and therefore cannot have economic effect.[97] The regulations also mention allocations attributable to nonrecourse liabilities, which have special rules contained in § 1.704-2, which are discussed in Chapter 6. The reason for special rules for nonrecourse deductions is that, in essence, the creditor, and not partners, bears the actual risk of economic loss.

Examples

1. Anders, Blake, Caleb, and Derek form the ABCD Partnership, in which each contributed an equal amount of cash. Although Anders is a one-fourth partner, the partnership agreement allocates 75% of the depreciation to him. The partnership agreement provides that capital accounts

---

90. Id.
91. Treas. Reg. § 1.704-1(b)(4)(ii).
92. Id.
93. Id.
94. Id. Investment tax credits are controlled by Treas. Reg. § 1.46-3.
95. Treas. Reg. § 1.704-1(b)(4)(ii).
96. Treas. Reg. § 1.704-1(b)(4)(iii).
97. Id.

4. Partnership Allocations Part I: § 704(b) and Substantial Economic Effect

will be determined and maintained in accordance with the Treasury Regulations and that liquidating distributions will be made in accordance with positive capital account balances. However, the agreement further provides that, if a partner has a deficit capital account upon liquidation, each partner will be required to contribute on an equal basis to remedy the deficit. The partnership agreement has no other relevant provision. Evaluate the propriety of the depreciation allocation.

2. The Beta Partnership has three equal partners—Edward, Francis, and Gary. Each of the partners contributed $50,000 to the partnership in exchange for their partnership interests. The partnership used the contributed cash to purchase depreciable equipment for $150,000. Assume that the depreciation on the equipment is straight-line in the amount of $30,000 per year. The partnership agreement contains provisions that require the proper maintenance of capital accounts, liquidation in accordance with positive capital account balances, and a deficit restoration obligation. Assume that items of partnership income equal items of partnership expense, except for depreciation. The partnership agreement allocates depreciation exclusively to Edward. At the end of Year 3, the partnership decides to liquidate, and it sells its property for its then-book value. Determine whether the allocations of depreciation for Years 1 through 3 are respected and calculate the amounts that the partners are entitled to receive upon the liquidation at the end of Year 3.

3. Hazel and Irene start the HI Partnership with cash contributions of $200,000 each. The partnership, in turn, uses that cash to purchase depreciable property for $400,000. The partnership agreement provides that the partners will share equally in items of income and loss, except for depreciation, which it exclusively allocates to Hazel. The partnership agreement provides that capital accounts will be properly determined and maintained and that liquidating distributions will be made in accordance with positive capital account balances. The partnership agreement does not contain a deficit restoration obligation, but it does contain a qualified income offset provision.

    The partnership recognizes income equal to its expenses, except for its depreciation expense. At the end of each taxable year, future distributions and the like are not reasonably expected to occur. The depreciation expense is $100,000 in Year 1 and $125,000 in Year 2. Analyze the allocation of depreciation deductions for the partnership's first two taxable years. What if, alternatively, Hazel had also contributed a promissory note with a principal balance of $25,000?

4. Jana and Kyra are equal partners in an investment partnership; the partnership owns various stocks and bonds. For the foreseeable future, Jana

4. Partnership Allocations Part I: § 704(b) and Substantial Economic Effect

expects to be in the 37% marginal tax bracket, and Kyra expects to be in the 12% marginal tax bracket. Also, for the foreseeable future, the partnership expects to receive a similar and stable amount of tax-exempt interest and taxable dividends. Although they are equal partners and have generally agreed to share partnership tax items equally, the partnership agreement provides that tax-exempt interest will be allocated 90% to Jana and 10% to Kyra, and that the taxable dividends will be allocated exclusively to Kyra. The partnership agreement provides for all elements for the main test of economic effect. Analyze the above special allocations if the partnership recognizes $10,000 of tax-exempt interest income and $10,000 of taxable dividend income.

5. Lana and Mae are equal partners in the Sunny Partnership, which operates an active business. In addition to its active business operations, the partnership agrees to invest for three years surplus funds into various financial investments, which include tax-exempt bonds and corporate stocks. Given Lana's other sources of income, she is in a much higher tax bracket than Mae. During the times of these surplus investments, Lana will be allocated 80% of any tax-exempt interest income (like municipal bond income) and Mae will be allocated 20% of tax-exempt income. Conversely, Lana will be allocated 20% of taxable investment income, and Mae will be allocated 80% of such taxable investment income. At the time these allocation decisions are made, though, it is unclear how much of each type of investment income will be generated due to uncertain economic conditions and financial markets. The partnership agreement contains the three standard provisions for satisfying the main test for economic effect. Analyze the issues and concerns, if any, with the stated special allocations of investment income.

6. Let's continue with Lana, Mae, and the Sunny Partnership (from Example 5). After further reflection, the partners decide to keep their 80/20 split on tax-exempt income and 20/80 split on taxable investment income, but they want to be more egalitarian. Therefore, they now stipulate that these special allocations will apply only for the first $20,000 of the respective type of income and that they will apply only for the first taxable year; after that threshold, the partners will then split items equally, and, in any event, they will share equally in all years other than the first taxable year. So, for example, if the partnership earns $25,000 of tax-exempt investment income, Lana is allocated 80% of $20,000, which equals $16,000, and then half of the $5,000 (the amount over $20,000), resulting in a total allocation of tax-exempt investment income of $18,500, and Mae would be allocated $6,500. Analyze the issue and

4. Partnership Allocations Part I: § 704(b) and Substantial Economic Effect

concerns, if any, with the revised special allocations of the investment income.

Explanations

1. The issue here is the application of the main test for economic effect. It has three requirements: (1) the capital account requirement, (2) the liquidation requirement, and (3) the deficit restoration obligation requirement. Here, the special allocation cannot have economic effect because the partnership agreement does not satisfy the deficit restoration obligation requirement. Additionally, the allocation cannot likewise be justified under the alternate test because the partnership does not have a qualified income offset provision, which is required under the alternate test. Because the allocation of depreciation does not have economic effect, it must be allocated in accordance with the partners' interest in the partnership.

2. The issue here is the application of the main requirements for economic effect. As noted, the partnership agreement satisfies the three requirements for economic effect under the § 704(b) regulations. The following table provides the changes in the partners' capital accounts for the three years.

	Capital Account		
	Edward	Francis	Gary
Contributions of money	$50,000	$50,000	$50,000
Allocation of Year 1 depreciation	($30,000)	–	–
End of Year 1 capital account	$20,000	$50,000	$50,000
Allocation of Year 2 depreciation	($30,000)	–	–
End of Year 2 capital account	($10,000)	$50,000	$50,000
Allocation of Year 3 depreciation	($30,000)	–	–
End of Year 3 capital account	($40,000)	$50,000	$50,000

At the end of Year 3, the equipment has a book value of $60,000, which the partnership translates into cash (upon the liquidation). To satisfy the liquidation requirement, Francis and Gary must receive $50,000 each. To satisfy the deficit restoration obligation, Edward must contribute an additional $40,000 to restore his capital account deficit. Between the $40,000 additional that Edward must contribute and the $60,000 from the cash from the sale of the equipment, Francis and Gary can receive the required amount of $50,000 each under the liquidation requirement.

4. Partnership Allocations Part I: § 704(b) and Substantial Economic Effect

In sum, the allocation of depreciation is respected under the main test because the three requirements are satisfied.[98] Because of that, there is no issue with Edward having a deficit (negative) capital account balance. But, upon liquidation, Edward must remedy that deficit. To satisfy the liquidation requirement, Francis and Gary must each receive $50,000 in liquidation, and to satisfy the deficit restoration obligation, Edward must contribute an additional $40,000. Importantly, the deficit restoration obligation must be satisfied "by the end of such taxable year (or, if later, within 90 days after the date of such liquidation)."[99]

3. This example tests the application of the alternate test for economic effect. It is based on Example 1 in the regulations.[100] The main test for economic effect cannot be satisfied because of the lack of a deficit restoration obligation for both partners. Consequently, the analysis focuses on the alternate test for economic effect. The alternate test requires three elements, the first two of which correspond to the main test. The first requirement is that capital accounts must be properly determined and maintained in accordance with the § 704(b) regulations. The second requirement is that liquidating distributions need to be made in accordance with positive capital account balances. The third requirement is that the partnership agreement must contain a qualified income offset provision. Under the alternate test, moreover, allocations can have economic effect to the extent they neither create nor increase a capital account deficit balance.

The partnership agreement satisfies the requirements under the alternate test. The following table demonstrates the capital account changes for the first taxable year.

	Capital Account	
	Hazel	Irene
Contributions of money	$200,000	$200,000
Less Year I depreciation	($100,000)	
Year I ending balance	$100,000	$200,000

Under the alternate test, therefore, the allocation in Year 1 to Hazel has economic effect because it neither creates nor increases a capital account deficit.

---

98. Technically, a full analysis would also consider *substantiality* here, too (as allocation must have *substantial* economic effect). The allocation as described, though, is substantial. It is neither a shifting nor transitory allocation, and the allocation does, in fact, affect the amounts the partners would receive, as the example demonstrates (for instance, in the absence of the allocation, the partners would bear the depreciation expense equally).
99. Treas. Reg. § 1.704-1(b)(2)(ii)(b)(3).
100. Treas. Reg. § 1.704-1(b)(5).

4. Partnership Allocations Part I: § 704(b) and Substantial Economic Effect

The following table demonstrates the capital account changes for the second taxable year.

	Capital Account	
	Hazel	Irene
Year 2 beginning capital account	$100,000	$200,000
Less Year 2 depreciation	($125,000)	
Year 2 ending balance	($25,000)	$200,000

The Year 2 depreciation allocation satisfies the alternate test only to the extent of $100,000. That is, it is not respected to the extent it creates or increases a deficit capital account, which is $25,000. Therefore, $25,000 of the depreciation expense must be allocated in accordance with the partners' interest in the partnership.

The partners' interest in the partnership corresponds to how they have agreed to share the economic benefits and burdens of the partnership items.[101] This determination is made by "taking into account all facts and circumstances relating to the economic arrangement of the partners."[102] The factors include, among other things, the rights to partners upon distributions of capital upon liquidation. Here, if the partnership sold its single asset (the depreciable property) for its tax basis (presently $175,000), those proceeds would be distributed to Irene (as she has a positive capital account balance of $200,000). Therefore, Irene bears the burden of the depreciation deduction that generates the deficit capital account balance to Hazel (that is, Irene is not being made whole as the partnership has only $175,000 although it is "supposed" to distribute $200,000 to her). Consequently, that $25,000 of depreciation is allocated to Irene.

In the alternative situation, the presence of Hazel's promissory note potentially changes the economic effect analysis. A partner is treated as having a deficit restoration obligation to the extent of any outstanding principal balance of a promissory note of which the partner is a maker.[103] This rule also generally requires that the promissory note must be satisfied "at a time no later than the end of the partnership taxable year in which such partner's interest is liquidated (or, if later, within 90 days after the date of such liquidation)."[104] If the note provides that Hazel is unconditionally obligated to pay the note in accordance with the timing rules, then Hazel is treated as having a limited deficit restoration

---

101. Treas. Reg. § 1.704-1(b)(3)(i).
102. Id.
103. Treas. Reg. § 1.704-1(b)(2)(ii)(c)(1).
104. Treas. Reg. § 1.704-1(b)(2)(ii)(c)(2). There are different rules for negotiable notes.

4. Partnership Allocations Part I: § 704(b) and Substantial Economic Effect

obligation. Consequently, because the deficit balance does not exceed her deemed limited deficit restoration obligation, the entire depreciation allocation now satisfies the alternate economic effect test.

4. The issue here is whether the allocations are *substantial*.[105] Because the partnership agreement contains all the elements for the main test ((1) the capital account requirement, (2) the liquidation requirement, and (3) the deficit restoration obligation requirement), the special allocation of tax-exempt interest has economic effect. We must analyze, then, whether that economic effect is *substantial*. Indeed, the whole object behind the substantiality requirement is the recognition that allocations can pass the main or alternate test but not affect a pocketbook (but it can affect a tax liability). As emphasized by the regulation, an allocation is substantial "if there is a reasonable possibility that the allocation (or allocations) will affect substantially the dollar amounts to be received by the partners from the partnership, independent of tax consequences."[106]

The regulations chart three ways to test for substantiality: (1) the general rule, (2) shifting tax consequences, and (3) transitory allocations. Under the general test, an allocation is not substantial if (1) the after-tax consequences of at least one partner is made better off with the allocation (compared to no special allocation), and (2) there is a *strong likelihood* that the after-tax consequences of no partner is substantially diminished with the allocation (compared to no allocation). Naturally, this requires a consideration of two universes—one with the allocation and one without the allocation. The following tables summarize these two alternative universes. The first table demonstrates the "with allocation" universe.

	With Allocation	
	Jana (37% bracket)	Kyra (12% bracket)
Tax-exempt interest allocated and distributed	$9,000	$1,000
Income tax on tax-exempt interest	0	0
Taxable dividends allocated and distributed	0	$10,000
Income tax on taxable dividends	0	($1,200)
After-tax income	$9,000	$9,800

The next table demonstrates the "without allocation" universe. In this situation, the partners would share equally in each tax item.

---

105. Treas. Reg. § 1.704-1(b)(5). This is based on Example 5 in the regulation.
106. Treas. Reg. § 1.704-1(b)(2)(iii)(a).

4. Partnership Allocations Part I: § 704(b) and Substantial Economic Effect

	Without Allocation	
	Jana (37% bracket)	Kyra (12% bracket)
Tax-exempt interest allocated and distributed	$5,000	$5,000
Income tax on tax-exempt interest	0	0
Taxable dividends allocated and distributed	$5,000	$5,000
Income tax on taxable dividends	($1,850)	($600)
After-tax income	$8,150	$9,400

The next table demonstrates the comparison of the two alternative universes.

	Jana			Kyra		
	With Allocation	Without Allocation	Difference	With Allocation	Without Allocation	Difference
After-tax income	$9,000	$8,150	$850	$9,800	$9,400	$400

The issue, then, is whether this satisfies the general test for substantiality. The first part is clearly satisfied because Jana is made better off, after-tax, with the allocation than compared without the allocation. The second part queries whether a partner's position is *substantially diminished* with the allocation compared to without the allocation. Here, Kyra's position is actually increased (and not diminished) on an after-tax basis. Consequently, the allocation is not substantial. This example does not discusss the strong likelihood standard, which is addressed in more detail in the next example.

5. The issue here, like with the prior example, focuses on whether these special allocations are substantial.[107] The allocations satisfy the main test for economic effect per the stated facts about the partnership agreement. Observe that the example makes special allocations based on *character*, which give rise to substantiality concerns, as many rate preferences hinge on the character of items. The acute concern, of course, is that partners are not changing the magnitude of what they may otherwise be allocated, but rather seeking to change the character of that allocated income. Here the concern is the allocation of tax-exempt income to one partner and taxable income to the other, which is based on a strategic analysis of their individual tax rates.

The core issue will be whether, at the time the allocations became part of the partnership agreement, there was a *strong likelihood* that the amount of tax-exempt income and taxable investment income will

---

107. This is based on Example 7 of Treas. Reg. § 1.704-1(b)(5).

4. Partnership Allocations Part I: § 704(b) and Substantial Economic Effect

differ substantially. If the amounts won't differ substantially, this gives rise to *transitory allocations*. Transitory allocations are ones in which the net increases and decreases in the partners' capital accounts with the allocations do not differ substantially than without the allocation, and the total tax liability of the partners for the respective years are less with the allocation than without the allocation.

For example, assume that the tax-exempt income is $2,000, $4,000, and $4,000 over the three years, and taxable investment income is $4,000, $5,000, and $1,000 over the same period. Over those three-years, Lana is allocated $8,000 of tax-exempt income and $2,000 of taxable investment income; Mae is allocated $2,000 of tax-exempt income and $8,000 of taxable investment income. So, they were each allocated $10,000 of income over the three-year period due to the special allocation. Each partner, therefore, has a net $10,000 increase to their capital accounts over the three-year period. A summary of the tax impact follows in the next table; recall also that Lana has a higher marginal tax rate.

	With Allocation	
	Lana (40% bracket)	Mae (15% bracket)
Tax-exempt interest allocated	$8,000	$2,000
Income tax on tax-exempt interest	0	0
Taxable investment income allocated	$2,000	$8,000
Income tax on taxable dividends	($800)	($1,200)
After-tax income	$9,200	$8,800

In the absence of the special allocation, the equal partners would share each item equally over the three-years. So, Lana and Mae would each be allocated $5,000 of both tax-exempt income and taxable investment income. Like with the allocation, the partners similarly have a net increase of $10,000 to their respective capital accounts. A summary of tax impact of that Without Allocation scenario follows.

	Without Allocation	
	Lana (40% bracket)	Mae (15% bracket)
Tax-exempt interest allocated	$5,000	$5,000
Income tax on tax-exempt interest	0	0
Taxable investment income allocated	$5,000	$5,000
Income tax on taxable dividends	($2,000)	($750)
After-tax income	$8,000	$9,250

4. Partnership Allocations Part I: § 704(b) and Substantial Economic Effect

Observe that with the allocation, the total tax liability would be $2,000 between the two partners, and that without the allocation, the total tax liability is $2,750, which is *more*. Also observe that in either scenario (with and without the allocation) the partners each experienced a net increase of their capital accounts of $10,000.[108] Consequently, this may be a set of transitory allocations if, at the time these allocations became part of the partnership agreement, there was a *strong likelihood* that these net increases and decreases occur and that the total tax liability would be less with the allocation.

Back to the example, though, the issue is the *strong likelihood* standard. If there is a strong likelihood that the net increases and decreases to the capital accounts won't differ substantially, there is a credible substantiality concern. Here, however, the facts stated that, due to market conditions, it is unclear and uncertain what the specific returns of the investments will be. For example, if the investment returns differ wildly—for example, the tax-exempt investments yield $20,000 in income over the three years and the taxable investments only $3,000—then the special allocation does affect the economic rights of the partners by affecting how much of partnership assets they are now entitled, i.e., the capital account increases and decreases are not the same over the three-year period between the two partners. In other words, their pocketbooks are affected.

6. This example demonstrates again the substantiality concern.[109] The special allocation of investment income has economic effect because the partnership agreement satisfies the three main requirements. However, we are again faced with the issue of whether the allocation changes just tax consequences without economic consequences (which is the heart of the substantiality concern). These allocations are not substantial, and they represent a form of shifting tax consequences.[110] The shifting tax consequence test is like the transitory standard that we just considered. It is similar because it considers the (i) net increases and decreases to the partners' capital accounts, and (ii) the total tax liability borne by the partners. The difference, though, is that shifting tax consequences look within the same tax year (and transitory allocations can span several years).

---

108. This further emphasizes our concerns about affecting tax liability without affecting economic benefits and burdens. In other words, in each situation, the partners are entitled to an additional $10,000 of partnership assets (the net increase in their capital accounts) but their tax liabilities are different. The concern, then, is one of tax gamesmanship by using the partnership form of business.
109. This is based on Example 7(ii) of Treas. Reg. § 1.704-1(b)(5).
110. Treas. Reg. § 1.704-1(b)(2)(iii)(b).

4. Partnership Allocations Part I: § 704(b) and Substantial Economic Effect

Because the special allocation is for one year only, that essentially removes the concern for a set of transitory allocations. The concern for shifting tax consequences, though, remains. Like with the prior example, the key issue is whether there is a strong likelihood of whether the two types of income will be substantially similar. If both types of income are going to exceed $20,000, then the special allocation shifts only character and not magnitude, just like with the above example. This is demonstrated by the following analysis based on if the partnership generates $30,000 of each type of income.

The first table demonstrates the "with allocation" scenario. Lana is allocated the 80% of the first $20,000 of tax-exempt investment income and 50% of the amount over $20,000; Mae is allocated the remainder. Mae is allocated 80% of the first $20,000 of the taxable investment income and 50% of the amount over $20,000 and Lana is allocated the remainder.

	With Allocation	
	Lana (40% bracket)	Mae (15% bracket)
Tax-exempt interest allocated and distributed	$21,000	$9,000
Income tax on tax-exempt interest	0	0
Taxable dividends allocated and distributed	$9,000	$21,000
Income tax on taxable dividends	($3,600)	($3,150)
After-tax income	$26,400	$26,850
Net capital account increase	$30,000	$30,000

The next table demonstrates the "without allocation" scenario. Here, each partner is allocated 50% of each type of income.

	Without Allocation	
	Lana (40% bracket)	Mae (15% bracket)
Tax-exempt interest allocated and distributed	$15,000	$15,000
Income tax on tax-exempt interest	0	0
Taxable dividends allocated and distributed	$15,000	$15,000
Income tax on taxable dividends	($6,000)	($2,250)
After-tax income	$24,000	$27,750
Net capital account increase	$30,000	$30,000

4. Partnership Allocations Part I: § 704(b) and Substantial Economic Effect

As shown, in each scenario, the net increases to the partners' capital accounts are the same. And, with the allocation, the partners collectively have a lower tax liability (combined income tax liability of $6,750 in the with-allocation scenario versus $8,250 in the without-allocation scenario). Consequently, the allocation is a set of shifting tax consequences if there exists a strong likelihood at the time the allocations become a part of the partnership agreement that the net increases and decreases to the partners' capital accounts will not differ substantially than compared without the allocation.

Partnership Allocations Part II: § 704(c) and Built-In Gain or Loss

INTRODUCTION

In the last chapter, we covered the main rules under § 704(a) and (b), namely that, consistent with the flexibility afforded to partnerships under state law, the partnership agreement can specially allocate items to partners so long as the allocations have substantial economic effect. The goal of substantial economic effect is to ensure that tax benefits and burdens follow real economic benefits and burdens. We also saw that if a partnership allocation does not have substantial economic effect or if the partnership agreement did not allocate an item, then it will be allocated in accordance with the partner's interest in the partnership. This, too, is geared at ensuring tax and economic parity.

Stated simply, the Code desires that the *tax* consequences to follow the *economic* consequences. We have already seen how capital accounts represent the economic entitlements of the partners to the economic assets of the partnership, and we have recorded these items at their "book value." Thus, the *tax* consequences should correspond to the *book* consequences. In many cases, that does not pose a problem because the tax and book amounts are equal (for example, when a partnership purchases an item of depreciable property). However, with contributed property this will not be the case if the *tax* and *book* amounts do not start with the same amounts. Contributed property is recorded upon contribution with a book value equal to its then-fair market value. This may diverge from the contributed property's *tax* column amount, i.e., its inside basis, which will be the carry-over basis from

5. Partnership Allocations Part II: § 704(c) and Built-In Gain or Loss

the contributing partner. In these cases, then, a divergence arises between the *book* and *tax* amounts attributable to that piece of contributed property. We therefore need a method to account for this "book-tax disparity."

This chapter focuses on § 704(c), which is about contributed property and dealing with resulting book-tax disparities. The general rule here is that "income, gain, loss, and deduction with respect to property contributed to the partnership by a partner shall be shared among the partners so as to take account of the variation between the basis of the property to the partnership and its fair market value at the time of contribution."[1] From this sentence springs myriad considerations attributable to property with built-in gain or loss at the time of contribution. Two quick examples can show the mischief that § 704(c) is targeted at preventing.

Let's consider the AB Partnership, in which A and B are equal partners and agree to share all items of gain or loss equally. A contributes $10,000 cash, and B contributes an undeveloped piece of real property with a value of $10,000 and a basis in B's hands of $2,000. Under § 722, we know that A and B take an outside basis in their partnership interests of $10,000 and $2,000, respectively. Under § 723, the partnership has an inside basis of $2,000 in the real property. And, under § 721, there is no gain or loss recognized on any of these transfers. Consequently, the partnership balance sheet looks as follows:

AB Partnership					
Assets			Liabilities		
	Adj. Basis	Book Value	None		$0
Cash	$10,000	$10,000			
Real Property	$2,000	$10,000	Capital Accounts		
				Adj. Basis	Book Value
			A	$10,000	$10,000
			B	$2,000	$10,000
Total	$12,000	$20,000	Total	$12,000	$20,000

We previously examined how these sections — §§ 721, 722, and 723 — preserve the tax status quo ante. That is, A had no built-in gain pre-formation and thus has no gain inherent in his partnership interest. B, however, had a $8,000 gain inherent in his real property, which is now preserved in the outside basis of his partnership interest — that gain is *also* inherent in the inside basis of AB's basis in the real property.

Consider what would happen if the partnership sold the real property for $10,000 and allocates that gain equally. AB recognizes a tax gain of

---

1. I.R.C. § 704(c)(1)(A).

5. Partnership Allocations Part II: § 704(c) and Built-In Gain or Loss

$8,000 (the $10,000 amount realized less the $2,000 tax basis). Under the partnership agreement, that gain will be split $4,000 each to A and B. If this allocation is allowed, then B has been allowed to *shift* his *pre-contribution* gain to A! In other words, the entire $8,000 of gain arose during B's ownership of the property, but now he was able to shift that gain to A through Subchapter K.[2] Making the point more acute, consider if A and B are in markedly different tax brackets—for example, if A is in a lower marginal tax bracket compared to B. Then not only has B been able to shift gain to another taxpayer, through the partnership entity they've also lowered the taxes due on that gain.

The same concern arises for losses, too. Consider A and B again, but now instead of a pre-contribution gain, the real property now has a pre-contribution loss of $8,000. The balance sheet looks as follows:

AB Partnership					
Assets			*Liabilities*		
	Adj. Basis	Book Value	None		$0
Cash	$10,000	$10,000			
Real Property	$18,000	$10,000	*Capital Accounts*		
				Adj. Basis	Book Value
			A	$10,000	$10,000
			B	$18,000	$10,000
Total	$28,000	$20,000	Total	$28,000	$20,000

Thus, when the property is sold for $10,000, the partnership now generates a $8,000 loss, which is purportedly allocated equally between A and B. Here, then, B has been able to *shift* his loss to A! The Code generally prevents these types of loss shifting transactions.[3] The same type of loss shifting should disallowed in partnership transactions.

Section 704(c) comes to the rescue here. Indeed, that is the entire import of § 704(c)(1)(A)—that the partners need to "take account of the variation between the basis of the property to the partnership and its

---

[2] At bottom, the concern here represents those common to assignment of income generally, that is, the ability to shift income between taxpayers. This concern is particularly acute among related taxpayers, such as families and its manifestation in family partnerships; for example, economically successful parents (likely in a high marginal tax bracket) who want to assign income to their children (likely in a lower marginal tax bracket).

[3] For example, consider § 1014, which is the basis section for gifts of property. Under this rule, the donee's basis for determining loss is limited to the fair market value at the date of the gift if the transferor's basis was more than the fair market value. This prevents the donor from gratuitously transferring the built-in loss to the donee. Additionally, consider § 267, which disallows losses arising from sales of property between related taxpayers.

5. Partnership Allocations Part II: § 704(c) and Built-In Gain or Loss

fair market value at the time of contribution."[4] In other words, the whole purpose of § 704(c) is that we do not want a partner to be able to shift that pre-contribution built-in gain or loss (e.g., the $8,000 gain and loss in the above examples). Thus, there are special rules that, for various purposes, account for this pre-contribution gain and loss. This is the focus of Chapter 5. Although the potential income-shifting abuse that § 704(c) is designed to prevent is most easily visible for the disposition of the contributed asset (like the examples above), § 704(c) applies to "income, gain, loss, and deduction" which means other items, such as depreciation.[5]

The key theme to this chapter, then, is when there is a difference between the book value (fair market value at date of contribution)[6] and basis, § 704(c) requires us to take that difference into account when dealing with the tax items generated by that piece of property. Indeed, the entire purpose of this rule, as explained by the regulations, "is to prevent the shifting of tax consequences among partners with respect to precontribution gain or loss."[7] To accomplish this goal, the regulations require that these allocations "must be made using a reasonable method that is consistent with the purpose of section 704(c)."[8] The regulations then provide three allocation methods that are generally reasonable: (1) the traditional method, (2) the traditional method with curative allocations, and (3) the remedial method. Each of these methods will be discussed in turn.[9] Importantly, the regulations provide that, although an allocation method may be literally described in the regulation, in certain situations, the "Commissioner can recast the contribution as appropriate to avoid tax results inconsistent with the intent of subchapter K."[10]

GENERAL MATTERS AND DEFINITIONS

Before we dive into the specifics of the three methods, the regulations unpack some operating rules and definitions. A primary operating rule is that the § 704(c) rules apply on a property-by-property basis.[11] Thus, we determine book-tax disparities on a property-by-property basis, as compared to a transferor-by-transferor basis. The partnership agreement can also use different allocations methods for different properties, provided that a

---

4. I.R.C. § 704(c)(1)(A).
5. Id.
6. Treas. Reg. § 1.704-3(a)(3)(i); Treas. Reg. § 1.704-1(b).
7. Treas. Reg. § 1.704-3(a)(1).
8. Id.
9. Id.
10. Id.
11. Treas. Reg. § 1.704-3(a)(2).

single reasonable method is used for each item of property and the overall combination is still reasonable and consistent with § 704(c).[12]

The regulations also provide some salient definitions to understand the scope of the rules. A primary definition is for "section 704(c) property," which is defined as "property if at the time of contribution its book value differs from the contributing partner's adjusted tax basis."[13] Book value is "equal to fair market value at the time of contribution and is subsequently adjusted for cost recovery and other events that affect the basis of the property."[14] Thus, if the partnership is properly maintaining capital accounts, book value is the initial value used for capital account purposes and adjusted thereafter.[15] "Built-in gain" is defined as "the excess of the property's book value over the contributing partner's adjusted tax basis upon contribution."[16] Built-in loss is defined as "the excess of the contributing partner's adjusted tax basis over the property's book value upon contribution."[17]

THE TRADITIONAL METHOD

We can now turn to the methods prescribed by the § 704(c) regulations to take into account the book-tax disparity; the first method is the traditional method. The traditional method provides that "when the partnership has income, gain, loss, or deduction attributable to section 704(c) property, it must make appropriate allocations to the partners to avoid shifting the tax consequences of the built-in gain or loss."[18] The regulation then gives a few examples of how this method is operationalized. First it considers a sale of § 704(c) property and notes that "if the partnership sells section 704(c) property and recognizes gain or loss, built-in gain or loss on the property is allocated to the contributing partner."[19] If only a portion of § 704(c) property is sold, then a proportionate part of the built-in gain or loss similarly needs to be allocated to the contributing partner. Moreover, if the § 704(c) property is subject to cost recovery (like depreciation), those cost recovery items need to take into account the built-in gain or loss. Consequently, "tax allocations to the noncontributing partners of cost recovery deductions with respect to section 704(c) property generally must, to the extent

---

12. Id.
13. Treas. Reg. § 1.704-3(a)(3)(i).
14. Id.
15. Id.
16. Treas. Reg. § 1.704-3(a)(3)(ii).
17. Id.
18. Treas. Reg. § 1.704-3(b)(1).
19. Id.

5. Partnership Allocations Part II: § 704(c) and Built-In Gain or Loss

possible, equal book allocations to those partners."[20] There is an important limit here, though, which is known as the "ceiling rule": the "the total income, gain, loss, or deduction allocated to the partners for a taxable year with respect to a property cannot exceed the total partnership income, gain, loss, or deduction with respect to that property for the taxable year."[21]

Before we look at some examples of the traditional method, let's do a little more setup of its rationale, particularly with respect to cost recovery deductions. Under the § 704(b) capital account rules covered in the previous chapter, partners are credited in their capital accounts for the fair market value of property. For capital account purposes, items that arise from that property (like depreciation) are based on that fair market value (as of the contribution date). Recall that one of the purposes of the capital account rules was to track the economic consequences to the partners. Thus, the fact that a partner contributed a property with a spread (disparity) between its fair market value and tax basis ought not affect the economic consequences to *the other partners*. That's essentially the rationale of the traditional method: we need to take into account the variation between book value and tax basis (so that the contributing partner cannot shift income), but we don't want that to spillover and affect the noncontributing partners (unless absolutely needed). Stated more simply, it desires that the allocations to the noncontributing partner shouldn't be different for tax and book (i.e., capital account) purposes. But those items are different to the contributing partner (and that difference is rooted in the underlying book-tax disparity).

Let's consider an example using the traditional method.[22] A and B form the AB Partnership. A contributes a piece of depreciable property with a fair market value of $20,000 and a tax basis of $8,000; B contributes $20,000 cash. They agree that they will share items equally and will use the traditional method for § 704(c) purposes. After formation, the partnership balance sheet looks as follows, which demonstrates that A has a built-in gain of $12,000, representing the excess of the book value of his contributed property ($20,000) over its adjusted basis ($8,000) at the time of contribution. Notice that the $12,000 of built-in gain is readily observable in the difference between the tax and book columns on each side of the balance sheet.

---

20. Treas. Reg. § 1.704-3(b)(1).
21. *Id.*
22. Based on Example 1 of Treas. Reg. § 1.704-3(b)(2).

5. Partnership Allocations Part II: § 704(c) and Built-In Gain or Loss

AB Partnership					
Assets			Liabilities		
	Tax	Book	None		$0
Cash	$20,000	$20,000			
Depreciable Property	$8,000	$20,000	Capital Accounts		
				Tax	Book
			A	$8,000	$20,000
			B	$20,000	$20,000
Total	$28,000	$40,000	Total	$28,000	$40,000

Let's now consider how depreciation of the depreciable property works under § 704(c) principles and the traditional method. For simplicity, assume that the property is depreciated over 10 years and is straight-line depreciated at 10%. For *book purposes* (i.e., capital account purposes), there is $2,000 of depreciation expense (10% of the $20,000 book value), which is shared equally between the partners, i.e., $1,000 each. For *tax purposes*, however, there is only $800 of depreciation ($8,000 × 0.10 = $800). Under the traditional method, "tax allocations to the noncontributing partners of cost recovery deductions with respect to section 704(c) property generally must, to the extent possible, equal book allocations to those partners."[23] Here, that would be $1,000 (the amount of book depreciation allocated to B) — but there is only $800 of actual tax depreciation. This is the ceiling rule! In other words, we can't allocate more tax depreciation than that which actually exists, so $800 serves as a "ceiling" on the total amount of tax depreciation that can be allocated. Consequently, the entire $800 of tax depreciation is allocated to B; therefore, A is not allocated any tax depreciation.

If we further assume that other items of income equal expenses (other than the above depreciation), the balance sheet and capital accounts at the end of Year 1 would look as follows:

AB Partnership					
Assets			Liabilities		
	Tax	Book	None		$0
Cash	$20,000	$20,000			
Depreciable Property	$7,200	$18,000	Capital Accounts		
				Tax	Book
			A	$8,000	$19,000
			B	$19,200	$19,000
Total	$27,200	$38,000	Total	$27,200	$38,000

---

23. Treas. Reg. § 1.704-3(b)(1).

5. Partnership Allocations Part II: § 704(c) and Built-In Gain or Loss

Observe that the book basis amount for the depreciable property decreased by $2,000, which represents the calculated book depreciation; there is also a corresponding $2,000 reduction in the book capital accounts ($1,000 each for A and B). For tax purposes, the inside basis of the depreciable property has decreased by $800 (the amount of tax depreciation), all of which was allocated to B, which is why B's outside basis (the tax column under Capital Account) also decreased by $800. The definition of "built-in gain" under the § 704(c) regulation notes that, "[t]he built-in gain is thereafter reduced by decreases in the difference between the property's book value and adjusted tax basis."[24] Therefore, the built-in gain inherent in the depreciable property (attributable to A) is now $10,800 ($18,000 less $7,200), which is a $1,200 decrease from the initial $12,000 of built-in gain. Observe that the $1,200 decrease represents the disparity between the total book depreciation ($2,000) and the total tax depreciation ($800). Indeed, that is the entire purpose of these rules—to take into account the initial variation between basis and value, and to reduce that differential over time.

There is something else worth pointing out expressly here, too. Examine B's capital account balance and his outside basis. B now has more outside basis ($19,200) than the balance of his capital account ($19,000). In other words, B practically now has a loss inherent in his partnership interest; that is, if the partnership were to liquidate immediately, B would be entitled to $19,000 of partnership assets, but he has a basis of $19,200 (i.e., more basis than property, or a loss). Why is this the case? We need to zoom out a bit to appreciate this. Consider what would have happened had there been no variation between the depreciable property's basis and value (i.e., they were both $20,000). That would have generated tax depreciation of $2,000,[25] of which B would have been allocated $1,000. However, B did not actually get this much in tax depreciation; he had only $800 of tax depreciation allocated to him because of the ceiling rule (you can't allocate depreciation that doesn't exist). The beauty (and elegance) of this rule is that "missed" $200 of tax depreciation to B in Year 1 effectively gets stored in his outside basis in the partnership. The rub, then, becomes one of timing: he will not get to benefit taxwise from this inherent loss in his partnership interest until he exits the partnership (or the partnership liquidates).[26]

Let's continue the example, and now assume that, at the beginning of Year 2, the partnership sells the property for its book value of $18,000. On this sale, the partnership recognizes tax gain of $10,800 and no book

---

24. Treas. Reg. § 1.704-3(a)(3)(ii).
25. That is, 10% of the tax basis of $20,000.
26. The delay in timing also gives rise to time value of money concerns with respect to waiting for the eventual benefit of that $200 for tax purposes. See Chapter 10 for a discussion of partnership exits and liquidations.

5. Partnership Allocations Part II: § 704(c) and Built-In Gain or Loss

gain.[27] Under the traditional method, the entire $10,800 of tax gain needs to be allocated to A because it represents the remaining built-in gain. After the sale and application of the traditional method, the balance sheet looks as follows:

AB Partnership					
Assets			*Liabilities*		
	Tax	Book	None		$0
Cash	$38,000	$38,000			
			Capital Accounts		
				Tax	Book
			A	$18,800	$19,000
			B	$19,200	$19,000
Total	$38,000	$38,000	Total	$38,000	$38,000

The cash balance of $38,000 represents the initial $20,000 plus the sale proceeds of $18,000. Observe how there is no longer variation between the total tax and book columns. This is because all the built-in gain has now been accounted for! Capital account book balances did not change because there was no book gain; but A's outside tax basis did change from $8,000 to $18,800, which is due to the $10,800 of tax gain that was allocated to him.

Let's zoom out and recap how the gain was treated in this example. Like we've seen in our prior chapters, a theme in partnership tax is that gain should not leak out—it must all be accounted for, either on a tax return or inherent in the basis of property. Partner A contributed property with $12,000 of gain inherent in it; he should not be able to use the partnership form of business to purge that gain. Partner A was allocated $10,800 of tax gain on the sale, which leaves $1,200 of the original built-in gain to account for. There is $200 of tax gain inherent in A's partnership interest, which leaves $1,000 of gain to account for. Recall that in Year 1 that A did not receive any tax depreciation, but he did receive $1,000 of book depreciation. Thus, the entire built-in gain has been accounted for between (1) the tax gain allocated to A, (2) the gain inherent in his partnership interest, and (3) the foregone tax depreciation.

Now, focus for a moment on Partner B. Partner B was supposed to get allocated $1,000 of tax depreciation, but due to the ceiling rule, he was allocated only $800—meaning there was $200 of a deduction/expense he was not afforded. All is not lost for B, though. Looking at his partnership

---

27. The tax gain calculation is the amount realized of $18,000 less the tax basis of $7,200, which equals $10,800; for book purposes, the amount realized is still $18,000 but the book basis is $18,000, too, which equals a gain of $0—that is, there is not a book gain.

5. Partnership Allocations Part II: § 704(c) and Built-In Gain or Loss

interest, we observe a $200 loss inherent in the interest, which he can benefit from later in time (for example, if he exits the partnership).

What if, though, instead of selling the property for exactly its book value, the partnership sells it for $20,000 (i.e., $2,000 over book value). Now there is both tax and book gain. The tax gain is calculated as $20,000 less $7,200, which equals $12,800; book gain is calculated as $20,000 less $18,000, which equals $2,000. So now we must allocate both gains. Like before, we must allocate the tax built-in gain to the contributing partner. Here that is still $10,800 (the amount of the difference between its book value and adjusted tax basis). So, of the $12,800 tax gain, the first $10,800 must be allocated to A. The remaining $2,000 of tax gain will be allocated in accordance with the partnership agreement, which states that items are shared equally between the partners.[28] The balance of the $2,000 tax gain will thus be allocated $1,000 each to A and B. Similarly, the book gain of $2,000 will be shared equally between the partners. After this transaction, the partnership balance sheet would be as follows:

AB Partnership					
Assets			Liabilities		
	Tax	Book	None		$0
Cash	$40,000	$40,000			
			Capital Accounts		
				Tax	Book
			A	$19,800	$20,000
			B	$20,200	$20,000
Total	$40,000	$40,000	Total	$40,000	$40,000

Notice here that, again, the disparity between the total tax and book columns has disappeared because, in the aggregate, the built-in gain has been accounted for. Moreover, observe that B still has more outside basis ($20,200) than capital account balance ($20,000) due to the ceiling rule preventing his full allocation of tax depreciation in Year 1 by $200. Symmetrically, A still has his $200 of gain inherent in his partnership interest. These amounts cancel out in the total tax column.

For completeness, let's consider a situation in which the property with a built-in gain is later sold for an amount less than book value—that is, the full built-in gain is not recovered. In this case, AB sells the depreciable property for $15,000. AB realizes a tax gain of $7,800. AB also has a "book" loss of $3,000 (the amount by which the book value of $18,000 exceeds the

---

28. This assumes their specified allocation of items has substantial economic effect or is otherwise in accord with the partners' interest in the partnership.

5. Partnership Allocations Part II: § 704(c) and Built-In Gain or Loss

sale price of $15,000). Under § 704(c), the entire tax gain is allocated to A; under the partnership agreement, the book loss is shared equally between the partners. After the sale and allocation, the balance sheet looks as follows:

AB Partnership					
Assets			Liabilities		
	Tax	Book	None		$0
Cash	$35,000	$35,000			
			Capital Accounts		
				Tax	Book
			A	$15,800	$17,500
			B	$19,200	$17,500
Total	$35,000	$35,000	Total	$35,000	$35,000

Observe that, in addition to the outside basis change to A (resulting from the allocation of the tax gain to him), A and B's capital accounts each decreased by $1,500 (the $3,000 of book loss).

Like before, let's see if this result makes conceptual sense. Partner A contributed property with a $12,000 built-in gain, which he should not be able to purge. As calculated above, he was allocated a tax gain of $7,800, which leaves $4,200 of the original built-in gain to account for. There is also a $1,700 gain inherent in his partnership interest, leaving $2,500 of the built-in gain to account for. The property, though, suffered a true economic loss, of which A bore $1,500 (by the reduction in his capital account, i.e., future economic entitlement to partnership assets). And, like with the prior example, the remaining $1,000 is reflected in the foregone tax depreciation.

TRADITIONAL METHOD WITH CURATIVE ALLOCATIONS

The next method allowed by the regulations is known as the traditional method with curative allocations. The entire reason behind this method is to cure the distortions that arise by operation of the ceiling rule, some examples of which were identified above. In a nutshell, the operation of the ceiling rule means that noncontributing partners may receive tax allocations that do not match their book allocations (like we saw with partner B in the earlier example). The ceiling rule basically operates to prevent a tax allocation that is greater than the tax item actually realized by the partnership. For example, in the AB Partnership example above, we could only allocate $800 of tax depreciation to B (the noncontributing partner) in Year 1 even

5. Partnership Allocations Part II: § 704(c) and Built-In Gain or Loss

though, in the absence of a book-tax disparity and § 704(c), his tax allocation would have been $1,000; this created a $200 tax distortion that would ultimately be remedied upon liquidation of B's partnership interest—a remedy that may be years away and that B does not want to wait for.

Under the regulations, the traditional method with curative allocations allows a partnership to "make reasonable curative allocations to reduce or eliminate disparities between book and tax items of noncontributing partners."[29] A curative allocation is defined as "an allocation of income, gain, loss, or deduction for tax purposes that differs from the partnership's allocation of the corresponding book item."[30] The regulation then proceeds to give a depreciation-specific example:

> if a noncontributing partner is allocated less tax depreciation than book depreciation with respect to an item of section 704(c) property, the partnership may make a curative allocation to that partner of tax depreciation from another item of partnership property to make up the difference, notwithstanding that the corresponding book depreciation is allocated to the contributing partner.[31]

Moreover, the partnership may limit curative allocations to one or more particular tax items (like depreciation or even with respect to specific properties). This is true even if the curative allocations do not fully cure the ceiling rule distortion. Importantly, "[a] partnership must be consistent in its application of curative allocations with respect to each item of section 704(c) property from year to year."[32] Another theme for curative allocations is that they need to be reasonable. To be reasonable, the amount of the curative allocation cannot be more than needed to offset ceiling rule effects for the current year. If the curative allocation is for a disposition of property, then the curative allocation cannot be more than cumulative effect of ceiling rule distortions.[33]

Additionally, the curative allocation needs to be one that is expected to have substantially the same effect on each partner's tax liability as the item limited by the ceiling rule.[34] As an example to this point, the regulations note that, if a tax-exempt partner's depreciation deductions were limited by the ceiling rule, then an allocation of dividend or interest income to that partner is not reasonable. An exception to this point, though, is that curative allocations from dispositions of property need not be of the same character as ceiling-rule limited depreciation deductions.[35]

---

29. Treas. Reg. § 1.704-3(c)(1).
30. Id.
31. Id.
32. Treas. Reg. § 1.704-3(c)(2).
33. Treas. Reg. § 1.704-3(c)(3)(i).
34. Treas. Reg. § 1.704-3(c)(3)(iii)(A).
35. Treas. Reg. § 1.704-3(c)(3)(iii)(B).

5. Partnership Allocations Part II: § 704(c) and Built-In Gain or Loss

Let's consider an example of the traditional method with curative allocations.[36] C and D form the CD Partnership, with each sharing 50% of all partnership items, and the partnership agreement provides that allocations will be made using the traditional method with curative allocations. C contributes equipment with a tax basis of $8,000, a fair market value of $20,000, and it has 10 years remaining of straight-line depreciation. D contributes $20,000 cash, which CD then uses to purchase inventory. Consequently, after formation and the purchase of the inventory (using D's contributed cash), the balance sheet and capital accounts look as follows:

CD Partnership					
Assets			*Liabilities*		
	Tax	Book	None		$0
Inventory	$20,000	$20,000			
Equipment	$8,000	$20,000	*Capital Accounts*		
				Tax	Book
			C	$8,000	$20,000
			D	$20,000	$20,000
Total	$28,000	$40,000	Total	$28,000	$40,000

As observed, C has a built-in gain of $12,000, representing the difference between the tax basis and fair market value at date of contribution; because of this built-in gain, the equipment is § 704(c) property.

Assume that, in Year 1, partnership revenues equal expenses other than depreciation. The equipment generates $2,000 of book depreciation and $800 of tax depreciation. At the end of Year 1, the partnership sells the inventory for $21,400, recognizing $1,400 of gain from the inventory. Further assume that the inventory gain is similar in character to the character of items that arise from the equipment (i.e., both give rise to ordinary income or loss).

Under the traditional method, C and D are each allocated $700 of income from the sale of the inventory for both book and tax purposes. For book purposes, the depreciation expense would be allocated $1,000 each. For tax purposes, under the ceiling rule, there is only $800 of depreciation to allocate; D, as the noncontributing partner, would be allocated $800 of tax depreciation and C would be allocated no tax depreciation. The balance sheet and capital accounts, after these Year 1 events, would look as follows under the traditional method:

---

36. Based on Example 1 of Treas. Reg. § 1.704-3(c)(4).

5. Partnership Allocations Part II: § 704(c) and Built-In Gain or Loss

CD Partnership					
Assets			Liabilities		
	Tax	Book	None		$0
Cash	$21,400	$21,400			
Equipment	$7,200	$18,000	Capital Accounts		
				Tax	Book
			C	$8,700	$19,700
			D	$19,900	$19,700
Total	$28,600	$39,400	Total	$28,600	$39,400

Let's drill down into the capital account changes. A breakdown of the beginning and ending capital accounts balances for C and D is as follows:

	C		D	
	Tax	Book	Tax	Book
Initial contribution	$8,000	$20,000	$20,000	$20,000
Depreciation	0	($1,000)	($800)	($1,000)
Income from inventory	$700	$700	$700	$700
Ending balance	$8,700	$19,700	$19,900	$19,700

Observe how the ceiling rule creates the $200 disparity for D, representing the difference (shortfall) between his book and tax depreciation.

The curative allocation seeks to remedy presently D's $200 disparity. In this case, the partnership can allocate to C an additional $200 from the sale of inventory for tax purposes, which simultaneously achieves a $200 reduction in the tax allocation to D. With this curative allocation, the capital accounts for C and D would be as follows:

	C		D	
	Tax	Book	Tax	Book
Initial contribution	$8,000	$20,000	$20,000	$20,000
Depreciation	0	($1,000)	($800)	($1,000)
Income from inventory	$900	$700	$500	$700
Ending balance	$8,900	$19,700	$19,700	$19,700

As shown, this curative allocation now equalizes the tax and book balances for D, the noncontributing partner. Let's reiterate what happened here. D entered the partnership with no disparity (i.e., no built-in gain) between his capital account (book) and outside basis (tax). The ceiling rule, however, limited D's ability to benefit from the full depreciation deduction for tax

5. Partnership Allocations Part II: § 704(c) and Built-In Gain or Loss

purposes, but not book purposes, by $200. This resulted in a $200 dollar disparity between D's tax and book balances. D would have eventually realized the benefit of this $200 for tax purposes, but it would have to wait for D to exit the partnership, which may be a long time away. The curative allocation provides a fix *now* (instead of waiting). The fix is to allocate to C additional income in the amount of $200, which has the concomitant benefit of lowering the allocation to D by $200, which is the equivalent of a $200 tax deduction. After that curative allocation, there is no longer a disparity between D's book and tax balances. It is important to realize, though, that the curative allocation was possible here because the partnership had *other* items of income that it could allocate (the inventory gain); had there been no inventory gain in this example there would have been no item to allocate in a curative fashion.

REMEDIAL ALLOCATION METHOD

The last method described in the regulations is known as the remedial allocation method. This method, like curative allocations, is designed to fix the distortions caused by the ceiling rule. Under the remedial method, the ceiling rule distortions are remedied by "creating remedial items and allocating those items to its partners."[37] After the ceiling rule limits the tax allocation of an item to a noncontributing partner, "the partnership creates a remedial item of income, gain, loss, or deduction equal to the full amount of the difference and allocates it to the noncontributing partner."[38] The partnership then "simultaneously creates an offsetting remedial item in an identical amount and allocates it to the contributing partner."[39]

The remedial allocations to the noncontributing partner must "have the same tax attributes as the tax item limited by the ceiling rule."[40] The offsetting allocations to the contributing partner must be "determined by reference to the item limited by the ceiling rule."[41] As an example, "if the ceiling rule limited item is loss from the sale of contributed property, the offsetting remedial allocation to the contributing partner must be gain from the sale of that property."[42] If the ceiling rule limits an item of depreciation or cost recovery, "the offsetting remedial allocation to the contributing

---

37. Treas. Reg. § 1.704-3(d)(1).
38. Id.
39. Id.
40. Treas. Reg. § 1.704-3(d)(3).
41. Id.
42. Id.

5. Partnership Allocations Part II: § 704(c) and Built-In Gain or Loss

partner must be income of the type produced (directly or indirectly) by that property."[43]

Remedial allocations do not affect the partnership's taxable income, nor do they effect the partnership's inside basis in its assets.[44] Importantly, remedial allocations are "notional tax items" that exist solely for tax purposes and do not affect capital accounts.[45] For tax purposes, though, these remedial items, although notional in nature, "have the same effect as actual tax items on a partner's tax liability and on the partner's adjusted tax basis in the partnership interest."[46]

Let's try an example of the remedial method that involves a sale of property.[47] E and F form the EF Partnership and agree to share partnership items equally. The partnership agreement provides that EF will use the remedial method to make § 704(c) allocations. E contributes real property, Greenacre, with a basis of $20,000 and a fair market value of $50,000; F also contributes a piece of real property, Redacre, that has a tax basis and value of $50,000. The balance sheet and capital accounts after formation are as follows:

EF Partnership					
Assets			Liabilities		
	Tax	Book	None		$0
Greenacre	$20,000	$50,000			
Redacre	$50,000	$50,000	Capital Accounts		
				Tax	Book
			E	$20,000	$50,000
			F	$50,000	$50,000
Total	$70,000	$100,000	Total	$70,000	$100,000

Given its built in gain, Greenacre is § 704(c) property. At the end of Year 1, the EF Partnership sells Greenacre for $45,000. For tax purposes, this sale generates capital gain of $25,000 ($45,000 less $20,000); for book purposes, it generates a book loss of $5,000 ($50,000 less $45,000). For simplicity, assume that there are no other items of income or loss. Applying the ceiling rule, E is allocated the recognized built-in gain of $25,000, and E and F are each allocated $2,500 of book loss. Consequently, their capital accounts would be as follows at the end of Year 1:

---

43. Id.
44. Treas. Reg. § 1.704-3(d)(4)(i).
45. Treas. Reg. § 1.704-3(d)(4)(ii).
46. Id.
47. Based on Example 2 of Treas. Reg. § 1.704-3(d)(7).

5. Partnership Allocations Part II: § 704(c) and Built-In Gain or Loss

	E		F	
	Tax	Book	Tax	Book
Initial contribution	$20,000	$50,000	$50,000	$50,000
Sale of Greenacre	$25,000	($2,500)	0	($2,500)
Ending balance (Year 1)	$45,000	$47,500	$50,000	$47,500

As evidenced in F's capital account balance, the ceiling rule injected a disparity between F's tax and book balances because no tax loss was allocated to F (as no tax loss existed). To fix that disparity for F, EF must make a remedial allocation of $2,500 of capital loss to F, and an offsetting remedial allocation to E of $2,500 of capital gain. After those allocations, the capital accounts will be as follows, in which the disparity caused by the ceiling rule is now remedied:

	E		F	
	Tax	Book	Tax	Book
Initial contribution	$20,000	$50,000	$50,000	$50,000
Sale of Greenacre	$25,000	($2,500)	0	($2,500)
Remedial allocations	$2,500		($2,500)	
Ending balance (Y1)	$47,500	$47,500	$47,500	$47,500

A special note is needed about calculating book depreciation under the remedial method. In short, partnerships using the remedial method must use a different method for calculating book depreciation than the method prescribed under the capital account rules.[48] Under the remedial method regulation, the book basis in the property needs to be split into two parts. The first part is the portion of book basis that is equal to the adjusted tax basis at the time of contribution to the partnership.[49] This portion of the basis "is recovered in the same manner as the adjusted tax basis in the property is recovered (generally, over the property's remaining recovery period under section 168(i)(7) or other applicable Internal Revenue Code section)."[50] The second part is equal to the remainder of the partnership's book basis in the property, i.e., "the amount by which book basis exceeds adjusted tax basis."[51] This second part is "recovered using any recovery period and depreciation (or other cost recovery) method (including first-year conventions) available to the partnership for newly purchased property (of the same type as the contributed property) that is placed in service at the time

---

48. Treas. Reg. § 1.704-3(d)(2).
49. Id.
50. Id.
51. Id.

5. Partnership Allocations Part II: § 704(c) and Built-In Gain or Loss

of contribution."[52] Importantly, for this second part, additional first-year depreciation under § 168(k) is not permissible.[53]

Let's go through an example of the remedial method involving cost recovery.[54] G and H form the GH Partnership and agree that they will share tax items equally; the partnership agreement provides that the remedial method will be used for § 704(c) property, and, if needed, the straight-line method will be used for excess depreciation. G contributes equipment with a tax basis of $12,000 and a fair market value of $30,000; the property had been depreciated using the straight-line method with a 10-year recovery period, in which 4 years remain. H contributes $30,000 in cash, which the partnership promptly uses to purchase a piece of real property. Consequently, after the formation and the purchase of the property, the partnership's balance sheet looks as follow:

GH Partnership					
Assets			Liabilities		
	Tax	Book	None		$0
Real property	$30,000	$30,000			
Equipment	$12,000	$30,000	Capital Accounts		
				Tax	Book
			G	$12,000	$30,000
			H	$30,000	$30,000
Total	$42,000	$60,000	Total	$42,000	$60,000

As is readily apparent, G contributed property with a § 704(c) built-in gain. For simplicity, assume that, except for depreciation, other expenses equal revenue. Let's first consider Years 1 through 4 of the GH Partnership, which coincides with the remaining recovery period for the equipment. To calculate the book depreciation, we need to split the book basis into the two parts. The first is equal to its tax basis at the time of contribution, which is $12,000. This part of the book basis is depreciated under the property's remaining recovery period, which is 4 years. Thus, the book depreciation on this part is $3,000 (that is, the $12,000 basis divided by 4 years, or $3,000 per year). The second part is the remainder of the book basis, i.e., the amount by which book basis exceeds tax basis; that amount is $18,000 (the $30,000 book amount less the $12,000 tax basis). This second part is depreciated over the recovery period for newly purchased property of the same type; we will assume that, too,

---

52. Id.
53. Id.
54. Adapted from Example 1 of Treas. Reg. § 1.704-3(d)(7).

5. Partnership Allocations Part II: § 704(c) and Built-In Gain or Loss

is 10 years. Thus, the book depreciation on the second part is equal to $1,800 ($18,000 divided by 10 years, or $1,800 per year). In total, the sum of the two parts equals $4,800, which is the total book depreciation. G and H are each then allocated $2,400 (one-half of the $4,800) of book depreciation.

For tax purposes, there is $3,000 of depreciation ($12,000 tax basis divided by 4). Of that $3,000, the first $2,400 is allocated to the noncontributing partner, H. G is allocated the balance of the tax depreciation ($600). In this case, therefore, no remedial allocation is needed; this is because the noncontributing partner (H) was not limited by the ceiling rule. In other words, H received the same amount of book and tax depreciation ($2,400 each for book and tax depreciation). This result will be similarly true for the rest of these 4 initial years. After 4 years, their capital accounts will look as follows:

	G		H	
	Tax	Book	Tax	Book
Initial contribution	$12,000	$30,000	$30,000	$30,000
Depreciation	($2,400)	($9,600)	($9,600)	($9,600)
Ending balance (Year 4)	$9,600	$20,400	$20,400	$20,400

Let's look at what happens in Year 5, though. Starting in Year 5, the first part of the basis (the initial tax basis) has been exhausted for book purposes. Thus, only the second part exists, which was $1,800 per year. Take note, however, that there is no tax depreciation! The property has been fully depreciated for tax purposes at the end of Year 4, as the tax depreciation was $3,000 for 4 years. So, in Year 5, we have our first application of the ceiling rule. In this case, then, G and H are both allocated $900 of book depreciation (half of the $1,800), but they are allocated no tax depreciation (as no tax depreciation exists). At the end of Year 5, then, the capital accounts would look as follows:

	G		H	
	Tax	Book	Tax	Book
Beginning of Year 5	$9,600	$20,400	$20,400	$20,400
Depreciation	0	($900)	0	($900)
Ending balance (Year 5)	$9,600	$19,500	$20,400	$19,500

As shown, the ceiling rule now creates a distortion in H's capital account because H cannot be allocated any tax depreciation. This is now where the remedial method steps in to remedy this distortion. To remedy the impact of the ceiling rule, the partnership must make a remedial allocation to H of

5. Partnership Allocations Part II: § 704(c) and Built-In Gain or Loss

$900 in tax depreciation each year for the remaining cost recovery period of the equipment (Years 5 through 10). As an offsetting allocation, the partnership must allocate to G an allocation of $900 of taxable ordinary income in each of those years, too. After application of the remedial and offsetting allocations, therefore, the capital accounts for the end of Year 5 would be as follows, in which you can observe that H no longer has a disparity between his tax and capital account balances.

	G		H	
	Tax	Book	Tax	Book
Beginning of Year 5	$9,600	$20,400	$20,400	$20,400
Depreciation	0	($900)	0	($900)
Remedial allocations	$900	0	($900)	0
Ending balance (Year 5)	$10,500	$19,500	$19,500	$19,500

Examples

1. Asher and Betsy form the AB Partnership. Asher contributes depreciable property with a basis of $400,000 and a value of $1,000,000; Betsy contributes $1,000,000 in cash. The property is depreciated on the straight-line method over a 10-year recovery period. The partnership agreement provides that partners will share items equally and that § 704(c) allocations will be made using the traditional method. Calculate the tax and book depreciation for Year 1. Additionally, evaluate the tax consequences if AB sells the property at the beginning of Year 2 for $900,000. First alternative: evaluate the tax consequences if AB sells the property for $1,000,000. Second alternative: evaluate the tax consequences if AB sells the property for $800,000.

2. Chloe and Darla form a partnership. Chloe contributes a piece of equipment that has an adjusted tax basis of $80,000 and a value of $200,000; Darla contributes $200,000 cash. After the formation, the partnership uses the cash to purchase inventory, which it plans to sell to customers. The partnership agreement provides that the partners will share equally in tax items, and that, for § 704(c) purposes, it will use the traditional method with curative allocations. In the first year, items of income equal items of expense, except for depreciation. The equipment is depreciated using the straight-line method over its remaining 10-year recovery period. Additionally, at the end of Year 1, the partnership sells the

5. Partnership Allocations Part II: § 704(c) and Built-In Gain or Loss

inventory for $214,000. Calculate the book and tax depreciation for Year 1, including the need, availability, and application of curative allocations, if any.

3. Elana and Felicia form a partnership in which they are equal partners. They each contributed a piece of depreciable property. Elana contributes property with a basis of $150,000 and a value of $500,000; Felicia contributes property with a basis of $300,000 and a value of $500,000. Assume that both pieces of property are depreciated using the straight-line method and have a 5-year recovery period remaining. For § 704(c) purposes, the partners agree to use the traditional method with curative allocations, but they further agree that curative allocations are limited to the extent the partnership has sufficient tax depreciation available. The partnership also generates $50,000 of operating income each year. Calculate the book and tax depreciation for Year 1, including the need, availability, and application of curative allocations, if any.

4. Gabriel and Hope form the GH partnership in which they are equal partners. Gabriel contributes depreciable property that has a tax basis of $80,000 and a value of $200,000; Hope contributes $200,000 in cash. After formation, the partnership uses the cash and purchases a piece of real property. The depreciable property is depreciated using the straight-line method and has four years remaining in its recovery period (it is 10-year property). The partnership agreement provides that the partners will equally share partnership items, and that, for § 704(c) purposes, it will use the remedial method and straight-line depreciation for recovery of excess book basis. For the first 10 years, assume that items of income equal items of expense, except for depreciation. Calculate (i) the book and tax depreciation, including remedial allocations, if any, for Years 1 through 4, and (ii) the book and tax depreciation, including remedial allocations, if any, for Years 5 through 10. Ignore any depreciation conventions and any additional first-year depreciation.

5. Ivory and Jonas form the IJ Partnership, each contributing a piece of property. Ivory contributes Greenacre, which has a tax basis of $100,000 and a value of $250,000; Jonas contributes Blueacre, which has a tax basis and value of $250,000. The partnership agreement provides that the partners share partnership items equally, and that the partnership will make § 704(c) allocations using the remedial method. At the end of its first tax year, the partnership sells Greenacre for $225,000; the partnership has no other items of income, gain, loss, or expense. Assume that the properties are capital assets in the hands of the partnership. Alternatively, what if the partnership sells Greenacre for $75,000? Evaluate the tax consequences of the sale of Greenacre.

5. Partnership Allocations Part II: § 704(c) and Built-In Gain or Loss

Explanations

1. The depreciable property is § 704(c) property because, at the time of its contribution, its book value differs from the contributing partner's tax basis.[55] The built-in gain is equal to $600,000. Under § 704(c), the allocations of depreciation and gain or loss from the property need to take into account that variation. The annual book depreciation is $100,000, of which $50,000 is allocated each to Asher and Betsy. The annual tax depreciation is $40,000, which is less than the book depreciation because of the book-tax disparity. In the absence of such disparity (and built-in gain or loss), Asher and Betsy would each be allocated $50,000 of tax depreciation (for a total of $100,000 per year). The traditional rule provides that "tax allocations to the noncontributing partners of cost recovery deductions with respect to section 704(c) property generally must, to the extent possible, equal book allocations to those partners."[56] The ceiling rule, however, limits the allocation of tax depreciation to the amount that exists. Consequently, the entire $40,000 of tax depreciation must be allocated to Betsy.

As a result of the allocations, the property's book value is now $900,000, which represents its initial book value less the full $100,000 book depreciation. The property's adjusted tax basis is $360,000, representing its initial inside tax basis less the $40,000 tax depreciation. Asher's built-in gain with respect to the property is now $540,000. The balance sheet for the AB Partnership at the end of Year 1 is as follows.

AB Partnership					
Assets			Liabilities		
	Tax	Book	None		$0
Property	$360,000	$900,000			
Cash	$1,000,000	$1,000,000	Capital Accounts		
				Tax	Book
			Asher	$400,000	$950,000
			Betsy	$960,000	$950,000
Total	$1,360,000	$1,900,000	Total	$1,360,000	$1,900,000

As you can see, the ceiling rule injected a book-tax disparity into Betsy's portion of the balance sheet. She now has a loss of $10,000 inherent in her partnership interest, which represents the amount of the tax depreciation that she did not receive in Year 1.

---

55. This problem is based on Example 1 of Treas. Reg. § 1.704-3(b)(2).
56. Treas. Reg. § 1.704-3(b)(1).

5. Partnership Allocations Part II: § 704(c) and Built-In Gain or Loss

When AB sells the property for $900,000, it realizes a tax gain of $540,000 ($900,000 less $360,000). It realizes no book gain ($900,000 less $900,000). Under the traditional method, built-in gain or loss must be allocated to the contributing partner. Here, therefore, the entire tax gain must be allocated to Asher because the entire tax gain represents built-in gain. In the first alternative ($1,000,000 sales price), the partnership realizes a tax gain of $640,000 ($1,000,000 less $360,000) and book gain of $100,000 ($1,000,000 less $900,000). Of the tax gain, $540,000 of it represents built-in gain and must be allocated to Asher; the remaining $100,000 of tax gain is shared equally between Asher and Betsy (given their partnership agreement). Similarly, the $100,000 book gain is shared equally between Asher and Betsy.

In the second alternative ($800,000 sales price), the partnership realizes a tax gain of $440,000 ($800,000 less $360,000) and a book loss of $100,000 ($900,000 less $800,000). The entire tax gain represents built-in gain and must be allocated to Asher. The book loss is shared equally between Asher and Betsy. Although Betsy suffered a book loss, no tax loss can be allocated to her because of the ceiling rule (i.e., a tax loss does not exist). A balance sheet of this alternative looks as follows.

AB Partnership					
Assets			Liabilities		
	Tax	Book	None		$0
Cash	$1,800,000	$1,800,000			
			Capital Accounts		
				Tax	Book
			Asher	$840,000	$900,000
			Betsy	$960,000	$900,000
Total	$1,800,000	$1,800,000	Total	$1,800,000	$1,800,000

It is worth examining the capital account and outside basis portion of the balance sheet to consider whether their values make conceptual sense. Observe that Asher has a $60,000 gain inherent in his partnership interest. This represents the remnants of his pre-contribution gain. Recall that he contributed property with a built-in gain of $600,000; he was allocated $440,000 of gain from the sale of the property. This leaves $160,000 of built-in gain left to account for.[57] Well, $60,000 of that gain is preserved in his partnership interest, as indicated. What about the other $100,000? Of that $100,000, $50,000 of it represents the loss in

---

57. Recall that we can't have gain evaporate (or leak) from the system.

5. Partnership Allocations Part II: § 704(c) and Built-In Gain or Loss

value that is allocable to his interest, the other $50,000 is the depreciation expense that he was not allocated in Year 1. In other words, between (1) the remaining built-in gain, (2) his proportionate share of the loss, and (3) the forgone depreciation, the entire $600,000 variation (book-tax disparity) has been accounted for with respect to Asher. Consider, now, the $60,000 loss that is inherent in Betsy's partnership interest. Of that loss, $50,000 represents the book loss that, because of the ceiling rule, she was not allocated a tax loss, and $10,000 represents the Year 1 depreciation she was not allocated (again due to the ceiling rule).

2. At the time of the Chloe's contribution, the equipment has a built-in gain of $120,000.[58] The equipment generates tax depreciation of $8,000 and book depreciation of $20,000 per year for the property's remaining recovery period. The sale of the inventory, moreover, generates $14,000 of ordinary income. Under the traditional method, Chloe and Darla are each allocated $10,000 of book depreciation. Due to the book-tax disparity, though, there is not enough tax depreciation to be allocated. Consequently, all the tax depreciation is allocated to Darla (the noncontributing partner). Additionally, without any curative allocation, the partners would be allocated $7,000 each of the ordinary income arising from the inventory gain. These transactions would manifest in the capital accounts as follows.

	Chloe		Darla	
	Tax	Book	Tax	Book
Initial contribution	$80,000	$200,000	$200,000	$200,000
Depreciation	–	($10,000)	($8,000)	($10,000)
Sales income	$7,000	$7,000	$7,000	$7,000
Ending balance	$87,000	$197,000	$199,000	$197,000

Observe that the ceiling rule injected a disparity in Darla's book-tax balances because she was not allocated an amount of tax depreciation equal to the amount allocated for book purposes. Thus, the ceiling rule created a $2,000 disparity.

A curative allocation is defined as "an allocation of income, gain, loss, or deduction for tax purposes that differs from the partnership's allocation of the corresponding book item."[59] Proper curative allocations need to be "reasonable."[60] The regulation further provides that, "[t]o be reasonable, a curative allocation of income, gain, loss, or deduction

---

58. This problem is based on Example 1 of Treas. Reg. § 1.704-3(c)(4).
59. Treas. Reg. § 1.704-3(c)(1).
60. Id.

5. Partnership Allocations Part II: § 704(c) and Built-In Gain or Loss

must be expected to have substantially the same effect on each partner's tax liability as the tax item limited by the ceiling rule."[61] Generally, one option would be to allocate depreciation from *another* piece of property to Darla—but there is not an additional piece of property here.[62] Another option implied by the regulation is to make a curative allocation of income to the contributing partner, but it must have the same impact on that partner as an allocation of income with respect to the contributed property.[63] Here, that option works because both the depreciable property and inventory generate ordinary income. Consequently, a proper curative allocation would be to allocate an additional $2,000 of income from the inventory sale to Chloe for tax purposes. That curative allocation would result in the following updated table.

	Chloe		Darla	
	Tax	Book	Tax	Book
Initial contribution	$80,000	$200,000	$200,000	$200,000
Depreciation	–	($10,000)	($8,000)	($10,000)
Sales income	$9,000	$7,000	$5,000	$7,000
Ending balance	$89,000	$197,000	$197,000	$197,000

Observe that the book columns *were not changed*; that is, the change is solely to the *tax columns*. Stated more directly, we "reallocated" $2,000 of the tax gain that would otherwise have been allocated to Darla and sent it to Chloe instead. The curative allocation has removed the book-tax disparity injected into Dara's accounts.

A last point here would be to demonstrate an example of an improper (i.e., unreasonable) curative allocation. Assume, for example, the partners agreed to allocate all the income from the inventory sale to Darla, but still agreed to share it equally for book purposes. This would be unreasonable because the allocation would exceed the amount needed to remedy the book-tax disparity created by the ceiling rule.

3. This is a § 704(c) problem because, at the time of contribution, each piece of contributed property has a built-in gain.[64] For ease, we will refer to the property as "Elana's property" and "Felicia's property" even

---

61. Treas. Reg. § 1.704-3(c)(3)(iii)(A).
62. Treas. Reg. § 1.704-3(c)(1) ("For example, if a noncontributing partner is allocated less tax depreciation than book depreciation with respect to an item of section 704(c) property, the partnership may make a curative allocation to that partner of tax depreciation from another item of partnership property to make up the difference, notwithstanding that the corresponding book depreciation is allocated to the contributing partner.").
63. Treas. Reg. § 1.704-3(c)(3)(iii)(A).
64. This is based on Example 2 of Treas. Reg. § 1.704-3(c)(4).

though the property is now owned by the partnership. Elana's property generates $30,000 of tax depreciation and $100,000 of book depreciation; Felicia's property generates $60,000 of tax depreciation and $100,000 of book depreciation.

Under the traditional method, each partner would be allocated $100,000 of book depreciation (there is $200,000 total book depreciation, which is shared equally). Without a book-tax disparity at contribution, then, the partners would each receive a total of $100,000 of book and tax depreciation. But there is a book-tax disparity. The tax depreciation on Elana's property is allocated exclusively to Felicia because there is not enough tax depreciation to allocate fully, so it goes to the noncontributing partner to the greatest extent possible to match the allocation of book depreciation. For Felicia's property, though, there is enough tax depreciation to allocate the full tax depreciation to Elana ($50,000, i.e., half of the $100,000 of book depreciation), and still have some remaining tax depreciation to allocate to Felicia (the remaining $10,000). These allocations are as follows.

	Elana		Felicia	
	Tax	Book	Tax	Book
Initial contribution	$150,000	$500,000	$300,000	$500,000
Elana's property depreciation	–	($50,000)	($30,000)	($50,000)
Felicia's property depreciation	($50,000)	($50,000)	($10,000)	($50,000)
Operating income	$25,000	$25,000	$25,000	$25,000
Ending balance	$125,000	$425,000	$285,000	$425,000

Let's summarize what happened: Elana was allocated a total of $50,000 in tax depreciation and Felicia was allocated $40,000 in tax depreciation; both were allocated $100,000 in book depreciation. Here, Elana was allocated *more* tax depreciation, even though she contributed the property with the *larger* book-tax disparity! In other words, Felicia contributed property with a lower built-in gain and thus a lower book-tax disparity, but she received *less* tax depreciation. An option here would be to make a curative allocation to allocate an additional $20,000 of tax depreciation to Felicia; this amount represents the amount needed to ratably reduce the differences between Elana and Felicia's book-tax disparity over the 5 years of depreciation (i.e., to reduce it proportionality). In other words, at formation, Felicia had a tax-to-book ratio of 60% (she had a tax basis that was 60% equal to her book basis), and Elana had a tax-to-book ratio of 30%. To keep those same percentages in the depreciation allocations for tax purposes, it would require Felicia to receive $60,000 of tax depreciation and for Elana to receive $30,000 of tax depreciation.

5. Partnership Allocations Part II: § 704(c) and Built-In Gain or Loss

4. This is a § 704(c) problem because, at the time of contribution, the contributed depreciable property has a built-in gain of $120,000.[65] Under the remedial method, we need to break the book depreciation into two parts. The first part is the portion of the book basis that is equal to its adjusted tax basis at the time of contribution; here, that is equal to $80,000. This portion is recovered in the same manner as the tax basis, i.e., using the property's remaining recovery period (here, 4 years). The book depreciation on this first portion, therefore, is equal to $20,000. The second portion is the amount by which the book basis exceeds the adjusted tax basis at contribution; here, that is equal to $120,000. This portion is recovered using "any recovery period and depreciation (or other cost recovery) method (including first-year conventions) available to the partnership for newly purchased property (of the same type as the contributed property) that is placed in service at the time of contribution."[66] The property is 10-year property, and the partnership agreement provides that straight-line depreciation will be used to recover excess book basis; the depreciation on this excess book basis is $12,000. The total book depreciation, therefore, is $32,000 (the sum of the depreciation on the two portions).

For years 1 through 4, the property generates $32,000 of book depreciation, and Gabriel and Hope are each allocated $16,000. The property generates $20,000 of tax depreciation. The remedial method starts with allocations of tax items in accordance with the traditional method.[67] Consequently, the noncontributing partner (Hope) is allocated $16,000 of tax depreciation, and Gabriel is allocated the remaining $4,000 of tax depreciation. No remedial allocation is needed because the noncontributing partner (Hope) did not receive a tax allocation of depreciation that was less than her book allocation. In other words, the ceiling rule did not limit her depreciation.

For years 5 through 10, though, the analysis is different. At the beginning of Year 5, the first portion of the book basis (the $80,000) has been completely recovered — so, too, has the tax basis. The excess book basis continues to be recovered, however. Thus, in Year 5 (and through Year 10), the partnership generates $12,000 of book depreciation but generates $0 tax depreciation. The ceiling rule is therefore in full effect: we cannot allocate tax depreciation that does not exist. In the absences of any remedial allocation, Gabriel and Hope are each allocated $6,000 of book depreciation but $0 tax depreciation. As applied to Hope, the ceiling rule creates an annual disparity of $6,000 between her book and tax

---

65. This problem is based on Example 1 of Treas. Reg. § 1.704-3(d)(7).
66. Treas. Reg. § 1.704-3(d)(2).
67. Treas. Reg. § 1.704-3(d)(1).

depreciation. To remedy that, the partnership must make an allocation of $6,000 in tax depreciation to Hope. The partnership must also create an offsetting remedial allocation of $6,000 in ordinary income to Gabriel (recall that offsetting allocations must be of the same character as the type of income generated by the property).

5. This is a § 704(c) problem because, at the time of its contribution, Greenacre has a built-in gain.[68] At its formation, the partnership balance sheet looks as follows.

IJ Partnership					
Assets			Liabilities		
	Tax	Book	None		$0
Greenacre	$100,000	$250,000			
Blueacre	$250,000	$250,000	Capital Accounts		
				Tax	Book
			Ivory	$100,000	$250,000
			Jonas	$250,000	$250,000
Total	$350,000	$500,000	Total	$350,000	$500,000

Upon the sale of Greenacre, the partnership realizes a tax gain of $125,000 (amount realized of $225,000 less tax basis of $100,000) and a book loss of $25,000 (book basis of $250,000 less amount realized of $225,000). Under the traditional method, the entire tax gain, which represents built-in gain, is allocated to Ivory (the contributing partner), and the partners are each allocated a $12,500 book loss. Although Jonas has a book loss, he cannot be allocated any tax loss because of the ceiling rule (as no tax loss exists). In the absence of any remedial allocation, the partners' book and tax accounts would be as follows.

	Ivory		Jonas	
	Tax	Book	Tax	Book
Initial contribution	$100,000	$250,000	$250,000	$250,000
Sale of Greenacre	$125,000	($12,500)	–	($12,500)
Ending balance	$225,000	$237,500	$250,000	$237,500

Observe how the ceiling rule creates a $12,500 disparity in Jonas's book and tax accounts (due to the presence of a book loss but no tax loss). Under the remedial method, IJ must make a remedial tax allocation of $12,500 of capital loss to Jonas. Symmetrically, it must also make

---

68. This problem is based on Example 2 of Treas. Reg. § 1.704-3(d)(7).

5. Partnership Allocations Part II: § 704(c) and Built-In Gain or Loss

an offsetting remedial allocation to Ivory of $12,500 of capital gain. Incorporating these remedial allocations results in the following book and tax accounts.

	Ivory		Jonas	
	Tax	Book	Tax	Book
Initial contribution	$100,000	$250,000	$250,000	$250,000
Sale of Greenacre	$125,000	($12,500)	–	($12,500)
Remedial allocations	$12,500		($12,500)	
Ending balance	$237,500	$237,500	$237,500	$237,500

In the alternative sale of Greenacre for $75,000, the partnership realizes a book and tax loss.[69] In particular, the partnership realizes a tax loss of $25,000 (which is a capital loss), and a book loss of $175,000. Each partner is allocated a book loss of $87,500. Under the traditional method and applying the ceiling rule, Jonas is allocated the entire tax loss—recall that we try to equalize the noncontributing partner first. Ivory is allocated none of the tax loss. The book and capital accounts would be as follows.

	Ivory		Jonas	
	Tax	Book	Tax	Book
Initial contribution	$100,000	$250,000	$250,000	$250,000
Sale of Greenacre	–	($87,500)	($25,000)	($87,500)
Ending balance	$100,000	$237,500	$225,000	$162,500

Observe how the ceiling rule injects a $62,500 disparity into Jonas's book and tax columns, due to the difference between his book and tax allocations. Consequently, the remedial method requires the partnership to make a remedial allocation of $62,500 of capital loss to Jonas. Symmetrically, it must also make an offsetting remedial allocation to Ivory of $62,500 of capital gain. Incorporating these remedial allocations results in the following book and tax accounts.

	Ivory		Jonas	
	Tax	Book	Tax	Book
Initial contribution	$100,000	$250,000	$250,000	$250,000
Sale of Greenacre	–	($87,500)	($25,000)	($87,500)
Remedial allocations	$62,500	–	($62,500)	
Ending balance	$162,500	$162,500	$162,500	$162,500

---

69. This problem is based on Example 3 of Treas. Reg. § 1.704-3(d)(7).

Partnership Liabilities

INTRODUCTION

So far in this book, the partnerships have had no liabilities (i.e., debt). More colloquially, they can be described as having "clean" balance sheets. Although that is true sometimes in the real world, it is also incredibly common for business enterprises—whether they are structured as corporations, partnerships, or LLCs—to have debt. The main topic of this chapter, therefore, is to walk through the consequences that introducing debt and liabilities has on the tax aspects of a partnership.

The main theme of this chapter is analyzing how partnership liabilities affect the outside bases of the partners (i.e., the basis they have in their partnership interest). Recall one of the themes that we previously saw in our discussion of partnership formation and basis rules is preserving the harmony between the partnership's aggregate inside basis of its assets and the partners' outside bases. Indeed, it was this harmonization that prevents the evaporation (or leakage) of the built-in gain. At a more zoomed-out level, it is this harmonization that helps us reconcile some of the distortions that would otherwise arise from treating the partnership as a separate entity.

The main section we deal with in this chapter is § 752. This section has four rules. The first rule is that an increase in a partner's share of partnership liabilities or an increase of his or her own liabilities by assuming a partnership liability is treated as a contribution of money by the partner to

6. Partnership Liabilities

the partnership.[1] The second rule is the symmetric opposite of the first, i.e., any decrease in the partner's share of partnership liabilities or a decrease of his or her own liabilities by reason of an assumption by the partnership is treated as a distribution of money to the partner by the partnership.[2] These first two rules are the main operating rules of § 752. The third rule provides that, "a liability to which property is subject shall, to the extent of the fair market value of such property, be considered as a liability of the owner of the property."[3] Finally, the fourth rule regards sales or exchanges of partnership interests,[4] of which we defer discussion until Chapter 10. As we go through this chapter, therefore, we need to be mindful of the impact of § 752 on the other sections we've discussed, such as § 722 (outside basis) and § 705 (adjustments to outside basis), as well as concepts to be covered later, such as distributions to a partner.

In summary, under § 752, an increase in the partner's share of partnership liabilities is treated as a contribution of money by the partner to the partnership. Under § 722, this results in an increase to the partner's outside basis in the partnership. This makes sense doctrinally. Indeed, the issue of how debt (and nonrecourse debt in particular) impacts basis and amount realized is not novel to partnership tax.[5] Conceptually, the Code treats debt as part of the basis of the property. One way to understand this is as an outgrowth of the *cost* basis of property. We know that, under § 1012, the basis of a purchased piece of property is its *cost*. If a taxpayer purchases Blackacre for $100,000 of cash and tenders a briefcase of cash at the closing table, we readily see that it "cost" him $100,000. What if, on the other hand, the taxpayer puts only $10,000 down of his own cash and borrows the remaining $90,000 from Big Bank? The loan from Big Bank is equivalent to Big Bank handing the taxpayer the money, who then tenders it at the closing table. Thus, in either situation, the taxpayer tenders $100,000 of cash and that represents his "cost" of the property.

Another way to view this is to consider that the debt repayment also constitutes "the cost" of the property (economically speaking). Translating back to our partnership situation, then, when a partner bears an economic obligation for a partnership debt, it is like that bank lent directly to the partner, who then transferred that money to the partnership—that is why §§ 752 and 722 treats it as such. The fact that we credit a partner for his or

---

1. I.R.C. § 752(a). Recall that capital accounts do not incorporate a partner's share of partnership liabilities. This makes conceptual sense because the capital accounts are essentially tracking a partner's equity in a partnership; a partner has no claim to an amount that is payable to a creditor.
2. I.R.C. § 752(b).
3. I.R.C. § 752(c).
4. I.R.C. § 752(d).
5. Similar issues were addressed in the canonical cases of Crane v. Comm'r, 331 U.S. 1 (1947), and Comm'r v. Tufts, 461 U.S. 300 (1983).

6. Partnership Liabilities

her share of the partnership liabilities is another facet of the aggregate versus entity distinction we've seen thematically in our study of partnership tax.

DETERMINING THE PARTNER'S SHARE OF LIABILITIES

Section 752 treats increases and decreases of the "partner's share of liabilities" as a contribution or distribution of money, respectively. The primary question, then, is how to determine a partner's share of liabilities. Before diving into those rules, though, we must first review the two main types of liabilities—recourse and nonrecourse liabilities. For state law purposes, a recourse debt (loan) is one in which the debtor is *personally* liable for the repayment of the debt—that is, the creditor has *recourse* against the debtor, and that is in addition to any underlying collateral. A nonrecourse liability, on the other hand, is one in which the creditor has no recourse against the debtor personally; for these liabilities, the creditor can look only to the underlying collateral for repayment. In economic terms, in a recourse loan, the debtor bears the risk of loss personally. In a nonrecourse loan, on the other hand, the debtor bears no economic risk of loss beyond the loss of the collateral.

The partnership tax regulations track this economic risk of loss concept in distinguishing between recourse and nonrecourse liabilities. For § 752 purposes, a recourse liability is a partnership liability "to the extent that any partner or related person bears the economic risk of loss for that liability under § 1.752-2."[6] Similarly, a nonrecourse liability is a partnership liability "to the extent that no partner or related person bears the economic risk of loss for that liability under § 1.752-2."[7] Before turning to Treas. Reg. § 1.752-2, let's first examine the term "liability." The regulations define a liability as an obligation—and obligation means an obligation to "make payment"[8]—that (1) creates or increases the basis of an obligor's assets (including cash), (2) gives rise to an immediate deduction to the obligor, or (3) gives rise to an expense that is neither deductible nor capitalized.[9]

---

6. Treas. Reg. § 1.752-1(a)(1).
7. Treas. Reg. § 1.752-1(a)(2).
8. Treas. Reg. § 1.752-1(a)(4)(ii).
9. Treas. Reg. § 1.752-1(a)(4). The regulations also provide for another type of liability in Treas. Reg. § 1.752-7. These are known as "§ 1.752-7 liabilities," and they are beyond the scope of this text. In short, § 1.752-7 liabilities are obligations that are not governed by the § 1.752-1(a)(4) rules, such as environmental obligations.

6. Partnership Liabilities

RECOURSE LIABILITIES

The regulations provide that "[a] partner's share of a recourse partnership liability equals the portion of that liability, if any, for which the partner or related person bears the economic risk of loss."[10] We determine whether a partner bears the economic risk of loss if the partner (or a related person) would be obligated to make a payment to satisfy that obligation upon a constructive liquidation.[11] In this hypothetical constructive liquidation, we assume that (1) all partnership liabilities become payable in full; (2) all partnership property, including cash, has a value of zero; (3) the partnership disposes of all property in a taxable transaction for no consideration; (4) all items of gain, loss, and the like are allocated; and (5) the partnership liquidates.[12] A partner's obligation to make a payment, moreover, is based on all the facts and circumstances and includes "[a]ll statutory and contractual obligations relating to the partnership liability," for example, guarantees and rights of reimbursement.[13]

Let's consider an example of this hypothetical constructive liquidation analysis.[14] A and B form the AB Partnership, which is a general partnership. They each contribute $100,000 in cash. After formation, the partnership purchases commercial real property for $1,000,000, which it uses its $200,000 cash, and finances the balance of the purchases price with a recourse loan. Take note that, given the nature of a general partnership and the nature of a recourse loan, A and B are, effectively, personally liable for the note (even if the loan is in the name of the AB Partnership). The partnership agreement specifies that items will be shared equally, except that tax losses will be shared 60% to A and 40% to B; it also provides for all the requirements of the main economic effect test, including deficit restoration obligations.

In the hypothetical constructive liquidation, the $800,000 liability becomes due, and all the partnership's assets are deemed to be worthless and sold for a value of zero. This results in a book loss of $1,000,000 (the book basis of $1,000,000 less the deemed amount realized of $0). To see the effects of this, it is helpful to construct capital accounts reflecting these items, which would be as follows:

---

10. Treas. Reg. § 1.752-2(a).
11. Treas. Reg. § 1.752-2(b)(1).
12. Id.
13. Treas. Reg. § 1.752-2(b)(3)(i).
14. Based on Treas. Reg. § 1.752-2(f)(1).

6. Partnership Liabilities

Capital Account Adjustments for Hypothetical Liquidation		
	A	B
	Book	Book
Initial contribution	$100,000	$100,000
Loss on hypothetical sale	($600,000)	($400,000)
Ending balance	($500,000)	($300,000)

Given the deficit restoration obligations, A and B would both need to make a make a payment to satisfy this obligation (in the amount of their capital account deficits). Because at least one partner bears the economic risk of loss, the liability is classified as a recourse obligation. A's share of the partnership liability is $500,000 based on his payment obligation (deficit restoration) in that amount, and B's share of the partnership liability is $300,000 based on his payment obligation (deficit restoration). As you can observe, this test is essentially asking who will have to repay the debt.

Let's examine another example.[15] B and C form the BC Limited Partnership. B, who will be the general partner, contributes $200,000 in cash; C, the limited partner, contributes $800,000 in cash. The partnership agreement allocates losses 20% to B and 80% to C until C's capital account is reduced to zero, after which losses will be allocated exclusively to B. The partnership purchases commercial real property for $2,500,000, of which it uses all its cash and finances the rest of the purchase with a $1,500,000 recourse loan. C guarantees the loan to the extent it remains unpaid after the lender has exhausted remedies against the partnership.

In the hypothetical constructive liquidation, (i) all assets are deemed worthless, (ii) those assets are sold for zero dollars, and (iii) the loan becomes due and payable. The worthlessness and sale of the commercial property generates a $2,500,000 book loss (the book basis of $2,500,000 less the deemed $0 amount realized). Capital account adjustments reflecting these items would be as follows:

Capital Account Adjustments for Hypothetical Liquidation		
	B	C
	Book	Book
Initial contribution	$200,000	$800,000
Loss on hypothetical sale	($1,700,000)	($800,000)
Ending balance	($1,500,000)	0

---

15. Based on Treas. Reg. § 1.752-2(f)(3).

6. Partnership Liabilities

Given the nature of B's status as general partner, state law obligates him to contribute to the partnership in the amount of his deficit, which is $1,500,000. In our hypothetical constructive liquidation, it is assumed that B will satisfy his obligation. Because of that, therefore, it is assumed that C would not need to satisfy his guarantee. The loan is treated as a recourse liability because at least one partner (B) bears the economic risk of loss. Moreover, B's share of the liability is $1,500,000, and C's share is zero.

NONRECOURSE LIABILITIES

Determining the share of a partner's share of nonrecourse liabilities is admittedly much more complicated. Definitionally, no partner bears a risk of economic loss for a nonrecourse liability. Therefore, we cannot use the hypothetical constructive liquidation approach that was used for determining a partner's share of recourse liabilities. Instead, the regulations prescribe a three-part formula.[16] A partner's share of the nonrecourse liabilities of a partnership is the sum of three tiers: (1) the partner's share of "partnership minimum gain," (2) the partner's § 704(c) gain, if any, assuming the partnership disposed of all the property subject to nonrecourse liabilities for an amount equal to the satisfaction of the liability, and (3) the partner's share of excess nonrecourse liabilities (i.e., those not allocated under (1) and (2)) as determined in accordance with the partner's share of partnership profits. Each of these items will be explained in turn.

Partnership Minimum Gain

The partner's share of partnership minimum gain is determined in accordance with the § 704(b) regulations,[17] namely Treas. Reg. § 1.704-2. Partnership minimum gain is defined as the excess of the amount of a nonrecourse liability secured by such property over the property's adjusted tax basis.[18] In other words, we calculate the amount of gain that would result if the partnership sold the property in an amount equal to the outstanding principal balance of the liability.[19] For example, consider a partnership that purchases commercial real estate for $50,000, using $5,000 in cash and financing the remainder with a nonrecourse loan ($45,000) that is initially interest-only (with a balloon payment later). The initial tax basis in

---

16. Treas. Reg. § 1.752-3(a).
17. Treas. Reg. § 1.752-3(a)(1).
18. Treas. Reg. § 1.704-2(b)(2).
19. Treas. Reg. § 1.704-2(d)(1).

6. Partnership Liabilities

the property is $50,000, so there is no partnership minimum gain because the tax basis exceeds the amount of the nonrecourse liability. That is, if the partnership sold the property for the amount of the nonrecourse liability ($45,000), it would not generate a tax gain. If, however, there is $10,000 of depreciation in Year 1, the partnership now has $5,000 of partnership minimum gain as of the end of the year; that is, if the partnership were to sell the property for an amount to satisfy the nonrecourse loan, which is $45,000, the partnership would realize a $5,000 gain ($45,000 amount realized less $40,000 adjusted tax basis).

Based on the definition of partnership minimum gain, it is not static—it necessarily ebbs and flows with changes in the amount of the liability or the tax basis of the encumbered property. Thus, like in the example above, depreciation of the encumbered property can increase partnership minimum gain; similarly, additional borrowing can increase partnership minimum gain. On the other hand, payments of principal on nonrecourse liabilities reduce partnership minimum gain.

Partnership minimum gain, moreover, is aggregated for the partnership.[20] That is, the partnership calculates "for each partnership nonrecourse liability any gain the partnership would realize if it disposed of the property subject to that liability for no consideration other than full satisfaction of the liability, and then aggregate[es] the separately computed gains."[21]

Nonrecourse Deductions

Before we turn squarely to determining a partner's share of partnership minimum gain, we need to unpack one more concept—that of nonrecourse deductions (because that's the measuring stick for determining a partner's share of the minimum gain, as we'll see later). Recall that the primary purpose of § 704 (partnership allocations) is to ensure that the tax consequences of an item follow the economic consequences (i.e., benefits and burdens); to accomplish that, the § 704(b) regulations advanced the substantial economic effect test. Allocations that relate to nonrecourse liabilities, however, definitionally lack economic effect because "the creditor alone bears any economic burden that corresponds to those allocations."[22] Later in this chapter we will discuss how nonrecourse liabilities affect our partnership allocation analysis. At this point, though, we need to understand that the regulations define, in principle, a "nonrecourse deduction" as "[a]llocations of losses, deductions, or section 705(a)(2)(B) expenditures attributable to partnership nonrecourse liabilities."[23]

---
20. Id.
21. Treas. Reg. § 1.704-2(d)(1).
22. Treas. Reg. § 1.704-2(b)(1).
23. Id.

6. Partnership Liabilities

In other words, we have special rules for deductions that are traceable to nonrecourse liabilities because the creditor (and not the partners) bears the economic risk of loss—and, further, recall our earlier principle that we want ensure that tax benefits and burdens follow the economic benefits and burdens.

Nonrecourse deductions are determined for each partnership taxable year.[24] Nonrecourse deductions for a particular tax year are equal to the net increase in partnership minimum gain for the year reduced by aggregate distributions of proceeds arising from a nonrecourse liability that is distributed to the partners.[25] This definition also gives rise to its natural opposite, i.e., a net decrease of partnership minimum gain. Finally, if there is a book-tax disparity for a property subject to a nonrecourse liability, the minimum gain calculations are based on the property's *book* value.

After we determine the amount of nonrecourse deductions, we must then allocate them to the partners, like we do with other partnership items. The full explication of this with respect to nonrecourse deductions is addressed later in this chapter. For present purposes, it is sufficient to understand that nonrecourse deductions need to be allocated in accordance with the partner's interest in the partnership;[26] this is satisfied if, among other things, the partnership agreement provides that the nonrecourse deductions will be allocated in a manner that is reasonably consistent with allocations that have substantial economic effect for some other significant item attributable to the underlying property.[27] For simplicity in the examples, we will assume that the general profit and loss sharing percentages meet this requirement (though, we will cover this in earnest later).

Partners' Share of Partnership Minimum Gain

Now that we have discussed nonrecourse liabilities, partnership minimum gain, and nonrecourse deductions, we can now turn to determining the partners' share of that partnership minimum gain,[28] which is the first part of determining a partner's share of the nonrecourse liabilities. A partner's share of partnership minimum gain is calculated as (1) the sum of the (i) amount of nonrecourse deductions allocated to the partner and (ii) distributions made to that partner from proceeds of a nonrecourse liability (allocable to an increase in partnership minimum gain), less (2) the sum of (i) the

---

24. Treas. Reg. § 1.704-2(c).
25. Id.
26. Treas. Reg. § 1.704-2(b)(1). Recall that a partner's interest in the partnership is the only permitted allocated method when it is impossible for the allocation to have substantial economic effect. *See* Chapter 4.
27. Treas. Reg. § 1.704-2(e)(2).
28. Treas. Reg. § 1.752-3(a)(1).

partner's aggregate share of net decrease in partnership minimum gain and (ii) the share of decrease resulting from revaluations of partnership property subject to nonrecourse liabilities.[29] In other words, that equation is:

Calculating a Partner's Share of Partnership Minimum Gain
+ Nonrecourse deductions allocated to the partner
+ Distributions from proceeds of a nonrecourse liability
− Partner's aggregate share of net decrease in partnership minimum gain
− Share of decrease resulting from revaluations of property subject to nonrecourse liabilities
= Partner's share of partnership minimum gain

Section 704(c) Gain

The second tier in allocating nonrecourse liabilities is the amount of gain allocated to the partner under § 704(c) if the partnership disposed of property subject to a nonrecourse liability for an amount in full satisfaction of the liability.[30] The full import of § 704(c) was discussed in the last chapter. As a quick review, the purpose of § 704(c) is to ensure that built-in gain or loss for contributed property is allocated to the contributing partner; it is an anti-income shifting provision. As we previously discussed, § 704(c) typically manifests in two situations. First, when a piece of contributed property is disposed of, that built-in gain or loss needs to be allocated in a manner that takes into account the pre-contribution gain or loss.[31] Second, if the contributed property is subject to cost recovery (e.g., depreciation), § 704(c) requires that those items be shared between the partners to account for the built-in gain or loss.

Partner's Share of Excess Nonrecourse Liabilities

The third tier in allocating nonrecourse liabilities is the "partner's share of the excess nonrecourse liabilities."[32] Excess recourse liabilities are those liabilities that are not allocated under the first two items (i.e., partnership minimum gain and § 704(c) gain). The partner's share of excess

---

29. Treas. Reg. § 1.704-2(g).
30. Treas. Reg. § 1.752-3(a)(2).
31. For § 704(c), take note that property initially purchased by the partnership (rather than contributed by a partner) can become § 704(c) property if the partnership revalues capital accounts. See Treas. Reg. § 1.704-3(a)(6). Such property is often referred to as "reverse § 704(c) property"; perhaps "*deemed* § 704(c) property" would be a more apt name.
32. Treas. Reg. § 1.752-3(a)(3).

6. Partnership Liabilities

nonrecourse liabilities needs to be determined in accordance with the partner's "interest in partnership profits."[33] This is determined by considering all the facts and circumstances. Importantly, the partnership agreement can specify the partners' interest in partnership profits for this purpose, as long as that allocation is "reasonably consistent" with allocations that have substantial economic effect for some other significant item of partnership income or gain.[34] The regulations refer to this as the "significant item method."[35]

Alternatively, the excess nonrecourse liabilities can be allocated in a manner that the partnership "reasonably expects" that deductions attributable to those nonrecourse liabilities will be allocated; this is known as the "alternative method."[36] In addition to the significant item and alternative methods, the regulations also permit a partnership to allocate excess nonrecourse liabilities to a partner up to the amount of that partner's § 704(c) gain and then the remaining amount of excess nonrecourse liabilities under one of the other methods; this is known as the "additional method."[37]

Now that we have unpacked the elements of allocating nonrecourse liabilities, let's try a simple example. D and E form the DE Partnership, in which D contributes $15,000 and E contributes $10,000. The partnership then purchases commercial real estate for $100,000, using $25,000 in cash and financing the balance with a nonrecourse liability; the nonrecourse liability is a note for five years with interest-only payments and a balloon payment of the full principal balance at the end of Year 5. The partnership agreement agrees to allocate partnership items, including profits and excess nonrecourse liabilities, 60% to D and 40% to E. Further assume that, except for depreciation, items of income equal items of loss, and that the building's depreciation is $10,000 per year. The partnership agreement satisfies the elements for the main economic effect test.

After formation and the purchase of the commercial real estate, the balance sheet is as follows, but note that this is *incomplete* because it does not account for the outside basis impact of the nonrecourse liability (as this part of the chapter is building up to that the answer):

---

33. Id.
34. Id.
35. Id.
36. Id.
37. Id.

6. Partnership Liabilities

DE Partnership						
Assets				*Liabilities*		
	Tax	Book				$75,000
Commercial property	$100,000	$100,000				
				Capital Accounts		
					Tax	Book
			D		$15,000	$15,000
			E		$10,000	$10,000
Total	$100,000	$100,000	Total		$25,000	$100,000

It is important to note that neither the purchase of the property nor the partnership's nonrecourse loan affected the capital accounts for D and E. It would be tempting to think there is now *imbalance* in the *balance* sheet, but that is not true for the book value columns. When we add the book value of the liability ($75,000) to the book values of D and E ($25,000), that right-hand side total book value equals the left-hand side total book value ($100,000). But we do have a *basis imbalance*—that's because we have not yet done the full § 752 analysis; recall what are we trying to ultimately answer here: the allocation of the nonrecourse liabilities to the partners, which will be treated as a contribution of money for outside basis purposes. Indeed, we observe a $75,000 imbalance in the right-hand side tax column because we have not allocated the liability, which is treated as a contribution of money and results in an increase in the partners' outside basis.

We now turn to finding the partners' share of nonrecourse liabilities. A partner's share of nonrecourse liabilities is the sum of the three tiers: (1) the partner's share of partnership minimum gain, (2) the partner's § 704(c) gain on property subject to nonrecourse liabilities, and (3) the partner's share of excess nonrecourse liabilities. We also need to be mindful of the point in time that we are calculating this because of the ebb and flow of partnership minimum gain. Let's first consider the moment immediately after the nonrecourse financing.

First, we must calculate the partnership minimum gain. At the purchase of the commercial real estate, there has not been any depreciation, so the property has a tax and book basis of $100,000. Given that the nonrecourse liability is still $75,000, there is no partnership minimum gain because no gain would be realized if it were sold in full satisfaction of the liability.[38] Because the property was purchased and not contributed, there is no § 704(c) gain. Therefore, the full $75,000 loan constitutes an excess

---

38. The deemed amount realized ($75,000) does not exceed the tax basis ($100,000), so no gain would occur on the hypothetical sale.

6. Partnership Liabilities

nonrecourse liability because none of it was accounted for by the first two items. The partnership agreement allocates excess nonrecourse liabilities 60% to D and 40% to E, which is reasonably consistent with an allocation with substantial economic effect of some other significant partnership item (i.e., the sharing of partnership profits). Consequently, the $75,000 of nonrecourse liabilities will be allocated $45,000 to D and $30,000 to E. Under § 752, this allocation is treated as a contribution by D and E of that amount, which concomitantly increases their outside basis.

The impact of the allocation of the nonrecourse liabilities is demonstrated in the following restated (and now correct) balance sheet:

DE Partnership (restated)					
Assets			Liabilities		
	Tax	Book			$75,000
Commercial property	$100,000	$100,000			
			Capital Accounts		
				Tax	Book
			D	$60,000	$15,000
			E	$40,000	$10,000
Total	$100,000	$100,000	Total	$100,000	$100,000

We now readily observe that the left-hand side and the right-hand side columns match and balance after the applying § 752's rule of treating allocation of nonrecourse liabilities as contributions of money, which increase a partner's outside basis. Take note, moreover, that the above balance sheet does not yet reflect the depreciation on the commercial property ($10,000 per year); accounting for that depreciation would reduce D and E's basis and capital accounts by $6,000 and $4,000, respectively, which would be as follows:

DE Partnership (end of Year 1)					
Assets			Liabilities		
	Tax	Book Value			$75,000
Commercial property	$90,000	$90,000			
			Capital Accounts		
				Tax	Book
			D	$54,000	$9,000
			E	$36,000	$6,000
Total	$90,000	$90,000	Total	$90,000	$90,000

6. Partnership Liabilities

Let's continue the same example into Year 2. For simplicity, again assume that items of income equal items of expenses, except for depreciation, which is still $10,000. At the end of Year 2, we need to assess the allocation of the nonrecourse liabilities, using the three-step process. Like before, there is still no partnership minimum gain, because the adjusted basis of the property, now $80,000 (reflecting the Year 2 depreciation), is still greater than the amount of the nonrecourse liabilities ($75,000). Because the property was not contributed, there is no § 704(c) gain. So, all the nonrecourse liabilities are considered excess nonrecourse liabilities under tier 3, which are allocated in accordance with the specified sharing of partnership profits. Thus, the allocation of the nonrecourse liabilities does not change. The balance sheet at the end Year 2 is as follows:

DE Partnership (end of Year 2)					
Assets			Liabilities		
	Tax	Book			$75,000
Commercial property	$80,000	$80,000			
			Capital Accounts		
				Tax	Book
			D	$48,000	$3,000
			E	$32,000	$2,000
Total	$80,000	$80,000	Total	$80,000	$80,000

Year 3 is more interesting because it gives rise to partnership minimum gain. After the $10,000 of depreciation in Year 3, the amount of the nonrecourse liability ($75,000) now exceeds the adjusted basis of the property ($70,000) by $5,000, which is now the amount of partnership minimum gain. It is worth emphasizing that we now also have the first net increase in partnership minimum gain under Treas. Reg. § 1.704-2. That is, the partnership minimum gain at the end of Year 2 was zero, and the partnership minimum gain at the end of Year 3 was $5,000, resulting in a net increase of $5,000, year-over-year. Now that we have a net increase in partnership minimum gain, we have nonrecourse deductions in the same amount ($5,000). These nonrecourse deductions will be allocated in the 60%/40% manner as the other items (we discuss a full treatment of nonrecourse deductions later in this chapter). Therefore, D and E have $3,000 and $2,000 of nonrecourse deductions, respectively. We must therefore compute their share of the partnership minimum gain:

6. Partnership Liabilities

	Calculating a Partner's Share of Partnership Minimum Gain	D	E
+	Nonrecourse deductions allocated to the partner	$3,000	$2,000
+	Distributions from proceeds of a nonrecourse liability	0	0
−	Partner's aggregate share of net decrease in partnership minimum gain	0	0
−	Share of decrease resulting from revaluations of property subject to nonrecourse liabilities	0	0
=	Partner's share of partnership minimum gain	$3,000	$2,000

Under the first part of our nonrecourse liability allocation, D and E are allocated $3,000 and $2,000 of the nonrecourse liability, respectively.

Second, and like before, there is not any § 704(c) gain because the property was purchased, not contributed. Third, the excess nonrecourse liabilities are now $70,000 (as $5,000 was allocated as partnership minimum gain). The $70,000 will be allocated 60%/40% per the partnership agreement; thus, D and E are allocated $42,000 and $28,000, respectively. In total, then, D is allocated $45,000 of the nonrecourse liability, and E is allocated $30,000 of the liability. After Year 3, therefore, the partnership balance sheet looks as follows:

DE Partnership (end of Year 3)					
Assets			*Liabilities*		$75,000
	Tax	Book Value			
Commercial property	$70,000	$70,000			
			Capital Accounts		
				Tax	Book Value
			D	$42,000	($3,000)
			E	$28,000	($2,000)
Total	$70,000	$70,000	Total	$70,000	$70,000

Note that, although D and E now have deficit capital account balances, it is not problematic because they have deficit restoration obligations, and the partnership agreement satisfied the main test for economic effect. Let's also review why D and E's outside tax bases are $42,000 and $28,000, respectively. Partner D started with an initial outside basis of $15,000 due to his cash contribution. Over the three years, he has been allocated a total of $18,000 in depreciation, which caused a reduction in outside basis. And, his current Year 3 allocation of the nonrecourse liability is $45,000. The sum of those amounts equals $42,000. For partner E, his initial outside basis was $10,000; he was allocated $12,000 of depreciation over the three

6. Partnership Liabilities

years; and his current share of the nonrecourse liabilities is $30,000. The sum of those amounts equals $28,000.[39]

Before we turn to the next subject, it is worth emphasizing the simplicity of the above example, which needed basically an analysis of excess nonrecourse liabilities. You can readily appreciate how much more complex this could be once we need to consider the implications of § 704(c) in this analysis. In other words, be mindful that a proper analysis of allocating nonrecourse liabilities can also necessitate the need to consider the interaction of other topics discussed so far, such as the traditional rule, ceiling rule, and the like, if applicable.

ALLOCATING NONRECOURSE DEDUCTIONS

In Chapter 4, we covered partnership allocations. Those rules allow the partnership flexibility in tailoring the sharing of partnership tax items between partners, but that tailoring will be respected only if it bears substantial economic effect. The purpose of that rule is to pair economic benefits and burdens with tax benefits and burdens. As we discussed there, it is a mirroring principle centering around "skin in the game"—that is, a partner should not get a tax benefit (like a tax loss) if that same partner does not bear the economic burden of that item (the economic loss). Similarly, in Chapter 5, we saw how § 704(c) seeks to prevent shifting of pre-contribution gain or loss. This is related to the general benefit-burden principle in § 704(b); a partner should have to bear the economic and tax benefits and burdens relating to their contributed property allocable to the period he or she owned it—in other words, a partner should not be able to use a partnership to purge built-in gain or loss.

With respect to nonrecourse liabilities, however, no partner bears the economic risk of loss due to the nonrecourse nature of the debt. Consequently, allocation of loss or deduction items attributable to nonrecourse liabilities do not have substantial economic effect. Stated more directly, the lender bears the economic risk of loss, not any particular partner. Because of that, allocations attributable to nonrecourse liabilities (known as nonrecourse deductions) need to be allocated in accordance with the partners' interest in the partnership.[40] This general framework was noted earlier in the chapter, and we dive deeper into it now.

The regulations provide a test that, if satisfied, will deem allocations of nonrecourse deductions to be made in accordance with the partners' interest in the partnership. If that test is not satisfied, however, then the

---

39. These analyses, such as the impact of depreciation and the nonrecourse liability allocations, are done on a year-by-year basis. It was presented as an aggregate here for simplicity.
40. Treas. Reg. § 1.704-2(b)(1).

6. Partnership Liabilities

nonrecourse deductions must be allocated "according to the partners' overall economic interest in the partnership."[41]

The safe-harbor test for allocations of nonrecourse deductions has four parts. First, for the "full term of the partnership," the partnership must abide the (i) capital account maintenance requirement, (ii) the liquidating distribution requirement, and (iii) partners with deficit capital accounts have an unconditional deficit restoration obligation or agree to a qualified income offset.[42] Thus, the first part of this test requires the partnership agreement to satisfy either the main or alternate test for economic effect under § 704(b) and Treas. Reg. § 1.704-1.

Second, in the first taxable year in which the partnership has nonrecourse deductions, the partnership agreement provides for "allocations of nonrecourse deductions in a manner that is *reasonably consistent* with allocations that have substantial economic effect of some other significant partnership item attributable to the property securing the nonrecourse liabilities."[43] This requirement must be met for the entire term of the partnership after the time when the partnership first has nonrecourse deductions.

Third, in the first taxable year in which the partnership has nonrecourse deductions or makes a distribution of proceeds from a nonrecourse liability that is allocable to partnership minimum gain, the partnership agreement contains a "minimum gain chargeback" provision.[44] This requirement must be met for the entire term of the partnership. A minimum gain chargeback provision is discussed in more detail shortly.

Fourth, "[a]ll other material allocations and capital account adjustments under the partnership agreement are recognized under § 1.704-1(b)."[45] This last requirement pairs with the first requirement. When put together, this test essentially requires the partnership to act in accordance with the § 704(b) regulations. A summary table of the safe harbor test for allocations of nonrecourse deductions follows.

Safe Harbor Test for Allocations of Nonrecourse Deductions [§ 1.704-2(e)]
1. Partnership agreement satisfies main or alternate test for economic effect.
2. Partnership agreement provides for allocations of nonrecourse deductions that are "reasonably consistent" with other allocation that has substantial economic effect relating to the property.
3. Partnership agreement has a minimum gain chargeback provision.
4. All other material allocations and capital account adjustments are recognized under § 1.704-1(b).

---

41. Id.
42. Treas. Reg. § 1.704-2(e)(1).
43. Treas. Reg. § 1.704-2(e)(2) (emphasis added).
44. Treas. Reg. § 1.704-2(e)(3).
45. Treas. Reg. § 1.704-2(e)(4). There is a carveout exception for allocations of adjusted tax basis and amount realized under I.R.C. § 613A(c)(7)(D) under Treas. Reg. § 1.704-1(b)(4)(v).

6. Partnership Liabilities

The regulations also define what constitutes a minimum gain chargeback provision. We saw earlier what happens with *increases* in partnership minimum gain—that is, we tie the allocation of nonrecourse deductions (and ultimately nonrecourse liabilities) to annual net increases in partnership minimum gain. The minimum gain chargeback provision relates to *decreases* in partnership minimum gain. If the partnership has a net decrease in partnership minimum gain for the taxable year, the minimum gain chargeback provision is triggered, and it requires that "each partner must be allocated items of partnership income and gain for that year equal to that partner's share of the net decrease in partnership minimum gain."[46] The partner's share of the net decrease in partnership minimum gain is defined as "the amount of the total net decrease multiplied by the partner's percentage share of the partnership's minimum gain at the end of the immediately preceding taxable year."[47]

Let's consider an example that incorporates some of the above concepts.[48] F and G form a limited partnership to purchase and rent commercial real property (a strip mall), in which F will be the limited partner and G will be the general partner. F contributes $18,000 and G contributes $2,000. The partnership then obtains a nonrecourse loan for $80,000, which is an interest-only loan with a balloon payment for the full principal amount due after five years. The partnership then purchases a strip mall for $100,000.

The partnership agreement provides that the partnership will properly maintain capital accounts and will make liquidating distributions in accordance with positive capital account balances. It further provides that G will need to restore any deficit in his capital account; F, as a limited partner, does not have this obligation. The agreement also contains a qualified income offset provision and a minimum gain chargeback provision. It is stipulated that none of the items in Treas. Reg. § 1.704-1(b)(2)(ii)(d)(4), (5), or (6) will cause or increase a deficit balance in F's capital account. Other than required from the qualified income offset and minimum gain chargeback provisions, tax items will be allocated 90% to F and 10% to G until the first time in which items of income and gain exceed items of loss and deduction; after that time, items will be allocated equally. The partnership agreement also specifies that it will use the significant-item method for allocating nonrecourse liabilities.

Before securing the financing and purchasing the property, the partnership balance sheet looks as follows:

---

46. Treas. Reg. § 1.704-2(f)(1).
47. Treas. Reg. § 1.704-2(g)(2).
48. Based on Example 1 of Treas. Reg. § 1.704-2(m).

6. Partnership Liabilities

FG Limited Partnership					
Assets			Liabilities		
	Tax	Book			0
Cash	$20,000	$20,000			
			Capital Accounts		
				Tax	Book
			F	$18,000	$18,000
			G	$2,000	$2,000
Total	$20,000	$20,000	Total	$20,000	$20,000

Upon the nonrecourse financing and purchase of the strip mall—before we can tackle the Year 1 operations—let's allocate the nonrecourse liabilities. Recall that a partner's share of the nonrecourse liabilities of a partnership is the sum of the three tiers: (1) the partner's share of partnership minimum gain, (2) the partner's § 704(c) gain, if any, assuming the partnership disposed of all the property subject to nonrecourse liabilities for an amount equal to the satisfaction of the liability, and (3) the partner's share of excess nonrecourse liabilities. Upon the purchase of the strip mall, there is no partnership minimum gain because the amount of the nonrecourse liability ($80,000) is not more than its book basis ($100,000). Moreover, there is no § 704(c) gain because the property was not contributed by a partner. The third tier (excess nonrecourse liabilities) operates, and the partnership agreement provided that nonrecourse liabilities will be allocated 90%/10%, which is consistent with the underlying tax item allocation, and thus consistent with the significant-item method. Consequently, after securing the financing and purchasing the strip mall, the balance sheet would look as follows:

FG Limited Partnership					
Assets			Liabilities		
	Tax	Book			$80,000
Strip mall	$100,000	$100,000			
			Capital Accounts		
				Tax	Book
			F	$90,000	$18,000
			G	$10,000	$2,000
Total	$100,000	$100,000	Total	$100,000	$100,000

Take note that F's basis was increased by $72,000 (90% of the $80,000 liability) under § 752, and G's basis was increased by $8,000 (10% of the $80,000 liability) for the same reason.

6. Partnership Liabilities

In Year 1, the partnership generates rental income of $9,500, interest expense of $8,000, other operating expenses of $1,000, and depreciation of $9,000; together, these items result in a tax loss of $8,500, which is allocated $7,650 and $850 to F and G, respectively. After Year 1, therefore, the partnership balance sheet would be as follows:

FG Limited Partnership (end of Year 1)					
Assets			Liabilities		
	Tax	Book			$80,000
Strip mall	$91,000	$91,000			
Cash	$500	$500	Capital Accounts		
				Tax	Book
			F	$82,350	$10,350
			G	$9,150	$1,150
Total	$91,500	$91,500	Total	$91,500	$91,500

As shown on the balance sheet, there is now a "Cash" asset on the balance sheet—the partnership received $9,500 in rental income and paid expenses of $9,000, and let's assume that all payments were made in cash. In any event, it's important to emphasize that, although the partnership had a tax loss, the depreciation expense (which essentially caused that loss) is a noncash expense. Further take note that adding the cash asset is what equalizes the left-hand and right-hand side of the balance sheet.

Assume that the partnership has the same results from operations in Year 2. Consequently, at the end of Year 2, the balance sheet would look as follows:

FG Limited Partnership (end of Year 2)					
Assets			Liabilities		
	Adj. Basis	Book Value			$80,000
Strip mall	$82,000	$82,000			
Cash	$1,000	$1,000	Capital Accounts		
				Adj. Basis	Book Value
			F	$74,700	$2,700
			G	$8,300	$300
Total	$83,000	$83,000	Total	$83,000	$83,000

The balance sheet reflects the additional $500 in cash and the deductions for depreciation across the book and basis columns. Again, take note that, as of the end of Year 2, there are still no recourse deductions because there

6. Partnership Liabilities

is not yet any partnership minimum gain, as the adjusted basis of the strip mall exceeds the nonrecourse liability. That changes, however, in Year 3.

In Year 3, assume the same results from operations as in Years 1 and 2, i.e., a net taxable loss of $8,500. If the partnership were to dispose of the property in full satisfaction of the nonrecourse liability, it would now recognize $7,000 of gain, that is, the amount of the liability ($80,000) in excess of the adjusted basis as of the end of Year 3 ($73,000). The partnership thus has a net increase in partnership minimum gain because there was no partnership minimum gain at the end of Year 2 and there is now $7,000 of partnership minimum gain at the end of Year 3. Because of that, we now have $7,000 in nonrecourse deductions (the amount of the net increase in the partnership minimum gain). The $7,000 in nonrecourse deductions consists of the depreciation deduction allocable to the building.

As we've been doing in this problem, tax items are shared 90% to F and 10% to G, which includes allocation of nonrecourse deductions. Here, this allocation of nonrecourse deduction satisfies the safe-harbor test in Treas. Reg. § 1.704-2(e) because it is reasonably consistent with allocations that have substantial economic effect with respect to the underlying property, and the other requirements of the safe harbor are met (e.g., having a minimum gain chargeback provision). In other words, it's helpful to think of the aggregate $8,500 loss as consisting of two items: (i) net loss without the nonrecourse deductions of $1,500, and (ii) the nonrecourse deductions of $7,000, each of which are allocated 90%/10%. Drilling down on the capital account changes in Year 3 would reveal the following:

Capital Accounts		
	F	G
	Book	Book
End of Year 2	$2,700	$300
Net loss (not including nonrecourse deductions)	($1,350)	($150)
Nonrecourse deductions	($6,300)	($700)
Ending balance	($4,950)	($550)

We now observe deficit balances in the capital accounts. For G, this is not problematic because he has a deficit restoration obligation. For F, however, we need to think more carefully about this because F does *not* have a deficit restoration obligation. Treas. Reg. § 1.704-2(g)(1), however, provides that "a partner's share of partnership minimum gain is added to the limited dollar amount, if any, of the deficit balance in the partner's capital account that the partner is obligated to restore."[49] In this case, then, F is *deemed* to

---

49. Treas. Reg. § 1.704-2(g)(1).

6. Partnership Liabilities

have a deficit restoration obligation in the amount of $6,300, which is his share of the partnership minimum gain. Consequently, under the alternate test, given the deemed deficit restoration obligation of F, the allocation has economic effect, notwithstanding the creation of the deficit balance for F.

It is important to realize why the regulations allow for this deemed deficit restoration obligation for F. Recall why the regulations reject tax allocations that create or increase capital account deficits for those without deficit restoration obligations: the partner would get more flow-through tax loss than his or her economic contribution; in other words, it upends the guiding principle that tax benefits and burdens should follow economic benefits and burdens.

The minimum gain chargeback provision, however, solves this concern. The minimum gain chargeback provision requires that, once it is triggered, "each partner must be allocated items of partnership income and gain for that year equal to that partner's share of the net decrease in partnership minimum gain,"[50] and it is triggered upon *net decreases* in partnership minimum gain.[51] What would cause a *decrease* in partnership minimum gain? One way is if the partnership sold the strip mall. Let's consider this next.

For simplicity, let's now assume that, in the beginning of Year 4, the partnership sells the strip mall, and its other income and expenses are equal, such that there is no net income or loss. If the partnership sells the strip mall for full satisfaction of the nonrecourse liability (presently $80,000), its partnership minimum gain would decrease from $7,000 to $0. That is, year over year, there has now been a net decrease in partnership minimum gain of $7,000 — in Year 3, the partnership minimum gain was $7,000 and now in Year 4 it is $0, which is a net decrease of $7,000. Because we have a decrease in partnership minimum gain, the minimum gain chargeback provision is triggered. The triggered minimum gain chargeback provision now requires that, in Year 4, each partner be allocated items of income and gain equal to his or her share of the net decrease in partnership minimum gain.

A partner's share of the net decrease in partnership minimum gain is defined as "the amount of the total net decrease multiplied by the partner's percentage share of the partnership's minimum gain at the end of the immediately preceding taxable year."[52] That is provided in the following table:

---

50. Treas. Reg. § 1.704-2(f)(1).
51. Id.
52. Treas. Reg. § 1.704-2(g)(2).

6. Partnership Liabilities

	Partner's Share of Net Decrease in PMG				
	Total PMG End of Y3 [A]	Partner's Share PMG End of Y3 [B]	Percentage Share PMG Y3 [B/A]	Total Net PMG Decrease Y4 [C]	Partner's Share of Decrease [C*(B/A)]
Partner F	$7,000	$6,300	90%	$7,000	$6,300
Partner G	$7,000	$700	10%	$7,000	$700

Consequently, with the sale of the strip mall, the minimum gain chargeback provision requires that F and G be allocated $6,300 and $700, respectively, of the gain from that sale.

The above example comprehensively shows the interaction of the allocation of nonrecourse liabilities, nonrecourse deductions, and minimum gain chargeback provisions. As you zoom out, be mindful of how the regulations try to ensure the matching of economic and tax benefits and burdens. The theme of the latter part of this chapter has been that it is more difficult to do this with nonrecourse liabilities due to the lack of personal obligation on the underlying debt repayment. The regulations patch that, in essence, by requiring that the nonrecourse deductions be tied to how items of gain and profit will be shared with respect to the underlying property.[53] The minimum gain chargeback provision, moreover, ensures that if a nonrecourse deduction causes or increases a deficit capital account balance, that a disposition of the asset will require a pairing of items of income and gain to offset that deficit.

Examples

1. Aimee contributes property with an adjusted basis of $100,000 and a value of $500,000 to a partnership in exchange for a one-third partnership interest. Prior to her contribution, the partnership does not have any liabilities. Aimee's property is subject to a recourse debt of $15,000. After her contribution, Aimee remains personally liable on the note and state law would not impute a liability to the other partners. Evaluate Aimee's basis in her partnership interest as a result of this transaction.

2. Bryon and Coral form a partnership by each contributing $350,000 in cash. After formation, the partnership purchases depreciable equipment for $3,500,000, paying $700,000 in cash and executing a note in favor of the seller for the difference. The note is executed on behalf of the

---

53. And those rules are based on the ironclad rule that the owner of property subject to nonrecourse debt cannot dispose of that property—even by abandonment—without having to include, at a minimum, the amount of the nonrecourse debt as an amount realized upon disposition of the property.

6. Partnership Liabilities

partnership. The partnership agreement provides that Bryon and Coral will share partnership items equally, except for losses, which will be allocated 75% to Bryon and 25% to Coral. The partnership agreement provides for the required items for the main test for economic effect. Evaluate whether the note represents a recourse or nonrecourse liability and how the partners must allocate the liability.

3. Dottie, Emili, and Fiona are equal members of DEF, LLC, which is taxed as a partnership for federal income tax purposes. The LLC borrows $10,000,000 from Big Bank. Dottie agrees to guarantee payment up to $3,000,000 of the liability if any amount of the full liability is not recovered by Big Bank. Emili agrees to guarantee payment up to $2,000,000, but only if Big Bank recovers less than $2,000,000. Dottie and Emili also agree to waive any right of contribution between the two of them. Evaluate the consequences under § 752 of this liability and guarantee arrangement.

4. Gwynn and Harvey form GH, LLC, in which they are equal members and that is taxed as a partnership for federal income tax purposes. At the beginning of the year, the LLC purchases depreciable property for $550,000, using a purchase money note in the name of the LLC. The note provides for interest-only payments for four years with a balloon payment due in the fifth year. The operating agreement provides that members will share tax items equally. The property depreciates at $110,000 per year. Evaluate the allocation of the liability at (i) the time of the equipment purchase and (ii) the end of the first year, incorporating the annual depreciation.

5. Gwynn and Harvey (described in Example 4) alternatively decide to allocate depreciation exclusively to Gwynn. The operating agreement further provides that it will allocate excess nonrecourse liabilities in the manner that it is reasonably expected that the deductions attributable to those nonrecourse liabilities will be allocated. For this problem, moreover, you may assume that the depreciation allocation comports with the § 704(b) requirements. Evaluate the allocation of the nonrecourse liability immediately after the purchase of the depreciable property.

6. Isabel and Jenna form the IJ Partnership in which they are equal partners. Isabel contributes $500,000 of cash in exchange for her partnership interest. Jenna contributes two pieces of property in exchange for her partnership interest. The first property, Redacre, has a value of $500,000 and a basis of $300,000; it is subject to a nonrecourse liability of $350,000. The second property, Greenacre, has a value of $850,000 and a basis of $300,000; it is subject to a nonrecourse liability of $500,000. After the formation, the partnership refinances the liabilities into a single $850,000 nonrecourse liability. The partnership agreement provides that excess nonrecourse liabilities will be allocated in accordance with the

6. Partnership Liabilities

"additional method" provided for in the § 1.752-3 regulation and any remaining amounts allocated equally between the partners. Evaluate the how the nonrecourse liabilities are allocated between Isabel and Jenna immediately after the refinancing.

Explanations

1. This problem involves some of the basic rules and definitions of Treas. Reg. § 1.752-1.[54] The first issue to consider is the impact of contributing property subject to a liability. The regulation provides that, "[i]f property is contributed by a partner to the partnership or distributed by the partnership to a partner and the property is subject to a liability of the transferor, the transferee is treated as having assumed the liability, to the extent that the amount of the liability does not exceed the fair market value of the property at the time of the contribution or distribution."[55] Consequently, the partnership is deemed to have assumed the entire liability because the property's value exceeds the amount of the liability. This deemed assumption causes Aimee's individual liabilities to decrease by $15,000. At the same time, however, her share of partnership liabilities has increased by $15,000. In other words, because no other partner is liable for this debt (per the facts), she bears the partnership's deemed $15,000 liability. The regulations further provide that, if a partner has an increase and decrease of liabilities (at the partner or partnership levels), then § 752 considers only the *net increase* or *net decrease*.[56] As applied here, then, Aimee has no *net change* in her liabilities, and therefore she is not treated as having contributed or received money under § 752. Her basis in the partnership interest is $100,000 (the basis of her contributed property under the normal contribution rules).

2. The example first requires us to determine whether a partner bears an economic risk of loss.[57] A partner bears an economic risk of loss if he or she would be required to make a payment to any person upon a constructive liquidation. The constructive liquidation analysis requires us to evaluate the consequences if all the following simultaneously occur: (1) all partnership liabilities become payable in full, (2) all partnership assets are worthless, (3) the partnership disposes of all property in a taxable transaction for no consideration, (4) partnership tax items are then allocated, and (5) the partnership liquidates.[58]

---

54. This is based on Example 1 of Treas. Reg. § 1.752-1(g).
55. Treas. Reg. § 1.752-1(e).
56. Treas. Reg. § 1.752-1(f).
57. This is based on Example 1 of Treas. Reg. § 1.752-2(f)(1).
58. Treas. Reg. § 1.752-2(b)(1).

6. Partnership Liabilities

Given its single asset and single liability, the partnership's constructive liquidation analysis is straightforward. The partnership's $2,800,000 note becomes immediately payable. The equipment is now worthless and is sold for no consideration. This generates a $3,500,000 tax and book loss. That loss is allocated $2,625,000 to Bryon (75% of the loss) and $875,000 to Coral (25% of the loss). Those allocations would have the following impact on the partners' capital accounts.

Capital Account Adjustments for Hypothetical Liquidation		
	Bryon	Coral
	Book	Book
Initial contribution	$350,000	$350,000
Loss on hypothetical sale	($2,625,000)	($875,000)
Ending balance	($2,275,000)	($525,000)

The $2,800,000 liability is classified as a recourse liability because one or more partners bear an economic risk of loss for nonpayment. In other words, if the partnership did not repay the liability, Bryon and Coral would be obligated to jointly repay the full balance ($2,275,000 + $525,000 = $2,800,000), as the constructive liquidation analysis reveals.

Continuing the analysis, a partner's share of a recourse liability "equals the portion of that liability, if any, for which the partner or related person bears the economic risk of loss."[59] The amounts that the partners are obligated to make a payment (their economic risk of loss) is reflected in their deficit capital account balances. Bryon and Coral are therefore allocated $2,275,000 and $525,000, respectively, of the partnership liability. Finally, these amounts represent an increase of the partners' share of partnership liabilities and are therefore treated as additional contributions under § 752 by Bryon and Coral.

3. This example requires an analysis of "bottom dollar" guarantees.[60] Bottom dollar payment obligations are not recognized as an obligation to make a payment under § 752.[61] As applied to a guarantee, a bottom dollar payment obligation is one that is the same or similar as "any payment obligation other than one in which the partner or related person is or would be liable up to the full amount of such partner's or related person's payment obligation if, and to the extent that, any amount of the partnership liability is not otherwise satisfied."[62] In essence, we are

---

59. Treas. Reg. § 1.752-2(a).
60. This problem is based on Example 10 of Treas. Reg. § 1.752-2(f)(10).
61. Treas. Reg. § 1.752-2(b)(3); Treas. Reg. § 1.752-2(b)(3)(ii)(A).
62. Treas. Reg. § 1.752-2(b)(3)(ii)(C)(1)(i).

6. Partnership Liabilities

evaluating whether the guarantees made by these members should be respected as actually bearing an economic risk of loss. A concern with bottom dollar arrangements is that they are "structured to insulate the obligor from having to pay their obligations."[63]

Dottie's guarantee is *not* a bottom dollar payment obligation. This is because her guarantee is triggered if *any amount* of the full liability is not recovered. Emili's guarantee, however, is a bottom dollar payment obligation. This is because Emili is obligated to pay *if and only if and to the extent* that Big Bank recovers less than $2,000,000. So, for example, if Big Bank recovers $3,000,000, Emili's guarantee would not be triggered, even though the Bank is still owed $7,000,000 more (note, though, Dottie's guarantee *would* be triggered here). Because it is a bottom dollar payment obligation, it is not recognized as a payment obligation; therefore, Emili does not bear any economic risk of loss for the liability.

To recap, let's ensure that we appreciate the economic difference between Dottie and Emili's guarantees. Dottie guarantees up to $3,000,000 if *any* amount of the debt is not recovered. So, if Big Bank recovers $4 million, Dottie is "on the hook" for $3 million more. If Big Bank recovers $9 million, Dottie is on the hook for $1 million. Compare that with Emili's guarantee. As soon as Big Bank recovers more than $2 million, Emili is "off the hook." So, if Big Bank recovers $4 million—still $6 million short—Emili has no personal liability on her guarantee. As you can see, Dottie and Emili have substantially different repayment risks—Dottie's is much more likely to be triggered. Consequently, the regulations recognize this difference in the legitimacy of Dottie and Emili's economic risks of loss; it recognizes Dottie's but not Emili's. As well, it is important to emphasize that the fact that the guarantees have maximum limits are not relevant to the bottom dollar determination.[64]

Finally, we must allocate the liability under § 752. As noted above, Dottie's guarantee is respected as a payment obligation under Treas. Reg. § 1.752-2(a). Therefore, Dottie is allocated $3,000,000 due to bearing an economic risk of loss. The remaining $7,000,000 is allocated under Treas. Reg. § 1.752-3 as a nonrecourse liability (recall that members of an LLC are not personally liable for the entity's debts except as they agree to personally, like Dottie).

---

63. 84 Fed. Reg. 54014.

64. Treas. Reg. § 1.752-2(b)(3)(ii)(C)(2) ("A payment obligation is not a bottom dollar payment obligation merely because a maximum amount is placed on the partner's or related person's payment obligation, a partner's or related person's payment obligation is stated as a fixed percentage of every dollar of the partnership liability to which such obligation relates, or there is a right of proportionate contribution running between partners or related persons who are co-obligors with respect to a payment obligation for which each of them is jointly and severally liable.").

6. Partnership Liabilities

4. The initial issue here is to determine whether the note represents a recourse or a nonrecourse liability.[65] A recourse liability, of course, is one in which a partner would bear the economic risk of loss (i.e., have a payment obligation). In an LLC, however, members do not have personal liability for entity debts—unless, of course, a member agrees to guarantee the note, which did not happen here. Thus, the note represents a nonrecourse liability.[66]

    Nonrecourse liabilities are allocated under Treas. Reg. § 1.752-3. There are three tiers: (1) the partner's share of partnership minimum gain, (2) the amount of § 704(c) gain arising from a disposition of property subject to a nonrecourse liability, and (3) excess nonrecourse liabilities. Partnership minimum gain is the amount of gain, if any, if property subject to a nonrecourse liability were sold for no consideration other than full satisfaction of the liability.[67] Upon the date of purchase, there is no partnership minimum gain because the amount of the debt equals the basis of the property. Additionally, there is no § 704(c) gain because the property was not contributed. Therefore, the entire liability consists of excess nonrecourse liabilities. The default rule is that excess nonrecourse liabilities are allocated in accordance with the partner's share of partnership profits.[68] Because the partners share the profits equally, Gwynn and Harvey will share the allocation of the liability equally, i.e., $275,000 each. Under § 752, then, they are each treated as contributing an additional $275,000 to the partnership.

    At the end of the year, the analysis is different. The liability is still a nonrecourse liability. However, there is now partnership minimum gain. If the LLC were to sell the property in full satisfaction of the liability ($550,000), it would generate a tax gain of $110,000 (the property's adjusted basis after the Year 1 depreciation is $440,000). As relevant here, a partner's share of partnership minimum gain is equal to the sum of the nonrecourse deductions allocated to that partner.[69] The presence of partnership minimum gain also triggers the nonrecourse deduction rules. The amount of a partnership's nonrecourse deductions for a year, as relevant here, equals the net increase of the partnership minimum gain for the year. Here, that amount is $110,000. Allocations of nonrecourse deductions need to be in accordance with the partners' interest in the partnership. That requires, among other things, that they be allocated reasonably consistent with some other allocation that has

---

65. This is based on Example 1 of Treas. Reg. § 1.752-3(c).
66. Formally, we would need to do a full constructive liquidation analysis to arrive at this conclusion, but that is omitted because it has been addressed in prior examples.
67. Treas. Reg. § 1.704-2(d)(1).
68. Treas. Reg. § 1.752-3(a)(3).
69. Treas. Reg. § 1.704-2(g)(1).

6. Partnership Liabilities

substantial economic effect.[70] Here, that is satisfied because the members are sharing all tax items equally. Therefore, the nonrecourse deduction (the depreciation) will be shared equally between the members. Thus, each member is allocated $55,000 of the liability under the first tier of allocating nonrecourse liabilities. Like before, moreover, there is no § 704(c) gain. There remains $440,000 of the liability to be allocated under the last tier as excess nonrecourse liabilities, which will be shared equally in accordance with the members' profit-sharing agreement. In sum, Gwynn and Harvey are each allocated $55,000 under the first tier and $220,000 under the third tier of Treas. Reg. § 1.752-3.

5. This problem focuses on methods to allocate excess nonrecourse liabilities.[71] As described in the prior example, the default method to allocate excess nonrecourse liabilities is in accordance with the partner's interest in partnership profits. An alternative method provided by the regulation is that excess nonrecourse liabilities can be allocated "in accordance with the manner in which it is reasonably expected that the deductions attributable to those nonrecourse liabilities will be allocated."[72] The regulations label this the "alternative method."[73] At the time of purchase, there is neither partnership minimum gain nor is there § 704(c) gain; thus, all of the nonrecourse liability is to be allocated as excess nonrecourse liabilities. If the allocation to Gwynn of the depreciation is valid—and the facts stipulate that is the case—then she will be allocated all the excess nonrecourse liability because she will be receiving all the nonrecourse deductions with respect to the property. Consequently, Gwynn will be allocated the $550,000 nonrecourse liability.

6. The problem requires us to allocate a liability among multiple properties and to apply the "additional method."[74] As we've seen, nonrecourse liabilities are allocated in a three-tier manner as provided in Treas. Reg. § 1.752-3. The first tier allocates based on partnership minimum gain. Here there is no partnership minimum gain; if the properties were sold for the amount of the nonrecourse liability ($850,000), there would be no gain (as the combined book value is $500,000 + $850,000 = $1,350,000). It is important to recognize here that we used *book values* instead of *tax basis* in this particular partnership minimum gain calculation. The reason for that is found in the § 1.704-2 regulation, which provides that if property subject to one or more nonrecourse liabilities has a book-tax disparity

---

70. Treas. Reg. § 1.704-2(e).
71. This is based on Example 2 of Treas. Reg. § 1.752-3(c).
72. Treas. Reg. § 1.752-3(a)(3).
73. Id.
74. This is based on Example 3 of Treas. Reg. § 1.752-3(c).

6. Partnership Liabilities

(i.e., its tax basis differs from its book value), then book values are used for partnership minimum gain calculations.

The second tier is the amount of taxable gain that would be allocated under § 704(c) if the partnership disposed of the property subject to the liability in full satisfaction thereof. The issue here is that we have two properties now subject to a single nonrecourse liability. Thus, we need to allocate this single liability across these two properties to be able to calculate the resulting § 704(c) gain. The regulations provide that "if a partnership holds multiple properties subject to a single nonrecourse liability, the partnership may allocate the liability among the multiple properties under any reasonable method."[75] Importantly, "[a] method is not reasonable if it allocates to any item of property an amount of the liability that, when combined with any other liabilities allocated to the property, is in excess of the fair market value of the property at the time the liability is incurred."[76]

For this problem, let's assume that the partners agree to allocate the nonrecourse liability equally between the properties. Thus, it is like each property is subject to a $425,000 liability. We can now calculate the second tier (§ 704(c) gain) for each property. If Redacre were sold in full satisfaction of its $425,000 deemed liability, it would generate $125,000 of § 704(c) gain ($425,000 less $300,000), which would be allocable to Jenna. If Greenacre were sold in full satisfaction of its $425,000 deemed liability, it would generate $125,000 of gain ($425,000 less $300,000), which is likewise allocable to Jenna. Jenna would therefore be allocated a total of $250,000 of the nonrecourse liability under tier 2. Isabel has not been allocated any of the liability yet.

The third and last tier is excess nonrecourse liabilities. Those are liabilities that have not been allocated under the earlier tiers. Here, that is equal to $600,000 ($850,000 – $250,000). Excess nonrecourse liabilities can be allocated in several ways that are provided by the regulation. As noted in the facts, the partners have agreed to the "additional method." The additional method is a shorthand description for allocations that "first allocate an excess nonrecourse liability to a partner up to the amount of built-in gain that is allocable to the partner on section 704(c) property . . . where such property is subject to the nonrecourse liability to the extent that such built-in gain exceeds the gain described in [the second tier] with respect to such property."[77]

Applying the additional method here requires us to first allocate based on their remaining § 704(c) gain. Isabel did not contribute property, so she does not have any § 704(c) gain. Jenna did contribute

---

75. Treas. Reg. § 1.752-3(b)(1).
76. Id.
77. Treas. Reg. § 1.752-3(a)(3).

6. Partnership Liabilities

property with a book-tax disparity, so she has § 704(c) gain. Some of that § 704(c) gain was handled under the second tier, but not all of it. Redacre has $200,000 of built-in gain ($500,000 less $300,000), of which $125,000 was addressed in the second tier, meaning there remains $75,000 of built-in gain. Greenacre has $550,000 of built-in gain ($850,000 less $300,000), of which $125,000 was addressed in the second tier, meaning there remains $425,000 of built-in gain. Between the two properties, there is $500,000 of remaining built-in gain. Jenna is thus allocated an additional $500,000 of the nonrecourse liability. There is $100,000 of the nonrecourse liability remaining, which the partners have agreed to allocate equally; this allocation is respected, too, because it is in accordance with their interests in the partnership profits; Isabel and Jenna are each allocated $50,000 of the remaining liability. In summary, neither partner is allocated any of the liability under tier one (partnership minimum gain). Jenna is allocated $250,000 under tier two (§ 704(c) gain). Isabel and Jenna are allocated $50,000 and $550,000, respectively, under the third tier (excess nonrecourse liabilities) using the additional method.

Distributions and Payments from a Partnership

INTRODUCTION

In this chapter, we cover a topic that is critical to a partner: getting cash or property out of the partnership. Conceptually, there are several ways that a partner can get a payment of value—whether that is cash or property—out of a partnership. First, a partnership can make a distribution to its partners, which are known as operating (or "current") distributions; this is the partnership distributing the profits out to its partners. Second, the partner may exit the partnership, resulting in a termination of his or her interest, and, colloquially speaking, gets "paid out," which is known as a liquidating distribution. Third, the partner may be acting (i.e., contracting) with the partnership in a non-partner capacity, which the Code may respect and treat as non-partner payments, known as § 707(a) payments. Fourth, the partner may receive payments for services that are determined without regard to the profits of the partnership, which are known as § 707(c) guaranteed payments. This chapter addresses operating and liquidating distributions. The other types of payments are addressed in later chapters.

At the outset of this chapter, it is also important to be clear about some terminology. When we speak of a "distribution," we mean getting "stuff" out of (or from) the partnership. This is *not* to be confused with a partner's "distributive share" under § 704. This terminology is admittedly unfortunate. Although a partner annually is allocated a "distributive share" of tax items (like income and deduction) from a partnership, that does not mean that the partnership actually *distributed* cash or property to the partner. In other words, for example, a partner may receive a $100 distributive share of income but no present cash or property.[1] Importantly—and to emphasize—this partner must include $100 on his or her tax return *even* if no property is currently distributed. In sum, then, we need to be careful and precise with our language such that we don't confuse distributions with distributive income. Consequently, this book generally prefers using the term allocation or allocative share to describe § 704 flow-through of items of income, gain, loss, deduction, and the like because it further distinguishes the concept from distributions of property.

Throughout this chapter, we will continue to see the theme of aggregate versus entity approaches to partnership taxation. For example, given the nature of the distributive share of § 704, reviewed above, partners are taxed on their share of partnership items whether or not partnership assets are actually distributed. Conceptually, then, when a distribution of property occurs, it may be a distribution of property upon which the partner has already included in income; if so, the distribution itself is not a taxable event. This represents an aggregate theory of a partnership: The partnership is a group of partners that, in the aggregate, own proportionate parts of partnership property. The entity, then, is just a conduit through which tax consequences flow. Thus, when those assets are paid to them, it is simply a return of capital and not separately taxable; distinguishing between new capital and already-taxed capital is tracked through the concept of basis.

OPERATING DISTRIBUTIONS

The first kind of distribution covered by this chapter is known as an operating (or current) distribution. The regulations make a distinction between distributions that result in the "termination of a partner's entire interest in a partnership"[2] (i.e., liquidating distributions) and those that do not. Thus, if a distribution is not a liquidating distribution, the regulations classify it as a "current distribution."[3] The main rule for operating distributions is found in § 731, and it is relatively simple. It provides that "gain shall not be recognized to such partner, except to the extent that any money distributed exceeds the adjusted basis of such partner's interest in the partnership

---

1. This reinforces the need to carefully review and draft the provisions in a partnership or operating agreement concerning distributions. A well-drafted instrument will have provisions about "tax distributions," meaning the entity should make distributions to cover the tax costs associated with the distributive share of income items.
2. Treas. Reg. § 1.761-1(d).
3. Id.

7. Distributions and Payments from a Partnership

immediately before the distribution."[4] Loss is not recognized on operating distributions; loss can be recognized only on liquidating distributions.[5] Any gain or loss that is recognized under § 731 on an operating distribution is "considered as gain or loss from the sale or exchange of the partnership interest of the distributee partner."[6]

Stated more simply, operating distributions are not included in *income* (i.e., are income-tax free) and require only the recognition of *gain* when the partner receives more money than his or her outside basis. Now, at first blush, this may seem too good to be true because the distribution can be entirely income-tax free. But recall that as items of income and gain have been allocated to the partner under § 704—and therefore included in the partner's income—the partner has been increasing his or her outside basis commensurately with those flow-through items under § 705. Thus, to the extent a partner receives a distribution of property that is less than his or her outside basis, the partner has not received property that has not been taxed yet. In other words, to the extent that the partner has received a distribution of property less than outside basis, that property (or money) has already been included in the partner's income-tax base and does not represent an accession to wealth—it merely represents a return of already-taxed property (or money)!

Continuing this process of trying to track how much the distribution of property reflects already-taxed property, we need to consider how the distribution affects the partner's basis in the partnership (i.e., outside basis). Section 705 provides that a partner's outside basis is decreased by "distributions by the partnership as provided in section 733."[7] For its part, § 733 provides that, in the case of a distribution (other than a liquidating distribution), the partner's outside basis shall be reduced (but not below zero) by (1) the amount of money distributed to the partner and (2) the basis of property distributed to the partner determined under § 732. We will cover property distributions and § 732 shortly, but we first start with cash distributions.

Let's consider a very simple example here to illustrate these concepts. A and B form the AB Partnership, each contributing $10,000 in cash. At formation, the partnership balance sheet looks as follows:

---

4. I.R.C. § 731(a)(1).
5. *See* I.R.C. § 731(a)(2).
6. I.R.C. § 731(a) (flush language).
7. I.R.C. § 705.

7. Distributions and Payments from a Partnership

AB Partnership					
Assets			*Liabilities*		
	Basis	Book Value			
Cash	$20,000	$20,000			
			Capital Accounts		
				Basis	Book Value
			A	$10,000	$10,000
			B	$10,000	$10,000
Total	$20,000	$20,000	Total	$20,000	$20,000

If the partnership makes a distribution of $7,500 in cash to A, § 731 provides that no gain will be recognized by A, and §§ 705 and 732 provide that A must reduce his outside basis by $7,500. Conceptually, this makes sense—the distribution is equivalent to A receiving some of his initial contribution back, which is not an accession of wealth to A and it should not be treated as income (he's just getting his previously taxed money back). After the distribution, the balance sheet would be as follows:

AB Partnership					
Assets			*Liabilities*		
	Adj. Basis	Book Value			
Cash	$12,500	$12,500			
			Capital Accounts		
				Basis	Book Value
			A	$2,500	$2,500
			B	$10,000	$10,000
Total	$12,500	$12,500	Total	$12,500	$12,500

Take note that the distribution also required a reduction in A's capital account under § 704. This should also feel intuitive now as the capital account conceptually reflects A's entitlement to the assets of the AB partnership, which is diminished to the extent he just received a payment of those partnership assets.

Let's add net income to the example. Same facts as above, except that now, in Year 1, the partnership generates $5,000 in net income, which is allocated equally between the partners. A balance sheet that reflects that generation of income is as follows:

7. Distributions and Payments from a Partnership

AB Partnership						
Assets			Liabilities			
	Adj. Basis	Book Value				
Cash	$25,000	$25,000				
				Capital Accounts		
					Adj. Basis	Book Value
			A		$12,500	$12,500
			B		$12,500	$12,500
Total	$25,000	$25,000	Total		$25,000	$25,000

Observe that the capital accounts of the partners have been increased by $2,500 each, representing their distributive share of the partnership income. Each partner has $2,500 of partnership income that will be reported on his or her Form 1040 (Individual Income Tax Return). With that flow-through of partnership income, each partner increases his or her outside basis under § 705 by the same amount.

When the partnership distributes the $7,500 in cash to A, A does not have to include that distribution in income (because it does not exceed his outside basis). With the distribution, A then decreases his outside basis under § 705; similarly, the partnership reduces A's capital account under § 704. Consequently, after the distribution, the partnership balance sheet looks as follows:

AB Partnership						
Assets			Liabilities			
	Basis	Book Value				
Cash	$17,500	$17,500				
				Capital Accounts		
					Basis	Book Value
			A		$5,000	$5,000
			B		$12,500	$12,500
Total	$17,500	$17,500	Total		$17,500	$17,500

The above balance sheets demonstrate why the $7,500 distribution does not reflect income to A. It implicitly consists of two items. The first part is a distribution of the income that the partnership has generated. That income, though, was included in A's income when it was allocated to him—so it would result in a double tax (the same income would be taxed twice) if we also included the property or cash distribution in income, too, which is why this part of the distribution is *not* income. The second part is a return of

7. Distributions and Payments from a Partnership

A's initial capital contribution; conceptually, a return of your own money is not income because you don't have an accession to wealth; that is, a return of your basis is not taxable because basis represents already-taxed money.[8]

DISTRIBUTIONS OF PROPERTY OTHER THAN MONEY

In the above examples, the partnership distributed cash to A, which represents the simplest type of operating distribution. A partner may also be distributed property (other than money); this is known as a distribution "in-kind." The same rules for operating distributions apply here, too. That is, under § 731, a partner does not recognize gain except if the partner receives money in excess of his or her basis.[9] Thus, a distribution of property that does not result in a liquidation (termination) of a partner's interest will not generate recognized gain; similarly, no loss will be recognized under § 731(b).

The main rub with in-kind operating distributions, then, is how we determine the basis of the distributed property in the hands of the partner. Section 732 provides the answer, and it has two parts, one for operating distributions and one for liquidating distributions. For operating distributions, it provides that "[t]he basis of property (other than money) distributed by a partnership to a partner other than in liquidation of the partner's interest shall . . . be its adjusted basis to the partnership immediately before such distribution."[10] It also provides a limitation, however, that the basis of the distributed property cannot exceed the "adjusted basis of such partner's interest in the partnership reduced by any money distributed in the same transaction."[11]

---

8. The reason for this is more elongated. The reasoning is that the money or value that gave rise to the basis was taxed upstream. Consider, for example, an individual who receives a paycheck that, after taxes, is $100. That $100 has already been included in the individual's income (under § 61 when it was received as wages). Thus, if it gets invested in a piece of property—whether that is real property, like Blackacre, or a partnership interest—a return of that $100 does not represent new income or wealth, but rather a return of money that was previously taxed (upon its prior receipt as wages). Stated otherwise, to the extent that property returns you $100, you don't have an *accession* or *increase* in wealth, which is the touchstone of gross income under § 61. For greater clarity, rent and dividends are distinguishable (and those amounts are income), because those are not returns of the underlying property itself, but rather are new items of income generated by the property.

9. The reasoning for this rule will manifest itself as we unpack the basis rules; the carveout for money is because we cannot reduce its basis to preserve gain, like we can for in-kind (property) distributions.

10. I.R.C. § 732(a)(1).

11. I.R.C. § 732(a)(2).

7. Distributions and Payments from a Partnership

Let's continue with the AB example from earlier. Assume that after the formation of the partnership, the partnership buys two pieces of property for $5,000 each and that are classified as capital assets.[12] The balance sheet would look as follows:

AB Partnership						
Assets			*Liabilities*			
	Adj. Basis	Book Value				
Property 1	$5,000	$5,000				
Property 2	$5,000	$5,000		*Capital Accounts*		
Cash	$10,000	$10,000			Adj. Basis	Book Value
			A		$10,000	$10,000
			B		$10,000	$10,000
Total	$20,000	$20,000	Total		$20,000	$20,000

The simplest example would be to consider the consequences if the partnership were to distribute Property 1 to Partner A. In that case, A does not recognize any gain or loss on that distribution under § 731(a). The partnership also does not recognize any gain or loss under § 731(b). Under § 732, A takes a basis in Property 1 equal to its inside basis, which does not exceed A's outside basis. Under § 733, A must reduce his outside basis by the amount of the basis of the distributed property. And, finally, A's capital account gets reduced by the amount of the distribution under § 704. After the distribution, the balance sheet would look as follows:

AB Partnership						
Assets			*Liabilities*			
	Adj. Basis	Book Value				
Property 2	$5,000	$5,000				
Cash	$10,000	$10,000		*Capital Accounts*		
					Adj. Basis	Book Value
			A		$5,000	$5,000
			B		$10,000	$10,000
Total	$15,000	$15,000	Total		$15,000	$15,000

In addition to the balance sheet values above, A would also own Property 1 with an adjusted basis of $5,000.

---

12. The classification as capital assets is to obviate the § 751 issues discussed later.

7. Distributions and Payments from a Partnership

What if, though, the partner's outside basis is less than the basis of the distributed property. Consider the following balance sheet:

AB Partnership						
Assets			Liabilities			
	Adj. Basis	Book Value				
Property 1	$10,000	$5,000				
Property 2	$5,000	$5,000		Capital Accounts		
Cash	$5,000	$5,000			Adj. Basis	Book Value
			A		$5,000	$10,000
			B		$15,000	$5,000
Total	$20,000	$15,000	Total		$20,000	$15,000

Assume that Partner A receives a distribution of $1,000 in cash and Property 1. In this case, the normal rule of § 732(a)(1) doesn't work because Partner A doesn't have enough outside basis to "absorb" the full amount of the cash and basis of property distributed to him. In other words, the distribution of the $1,000 in cash reduces A's outside basis to $4,000, which triggers the limitation in § 732(a)(2); this limitation provides that the basis to the distributee partner cannot exceed his outside basis reduced by money received in the same transaction. This situation triggers the rules of § 732(c).

Section 732(c) provides an allocation system—that is, a specific order by which we pour the partner's outside basis into the distributed property. It provides that basis shall be first allocated to "unrealized receivables," a type of property we discuss in more detail later. If the outside basis is less than the basis of the distributed property, though, then we need to allocate, in a particular order, the amount needed to equalize them; this is known as "allocating decrease." If there is more than one property, we first assign to each property an amount of basis equal to its inside basis to the partnership. If there is not enough outside basis to do that, we then allocate the decrease needed to equalize them in a particular order.

Those instructions may seem opaque. Let's apply them to the simple example we have so far. In the above example, Property 1 is not an unrealized receivable. We want to assign a basis of $10,000 to Property 1 in the hands of Partner A, but we can't, due to his current outside basis of $4,000.[13] Therefore a "decrease in basis" of $6,000 is required. Here, because there is only one piece of property, the entire decrease in basis is

---

13. Recall, it's $4,000 after the application of the $1,000 cash distributed in the same transaction.

7. Distributions and Payments from a Partnership

allocated to Property 1. Thus, Partner A will take a basis in Property 1 of $4,000; A simultaneously reduces his outside basis to zero under § 733.

Let's consider a more complicated example that requires a full application of the basis allocation rules. Consider the following balance sheet:

AB Partnership						
Assets				Liabilities		
	Adj. Basis	Book Value				
Real Property 1	$75,000	$60,000				
Real Property 2	$5,000	$10,000		Capital Accounts		
Real Property 3	$40,000	$50,000			Adj. Basis	Book Value
Inventory	$40,000	$40,000	A		$50,000	$150,000
Cash	$40,000	$40,000	B		$150,000	$50,000
Total	$200,000	$200,000	Total		$200,000	$200,000

Assume that Partner A receives a distribution that consists of $10,000 in cash, $15,000 of inventory (that has a basis of $15,000), Real Property 1, and Real Property 2.[14] In sum, A is distributed cash of $10,000 and property that has a total book value of $85,000 ($60,000 + $10,000 + $15,000) and basis of $95,000 ($75,000 + $5,000 + $15,000). As before, given A's outside basis of $50,000, the general rule of § 732(a)(1) doesn't work. Here, § 732(a)(2) operates to limit the basis in the distributed property to $40,000, which is the outside basis of $50,000 less the $10,000 cash distributed.

Given the $40,000 limitation under § 732(a)(2), there is a decrease in basis required of $55,000, which represents the difference in the basis of the property distributed ($95,000) and our outside basis ($40,000, after the cash distribution). We now turn to § 732(c) to see which property bears that decrease in basis. Section 732(c)(1)(A)(i) provides that basis is poured first into unrealized receivables and inventory items. No unrealized receivables were distributed, but inventory was distributed, so we pour $15,000 of the $40,000 basis into the inventory, matching its inside basis to the partnership. There is $25,000 basis remaining to be poured into the two pieces of real property.

Section 732(c)(1)(B) provides that we pour the remaining basis to the other distributed property in a two-step process: first, we assign to the property a basis equal to its inside basis, and second, we then need to adjust those bases by the needed amount of increase or decrease. Assigning a basis

---

14. This example does not discuss the wisdom of this distribution; the numbers were designed to illustrate the need for allocating a decrease in basis in § 732(c); to illustrate § 732(c) squarely, it also assumes that another section or rule does not prevent this distribution.

7. Distributions and Payments from a Partnership

of $75,000 to Real Property 1 and a $5,000 basis to Real Property 2 results in a decrease needed of $55,000 ($80,000 less $25,000). In other words, we would ideally want to assign a basis to the distributee partner equal to the prior inside basis to the partnership; however, we are limited by the § 732(b) outside-basis limit.

Allocating decrease is found in § 732(c)(3). It provides that decrease is allocated first to properties with unrealized depreciation in proportion to such unrealized depreciation, but only to the extent of the unrealized depreciation.[15] Unrealized depreciation occurs when property has a book value less than tax basis.[16] After the allocation based on unrealized depreciation, decrease is then allocated in proportion to the adjusted bases of the property.[17] As applied here, we observe there is unrealized depreciation of $15,000 and $0, in Real Property 1 and Real Property 2, respectively. The first $15,000 of decrease, therefore, is allocated to Real Property 1 (the extent of its unrealized depreciation). There is still $40,000 of decreases needed (the initial $55,000 decrease less the $15,000 of unrealized depreciation). We allocate the remaining $40,000 in proportion to the adjusted bases of the property (incorporating the adjustments based on unrealized depreciation). The following table shows this calculation. Observe that Real Property 1 already reflects its allocated decrease (its inside basis of $75,000 less the $15,000 decrease already allocated).

Allocating Decrease in Basis under § 732(c)					
	Inside Basis [A]	Proportionate Share of Basis	Decrease to Allocate	Share of Decrease [B]	Outside Basis [A] − [B]
Real Property 1	$60,000	$60,000/$65,000 = 92.31%	$40,000	$36,924	$23,076
Real Property 2	$5,000	$5,000/$65,000 = 7.69%	$40,000	$3,076	$1,924
Total	$65,000	100%		$40,000	$25,000

Observe that Partner A has the following bases in his distributed assets: cash, $10,000; inventory, $15,000; Real Property 1, $23,076; and Real Property 2, $1,924; these amounts sum to $50,000, which was A's outside basis before the distribution.[18]

---

15. I.R.C. § 732(c)(3)(A).
16. See Treas. Reg. § 1.732-1(c)(4) Example 2.
17. I.R.C. § 732(c)(3)(B).
18. Although this example demonstrated the application of § 732, it is important to note that the distribution of the inventory gives rise to concerns under § 751(b), which is discussed later in this chapter.

7. Distributions and Payments from a Partnership

The partnership balance sheet looks as follows after the distribution.

AB Partnership					
Assets			Liabilities		
	Adj. Basis	Book Value			
Real Property 3	$40,000	$50,000			
Inventory	$25,000	$25,000		Capital Accounts	
Cash	$30,000	$30,000		Adj. Basis	Book Value
			A	$0	$55,000
			B	$150,000	$50,000
Total	$95,000	$105,000	Total	$150,000	$105,000

Observe that A's outside basis is $0 and his capital account now has a value of $55,000, which represents an inherent built-in gain of $55,000. As well, A has a total basis in his distributed property of $50,000 with a total value of $95,000, which translates into an inherent gain in the distributed property of $45,000. In sum, between his partnership interest and the distributed property, A has a total inherent gain of $100,000. Note that this amount equals the gain inherent in his partnership interest *before* the distribution (he had an outside basis of $50,000 and a capital account of $150,000), representing an inherent gain of $100,000. Thus, we see that § 732 preserved the status quo ante and that no gain leaked out of the system. All of the gain that existed before the distribution is inherent in the distributed property and the partnership interest.

Now you may observe an *imbalance* between our inside bases and outside bases. The inside basis of the partnership assets is $95,000, but the total outside basis is $150,000. This was caused by distributing built-in loss property to A when A did not have any loss inherent in his partnership interest (the built-in loss belonged, conceptually, to B). The partnership could remedy this by way of a § 754 election. A § 754 election would allow the partnership to adjust the basis of undistributed partnership property as allowed by § 734.

Section 734 provides that

> The basis of partnership property shall not be adjusted as the result of a distribution of property to a partner unless the election, provided in section 754 (relating to optional adjustment to basis of partnership property), is in effect with respect to such partnership or unless there is a substantial basis reduction with respect to such distribution.[19]

---

19. I.R.C. § 734(a).

7. Distributions and Payments from a Partnership

Thus, we see the general rule that a distribution of property does not cause an adjustment to the inside basis of partnership property. We also see an exception in the case of a § 754 election. A § 754 election allows a partnership to adjust the inside basis of property under §§ 734 and 743.

Under § 734, the basis of partnership property can either be increased or decreased. A partnership *increases* the inside basis of partnership property by the sum the of (i) the amount of gain recognized by the distributee partner, and, in the case of distributed property to which § 732(a)(2) or (b) applies, (ii) the excess of the inside basis of the distributed property over the basis of the property to the distributee partner.[20] A partnership *decreases* the inside basis of property by the sum of (i) amount of the loss recognized to the distributee under § 731(a)(2), and, in the case of property to which § 732(b) applies, (ii) the excess of the basis of the distributed property over the inside basis of the property before the distribution.[21]

In this example, Partner A neither recognized a gain nor a loss. The inside basis of the distributed property immediately before the distribution was $95,000 and the basis of the property in the hands of the distributee partner is $40,000. We thus observe a $55,000 difference between the inside basis before distribution and the basis to the distributee partner. This results in a calculated increase of $55,000 under § 734(b)(1). Now that we know we can adjust the inside basis of the remaining property by $55,000, we now must decide *how* to allocate that basis. This allocation is provided by § 755.[22]

Section 755 provides that, generally, the allocation of basis under a § 734 or § 743 election shall be made "in a manner which has the effect of reducing the difference between the fair market value and the adjusted basis of partnership properties"[23] or as provided by regulation.[24] The § 755 regulation provides a two-step process. First, the partnership must determine the value of its remaining assets. Second, it must allocate the basis between two classes of assets ((i) capital assets and § 1231 property and (ii) any other property).

Section 755 allocation requires use of the assets' current fair market value, not necessarily their current book values. For partnerships that constitute a trade or business, the residual method under § 1060 must be used to assign value to § 197 intangibles. For the second step, the regulations provide that, "the adjustment must be allocated to remaining partnership property of a character similar to that of the distributed property with respect

---

20. I.R.C. § 734(b)(1).
21. I.R.C. § 734(b)(2).
22. I.R.C. § 734(c).
23. I.R.C. § 755(a)(1).
24. I.R.C. § 755(a)(2).

7. Distributions and Payments from a Partnership

to which the adjustment arose."[25] So, for example, "when the partnership's adjusted basis of distributed capital gain property immediately prior to distribution exceeds the basis of the property to the distributee partner (as determined under section 732), the basis of the undistributed capital gain property remaining in the partnership is increased by an amount equal to the excess."[26] A special rule also provides that, "[w]here there is a distribution resulting in an adjustment under section 734(b)(1)(A) or (b)(2)(A) to the basis of undistributed partnership property, the adjustment is allocated only to capital gain property."[27] Observe that this special rule is triggered when a partner has recognized a gain or loss on the distribution.

When we need to allocate to several properties within the same class (e.g., there are several remaining capital gain properties), the increase is allocated based on unrealized appreciation within the class (to the extent of each property's unrealized appreciation), and then the remaining excess, if any, is based in proportion to fair market value.[28] A similar rule applies to allocations of decrease, but it is based on unrealized depreciation and then adjusted basis.[29]

Back to our in-text example of allocating an increase of $55,000. When A received his property, he was able to pour the inside basis fully into the inventory property. Thus, any increase needed under § 734 is traceable to the capital gain property distributed, which did not receive its full basis in the distribution. Therefore, the $55,000 of basis is allocable to capital gain property. The partnership has only one remaining capital gain property, Real Property 3, which will receive the entire increase. After the increase under § 734, the partnership balance sheet looks as follows, which, as you can observe, now equalizes the bases columns.

AB Partnership					
Assets			Liabilities		
	Adj. Basis	Book Value			
Real Property 3	$95,000	$50,000			
Inventory	$25,000	$25,000	Capital Accounts		
Cash	$30,000	$30,000		Adj. Basis	Book Value
			A	$0	$55,000
			B	$150,000	$50,000
Total	$150,000	$105,000	Total	$150,000	$105,000

---

25. Treas. Reg. § 1.755-1(c)(1)(i).
26. Id.
27. Treas. Reg. § 1.755-1(c)(1)(ii).
28. Treas. Reg. § 1.755-1(c)(2)(i).
29. Treas. Reg. § 1.755-1(c)(2)(ii).

7. Distributions and Payments from a Partnership

Let's now consider an operating distribution that consists of property and money. Continuing with the earlier AB example, the partnership now distributes $7,500 to A, consisting of Property 1 and $2,500 of money. Like before, A does not recognize any gain or loss on that distribution under § 731(a). The partnership also does not recognize any gain or loss under § 731(b). Under § 732, A takes a basis in Property 1 equal to its inside basis; note that this basis *does not* exceed the partner's inside basis ($10,000) reduced by money distributed to him ($2,500). Under § 733, A must reduce his outside basis by the amount of the basis of the property and money distributed to him. And, finally, A's capital account gets reduced by the amount of the distribution under § 704. Consequently, the balance sheet after the distribution looks as follows:

AB Partnership					
Assets			*Liabilities*		
	Basis	Book Value			
Property 2	$5,000	$5,000			
Cash	$7,500	$7,500	*Capital Accounts*		
				Basis	Book Value
			A	$2,500	$2,500
			B	$10,000	$10,000
Total	$12,500	$12,500	Total	$12,500	$12,500

In addition, Partner A owns Property 1 with an adjusted basis of $5,000 and cash (with a basis of $2,500).

LIQUIDATING DISTRIBUTIONS

The next type of distributions we examine are liquidating distributions. Liquidating distributions are distributions that terminate (i.e., "pay out") the partner's complete interest in the partnership. Unless an exception applies—namely § 737 or § 751(b), both of which are discussed later—the same rules that we discussed above for operating distributions (e.g., § 731) apply for liquidating distributions. In short, the distributions can be entirely income-tax-free to the partner and the partnership.

Consider the following simple example of a liquidating distribution. The ABC Partnership has the following balance sheet:

7. Distributions and Payments from a Partnership

ABC Partnership					
Assets			*Liabilities*		
	Basis	Book Value			
Cash	$50,000	$50,000			
Blackacre	$10,000	$25,000	*Capital Accounts*		
				Basis	Book Value
			A	$20,000	$25,000
			B	$20,000	$25,000
			C	$20,000	$25,000
Total	$60,000	$75,000	Total	$60,000	$75,000

Let's analyze what happens if the partnership distributes Blackacre, which is real property, to A in full liquidation of A's partnership interest. Under § 731, gain is recognized to a partner upon a distribution only if he or she receives more money than outside basis.[30] In this example, A does not receive any cash, so gain under § 731(a) is not triggered. Consequently, A receives Blackacre without the recognition of any gain; similarly, the partnership does not recognize gain under § 731(b).

In operating distributions, we examined § 732(a) to determine the basis of the distributed property in the hands of the distributee partner. In a liquidating distribution, though, § 732(b) now governs. It provides a simple rule that "[t]he basis of property (other than money) distributed by a partnership to a partner in liquidation of the partner's interest shall be an amount equal to the adjusted basis of such partner's interest in the partnership reduced by any money distributed in the same transaction."[31] Thus, A will have a basis of $20,000 in Blackacre after the distribution.[32]

After the liquidating distribution to A, the balance sheet of the partnership will look as follows:

---

30. I.R.C. § 731(a).
31. I.R.C. § 732(b).
32. Had this been a non-liquidating distribution, A's basis in Blackacre would be limited to $10,000. In a liquidating distribution, all of A's outside basis has to be poured into the distributed property because no partnership interest remains.

7. Distributions and Payments from a Partnership

BC Partnership					
Assets			*Liabilities*		
	Basis	Book Value			
Cash	$50,000	$50,000			
			Capital Accounts		
				Basis	Book Value
			B	$20,000	$25,000
			C	$20,000	$25,000
Total	$50,000	$50,000	Total	$40,000	$50,000

Now, you may observe that the outside basis of B and C (total of $40,000) does not equal the inside tax basis of the partnership property (the cash of $50,000). Note that this makes conceptual sense here. If the partnership were to distribute the cash here, each partner would be entitled to $25,000, which would result in a $5,000 gain each under § 731(a)(1) (i.e., each partner receives $25,000 cash in liquidation of their partnership interest with a tax basis of $20,000). Recall there was a total of $15,000 of gain inherent in Blackacre before its distribution. The rule ensures that the $5,000 of inherent gain is preserved for the remaining partners; for A, his share of the gain is built into the basis of Blackacre (i.e., Blackacre is worth $25,000 and A has a tax basis of $20,000 in it).

Speaking of cash liquidating distributions, let's consider one. Assume the earlier ABC Partnership with the following balance sheet (like before):

ABC Partnership					
Assets			*Liabilities*		
	Adj. Basis	Book Value			
Cash	$50,000	$50,000			
Blackacre	$10,000	$25,000			
			Capital Accounts		
				Adj. Basis	Book Value
			A	$20,000	$25,000
			B	$20,000	$25,000
			C	$20,000	$25,000
Total	$60,000	$75,000	Total	$60,000	$75,000

Assume now that, instead of distributing Blackacre to A, the partnership distributes $25,000 in cash to A in liquidation of his interest. This now triggers § 731(a)(1) because now the money that the partner received exceeded his adjusted basis. Thus, A will recognize gain of $5,000 on the liquidating distributions. Under § 731(a), moreover, this $5,000 gain will be considered a "sale or exchange of the partnership interest of the distributee

7. Distributions and Payments from a Partnership

partner."[33] Observe that this treatment is consistent with the general rules for exchanging property under § 1001—that is, a taxpayer recognizes gain to the extent the amount realized exceeds adjusted basis.

Now let's understand why the different tax treatment between the examples of a property-only liquidating distribution and a cash-only liquidating distribution. In the property-only liquidating distribution, there was no gain recognized; the underlying reasoning for this is that we can preserve the gain inherent in the partnership interest by way of the basis rules.[34] We ported A's outside basis to his newly distributed property—this preserved the built-in gain economically inherent in his partnership interest. Indeed, take note above of his capital account balance of $25,000 and outside basis of $20,000—he had a $5,000 gain inherent in his partnership interest, which was preserved in Blackacre. With a cash-only liquidating distribution, however, there is no way to preserve inherent gain with basis. At an even more conceptual level, in a property-only liquidating distribution, it is akin to other nonrecognition sections in that the Code treats it as changing the nature of the investment rather than exiting of the investment. This even harkens back to our foundational question of what a partnership is for tax purposes—is it an entity or an aggregation of property interests? Here, we see an aggregate approach, i.e., the partner is simply treated as getting his or her own property back. With a cash-only liquidating distribution, however, it is fundamentally exiting the partnership investment and ought to trigger gain.

We have observed what happens in property-only and cash-only liquidating distributions. What if, though, it is a mixture of property and cash in the liquidating distribution? To unpack this, consider the ABC Partnership, which has the following balance sheet:

ABC Partnership					
Assets			*Liabilities*		
	Basis	Book Value			
Cash	$100,000	$100,000			
Blackacre	$10,000	$25,000	*Capital Accounts*		
Redacre	$10,000	$25,000		Basis	Book Value
			A	$40,000	$50,000
			B	$40,000	$50,000
			C	$40,000	$50,000
Total	$120,000	$150,000	Total	$120,000	$150,000

---

33. I.R.C. § 731(a) (flush language).
34. Indeed, this reinforces a point made throughout the text. The rules are designed to prevent the transformation of ordinary loss into capital loss and deferring the loss until the distributed property is later sold.

7. Distributions and Payments from a Partnership

Now assume that A receives a liquidating distribution of Blackacre and $25,000 in cash.[35] Recall that § 731(a) provides that "gain shall not be recognized to such partner, except to the extent that any money distributed exceeds the adjusted basis of such partner's interest in the partnership immediately before the distribution."[36] In this example, then, A would not recognize any gain because the amount of the cash distributed ($25,000) does not exceed the outside basis immediately before the distribution ($40,000).

Let's now consider the basis implications for the distributed property. Section 732(b) provides that "[t]he basis of property (other than money) distributed by a partnership to a partner in liquidation of the partner's interest shall be an amount equal to the adjusted basis of such partner's interest in the partnership reduced by any money distributed in the same transaction."[37] A would therefore take a basis of $15,000 in Blackacre ($40,000 outside basis less the $25,000 distributed cash).

It is worth emphasizing the elegance of these liquidating distribution rules. Observe that before the liquidating distribution A has a $10,000 gain inherent in his partnership interest. In liquidation of his interest, he received two items (the cash and real property) but did not recognize any gain on receipt of those items. The § 732(b) basis rules preserved the $10,000 gain by mandating a $15,000 basis in Blackacre, which has a value of $25,000. In short, even though no gain was recognized on the liquidation, the inherent gain was preserved in the distributed property.

Let's now consider a liquidating distribution in which there is a loss. Consider the ABC Partnership, which now has the following balance sheet:

ABC Partnership						
Assets			Liabilities			
	Basis	Book Value				
Cash	$150,000	$150,000				
				Capital Accounts		
					Basis	Book Value
			A		$75,000	$50,000
			B		$25,000	$50,000
			C		$50,000	$50,000
Total	$150,000	$150,000	Total		$150,000	$150,000

Here A receives a liquidating distribution of $50,000 in cash. Consider § 731(a)(2), which provides that loss is not recognized in a distribution

---

35. Note that the book values of these two items equals $50,000, which is the balance of A's capital account.
36. I.R.C. § 731(a) (emphasis added).
37. I.R.C. § 732(b).

7. Distributions and Payments from a Partnership

unless it is a liquidating distribution in which the partner receives (i) only money and hot assets (unrealized receivables and inventory), and (ii) the partner's outside basis exceeds the amount of money and hot assets received. That is triggered here because A's distribution is in liquidation of his interest, he received only money or hot assets, and his outside basis exceeds that sum. Consequently, A would recognize a $25,000 loss, which would be a considered a loss from the sale or exchange of his partnership interest.[38]

What if, though, instead of a cash-heavy balance sheet, the ABC Partnership's balance sheet looked as follows:

ABC Partnership					
Assets			Liabilities		
	Basis	Book Value			
Blackacre	$40,000	$50,000			
Redacre	$40,000	$50,000		Capital Accounts	
Greenacre	$40,000	$50,000		Basis	Book Value
			A	$75,000	$50,000
			B	$25,000	$50,000
			C	$20,000	$50,000
Total	$120,000	$150,000	Total	$120,000	$150,000

Assume now that ABC distributes Blackacre to A in full liquidation of his interest. In this case, then, A does not recognize a gain or loss on this liquidation;[39] to be clear, he cannot recognize a loss under § 731(a)(2) because, although the amount distributed is less than his outside basis, he did not receive only money or hot assets (he received real property). What happens, then, to the loss he has inherent in his partnership interest (he has a basis of $75,000 but received only $50,000 in exchange for it)?

As before, this is remedied by the basis rules in § 732(b). Recall that § 732(b) provides that for liquidating distributions, "[t]he basis of property (other than money) distributed by a partnership to a partner in liquidation of the partner's interest shall be an amount equal to the adjusted basis of such partner's interest in the partnership reduced by any money distributed in the same transaction."[40] Therefore, A will take a $75,000 basis in Blackacre, which preserves the loss he had inherent in his partnership interest before liquidation. If multiple properties were received, then an allocation of basis, including allocating increase or decrease, would be calculated under § 732(c), which was discussed earlier.

---

38. I.R.C. § 731(a).
39. ABC Partnership similarly does not recognize a gain or loss under § 731(b) — this is a *per se* rule.
40. I.R.C. § 732(b).

CHARACTER ISSUES AND HOLDING PERIOD

Common to both current and liquidating distributions is that we must also consider the character of any gain or loss inherent in the distributed property. Like we've seen before, partnership tax rules are concerned with the ability to effectuate a character change.[41] Section 735(a) provides rules to prevent certain character changes. It provides two rules. First, the gain or loss on a disposition by a distributee partner of *unrealized receivables* shall be ordinary income or ordinary loss.[42] This ordinary character classification is forever—it is not time bounded. The second rule is that the gain or loss on a disposition by a distributee partner on *inventory items* shall be ordinary income or loss if the sale or exchange happens within five years of the distribution.[43] Thus, for inventory items, there is a five-year window in which the property retains its ordinary-income status. After that five-year window, the gain (or loss) may be capital in nature, if the asset is a capital asset in the hands of the distributee partner.

Lastly, we must consider the holding period of the distributed property. Section 735(b) provides a simple rule that the holding period to the distributee partner tacks on the holding period of the partnership.[44] Importantly, though, this rule does not apply in determining the five-year window for purposes of the ordinary-income characterization from § 735(a)(1).

DISTRIBUTIONS OF "HOT ASSETS" AND § 751(B)

The above rules about operating (current) distributions and liquidating distributions are relatively straightforward. Generally, no gain or loss is recognized to the distributee partner, and that partner takes a "carry over" basis in the distributed assets, subject to the outside basis limitation. Alas, the rules get immensely more complicated, though, once our partnership distributions start affecting items colloquially known as "hot assets." Before we dive into the mechanics, though, let's try to get a feel for the concern that these rules are trying to police. Again, if we understand the reason, the object, and the "why" of the rules, the mechanics become more intuitive.

We have already seen and examined safeguards to prevent income shifting, namely § 704(c). Recall that § 704(c) requires partnerships to take into account pre-contribution gain or loss in allocating partnership tax items.

---

41. Indeed, this was one of the main themes of partnership tax discussed in Chapter 1.
42. I.R.C. § 735(a)(1).
43. I.R.C. § 735(a)(2).
44. I.R.C. § 735(b).

7. Distributions and Payments from a Partnership

Most directly, if a partner contributes property with a built-in gain, that partner must be allocated that gain upon the partnership's disposition of the asset. This prevents the partner from shifting that pre-contribution gain to another partner. In addition to guardrails about the *magnitude* (or size) of income and gain, we must also have rules that guard the *character* of income and gain. That is, even if we protect and preserve the magnitude of the gain, if the partners can change the character of the gain, say, from ordinary to capital in nature, that results in a lowering of taxes paid by the partner simply due to moving things around in a partnership.

The motivation for these rules can be illustrated in the following example. Consider the CDE Partnership, in which C, D, and E are equal partners, with each partner originally contributing $100,000 in cash. Assume that, over time, the partnership has acquired two assets, a piece of real property and inventory. Consider the CDE Partnership balance sheet, which looks as follows:

CDE Partnership					
Assets			*Liabilities*		
	Basis	Book Value			
Cash	$90,000	$90,000			
Inventory	$50,000	$100,000	*Capital Accounts*		
Real property	$10,000	$110,000		Basis	Book Value
			A	$50,000	$100,000
			B	$50,000	$100,000
			C	$50,000	$100,000
Total	$150,000	$300,000	Total	$150,000	$300,000

The motivation behind § 751 is best illustrated by a partner who is "walking away," i.e., leaving the partnership and receiving a liquidating distribution. Observe the built-in gain inherent in the partnership presently. There is a total of $150,000 of gain, which is spread between the $50,000 gain in the inventory and the $100,000 gain in the real property, which let's assume is capital in nature. Given that CDE are equal partners, conceptually they each have $50,000 of that gain allocable to them. More importantly, consider the *character* of that gain—it is a mix of ordinary and capital gain; that is, they each have a portion of the ordinary and capital gain inherent in their interest.

Assume that the partnership distributes the inventory to C. Under the general nonrecognition framework we covered earlier, neither C nor the partnership would recognize income upon that distribution, and C would take a basis of $50,000 in the inventory, which also preserves the gain in the inventory, and reduces C's partnership basis to zero. At a surface level,

7. Distributions and Payments from a Partnership

this seems to handle the concerns about income shifting—and it does with respect to the *magnitude* of gain, as the $50,000 gain still inherent in the inventory preserves the gain that was inherent both in itself and the gain in C's outside basis, so no gain leaked out of the system.

Although there was no leakage of gain or shifting of the magnitude of gain between partners, something did shift between the partners—the *character* of the gain. After the distribution, C has all the ordinary gain inherent in his inventory; D and E no longer have any ordinary income (as the partnership no longer has an ordinary income asset), they have only capital gain. Stated more clearly, after the liquidating distribution, the remaining gain in the partnership ($100,000) is capital in nature (as it is traceable to the capital asset)—if this is allowed, D and E have shifted the character of their gain. As this example demonstrates, therefore, we need guardrails that not only prevent the shifting of the *magnitude* of gain, but also prevent the shifting of the *character* of gain. This is the purpose of § 751 and, as discussed more particularly, § 751(b).

The essence of § 751(b) is to ensure that the gain inherent in ordinary-income assets, like unrealized receivables and inventory items, will be recognized as ordinary income and can't be shifted between partners. We will refer to these as "hot assets." At a broad level, the rule operates such that if a partner receives a disproportionate share of hot assets, it triggers the § 751(b) rules. In other words, under § 751(b), if a partner receives more hot assets than his or her share, it considers that extra amount of distributed hot assets as received in exchange for partner's share of *other* assets. This is an important conceptual point that is worth being abundantly clear about. Consider the following simple example to illustrate this singular point. Assume the AB Partnership, with two equal partners, A and B. The AB Partnership has the following balance sheet:

AB Partnership					
Assets			*Liabilities*		
	Adj. Basis	Book Value			
Real property	$10,000	$20,000			
Unrealized receivable	$0	$10,000	*Capital Accounts*		
				Basis	Book Value
			A	$5,000	$15,000
			B	$5,000	$15,000
Total	$10,000	$30,000	Total	$10,000	$30,000

Right now, each partner has a $10,000 inherent gain in their partnership interest, which is traceable to the gain inherent in the unrealized receivable

7. Distributions and Payments from a Partnership

and the real property. If the partnership distributes the unrealized receivable to Partner B, § 751(b) operates. Conceptually, before the distribution, B has an entitlement to half the unrealized receivable ($5,000) and half of the real property ($10,000). After the distribution, B's capital account is now $5,000 (as it is reduced by the $10,000 distribution of the unrealized receivable), which represents now only a quarter of the real property. In essence, B has *exchanged* a portion of his interest in the real property for more of the unrealized receivable. Section 751(b) basically wants to treat this as a sale (as it views it as B selling his real property interest in exchange for the excess unrealized receivable interest).

Now that we have a feel for the backdrop of § 751(b), let's unpack the items to which it applies. By its terms, § 751(b) applies to unrealized receivables and "substantially appreciated" inventory items—these are the previously discussed "hot assets."[45] The term "unrealized receivables" means an amount "to the extent not previously includible in income under the method of accounting used by the partnership, any rights (contractual or otherwise) to payment for . . . goods delivered, or to be delivered, to the extent the proceeds therefrom would be treated as amounts received from the sale or exchange of property other than a capital asset" and "services rendered, or to be rendered."[46] The statute also includes other specific items in the § 751(c) flush language, such as stock in a DISC, farm land, trademarks and trade names, and other items.[47]

Inventory items are defined as property described in § 1221(a)(1) (e.g., stock in trade),[48] "other property of the partnership which, on sale or exchange by the partnership, would be considered property other than a capital asset and other than property described in section 1231,"[49] and "other property held by the partnership which, if held by the selling or distributee partner, would be considered [an inventory item]."[50] To be substantially appreciated, the inventory item's fair market value must exceed 120% of the partnership's inside basis in the item;[51] this determination is made at the aggregate level, not an item-by-item basis.[52] For example, if a partnership holds total inventory with an inside basis of $10,000 and a fair market value of $15,000, then all of the inventory is considered substantially appreciated; this is true even if the partnership were to distribute an individual item of inventory in which the basis equaled its fair market value.

---

45. I.R.C. § 751(b)(1)(A).
46. I.R.C. § 751(c), (c)(1), (2).
47. I.R.C. § 751(c) (flush language).
48. I.R.C. § 751(d)(1).
49. I.R.C. § 751(d)(2).
50. I.R.C. § 751(d)(3).
51. I.R.C. § 752(b)(3).
52. Treas. Reg. § 1.751-1(d)(1).

7. Distributions and Payments from a Partnership

Now that some preliminary concepts and terms have been unpacked, we can turn to the operation of § 751(b). The first consideration is whether § 751(b) even applies to the distribution. By its terms, § 751(b) applies only if the partner (i) receives a distribution of unrealized receivables or substantially appreciated inventory items (i.e., hot assets) or (ii) receives other partnership property (including money) in exchange for his or her interest in the partnership's hot assets. In other words, every distribution of property—even if the partnership has hot assets—does not necessarily trigger the full effect § 751(b). That does not mean, however, that we do need to test for the application of § 751(b). An easy shortcut to consider here is whether a pro rata (in terms of value) distribution to all partners was made; if a pro rata distribution to all partners was made, that would not trigger an "exchange" for § 751(b) because the owners could not have shifted their respective ownership in the remaining assets. Consider the following example illustrating this.

The EFG Partnership, in which each partner is an equal partner in all items, has the following balance sheet:

	EFG Partnership				
	Assets			Liabilities	
	Basis	Book Value			
Real property	$5,000	$20,000			
Unrealized receivable	$0	$30,000		Capital Accounts	
Cash	10,000	$10,000		Basis	Book Value
			E	$5,000	$20,000
			F	$5,000	$20,000
			G	$5,000	$20,000
Total	$15,000	$60,000	Total	$15,000	$60,000

If the partnership were to distribute the unrealized receivable equally to each partner ($10,000 each), this would not trigger § 751(b) because a partner did not *exchange* hot assets in exchange for other partnership property (as each partner got their allocable share of the unrealized receivable), and the partners did not *exchange* other property in exchange for hot assets. In other words, the partners will fully realize their allocable share of the ordinary income inherent in the unrealized receivable. This demonstrates a helpful shortcut: a pro rata (proportionate) distribution of property (hot assets or otherwise) will not trigger § 751(b).

Consider the contrary result, however, if the partnership distributes $15,000 of the unrealized receivable to E. In this case, then, § 751(b) is triggered because E receives more than his or her share of the unrealized

7. Distributions and Payments from a Partnership

receivable (i.e., receiving $15,000 instead of $10,000). There is now an *exchange*—that is, E is deemed to have exchanged a portion of his or her interest in the other partnership property (the real property and the cash) in *exchange* for the extra $5,000 of the unrealized receivable. This demonstrates the implied negative of the hot asset shortcut: a non-proportionate distribution of property raises § 751(b) concerns.

Let's now dive deep into the mechanical operation of § 751(b). For tractability, we will first explore these mechanics in a liquidating distribution context. The first step in a § 751(b) analysis is to properly classify partnership property as either a hot asset or not a hot asset (i.e., a "cold asset"). We can only measure if a disproportionate distribution of hot assets has occurred if we fully appreciate the extent of the partnership's hot assets. An important implication of this, then, is that if a partnership does not have any hot assets, then § 751(b) would not even apply. On the flip side, if a partnership has *only* hot assets, then § 751(b) similarly would not have any sting because it would be impossible to make a disproportionate distribution (as it could *only* distribute hot assets).

After the partnership's assets have been properly classified (as hot assets or cold assets), we need to determine the distributee partner's interest in each asset both before the distribution and after the distribution. Due to the flexibility in allocations, though, this step can be quite complex; for example, a partner may have a special allocation of a certain type that may increase or decrease his or her interest in a piece of property. Consider, as well, the impact that abiding the principles of § 704(c) may play here. For present purposes and tractability, though, we will assume for a simplifying convention that a partner has the same interest in each type of asset. Consequently, a partner's interest in a partnership asset will be his interest in partnership items and capital multiplied by the value of the asset.

Let's revisit the EFG Partnership, which now has the following balance sheet:

EFG Partnership					
Assets			*Liabilities*		
	Basis	Book Value			
Real property	$15,000	$45,000			
Unrealized receivable	$0	$30,000		*Capital Accounts*	
Cash	45,000	$45,000		Basis	Book Value
			E	$20,000	$40,000
			F	$20,000	$40,000
			G	$20,000	$40,000
Total	$60,000	$120,000	Total	$60,000	$120,000

7. Distributions and Payments from a Partnership

To review our analysis so far, the partnership has hot assets and non-hot assets. The hot asset is the unrealized receivable, and the cold (non-hot) assets are the remaining assets (the real property and cash). Each partner has an equal share of profits, losses, and capital; therefore, each partner's interest in the assets is $15,000, $10,000, and $15,000 of the real property, unrealized receivable, and cash, respectively. This is summarized in the following table:

Partners' Interest in Partnership Property Pre-Distribution				
	E	F	G	Total
Real property	$15,000	$15,000	$15,000	$45,000
Unrealized receivable	$10,000	$10,000	$10,000	$30,000
Cash	$15,000	$15,000	$15,000	$45,000

The next step is intuitive from the above table: We need to compare the post-distribution interest in property to the pre-distribution interests to see if a disproportionate distribution of hot assets has occurred. This is easiest to see in a liquidating distribution because the distributee partner's interest will be zero across non-distributed partnership property after the distribution. Therefore, let's assume that E is receiving a liquidating distribution of $40,000 in cash. The post-distribution interest table would be as follows:

Partners' Interest in Partnership Property Post-Distribution				
	E	F	G	Total
Real property	$0	$22,500	$22,500	$45,000
Unrealized receivable	$0	$15,000	$15,000	$30,000
Cash	$40,000	$2,500	$2,500	$45,000

If we combine the two tables, we can readily observe how the distribution caused a change in the share of the partnership assets; consider the following table, in which the difference column represents the difference between the post-distribution and pre-distribution entitlements:

Comparison of Partners' Interest in Property Pre- and Post-Distribution									
	E			F			G		
	Post	Pre	Diff.	Post	Pre	Diff.	Post	Pre	Diff.
Real property	$0	$15,000	($15,000)	$22,500	$15,000	$7,500	$22,500	$15,000	$7,500
Unrealized receivables	$0	$10,000	($10,000)	$15,000	$10,000	$5,000	$15,000	$10,000	$5,000
Cash	$40,000	$15,000	$25,000	$2,500	$15,000	($12,500)	$2,500	$15,000	($12,500)

7. Distributions and Payments from a Partnership

E's column shows that he now has $40,000 of (former) partnership cash—this is $25,000 *more* than he was entitled to pre-distribution. This illustrates the motivation behind § 751(b): Why did the partnership give him more cash than he was entitled to in liquidation for this partnership interest? He must have implicitly sold his share of *other* partnership property for it. Indeed, that is exactly what we see happened; we can observe that F and G have a smaller cash entitlement post-distribution (that adds up to $25,000), but they have *more* real property and unrealized receivables. In other words, it is *as* if E sold his slice of the real property and unrealized receivables in exchange for a slice of F and G's cash.

The next step encapsulates the discussion above. We need to isolate exactly what the distributee partner "purchased" and what that partner "sold." In the above EFG example, E purchased $25,000 in additional partnership cash by selling his share ($15,000) of the real property and his share ($10,000) of the unrealized receivable to F and G, jointly.

Like with any sale of property, we need to eventually calculate the gain or loss on sale—which is the ultimate goal of § 751(b)—but before that step, we must be able to determine the distributee partner's basis in the assets he or she sold. The regulations provide that the distributee partner's basis in the relinquished property is the basis the partner would have in the property as if the partnership had distributed it to the partner in a current distribution under § 732.[53]

The second-to-last step is to calculate the gain or loss on the deemed sale or exchange under § 751(b). The regulations provide that the distributee partner realizes gain or loss measured by the difference between the adjusted basis for the property relinquished (sold) in the exchange and the fair market value of the property received by him (either the additional § 751(b) property or any other property).[54] The character of the gain or loss depends on the nature of the distributed property. If the distributee partner receives additional § 751 property, the character of the gain is determined by the nature of the relinquished property.[55] If, on the other hand, the distributee partner receives additional non-§ 751 property, then the character of the gain is ordinary income (because he relinquished § 751 property).

In the EFG example, observe that it is as if E sold his slice of the real property and the unrealized receivable in exchange for the extra cash. Section 751(b) does not care, however, about the real estate portion of the transaction; it cares only about the disproportionate treatment of the hot asset, i.e., the unrealized receivable. That is, to the extent § 751(b) is not operating, the normal distribution rules apply—so the normal

---

53. *See* Treas. Reg. § 1.751-1(b)(2)(iii); Treas. Reg. § 1.751-1(b)(3)(iii).
54. Treas. Reg. § 1.751-1(b)(2)(iii); Treas. Reg. § 1.751-1(b)(3)(iii).
55. Treas. Reg. § 1.751-1(b)(2)(iii).

7. Distributions and Payments from a Partnership

distribution rules will apply for the portion of the distribution traceable to the real property. Concerning § 751(b), though, E must recognize $10,000 in ordinary income, which represents the difference between his basis in the unrealized receivable (here $0) and the fair market value of property and money received in exchange for his interest in the hot asset (here $10,000).

The last step is to consider the collateral tax impacts of the deemed § 751(b) sale. For example, the partnership may have gain or loss on the deemed sale of the property. Recall that § 751(b) treats this distribution as if the partnership sold other partnership assets to the distributee partner. Consequently, the regulations provide that the partnership may have income or loss on that sale, which will need to be allocated to the other partners as part of their distributive share, which will be separately reported under § 702(a)(7).[56]

A summary table of the § 751(b) steps is provided below:

Step	Steps in a § 751(b) Analysis — Description
1	Classify all partnership property as either a hot asset (§ 751 property) or not a hot asset (i.e., cold asset)
2	Does § 751(b) even apply? Recall the shortcuts: (1) Does the partnership have hot assets? (2) Is the distribution pro rata in value with respect to all the partners?
3	Determine the distributee partner's interest in each partnership asset *before* the distribution. (Note: in a more complicated scenario, you can aggregate this into the aggregate share of hot assets and aggregate share of cold assets)
4	Determine the distributee partner's interest in each partnership asset *after* the distribution
5	Calculate the difference in interests between pre- and post-distribution
6	Determine whether a § 751(b) distribution occurred. Look at the difference columns for the non-distributee partners. If they have a difference for a hot asset, a § 751(b) distribution occurred.
7	Isolate exactly what the distributee partner "purchased" and what that partner "sold"
8	Determine the distributee partner's basis in the assets sold
9	Calculate the gain or loss on the deemed sale or exchange for the distributee partner
10	Determine and calculate collateral tax consequences (namely the gain or loss to the partnership and resulting distributive share items to non-distributee partners)

---

56. *See* Treas. Reg. § 1.751-1(b)(2)(ii); Treas. Reg. § 1.751-1(b)(3)(ii). Note that although the regulations cite to § 702(a)(8), this is the result of a historical renumbering in which the § 751 regulations were not renumbered accordingly.

7. Distributions and Payments from a Partnership

Examples

1. Amelia is a partner in the AB Partnership. She has an outside basis of $300,000 in her partnership interest and a capital account balance of $600,000. She receives an operating distribution of real property that had an inside basis of $200,000 and $40,000 in cash. Calculate the income tax consequences of this distribution to Amelia and the AB Partnership. What if, alternatively, Amelia had an outside basis of $100,000?

2. Beverly is a partner of the Beta Partnership. She has an outside basis in her partnership interest of $360,000. Her interest is being liquidated; she receives $60,000 of cash and real property with an inside basis of $180,000 and a fair market value of $420,000. What is her basis in the distributed property?

3. Carter is a one-fourth partner in the Gamma Partnership. He has an outside basis of $3,250,000. In a liquidating distribution, Gamma distributes (i) inventory with a basis of $500,000 and a value of $1,000,000, (ii) Blueacre with a basis of $250,000 and a value of $2,000,000, and (iii) Greenacre with a basis and value of $500,000. Both Blueacre and Greenacre are capital assets. Calculate the tax consequences of this liquidating distribution, focusing on the bases of the distributed assets.

4. Don is a one-third partner in the Epsilon Partnership, which has the following balance sheet (it has multiple depreciable properties, which are aggregated in the balance sheet). You may assume that the assets' fair market values are the same as their recorded book values and that the accounts receivable was recorded due to the sale of widgets on credit.

Epsilon Partnership						
Assets			Liabilities			$288,000
	Basis	Book Value				
Cash	$120,000	$120,000				
Accounts receivable	$72,000	$72,000	Capital Accounts			
Inventory	$168,000	$240,000		Basis	Book Value	
Depreciable properties	$336,000	$384,000	Don	$256,000	$200,000	
Land	$72,000	$72,000	Partner 2	$256,000	$200,000	
			Partner 3	$256,000	$200,000	
Total	$768,000	$888,000	Total	$768,000	$888,000	

The partnership makes a liquidating distribution to Don that consists of $80,000 in cash and some of the depreciable property, the portion of which

231

7. Distributions and Payments from a Partnership

has a value and inside basis of $120,000. Evaluate the tax consequences of this distribution to Don, the partnership, and the remaining partners.

5. Eliot is a partner of the Zeta Partnership, in which he is a one-third partner. In exchange for his interest, he contributed $750,000 in cash and Blackacre, which has a value of $750,000 and a basis of $375,000. The other two partners each contributed $1.5 million in cash. After the formation, the partnership uses the cash to purchase additional assets, including inventory. After several years, the partnership has the following balance sheet. For simplicity, further assume that book values reflect current fair market values.

Zeta Partnership					
Assets			*Liabilities*		
	Basis	Book Value			$0
Blackacre	$375,000	$1,125,000			
Redacre	$1,500,000	$1,762,500		*Capital Accounts*	
Greenacre	$750,000	$900,000		Basis	Book Value
Inventory #1	$600,000	$675,000	Eliot	$1,125,000	$1,800,000
Inventory #2	$750,000	$900,000	Partner 2	$1,500,000	$1,800,000
Inventory #3	$150,000	$37,500	Partner 3	$1,500,000	$1,800,000
Total	$4,125,000	$5,400,000	Total	$4,125,000	$5,400,000

The partnership distributes Greenacre and Inventory #2 to Eliot in complete liquidation of his interest in the partnership. All of the real property is capital gain property, and the inventory items are ordinary income property. The partnership has a § 754 election in effect. Evaluate the tax consequences to Eliot and the partnership for this liquidating distribution, focusing on the allocation of Eliot's basis and the impact of the § 754 election on the remaining partnership assets.

Explanations

1. This is a straightforward example of § 731 and related rules concerning operating (current) distributions.[57] Under § 731(a), Amelia does not recognize any gain because she did not receive more money than her outside basis. Similarly, the AB Partnership never recognizes a gain (or loss) on a distribution of property to a partner.[58] Because this is a

---

57. This is based on Example 1 of Treas. Reg. § 1.732-1(a).
58. I.R.C. § 731(b). Note that this is in stark contradistinction to a corporation, including an S corporation, which would have to recognize any built-in gain on distributed property.

7. Distributions and Payments from a Partnership

distribution other than a liquidating distribution, § 732(a) governs the basis analysis. Section 732(a) provides that the basis of property distributed (other than money) shall be its inside basis before distribution. Under § 732(b), this is limited to the partner's outside basis reduced by any money distributed in the same transaction. Here, there is not a § 732(b) limitation because Amelia has sufficient basis. Amelia therefore takes a $200,000 basis in the real property. Under §§ 733 and 705, moreover, Amelia must reduce her outside basis by the basis of her distributed property, namely the $200,000 of real property and $40,000 of cash; therefore, her outside basis after the distribution is now $60,000 (starting outside basis of $300,000 less the $200,000 of basis poured into the real property and the $40,000 basis present in the cash). Lastly, her capital account must also be reduced by the value of the property distributed.

In the alternative, the differential is now the application of § 732(b)'s basis limitation. Her outside basis before the distribution was $100,000 and must be reduced by the amount of money distributed ($40,000). Therefore, she only has $60,000 to pour into the basis of the real property.

2. This is another simple example of the basis rules for distributions, here focusing on liquidating distributions.[59] The governing rule is § 732(b), which provides that, in a liquidating distribution, "[t]he basis of property (other than money) distributed by a partnership to a partner in liquidation of the partner's interest shall be an amount equal to the adjusted basis of such partner's interest in the partnership reduced by any money distributed in the same transaction."[60] Applying that simple rule here, Beverly will take a basis of $300,000 in the real property.

3. Because Carter did not receive any money, he cannot recognize any gain on the liquidating distribution under § 731(a).[61] Moreover, he cannot recognize any loss on this liquidating distribution under § 731(a)(2) because he received property other than money and hot assets. Similarly, the partnership does not recognize gain or loss on this distribution under § 731(b).

The real issue here is the allocation of basis in the distributed assets under § 732(b) and (c). Because he did not receive any money in the liquidating distribution, the total basis in the distributed assets must equal his outside basis before the liquidation ($3,250,000). Under Treas. Reg. § 1.732-1(c), basis is first allocated to hot assets. Here that

---

59. This is based on the Example of Treas. Reg. § 1.732-1(b).
60. I.R.C. § 732(b).
61. This is based on Example 1 of Treas. Reg. § 1.732-1(c)(4).

is the distributed inventory. Thus, $500,000 of basis is first poured into the distributed inventory. This leaves $2,750,000 to pour into the distributed cold assets.

After the basis has been poured into the hot assets, we then assign to each distributed property a basis equal to its inside basis.[62] We thus pour $250,000 into the basis of Blueacre and $500,000 into the basis of Greenacre. As you see, though, we have *excess* basis remaining; that is, there is still $2,000,000 of outside basis remaining, and under the liquidating distribution rules, we must pour *all* of it into the distributed property.

We therefore must make an adjustment to the basis allocation that results in an *increase* to the basis of the distributed properties. This is governed by Treas. Reg. § 1.732-1(c)(2)(ii). It provides that increases are made to cold assets first with "unrealized appreciation in proportion to each property's respective amount of unrealized appreciation before any increase (but only to the extent of each property's unrealized appreciation)."[63] Any remaining increase is "allocated to the distributed property (other than unrealized receivables or inventory items) in proportion to the fair market value of the distributed property."[64]

Blueacre has unrealized appreciation of $1,750,000 and Greenacre has $0 in unrealized appreciation. Therefore, Blueacre is assigned the first $1,750,000 of the remaining excess basis. This leaves $250,000 of basis to pour, which we pour in accordance with the fair market value property. The total fair market value of the properties is $2,500,000. Blueacre is thus allocated $200,000 [$250,000 × ($2,000,000 / $2,500,000)] and Greenacre is allocated $50,000 [$250,000 × ($50,000 / $2,500,000)].

In sum, then, Carter has the following basis in the properties that he received in his liquidating distribution: inventory, $500,000; Blueacre, $2,200,000; and Greenacre, $550,000.

4. This problem focuses on the interaction between liquidating distributions and hot assets under § 751.[65] As an introductory matter, because Don's entire interest is being liquidated, § 736 is implicated—that is, Don's interest as a partner is being terminated.[66] Don's payment is a § 736(b) payment for partnership property because it is being made in exchange for his interest in the partnership property. Note also that the

---

62. Treas. Reg. § 1.732-1(c)(1)(ii).
63. Treas. Reg. § 1.732-1(c)(2)(ii).
64. Id.
65. This is based on Example 2 of Treas. Reg. § 1.751-1(g).
66. Section 736 is discussed more in Chapter 10.

7. Distributions and Payments from a Partnership

partnership does not have assets that are subject to the § 736(b) carve-out, namely unrealized receivables and goodwill. Thus, the payment will be governed by the distribution rules. We can now turn to the hot asset analysis.

We must determine whether § 751(b) applies. Our analytical shortcut is twofold: First, does the partnership have hot assets? Second, is the distribution pro rata with respect to all the partners? As to the first question, we see that the partnership has inventory as an asset. In addition to the inventory, though, the partnership also has accounts receivable, which counts as inventory for § 751 purposes because it would generate ordinary income upon its sale or transfer.[67] For distributions, though, inventory is a hot asset only if it is "substantially appreciated."[68] Inventory is substantially appreciated if its fair market value exceeds 120% of its inside basis. Here, that test is satisfied because the value of the inventory is $312,000, which is 130% of the book basis of $240,000 ($168,000 + $72,000). The answer to the second question is that there is a non-pro rata distribution of property—that is readily observable because Don is not receiving any hot asset in his liquidating distribution.

As noted, there are two hot assets—the inventory and the accounts receivable. Step 3 requires us to determine the distributee partner's interest in each partnership asset before the distribution. In the absence of § 704(c) and other complications, we assume that the partners are equal partners in the assets such that Don is a one-third partner in each asset. Thus, his pre-distribution share of each asset is as follows.

Partners' Interest in Partnership Property Pre-Distribution				
	Don	P2	P3	Total
Cash	$40,000	$40,000	$40,000	$120,000
Accounts receivable	$24,000	$24,000	$24,000	$72,000
Inventory	$80,000	$80,000	$80,000	$240,000
Depreciable properties	$128,000	$128,000	$128,000	$384,000
Land	$24,000	$24,000	$24,000	$72,000

Step 4 requires us to determine the distributee partner's interest in each asset after the distribution, which is as follows.

---

67. I.R.C. § 751(d)(2).
68. This is in marked contradistinction to *sales* or *transfers* of partnership interests, which has no added requirement to the presence of inventory as a hot asset. Compare I.R.C. § 751(a)(2) with I.R.C. § 751(b)(A)(ii).

7. Distributions and Payments from a Partnership

Partners' Interest in Partnership Property Post-Distribution				
	Don	P2	P3	Total
Cash	$80,000	$20,000	$20,000	$120,000
Accounts receivable	$0	$36,000	$36,000	$72,000
Inventory	$0	$120,000	$120,000	$240,000
Depreciable properties	$120,000	$132,000	$132,000	$384,000
Land	$0	$36,000	$36,000	$72,000

Step 5 requires us to calculate the difference in pre- and post-distribution assets. We see that Don has increased his share of the cash and has decreased his share of all other partnership assets. Step 6 is to determine whether a § 751(b) distribution occurred, in which we see whether the non-distributee partners have a change in their hot assets. Steps 5 and 6 are depicted in the following table.

Comparison of Partners' Interest in Property Pre- and Post-Distribution (amounts in $)									
	Don			Partner 2			Partner 3		
	Post	Pre	Diff.	Post	Pre	Diff.	Post	Pre	Diff.
Cash	80,000	40,000	40,000	20,000	40,000	(20,000)	20,000	40,000	(20,000)
Accounts receivable	0	24,000	(24,000)	36,000	24,000	12,000	36,000	24,000	12,000
Inventory	0	80,000	(80,000)	120,000	80,000	40,000	120,000	80,000	40,000
Depreciable properties	120,000	128,000	(8,000)	132,000	128,000	4,000	132,000	128,000	4,000
Land	0	24,000	(24,000)	36,000	24,000	12,000	36,000	24,000	12,000

We observe that Partners 2 and 3 each have a difference for the accounts receivable and inventory rows, indicating that a distribution of hot assets occurred.

Step 7 requires us to isolate exactly what the distributee partner "purchased" and the what the distributee partner "sold." Here, Don received an additional $40,000 distribution of cash more than his share. In addition, by exiting the partnership—and no longer being liable for the partnership liabilities—he also has $96,000 of liability relief, which, under § 752, a reduction in a partner's share of partnership liabilities is treated as a distribution of money. In sum, he received $136,000 of excess value. He accomplished this by "giving up" his share of the accounts receivable ($24,000), inventory ($80,000), depreciable property ($8,000), and Land ($24,000), which also sum to $136,000. Stated otherwise, it is like he sold his interest in the accounts receivable, inventory, a portion of the

7. Distributions and Payments from a Partnership

depreciable property, and the land in exchange for the extra money and the liability assumption. Section 751(b), though, only concerns itself with the exchange of other property for § 751 property. The extent of the § 751 property is $104,000, which is Don's share of the inventory and accounts receivable.

Step 8 requires us to determine the distributee partner's basis in the assets sold. Before the deemed sale, Don is treated as if he received them in a current distribution. Don's basis in those assets, therefore, would be $56,000 for the inventory (one-third of the partnership's inside basis) and $24,000 for the accounts receivable (one-third of the partnership's inside basis). The total basis of the hot assets deemed distributed is therefore $80,000. Step 9 requires us to calculate the gain or loss on the deemed sale by the distributee partner. Here, Don is treated as selling his share of the assets for $104,000 that have a basis of $80,000, resulting in a gain of $24,000. Thus, Don must recognize $24,000 of ordinary income.

Step 10 requires us to calculate the collateral tax consequences. It is helpful here to consider the portion of the distribution that is governed under § 751(b) and the non-§ 751(b) portion. We also need to analyze the collateral consequences to the distributee partner and the other partners. First, let's consider the remaining tax consequences to Don. We already covered the § 751(b) consequences for Don (i.e., the ordinary income of $24,000). However, he also has a portion of the distribution not governed by § 751(b). Before the distribution, Don had an outside basis of $256,000, of which $96,000 was traceable to his share of partnership liabilities. His basis is reduced by the portion of the hot assets deemed distributed under § 751, which was earlier calculated as $80,000. Thus, Don has a basis of $176,000 for the remainder of the distribution. The total value distributed to Don was $296,000, consisting of the cash ($80,000), depreciable property ($120,000), and the liability relief ($96,000), which is treated as an additional distribution of money.

Because Don did not receive more than his share of the depreciable property, it could not constitute proceeds from the sale under § 751(b). Don did, however, receive more than his share of money; the sales proceeds—the tax consequences of which we determined in the § 751(b) portion of the analysis—must therefore consist of money, and since that portion of the money has already been covered, it must be subtracted from the liquidation analysis (as it was handled in the § 751(b) analysis). The property he is deemed to receive in liquidation (apart from the property covered in the § 751(b) analysis) is the depreciable property ($120,000) and $72,000 of money ($176,000 [total money]

7. Distributions and Payments from a Partnership

less $104,000 [sales proceeds]). Recall Don's outside basis is $256,000, so he has not received more money in liquidation than the outside basis; therefore, he does not recognize a gain under § 732(b). Relatedly, the basis in his depreciable property must be $104,000, which represents the remaining outside basis ($176,000) less the money reduced in the distribution ($72,000).

We can now turn to the tax consequences to the partnership and the remaining partners. Like with Don, it is helpful to bifurcate the analysis into the § 751(b) portion and the non-§ 751(b) portion. The § 751(b) portion is treated as a sale between Don and the partnership. Here the partnership did not sell any hot assets to Don (rather, it purchased them), so the partnership has no ordinary income on the deemed distribution. The partnership does, though, have a new cost basis in the inventory and accounts receivable that it purchased from Don. As well, the partnership is treated as having distributed Don's share of inventory and accounts receivable so it must also decrease its basis in those assets by the amount of basis distributed to Don. In short, the partnership is decreasing its basis in the inventory and accounts receivable by $80,000 (for the deemed distribution), and then also increasing its basis in the inventory and accounts receivable by $104,000 (for the amount it is deemed to have purchased those assets from Don). The difference is really attributable to the inventory (as there was no gain in the accounts receivable), such that the partnership's inside basis in the inventory is now increased by $24,000.

We must now apply §§ 731 through 736 for the remaining part of the distribution (i.e., the portion that is not governed by § 751(b)). To be clear, the portion of Don's distribution that is not governed by § 751(b) is the distribution of the depreciable property ($120,000) and $72,000 of money. Under § 731(b), the partnership does not recognize a gain or loss on a distribution. Under the main rule of § 734, moreover, the partnership does not adjust the inside basis of remaining partnership property unless a § 754 election is in effect. We will assume that no such election is in effect. Because the partnership distributed depreciable property with a basis of $120,000, it must have a remaining inside basis of $216,000 ($336,000 less $120,000). Lastly, the remaining partners now bear a greater share of the partnership liabilities (having absorbed Don's share) so they can each increase their outside basis under § 752 by $48,000.

In closing, the partnership would have the following balance sheet after the liquidation of Don's interest.

7. Distributions and Payments from a Partnership

Epsilon Partnership					
Assets			Liabilities		
	Basis	Book Value			$288,000
Cash	$40,000	$40,000			
Accounts receivable	$72,000	$72,000	Capital Accounts		
Inventory	$192,000	$240,000		Basis	Book Value
Depreciable property	$216,000	$264,000	Partner 2	$304,000	$200,000
Land	$72,000	$72,000	Partner 3	$304,000	$200,000
Total	$592,000	$688,000	Total	$608,000	$688,000

Observe that the basis columns do not equal—the partnership's inside bases do not equal the partners' outside bases. This is due to the lack of adjustment under § 734 and § 754.

5. This problem focuses on the allocation of basis to the distributed assets to the liquidated partner and the remaining assets inside the partnership.[69] An important observation needs to be made about the inventory items. Recall that § 751(b) can apply to liquidating distribution that results in a shifting of hot assets, such as inventory items. The partnership has a total basis of inventory items of $1,500,000, and a current value of $1,612,500—the value does not exceed 120% of the basis,[70] and therefore the inventory is not "substantially appreciated." Because they are not substantially appreciated, moreover, they are not inventory items for the purposes of § 751(b) and distributions. Therefore, at the time of the distribution, the partnership does not have hot assets that it can disproportionately distribute. Even though it is not a hot asset for § 751(b) purposes, it still constitutes "inventory" for purposes of allocation under § 732(c), described more below.

Under § 732(b), because no money was distributed, the bases of the distributed property must equal Eliot's outside basis before the liquidating distribution, which was $1,125,000. The inside basis of Greenacre and Inventory #2 was $750,000 and $750,000, respectively, which sums to $1,500,000. We thus observe that Eliot does not have enough outside basis to match fully the partnership's inside bases of the assets. Under § 732(c), the basis is allocated first to unrealized receivables and

---

69. This is based on the Example in Treas. Reg. § 1.755-1(c)(6).
70. This represents only an appreciation of 7.5%, which does not exceed the required 20%.

7. Distributions and Payments from a Partnership

inventory items. Eliot therefore pours $750,000 of basis into Inventory #2, matching the partnership's inside basis before the distribution. This leaves Eliot $375,000 of remaining basis, which can be poured into Greenacre. In short, the only remaining property (Greenacre) necessarily bears the required basis reduction of $375,000 under § 732(c).

Turning to the partnership, the general rule of § 734(a) is that the inside basis of remaining property is not adjusted because of a distribution to a partner. The exception, of course, is if a § 754 election is in place, which is the case here. A § 754 election permits a change in basis under § 734(b), which can result in an inside basis increase or decrease. An inside basis *increase* results if the inside basis of the distributed property exceeds the basis of the property in the hands of the distributee partner; this is the case here.[71] The partnership distributed property with a total basis of $1,500,000, which exceeds the total basis of that property in Eliot's hands of $1,125,000 under § 732(b). The difference is $375,000, which must be allocated under § 755.[72]

The § 755 regulations provide a three-step process for allocating adjustments under § 734(b).[73] First, the value of each partnership asset must be determined. Second, the basis adjustment is allocated between two classes of property, (i) capital assets and § 1231(b) property and (ii) and any other property (i.e., ordinary income property). Here, the facts stipulated that book values reflected current fair market values.[74] Third, the basis adjustment is allocated among the items within each class.

Because we already have fair market values, we can start with Step 2. The regulations provide that "the adjustment must be allocated to remaining partnership property of a character similar to that of the distributed property with respect to which the adjustment arose."[75] An example of this is "when the partnership's adjusted basis of distributed capital gain property immediately prior to distribution exceeds the basis of the property to the distributee partner (as determined under section 732), the basis of the undistributed capital gain property remaining in the partnership is increased by an amount equal to the excess."[76] This is the case here because the partnership's inside basis of the distributed capital gain property (Greenacre) was $750,000, which exceeds the basis of $375,000 in Eliot's hands. We therefore need to make a $375,000 increase to the remaining capital assets of the partnership.

---

71. This ignores the impact of gain or loss in the § 734(b) calculation because it was not recognized by Eliot. *See* I.R.C. § 734(b)(1)(A) and (2)(A).
72. I.R.C. § 734(c).
73. Treas. Reg. § 1.755-1(c).
74. Please observe that this is generally a simplifying convention for this text and is not generally true in the real world.
75. Treas. Reg. § 1.755-1(c)(1)(i).
76. Id.

7. Distributions and Payments from a Partnership

The third step is to allocate our increase ($375,000) within property of the capital gain property class, which consists of Blackacre and Redacre. The regulations provide that increases are allocated first to properties in proportion of their unrealized appreciation (to the extent thereof), and any remaining increase is then allocated in proportion to fair market values. Unrealized appreciation is the difference between the property's fair market value and their inside basis. Blackacre and Redacre have unrealized appreciation of $750,000 and $262,500, respectively. The following table demonstrates the allocation based on unrealized appreciation, including their new adjusted inside basis in the far-right column.

	Allocating Increase in Basis Under § 755 Based on Unrealized Appreciation						
	Inside Basis [A]	Fair Market Values [B]	Unrealized Appreciation [B] − [A]	% of UA [C]	Increase to Allocate [D]	Allocated Increase [C] x [D]	Adjusted Basis [A] + ([C] x [D])
Blackacre	$375,000	$1,125,000	$750,000	74.07%	$375,000	$277,763	$652,763
Redacre	$1,500,000	$1,762,500	$262,500	25.93%	$375,000	$97,238	$1,597,238
Total	$1,875,000	$2,887,500	$1,012,500	100%		$375,000[77]	$2,225,000[78]

---

77. Technically $375,001 due to rounding.
78. Technically $2,225,001 due to rounding.

Payments Between a Partnership and its Partners: § 707

INTRODUCTION

In the last chapter, we covered partnership distributions, which are payments of property including money from a partnership to a partner by reason of being a partner. The distribution framework implicitly recognized that, unless a partner receives more money than outside basis, such a distribution essentially represents a return of previously taxed capital, and, as such, need not be reported again on the partner's individual tax return. What if, though, a partner receives a payment that is unconnected with his or her role as a partner? For example, if a partner renders services to the partnership—like that of an attorney, accountant, or other professional—and is paid for those services? Similarly, what if a partner receives a payment from a partnership that is "guaranteed" and not dependent on any profits, economic return, or entrepreneurial risk of the partnership? These two types of payments are conceptually different than a distribution of previously taxed partnership profits (i.e., current or liquidating distributions) connected with the status of being a partner.

Consequently, there is a separate section that governs these types of payments. Section 707 resolved a tension in the case law that hinged on the nature of a partnership—a theme that we have already seen—namely whether a partnership is an entity or an aggregate. Consider, for example, a partnership involved in buying and selling financial investments, and a partner that sells on his own account (that is, he buys his own investments through the partnership). As is typical with investments, a commission

8. Payments Between a Partnership and its Partners: § 707

is typically paid on the purchase or sale of securities. Under an entity approach, a partner would be taxable on his distributive share of partnership income—even that portion of the commissions he paid himself. On the other hand, under an aggregate approach, a partner should not be taxed on money that he essentially paid to himself.[1]

Section 707, therefore, resolves this conceptual conflict, and it provides clarity on how to treat transactions between a partnership and a partner. It is helpful to appreciate the statutory framework here and how § 707 clarifies it. Under Subchapter K, an allocation or distribution for the provision of services can be handled in three ways, two of which are the focus of this chapter. First, the payment can simply be part of the partner's distributive share under § 704(b), a topic covered in earlier chapters. Second, the payment can be a "guaranteed payment" under § 707(c), which essentially means the payment does not depend on the underlying profitability of the partnership. Third, the payment can be treated just like if the partner was not a partner (e.g., like a vendor or contractor), which is the focus of § 707(a).

This chapter focuses on the second and third ways of handling the provision of services to the partnership by a partner. Section 707(a) governs transactions and payments between a partnership and a partner when that partner is not acting in a partner-capacity (but is, instead, operating like a vendor, for example). Section 707(c) governs payments known as "guaranteed payments"; these are payments to a partner that are "guaranteed" and do not depend on partnership income. These first two rules are expressly provided for in § 707. Identifying features of the proper classification depends on what "hat" the partner is wearing while performing the services—that is, a partner hat or a non-partner hat. Also, another critical feature is whether the payment is subject to entrepreneurial risk—that is, is the payment guaranteed or is it contingent on partnership operations.

Before we dive into the mechanics of these two new rules (§§ 707(a) and (c)), a quick example illustrates when they apply. For example, consider a real estate partnership in which one of the partners is also a bookkeeper, but he is not required under the partnership agreement to render bookkeeping services to the partnership. If the partnership decides to engage the partner as its bookkeeper, and the partner-bookkeeper bills the partnership just like he or she would any other client, then § 707(a) applies and it treats these payments like the partner-bookkeeper was not a partner. If, on the other hand, the partnership offers to pay the partner a guaranteed sum of $25,000 annually, regardless of partnership profits—perhaps to entice him or her to be a partner—this represents a guaranteed payment under § 707(c). Lastly, if the partnership agrees to pay the partner-bookkeeper the first $25,000 of partnership income as payment for services rendered, this

---

1. *See* Benjamin v. Hoey, 139 F.2d 945, 946 (2d Cir. 1944); *see also* WILLIAM S. McKEE ET AL., FEDERAL TAXATION OF PARTNERSHIPS ¶ 14.01 (2024).

8. Payments Between a Partnership and its Partners: § 707

payment may represent neither a § 707(a) nor § 707(c) payment—it may be a payment of partnership distributive income.

PARTNER ACTING IN A NON-PARTNER CAPACITY: § 707(A) PAYMENTS

The first rule is found in § 707(a)(1), which provides that "[i]f a partner engages in a transaction with a partnership other than in his capacity as a member of such partnership, the transaction shall, except as otherwise provided in this section, be considered as occurring between the partnership and one who is not a partner."[2] As described in the regulations, these transactions result in treating the partner "as if he were not a member of the partnership with respect to such transaction."[3]

The regulations give examples of prototypical § 707(a) transactions:

> Such transactions include, for example, loans of money or property by the partnership to the partner or by the partner to the partnership, the sale of property by the partner to the partnership, the purchase of property by the partner from the partnership, and the rendering of services by the partnership to the partner or by the partner to the partnership.[4]

Similarly, if a partner leases property for partnership use that is also a § 707(a) transaction.[5] In summary, then, the regulations offer four genres of prototypical transactions between a partner and the partnership that triggers the non-partner treatment under § 707(a): (1) loans, (2) sales of property, (3) rendering services, and (4) leasing property.

Once § 707(a) applies to a payment, the typical rules that accompany that type of payment apply—for example, with respect to the payment's character, inclusion timing, and deduction timing. This is implied by the exhortation of § 707(a) to consider the payment as "occurring between the partnership and one who is not a partner."[6]

Consider the following example. The ABC Partnership is involved in buying and renting residential rental property. It outsources the day-to-day management of the property—e.g., handling the collection and depositing of rent and handyman repairs across its rental portfolio—to one of its partners, A. As part of this contract, it pays A $5,000 per month, which we will

---

2. I.R.C. § 707(a)(1).
3. Treas. Reg. § 1.707-1(a).
4. Id.
5. Id.
6. I.R.C. § 707(a)(1).

8. Payments Between a Partnership and its Partners: § 707

assume is commensurate with typical management contracts of this sort. For present purposes, let's assume that this is a type of payment contemplated by § 707(a), i.e., A is being paid for rendering services to the partnership.[7] Consequently, this "transaction" is treated as one between the partnership and one who is not a partner. Thus, assuming A is a cash-method, calendar-year taxpayer, he receives $5,000 of ordinary income under § 61 upon the actual or constructive receipt of the monthly fee. Similarly, the partnership incurs and deducts $5,000 as an ordinary and necessary business expense under § 162 for each payment.

Although § 707(a) provides that these payments are to be treated as between a partnership and a non-partner, there are other sections that may affect the timing of the deduction. Generally, a partnership may deduct a deductible item (like a business expense) consistent with its method of accounting. Thus, a cash-method partnership can deduct the expense when actually paid,[8] and an accrual-method partnership can deduct the expense when the all-events test has been satisfied.[9] However, the partner and partnership need to be mindful of the impact of § 267 on these § 707(a) payments.

Section 267 regards transactions between related persons. A key provision of § 267 is subsection (a)(2), which provides a matching rule between related persons. Under this rule, a related payor cannot properly deduct an item until the related payee includes the item in income. For this rule, a partner is a related person.[10] This rule most clearly manifests when you have an accrual-method partnership and a cash-method partner-payee.

Let's illustrate this using a modification of the earlier example. Assume that the ABC Partnership is now an accrual-method taxpayer and Partner A is a cash-method taxpayer, both of whom are on a calendar-year tax year. Assume that for the services rendered in December, the partnership does not, in fact, pay Partner A until the following January. In this case, the amount would ordinarily still be deductible by ABC in December Year 1 when the liability satisfies the all-events test, and includible by A when received in January Year 2.[11] Section 267(a)(2), however, provides that the partnership

---

7. As unpacked in our discussion later in the chapter, given the nature of the partnership, it is possible that this may be classified as his share of distributive income if he is doing this whilst wearing a partner hat.
8. Treas. Reg. § 1.461-1(a)(1) ("Under the cash receipts and disbursements method of accounting, amounts representing allowable deductions shall, as a general rule, be taken into account for the taxable year in which paid.").
9. Treas. Reg. § 1.461-1(a)(2)(i) ("Under an accrual method of accounting, a liability . . . is incurred, and generally is taken into account for Federal income tax purposes, in the taxable year in which all the events have occurred that establish the fact of the liability, the amount of the liability can be determined with reasonable accuracy, and economic performance has occurred with respect to the liability.").
10. I.R.C. § 267(e).
11. Assuming, of course, no constructive receipt issues to accelerate the inclusion into December.

8. Payments Between a Partnership and its Partners: § 707

may not deduct the payment until Year 2 (when Partner A properly includes it in his income).

In addition, loans between the partner and partnership are transactions listed in the § 707 regulations that may be treated as occurring between the partnership and a non-partner.[12] It may be helpful to explain why the § 707 regulations require this treatment. Because interest paid on loans can be tax deductible, there may be an incentive to classify contributions to a partnership as a loan; this concern is allayed, of course, because although the partnership may receive an interest deduction, the partner would have a corresponding interest income inclusion.[13] Relatedly, there may be an incentive to classify a distribution to a partner as a loan—for example, when the distribution exceeds the partner's outside basis, which would typically trigger a gain under § 731. The exhortation, then, under § 707 is to treat items as loans which are, in substance, actually loans.[14] In addition to loans, the regulations also highlight transactions in which "a partner retains the ownership of property but allows the partnership to use such separately owned property for partnership purposes."[15]

Sales of Property Between a Partnership and a Partner Acting in a Non-Partner Capacity

The § 707 regulations provide that the "the sale of property by the partner to the partnership" and "the purchase of property by the partner from the partnership" can be transactions governed by § 707(a).[16] The concern here is to distinguish between *bona fide* sales of property, which are governed by § 707, and contributions of property, which are governed by § 721. Consider the example in which Partner A sells Blackacre, worth $100,000 with a basis of $25,000 to his partnership for $100,000 of cash. At first blush, you may be wondering why A would ever want sales treatment here, which would trigger immediate gain recognition, instead of the deferral allowed under § 721. One response is character planning. In other words, assume in this example that Blackacre is a capital asset in the hands of A, but would be an ordinary income asset in the hands of the partnership (because, say, the partnership will be in the land development business). By structuring this as a § 707 transaction, A can be assured of the capital gain nature of that built-in gain, rather than a later sale by the partnership of the asset, which would be ordinary income.

---

12. Treas. Reg. § 1.707-1(a).
13. The analysis becomes more complicated for non-U.S.-based partners. *See* I.R.C. § 871.
14. Treas. Reg. § 1.707-1(a).
15. Id.
16. Id.

8. Payments Between a Partnership and its Partners: § 707

Disguised Payments for Services and Sales

Section 707 is not only concerned with transactions that are expressly structured as sales or payments for services, like the earlier examples, but it is also concerned with transactions that, although structured like a contribution or distribution are, in substance, sales or payments for services. These are known as disguised payments, which are also controlled by § 707. Understanding the rules about disguised payments are best served by appreciating the prototypical transaction it is seeking to ferret out; let's consider an example of a disguised sale.

Partner A contributes Blackacre with a basis of $25,000 and a fair market value of $100,000 to a partnership in exchange for his partnership interest. The partnership then transfers $25,000 in cash to him, and it also agrees to increase A's share of partnership income by $75,000 in total over the next three years. Take note that the special allocation here has the concomitant effect of reducing the other partners' taxable income by $75,000 (akin to a business deduction), which is a point worth emphasizing: If the transaction was styled as a *purchase of property* by the partnership, on the other hand, there would be *no* current income deduction because of the capitalization rules of § 263.[17] As well, if the distribution of cash is respected as a distribution under § 731, it does not exceed A's outside basis in his partnership and thus would not be presently taxable. In sum, A has deferred the recognition of gain on this transaction (by way of § 731 and the future allocations of income) and the other partners have similarly secured an equivalent deduction over the next few years, short-circuiting the capitalization rules.[18]

Section 707(a)(2) therefore provides rules that would prevent the above capitalization-avoidance tax treatment. There are two main rules of § 707(a)(2), which are both further defined by regulations. The first, contained in subparagraph (A), regards certain performances of services and property transfers, and the second, contained in subparagraph (B), regards property transfers, including money. The essence of both rules is the same, though. In both, if a partner (i) transfers property or performs services, (ii) there is a related direct or indirect allocation or transfer to such partner, and (iii) such transfer or performance and the allocation, when viewed together, are properly characterized as transaction between a partner and a non-partner or as a sale, then it will be treated as such. In other words, we need to view the transfer of property or performance of services along

---

17. Indeed, preventing the end-run around the capitalization rules of § 263 is a core motivation of § 707(a). *See, e.g.*, Disguised Payment for Services, 80 Fed. Reg. 43652-01, 2015-32 I.R.B. 158 (proposed July 23, 2015).
18. To be sure, some of the property may be depreciable under §§ 167 and 168, so this arrangement may be more of a timing issue for the other partners; that is, the timing of the special allocations may be quicker than the depreciation schedule required under § 168.

8. Payments Between a Partnership and its Partners: § 707

with any allocations to that partner to see if they really represent a disguised payment for services or a disguised sale of property. Each disguised payment will be considered in turn.

Disguised Payments for Services

Take note that, on its face, unlike § 707(a)(1), subsection (a)(2) is not self-executing; that is, it requires regulations to operate. Although there are final regulations concerning disguised sales under § 707(a)(2)(B), there are only *proposed* regulations, which were issued in 2015, concerning disguised payments for services. As the proposed regulations explain, the expressed concern justifying § 707(a)(2)(A) was the view that "partnerships and service providers were inappropriately treating payments as allocations and distributions to a partner even when the service provider acted in a capacity other than as a partner."[19] The Treasury further explained that Congress contemplated that the regulations would use five factors to determine whether a service provider is acting in its capacity as a partner;[20] Treasury also added a sixth factor.[21]

The first factor is whether the "arrangement lacks significant entrepreneurial risk," which is the most important factor.[22] The second factor is whether the "[t]he service provider holds, or is expected to hold, a transitory partnership interest or a partnership interest for only a short duration."[23] The third factor is whether the "service provider receives an allocation and distribution in a time frame comparable to the time frame that a non-partner service provider would typically receive payment."[24] The fourth factor is whether the "service provider became a partner primarily to obtain tax benefits that would not have been available if the services were rendered to the partnership in a third party capacity."[25] The fifth factor is "[t]he value of the service provider's interest in general and continuing partnership profits is small in relation to the allocation and distribution."[26] The sixth factor regards whether allocations and distributions differ with

---

19. Disguised Payment for Services, 80 Fed. Reg. 43652-01, 2015-32 I.R.B. 158 (proposed July 23, 2015).
20. Id.; H.R. Rep. No. 432 (Pt. 2), 98th Cong., 2d Sess. 1216-21 (1984) at 1219-20; S. Prt. No. 169 (Vol. 1), 98th Cong., 2d Sess. 223-32 (1984) at 227.
21. Disguised Payment for Services, 80 Fed. Reg. 43652-01, 2015-32 I.R.B. 158 (proposed July 23, 2015).
22. Prop. Treas. Reg. § 1.707-2(c)(1), 80 Fed. Reg. 43652-01 (July 23, 2015).
23. Prop. Treas. Reg. § 1.707-2(c)(2), 80 Fed. Reg. 43652-01 (July 23, 2015).
24. Prop. Treas. Reg. § 1.707-2(c)(3), 80 Fed. Reg. 43652-01 (July 23, 2015).
25. Prop. Treas. Reg. § 1.707-2(c)(4), 80 Fed. Reg. 43652-01 (July 23, 2015).
26. Prop. Treas. Reg. § 1.707-2(c)(5), 80 Fed. Reg. 43652-01 (July 23, 2015).

8. Payments Between a Partnership and its Partners: § 707

respect to the services rendered, whether those persons are related, and varying levels of entrepreneurial risk.[27]

Importantly, these factors help illuminate whether the required statutory and regulatory elements of § 707(a)(2)(A) are present, which are:

> (i) A person (service provider), either in a partner capacity or in anticipation of becoming a partner, performs services (directly or through its delegate) to or for the benefit of a partnership; (ii) There is a related direct or indirect allocation and distribution to such service provider; and (iii) The performance of such services and the allocation and distribution, when viewed together, are properly characterized as a transaction occurring between the partnership and a person acting other than in that person's capacity as a partner.[28]

This analysis happens "at the time the arrangement is entered into or modified and without regard to whether the terms of the arrangement require the allocation and distribution to occur in the same taxable year."[29] If the arrangement is classified as a payment for services, it is treated as such for all tax purposes, including timing issues.

Let's consider an example based on the application of the proposed regulations. Assume that the Alpha Partnership constructs a building that is forecasted to generate $100,000 of revenue each year.[30] Partner A is an architect who performs services for the partnership and his normal fee would be about $40,000 for the contemplated work for the partnership. Partner A contributes cash that grants him a 25% interest in the partnership. In addition, the partnership specially allocates him $20,000 of partnership *gross income* for the first two years. The regulations conclude that this arrangement lacks significant entrepreneurial risk. The regulations note that the special allocation to A is capped, and the cap is reasonably expected to apply (e.g., the building will generate sufficient income). The special allocation is also of partnership *gross income*. Because the allocation lacks significant entrepreneurial risk, the arrangement is deemed to be a disguised payment for services.

Disguised Sales

As noted, § 707 is not only concerned with transactions that are expressly structured as sales, but also transactions that are structured like a contribution or distribution but are, in substance, sales. The regulations provide that

---

27. Prop. Treas. Reg. § 1.707-2(c)(6), 80 Fed. Reg. 43652-01 (July 23, 2015).
28. Prop. Treas. Reg. § 1.707-2(b), 80 Fed. Reg. 43652-01 (July 23, 2015).
29. Prop. Treas. Reg. § 1.707-2(b)(2), 80 Fed. Reg. 43652-01 (July 23, 2015).
30. Based on Example 1 of Prop. Treas. Reg. § 1.707-2(d), 80 Fed. Reg. 43652-01 (July 23, 2015).

8. Payments Between a Partnership and its Partners: § 707

if "transfers of property" by a partner to a partnership and "one or more transfers of money or other consideration" by partnership to a partner meet the requirements of subsection (b)(1) of the regulations, it will be treated as a sale (either in whole or in part).[31]

Subsection (b)(1) provides that a transfer and return consideration will be treated as a sale if, based on all the *facts and circumstances*, (1) the transfer of money or consideration would not have been made but for the transfer, and (2) if the transfers are not simultaneous, the later transfer is not dependent on entrepreneurial risks of partnership operations.[32] We thus distill some key points here. First, the nature of the facts and circumstances are critically important; second, the articulation of a "but for" standard; and third, an analysis of entrepreneurial risks for transfers separated by time.

The regulations further unpack the facts and circumstances analysis needed here. It notes that the weight given to each fact depends on the particular case; it further notes that the facts and circumstances are to be examined as of the date of the earliest transfer. It lists several facts and circumstances to consider, such as the certainty with which the timing and amount of a later transfer can be determined, a legally enforceable right to a later transfer, whether a transfer is secured, and partnership distributions allocations, or control of operations, among others.[33]

In addition to the facts and circumstances test, the regulations also provide that, transfers occurring within two years of each other are *presumed* to be a sale of property to the partnership unless the facts and circumstances *clearly* establish the transfers are not a sale; relatedly, this two-year timing rule also mandates disclosure to the Service if the parties are treating it not as a sale.[34] Just like this two-year rule makes a presumption of a sale, if the transfers happen more than two years apart, the regulations provide the transfers are not presumptively a sale, unless the facts and circumstances clearly established it was a sale.[35]

Let's work through these rules with some examples. Consider first that A transfers Blackacre to the AB Partnership in exchange for a partnership interest.[36] At the time of transfer, Blackacre has a fair market value of $400,000 and a tax basis of $120,000; after the transfers, the partnership transfers $300,000 in cash to A. Given the facts, circumstances, and timing of these transfers (e.g., within the two-year presumption period), assume that the transfer of cash to A is treated as a part sale of Blackacre. Because the cash received by A does not equal the full fair market value of Blackacre, A is

---

31. Treas. Reg. § 1.707-3(a)(1).
32. Treas. Reg. § 1.707-3(b)(1).
33. Treas. Reg. § 1.707-3(b)(2).
34. Treas. Reg. § 1.707-3(c)(2).
35. Treas. Reg. § 1.707-3(d).
36. Based on Example 1 of Treas. Reg. § 1.707-3(f).

8. Payments Between a Partnership and its Partners: § 707

deemed to have sold a portion of property to the partnership that was worth $300,000 in exchange for the cash. Consequently, A must recognize gain on the sale portion of the transfer. Partner A first determines his adjusted basis allocated to the sale portion; that is calculated by multiplying his adjusted basis by the ratio of the sales prices over the fair market value—that is, $120,000 \times (\$300,000 / \$400,000) = \$90,000$. Thus, the gain realized is calculated as the amount realized ($300,000) less the adjusted basis ($90,000), which equals $210,000 of gain. This transaction was only part sale. The balance of the transfer was thus a § 721 contribution; that is, here, A is still considered to have contributed a piece of property worth $100,000 (the fair market value over the deemed sales price) and an adjusted basis of $30,000 (the basis that was not allocated to the deemed sale).

The prior example was relatively straightforward due to the timing, i.e., the transfers happened at the same time. What if, though, we take the example above, and space the transfers by one year—that is, assume now that the partnership transfers the $300,000 one year after A transfers Blackacre to the partnership. The first issue to decide is whether this is a disguised sale under § 707(a)(2)(B). As noted earlier, the general test under the regulations is a "but for" test that examines whether the transfer of property by the partner would not have been made but for the return transfer of property.[37] And, the regulations further provide that, when the transfers are not made simultaneously—like here—you must also consider if the "the subsequent transfer is not dependent on the entrepreneurial risks of partnership operations."[38] The analysis is simplified because the transactions occur within two years of each other, which triggers the presumption in the regulations that the transfers are presumed to be a sale.[39]

Now that the regulations presume that our one-year-spaced transfers are a disguised sale, we need to apply the operative rules. An item to highlight early is when the sale is deemed to occur—does it happen upon the transfer to the partnership or upon the later-in-time transfers of cash to the partner (here, one year later). The regulations provide that the "[t]he sale is considered to take place on the date that, under general principles of Federal tax law, the partnership is considered the owner of the property."[40] The regulations further clarify the impact of the time spacing: "If the transfer of money or other consideration from the partnership to the partner occurs after the transfer of property to the partnership; the partner and the partnership are treated as if, on the date of the sale, the partnership

---

37. Treas. Reg. § 1.707-3(b)(1)(i).
38. Treas. Reg. § 1.707-3(b)(1)(ii).
39. Treas. Reg. § 1.707-3(c). This is rebuttable, if it can be shown that the transfers "clearly establish" the transfers do not constitute a sale. Treas. Reg. § 1.707-3(c)(1).
40. Treas. Reg. § 1.707-3(a)(2).

8. Payments Between a Partnership and its Partners: § 707

transferred to the partner an obligation to transfer to the partner money or other consideration."[41]

In our example, then, the partner sells a portion of Blackacre to the partnership and the partnership gives the partner an obligation (i.e., essentially a promissory note) to transfer the sales price in the future. Importantly, this triggers application of § 1274, which determines the issue price of debt obligation.[42] Under § 1274, assume the imputed principal amount of the partnership's obligation is $272,109,[43] which represents A's amount realized. To calculate his gain, we need to allocate his basis: $120,000 × ($272,109 / $400,000) = $81,633. Thus, his gain is calculated as the amount realized of $272,109 less the adjusted tax basis of $81,633, which equals $190,476. To complete the example, A is therefore considered to have contributed $127,891[44] of the fair market value of Blackacre to the partnership with an adjusted tax basis of $38,367.[45] Furthermore, the amount that the $300,000 payment exceeds the obligation value (i.e., $27,891) will be recognized under § 1272.

Let's do another example that probes the two-year presumption.[46] Assume that A transfers Redacre, which is undeveloped land, to the AB Partnership in exchange for his partnership interest. The partnership intends to build rental condominiums on the land, and, at the time of contribution, it is unencumbered. The partnership agreement provides that upon the completion of construction, the partnership will distribute $500,000 to A.

Consider the results if construction is completed within two years and the $500,000 transfer is made to A — this would trigger the two-year presumption, requiring that the transfer be presumed to be in part a sale of Redacre to the partnership. This presumption may be rebutted, however, on two grounds: First, if A can show that the $500,000 transfer would have been made without regard of his transfer of Redacre to the partnership. Second, if A can show that the partnership's obligation or ability to make the $500,000 transfer depends on the entrepreneurial risks of partnership operations. Some factors that may bear on this include, for example, if the partnership's ability to fund the transfer depends on its ability to obtain loan proceeds that exceed the cost of construction. Similarly, another factor may be if the partnership is only able to finance the cost of construction, which

---

41. Id.
42. I.R.C. § 1274 is not a partnership tax section and its intricacies and operations are beyond the scope of this text.
43. Like the example in the regulation, this is assuming an applicable Federal short-term rate of 10%, compounded semiannually. In other words, the $272,109 is the present value of a $300,000 future value, in one year, discounted at 10% compounded semiannually.
44. This is the full fair market value of $400,000 less the deemed sales price of $272,109.
45. This is the full adjusted tax basis of $120,000 less the amount allocated to the sale of $81,633.
46. Based on Example 3 of Treas. Reg. § 1.707-3(f).

8. Payments Between a Partnership and its Partners: § 707

limits the partnership's ability to make the later transfer to A. Both of these would be enhanced, moreover, if at the time of transfer, there is not even a lender arranged.

GUARANTEED PAYMENTS

The next type of payment to consider under § 707 is known as a "guaranteed payment" and it is covered under § 707(c). Section 707(c) provides, in full:

> To the extent determined without regard to the income of the partnership, payments to a partner for services or the use of capital shall be considered as made to one who is not a member of the partnership, but only for the purposes of section 61(a) (relating to gross income) and, subject to section 263, for purposes of section 162(a) (relating to trade or business expenses).[47]

The critical requirement, then, of a guaranteed payment is that the payment is made "without regard to the income of the partnership."[48] Like § 707(a)(1) payments, guaranteed payments are treated as being made to a non-partner, but unlike § 707(a)(1) payments, this non-partner treatment applies only for § 61(a) and § 162(a) purposes. In other words, they are treated as non-partner payments only for inclusion and deductibility purposes.

In addition to the payment being "guaranteed"—meaning not dependent on the income of the partnership—the payment must also be made to a partner who is acting in the capacity of a partner. This is admittedly not express on the face of § 707, but it is implied in the operation of the § 707 regulations. In other words, if the payment is to a partner acting in a non-partner capacity, then the payment is covered under § 707(a)(1) and not § 707(c). Despite the import of the hat-wearing-status of the partner (i.e., is the partner wearing a partner or a non-partner hat) in a particular transaction, there is no clear delineation of this line in either the statute or the regulations. In one case, though, the Tax Court held that receiving fees for "performing services within the normal scope of their duties as general partners and pursuant to the partnership agreement" were received in the capacity of being a partner and therefore were not § 707(a) payments.[49] On appeal, the Fifth Circuit agreed and noted that "the duties to be performed

---

47. I.R.C. § 707(c).
48. I.R.C. § 707(c); Treas. Reg. § 1.707-1(c).
49. Pratt v. Comm'r, 64 T.C. 203, 211–12 (1975), aff'd in part, rev'd in part, 550 F.2d 1023 (5th Cir. 1977).

8. Payments Between a Partnership and its Partners: § 707

were activities for which the partnership was created in the first place."[50] On the other hand, the Service has held that a partner was acting as a nonpartner when it rendered investment advising services that were "substantially the same as those it renders as an independent contractor or agent for persons other than [the partnership] and, under the agreement, the adviser is not precluded from engaging in such transactions with others."[51]

The following example demonstrates a guaranteed payment.[52] Consider the ABC Partnership, in which Partner A is entitled to $25,000 for services rendered to the partnership, without regard to the income of the partnership. Assume also that A's distributive share is 10% of partnership income and, after deducting the guaranteed payment, the partnership has $300,000 of ordinary income. Consequently, A must include $55,000 as ordinary income, which traces to his $25,000 guaranteed payment and his $30,000 distributive share.

Instead of fixed dollar amounts, like the above example, guaranteed payments may also be expressed as a fixed minimum amount; this is demonstrated in the following example.[53] The CD Partnership provides that Partner C will receive 20% of partnership income as determined before any guaranteed payments but in no event less than $15,000. If the partnership income is $200,000, C's distributive share is $40,000 and therefore none of the amount is a guaranteed payment. If, however, the partnership income was only $50,000, C's distributive share would be $10,000, meaning he would need to receive an additional $5,000, which would be a guaranteed payment.

Importantly, proposed regulations would change the analysis in the above paragraph.[54] Consider the example in the proposed regulation:

> Partner C in the CD partnership is to receive 30 percent of partnership income, but not less than $10,000. The income of the partnership is $60,000, and C is entitled to $18,000 (30 percent of $60,000). Of this amount, $10,000 is a guaranteed payment to C. The $10,000 guaranteed payment reduces the partnership's net income to $50,000 of which C receives $8,000 as C's distributive share.[55]

Under the current rule, if the partnership income is $60,000, none of the payment represents a guaranteed payment because C's 30% income share ($18,000) is *above* the minimum. On the other hand, if the income allocation is

---

50. 550 F.2d 1023, 1026 (5th Cir. 1977).
51. Rev. Rul. 81-301, 1981-2 C.B. 144.
52. Example 1 of Treas. Reg. § 1.707-1.
53. Example 2 of Treas. Reg. § 1.707-1.
54. Example 2 of Prop. Treas. Reg. § 1.707-1, 80 Fed. Reg. 43658 (July 23, 2015).
55. Id.

8. Payments Between a Partnership and its Partners: § 707

less than the guaranteed amount (say 30% of $20,000 or $6,000) only the difference (now $4,000 to arrive at the guaranteed minimum) represents the guaranteed payment. Under the proposed amendment to the example, though, the Service would treat the minimum as a guaranteed payment. In its explanation of the proposed regulations, the Service explained Example 2 as currently written is "inconsistent with the concept that an allocation must be subject to significant entrepreneurial risk to be treated as a distributive share under section 704(b)."[56] Thus, the proposed rule would "provide that the entire minimum amount is treated as a guaranteed payment under section 707(c) regardless of the amount of the income allocation."[57]

As noted earlier, guaranteed payments are treated as non-partner payments for § 61(a) and § 162(a) purposes. However, unlike § 707(a), which piggybacks on the service partner's method of accounting for inclusion timing, guaranteed payments under § 707(c) have an express timing rule provided in the regulation. The regulation provides that the partner must include guaranteed payments as ordinary income in the "taxable year within or with which ends the partnership taxable year in which the partnership deducted such payments as paid or accrued under its method of accounting."[58] This timing difference is therefore a critical difference in the consequences between § 707(a) and § 707(c) payments. An application of the timing rules of guaranteed payments is provided in the following example.

Ethan is a calendar year, cash-basis taxpayer.[59] He is a member of the Bravo Partnership, also a cash-basis taxpayer, which has a fiscal year that ends on June 30. For the partnership year that ends on June 30, Year 2, the partnership made guaranteed payments of $100,000 to Ethan for services provided; specifically, the partnership paid him $25,000 on July 31, Year 1; December 31, Year 1; March 31, Year 2, and June 30, Year 2. Despite the timing of the guaranteed payments that span Years 1 and 2, Ethan will report the entire $100,000 in his Year 2 income tax return.

SECTION 707 SYNTHESIS

After this chapter, we can now appreciate the statutory framework of Subchapter K that allows for three paths for a payment for services to a

---

56. Disguised Payment for Services, 80 Fed. Reg. 43652-01, 2015-32 I.R.B. 158 (proposed July 23, 2015).
57. Id.
58. Treas. Reg. § 1.707-1(c); *see also* Treas. Reg. § 1.706-1(a)(1) ("A partner must also include in taxable income for a taxable year guaranteed payments under section 707(c) that are deductible by the partnership under its method of accounting in the partnership taxable year ending within or with the partner's taxable year.").
59. Based on the Example of Treas. Reg. § 1.706-1(a)(2).

8. Payments Between a Partnership and its Partners: § 707

partner by a partnership: (1) § 707(a) non-partner payment, (2) § 707(c) guaranteed payment, and (3) a distributive share under § 704. The first critical juncture in the analytical framework is to determine whether a partner is acting in his or her capacity of partner. Although it's a simple rule to state—and despite its importance—this first decision is not well defined. A main case in this space, as noted above, is *Pratt v. Commissioner*.[60] There, the Tax Court held—and the Fifth Circuit affirmed—that general partners who provided managerial duties that were integral and central to their duties under the partnership agreement were not § 707(a) payments, i.e., they were acting like partners.[61]

The two key administrative rulings are Revenue Ruling 81-300 and Revenue Ruling 81-301. In Revenue Ruling 81-300, the Service considered management fees paid to general partners in exchange for management services in a real estate partnership. There, the facts were that "the partnership agreement provides that the general partners must contribute their time, managerial abilities and best efforts to the partnership and that in return for their managerial services each will receive a fee of five percent of the gross rentals received by the partnership."[62] Although the ruling focused on the application of guaranteed-payment treatment under § 707(c), by holding that such an arrangement constituted § 707(c) payments, it necessarily implied that the payments were made in their partner capacities. In Revenue Ruling 81-301, discussed earlier, the Service found that payments paid to a partner who provided investment-adviser services were § 707(a) payments, i.e., not made in a partner capacity.[63] There, the Service focused on, among other things, that the adviser provided similar services to others as part of its regular businesses, the adviser could terminate its services upon giving notice, the adviser paid its own expenses relating to those services, and the services were supervised by other partners.[64]

If the conclusion to the first query is that the payment is being made in a non-partner capacity, then the analysis stops: it is treated as a § 707(a) payment and the partner is treated as an "outsider"—just like any other external vendor or contractor. If, on the other hand, the payment is being made in a partner capacity, then a second inquiry is needed—this second inquiry is to filter between guaranteed payments and distributive share payments. The second inquiry is whether the payment is determined without regard to the income of the partnership. If the payment is determined without regard to the income of the partnership, then it is treated as a

---

60. 64 T.C. 204 (1975), *aff'd in part, rev'd in part*, 550 F.2d 1023 (5th Cir. 1977).
61. *See also* Disguised Payment for Services, 80 Fed. Reg. 43652-01, 2015-32 I.R.B. 158 (proposed July 23, 2015).
62. 1981-51 I.R.B. 11, 1981-2 C.B. 143.
63. 1981-51 I.R.B. 12, 1981-2 C.B. 144.
64. *Id.*

8. Payments Between a Partnership and its Partners: § 707

guaranteed payment under § 707(c). Section 707(c) provides that guaranteed payments are treated like § 707(a) payments (i.e., a payment made to an outsider) but only for purposes of § 61(a) and § 162 (but subject to § 263 requirements). There is also the special timing rule for guaranteed payments: they are included by the partner in the year of partnership deduction. If a payment is neither a § 707(a) nor a § 707(c) payment, then it represents a payment of the partner's distributive share of partnership income; these payments are governed by § 704 and related rules.

Examples

1. In addition to her full-time job as a tax accountant, Ally is a one-third partner in the Lima Partnership that invests in various residential rental properties in her community. The partnership has recently lost its tax preparer, and Ally has agreed to prepare this year's federal and state partnership tax returns and related schedules for the partners. Ally charges the partnership $15,000 for the tax compliance work, which is commensurate with what she would charge a similarly situated, unrelated partnership. The partnership generates $300,000 in net partnership income for the year; Ally has an outside basis of $100,000 at the beginning of the year. Ally and the partnership are cash-basis, calendar-year taxpayers. Ally invoices the partnership for the compliance work in February, which it promptly pays in March of the same year. Evaluate the tax consequences for Ally and the partnership for the arrangement described.

2. Brodie is a partner in a partnership that manages and rents residential rental properties. Brodie is a contractor and handyman, and, as part of his duties under the partnership agreement, Brodie performs repair and maintenance services. The partnership agreement provides that Brodie is to receive 25% of partnership income determined before taking into account any guaranteed payments, but in no event less than $15,000 per year. For the current tax year, the partnership's income is $80,000. Based on this arrangement, what is the amount, if any, of Brodie's (i) § 707(a) payment, (ii) § 707(c) payment, and (iii) § 704 distributive income? Alternatively, what if the partnership's income was $45,000?

3. Casey is an investment adviser and stockbroker. She agrees to trade on behalf of the Sigma Partnership without charging her customary commission. Moreover, she contributes cash to the partnership in exchange for a 60% partnership interest. Additionally, the partnership agreement provides a special allocation of gross income to Casey that essentially approximates her foregone stock trading commission; in fact, the special allocation provision uses a methodology like that used by the brokerage to calculate the commission itself. The partnership agreement has all the

8. Payments Between a Partnership and its Partners: § 707

required provisions for the special allocation to have substantial economic effect. Evaluate the concerns and risks of this special allocation.

4. Frank and Gary are partners in the FG Partnership. The partnership agreement provides that Frank is to receive 30% of the partnership income as determined before taking into account any guaranteed amount, but no less than $100,000. The agreement also provides that any guaranteed amount will be treated as a partnership expense in any year that Frank's profit percentage is less than the guaranteed minimum. The partnership agreement provides that capital gain items will be shared like other items of income and loss. In the current year, the partnership generates partnership income of $200,000, of which $120,000 is ordinary income and $80,000 is capital gain. Determine the amounts of ordinary income and capital gains to be reported by the partners for the current tax year.

5. Hartley is a partner of a partnership, and she is entitled to a guaranteed payment of $80,000. Several years ago, the partnership purchased Blackacre, a piece of real property, for $50,000; it currently has a fair market value of $80,000. The partnership transfers Blackacre to Hartley in satisfaction of her guaranteed payment. Evaluate the tax consequences of this transaction, focusing on the partnership using Blackacre to satisfy its guaranteed payment obligation.

Explanations

1. The main issue here is the classification of the payment to Ally under § 707, as well as the collateral tax consequences that follow. The three options under § 707 are: (1) § 707(a) non-partner payment, (2) § 707(c) guaranteed payment, or (3) § 704 distributive share. The initial question is to determine what "hat" Ally is wearing here—is she wearing her partner hat or is she wearing her non-partner hat? As noted in the main text, there is unfortunately not clear, unequivocal guidance to answer this question. What we can piece together from legislative history, administrative materials, and some case law is that if the services are integral or central to the nature of the partnership, it is more likely to be a deemed a partner transaction, like in Pratt. On the other hand, if the rendered services are technical in nature, like that of a learned professional, it may be deemed a non-partner capacity, particularly if the partner renders those services to others, like the investment adviser in Revenue Ruling 81-301. Here, the services that Ally render are (i) limited in scope (tax return preparation), (ii) limited in time (for one tax year), (iii) not integral to the nature of the partnership (its main activity is real estate investing/management), and (iv) she offers to other persons these technical, professional services. On balance, then, it is very

8. Payments Between a Partnership and its Partners: § 707

likely that these will be deemed non-partner type services governed by § 707(a).

Once the payment is classified as a § 707(a) payment, the collateral consequences flow naturally. The payment is § 61 income to the partner; the payment is deductible by the partnership under § 162, subject to § 263 (capitalization), which is not implicated here based on the nature of the services. The timing of the inclusion and deduction depend on the taxpayer's method of accounting. Because both of the taxpayers are cash-method, calendar year taxpayers, the payment will be included by Ally when actually or constructively received by her; similarly, it will be deductible by Lima when actually paid, subject to § 267.

2. This problem requires an analysis of the nature and extent of various § 707 payments.[65] The initial inquiry is whether the any part of the payment is a § 707(a) non-partner payment. On balance, that does not appear to be the case. The services that Brodie renders are related to the underlying nature of the partnership (home maintenance and repair), and they are required under the partnership agreement. Continuing this analysis, then, it will be deemed that none of the payment represents a § 707(a) payment. With the first inquiry answered, the second inquiry is whether any portion of his payment is guaranteed such that it would be a § 707(c) payment. Based on the amount of partnership income, Brodie is entitled to $20,000 (25% of the $80,000). No part of this payment, therefore, represents a guaranteed payment. Because the payment is neither a § 707(a) nor a § 707(c) payment, the full payment represents his distributive share under § 704. In the alternative, Brodie is entitled to $15,000. Of that $15,000, $11,250 represents his share of distributive partnership income (25% of $45,000), the remaining $3,750 represents a guaranteed payment.

3. The concern here is whether the special allocation represents a disguised payment for services under § 707(a)(2)(A) and its accompanying proposed regulations.[66] Section 707(a)(2)(A) provides that, if there is a provision of services by a partner, and an allocation and distribution that when viewed together is properly viewed as a payment for services, it should be treated as such. The proposed regulations provide six factors to consider, which are described above in the main text.[67] The key factor is whether arrangements "lack significant entrepreneurial risk." There are several factors to analyze entrepreneurial risk, including whether there is an allocation of *gross* income and an allocation that is predominantly

---

65. This is based on Example 2 of Treas. Reg. § 1.707-1(c).
66. This is based on Example 2 of Prop. Treas. Reg. § 1.707-2(d), 80 Fed. Reg. 43658 (July 23, 2015).
67. Prop. Treas. Reg. § 1.707-2(c), 80 Fed. Reg. 43658 (July 23, 2015).

8. Payments Between a Partnership and its Partners: § 707

fixed (such as a formula).[68] Here, given that the allocation is of gross income and is predominantly fixed (using the formula), it is presumed that the special allocation lacks significant entrepreneurial risk. There are no facts provided to rebut this. The special allocation is thus treated as a disguised payment for services as of the date that Casey and the partnership enter into the agreement.

4. This problem is based on Revenue Ruling 69-180,[69] and it demonstrates how guaranteed payments interact with the sharing of other partnership tax items. For the current year, Frank's share of partnership profits is $60,000 ($200,000 × 30%). Because that is less than the $100,000 minimum, Frank also has a guaranteed payment of $40,000 under the current Treas. Reg. § 1.707-1(c).[70]

Now that we have ascertained the amount of the guaranteed payment, the partnership's ordinary income equals $80,000, which represents its gross ordinary income less the guaranteed payment (recall that guaranteed payments are deductible by the partnership under § 162 as a business expense). We must now determine how to allocate the $80,000 of partnership ordinary income (i.e., non-separately stated income) and the $80,000 of capital gain income (separately stated).

In the problem, capital gain items are shared in the same manner as other tax items.[71] As noted, the partnership taxable income for the year is a total of $160,000, of which Frank's distributive share is $60,000. Consequently, Gary's distributive share must be $100,000. From this, we observe that Frank has an effective profit-sharing ratio of 3/8, and Gary has an effective profit-sharing ratio of 5/8.[72] We can now use these profit-sharing ratios to allocate the ordinary and capital gain to the partners, factoring in the effect of the guaranteed payment; the following table demonstrates this.

Item	Frank	Gary	Total
Ordinary income	$30,000	$50,000	$80,000
Guaranteed payment	$40,000	$0	$40,000
Total ordinary income	$70,000	$50,000	$120,000
Capital gain	$30,000	$50,000	$80,000
Total	$100,000	$100,000	$200,000

---

68. Prop. Treas. Reg. § 1.707-2(c)(1)(iii), (iv), 80 Fed. Reg. 43658 (July 23, 2015).
69. 1969-1 C.B. 183.
70. In particular, Example 2 of Treas. Reg. § 1.707-1(c).
71. Note that, in the revenue ruling, the Services had to answer this preliminary point first; we provided it by the given facts.
72. That is, $60,000/$160,000 for Frank, which simplifies to 6/16, and further simplifies to 3/8, and $100,000/$160,000 for Gary, which simplifies to 10/16, and further simplifies to 5/8.

8. Payments Between a Partnership and its Partners: § 707

It is important to note that, like Example 2 in the current § 1.707-1(c) regulation, the Service has also noted that this revenue ruling is inconsistent with the proposed regulation—recall that the proposed regulation would treat the *entire* minimum amount as a guaranteed payment. Consequently, the Service has noted that it plans to obsolete this revenue ruling when it finalizes the § 707(c) regulations.[73]

5. This problem is based on Revenue Ruling 2007-40,[74] and it requires us to consider whether the transfer of property to satisfy a guaranteed payment constitutes (i) a sale or exchange under § 1001 or (ii) a distribution of property under § 731. In the ruling, the Service notes that, generally, "[a] taxpayer that conveys appreciated or depreciated property in satisfaction of an obligation, or in exchange for the performance of services, recognizes gain or loss equal to the difference between the basis in the distributed property and the property's fair market value."[75] Consequently, a transfer of property to satisfy an obligation to make a guaranteed payment constitutes a sale or exchange of property under § 1001. Because it is therefore a sale, it cannot be a distribution within the meaning of § 731; therefore, the nonrecognition rule of § 731(b) likewise does not apply. The partnership must recognize the gain when it transfers Blackacre in satisfaction of its § 707(c) obligation to Hartley—here, that gain is $30,000. As well, Hartley has a guaranteed payment of $80,000.

---

73. Disguised Payment for Services, 80 Fed. Reg. 43652-01, 2015-32 I.R.B. 158 (proposed July 23, 2015).
74. 2007-1 C.B. 1426.
75. Id.

Other Payments to Service Partners

INTRODUCTION

In the last chapter, we examined § 707, which provides a framework for analyzing certain payments made to partners as something other than a standard distribution. That framework hinges on whether the payment is made to a partner who is acting in a non-partner capacity or, alternatively, whether the payment is guaranteed. Each of those payments represents a way to compensate a service partner, i.e., a partner who provides valuable services to a partnership and is being remunerated in return. In this chapter, we explore additional methods that a partnership can compensate or pay a service-providing partner, namely by the way of additional grants of a partnership interest, either of partnership capital or profits. In other words, this chapter explores how partnership equity can be issued in exchange for providing services.

At the outset, it is worth underlining why this chapter does not just retrace § 721. Although we covered § 721 in the context of partnership formation, the section applies even for non-formation events. In other words, § 721 applies, too, when an existing partner contributes *additional property* in exchange for more partnership equity. In those cases, the elements of § 721 are still satisfied, namely the partner has contributed *property* in exchange for an interest in the partnership. This is confirmed by the regulations, which note that § 721 applies "whether the contribution is made to a partnership in the process of formation or to a partnership which is already formed and

9. Other Payments to Service Partners

operating."[1] The transactions contemplated by this chapter, however, are not initially covered by § 721 because the partner is contributing *services* not *property*, which automatically takes it outside of § 721.

This chapter therefore covers two methods, other than § 707(a) or § 707(c) payments, to compensate a partner that provides services to a partnership. The first method is payment with a "capital interest" in the partnership, and the second method is a payment with a "profits interest" in the partnership. Each method will be covered in turn, but before those are discussed, some additional introductory matters are addressed.

In the transactions contemplated by this chapter, the partner is being *compensated* for the services being provided to the partnership; the compensation is being paid in the form of an interest in the partnership, i.e., in property. Thus, the general § 61 framework is applicable here, just like with any compensatory arrangement. Consequently, the service partner should recognize ordinary income just like with any compensation arrangement. Similarly, just like if the partner were compensated with other property, the partner would take a tax cost basis in the received property. As with other transactions involving property received in exchange for services, there is a potential for the application of § 83. In addition, there are deduction implications for the payor-partnership under § 162 (and also potential capitalization implications under § 263, depending on the nature of the services provided).

This chapter covers two types of partnership interests—capital interests and profits interests. A capital interest can be defined as "an interest that would give the holder a share of the proceeds if the partnership's assets were sold at fair market value and then the proceeds were distributed in a complete liquidation of the partnership."[2] Importantly, "[t]his determination generally is made at the time of receipt of the partnership interest."[3] A profits interest, on the other hand, "is a partnership interest other than a capital interest."[4]

Before we continue, a quick example will demonstrate the difference between these two types of interests. Consider the AB Partnership, in which A and B both contributed $45,000 of cash to the partnership. Consequently, the AB Partnership balance sheet looks as follows:

---

1. Treas. Reg. § 1.721-1(a). As well, this is marked contrast to § 351 in the corporate context: Although § 721 applies to all partnership interests exchanged for a contribution of property, § 351 requires the "control" element to be satisfied for its application; no such requirement is present in § 721.
2. Rev. Proc. 93-27, 1993-2 C.B. 343. But *see* Notice 2005-43, 2005-1 C.B. 1221 (providing a proposed Revenue Procedure that would obsolete Rev. Proc. 93-27).
3. Rev. Proc. 93-27, 1993-2 C.B. 343.
4. Id.

9. Other Payments to Service Partners

AB Partnership						
Assets				Liabilities		
	Basis	Book Value				
Cash	$90,000	$90,000				
				Capital Accounts		
					Basis	Book Value
			A		$45,000	$45,000
			B		$45,000	$45,000
Total	$90,000	$90,000	Total		$90,000	$90,000

A and B agree to admit C into the partnership without C needing to make any contribution of capital, and they agree to share profits and losses equally, as well as crediting C with a one-third interest in the partnership capital (i.e., $30,000).

After C's admittance, the balance sheet looks as follows:

ABC Partnership						
Assets				Liabilities		
	Basis	Book Value				
Cash	$90,000	$90,000				
				Capital Accounts		
					Basis	Book Value
			A		$30,000	$30,000
			B		$30,000	$30,000
			C		$30,000	$30,000
Total	$90,000	$90,000	Total		$90,000	$90,000

Take note that A and B's outside bases and capital accounts in the aggregate have decreased by $30,000, representing the share that was, in essence, transferred to C. In other words, it is just like A and B, individually, gave C $15,000 each of their interest in the partnership. Indeed, it is this deemed transfer that is the heart of the tax consequences of a capital interest grant, which is detailed more below. C's interest is a capital interest because if the partnership were to liquidate immediately after C's admittance, C would be entitled to the $30,000 (his positive capital account balance).

On the other hand, let's observe how this would operate with a profits interest. Like before, the AB Partnership's balance sheet looks as follows before the grant:

9. Other Payments to Service Partners

AB Partnership					
Assets			*Liabilities*		
	Basis	Book Value			
Cash	$90,000	$90,000			
			Capital Accounts		
				Basis	Book Value
			A	$45,000	$45,000
			B	$45,000	$45,000
Total	$90,000	$90,000	Total	$90,000	$90,000

Now, in recognition of the services rendered (and to be rendered) by C, A and B agree to grant C a one-third profits interest in the partnership. After the grant, the partnership balance sheet would look as follows:

ABC Partnership					
Assets			*Liabilities*		
	Basis	Book Value			
Cash	$90,000	$90,000			
			Capital Accounts		
				Basis	Book Value
			A	$45,000	$45,000
			B	$45,000	$45,000
			C	$0	$0
Total	$90,000	$90,000	Total	$90,000	$90,000

Observe how C's outside basis and capital accounts are both $0. In other words, if the partnership were to liquidate immediately after the grant of C's profits interest, C would *not* be entitled to any of the partnership capital. Here, C is only entitled to future profits (and capital) of the partnership.

To illustrate the profits interest one step further, let's assume that at the end of the first year of the profits interest grant, the partnership earns $30,000 of net taxable income, which is equally allocated to the three partners, i.e., each partner receives a $10,000 § 704(b) allocation of income, but no distributions are made. Consequently, the partnership balance sheet would be as follows:

9. Other Payments to Service Partners

ABC Partnership					
Assets			Liabilities		
	Basis	Book Value			
Cash	$120,000	$120,000			
			Capital Accounts		
				Basis	Book Value
			A	$55,000	$55,000
			B	$55,000	$55,000
			C	$10,000	$10,000
Total	$120,000	$120,000	Total	$120,000	$120,000

You can readily see that C is now entitled to $10,000 in liquidation, which represents his share of the partnership profits (and resulting capital) after the grant of the profits interest. A and B, of course, report higher outside bases and capital accounts for their share of the new $30,000 of profits (and capital). This illustrates an important point: although a profits interest partner starts with an outside basis and capital account of $0, those balances do not remain at $0.

PAYMENT WITH A CAPITAL INTEREST IN THE PARTNERSHIP

Let's start with a partner (new or existing) receiving a "capital interest" in the partnership for payment for services. A helpful analogy will set the stage. Assume that instead of a capital interest in the partnership, the partner is compensated with Blackacre (real property) that is worth $100,000 and has a basis to the partnership of $20,000. And, to start with an even simpler example, let's assume the person isn't a partner—he or she is an employee.

First consider the tax consequences to the employee who is being paid "in-kind"—meaning with property instead of cash. The employee has $100,000 of compensation income under § 61.[5] Because of that $100,000 inclusion, the employee would therefore take a $100,000 "tax cost" basis in Blackacre. Stated simply, tax cost basis means that if receipt of an item generates an income inclusion, the corresponding basis in that item is the amount of the inclusion (generally its fair market value). This prevents a

---

5. In the employee context, these are also "wages" for employment tax purposes. I.R.C. § 3121(a).

9. Other Payments to Service Partners

double inclusion of the same value in the income tax base when the property is later sold. When the dust settles, the employee has $100,000 of compensation and holds Blackacre with a tax basis of $100,000.

For the partnership-employer, it has a few things going on. First, it must recognize the built-in gain on the disposition of Blackacre. In other words, using the property to pay a debt (the compensation obligation) is a realization event for the employer. Thus, the partnership has a $80,000 gain, the character and holding period of which depends on the nature of the property. Second, the partnership has a $100,000 § 162 deduction for the compensation payment to the employee.

This example thus demonstrates a few key points. First, the service provider has compensation in the amount of the fair market value of the property. Second, the service provider also takes a fair market value basis in the received property. Third, the payor must realize (and recognize) any built-in gain on the transfer of property for payment. Fourth, the payor receives a compensation deduction in the amount of the property transferred. This framework serves as a helpful base to build upon as we translate this into the partnership context.

Let's now translate this example into the partnership context with payment of a capital interest. Like before, let's use the AB Partnership, which has a single asset, Blackacre, that has an inside basis of $30,000 and a fair market value of $90,000. The balance sheet of the AB Partnership is as follows:

AB Partnership					
Assets			Liabilities		
	Basis	Book Value			
Blackacre	$30,000	$90,000			
			Capital Accounts		
				Basis	Book Value
			A	$15,000	$45,000
			B	$15,000	$45,000
Total	$30,000	$90,000	Total	$30,000	$90,000

The partnership is going to transfer a one-third capital interest to C in recognition of services rendered by C; assume also that these services do not require capitalization by AB. This transaction can actually be viewed as two different steps. The first step is that the partnership transfers one-third of Blackacre to C, and the second step is that C contributes that portion of Blackacre back to the partnership in exchange for his partnership interest.

The first step should trigger recognition of gain by the AB Partnership, like we illustrated earlier. Consequently, AB is treated as selling one-third of Blackacre, the allocable portion (one-third) of which has a value of

9. Other Payments to Service Partners

$30,000 and a basis of $10,000, triggering $20,000 of gain. This $20,000 of gain gets allocated to A and B under § 704. The partnership then transfers that one-third interest in Blackacre to C, as compensation, which similarly allows the partnership a $30,000 compensation deduction, which similarly flows through to A and B ($15,000 each). After this first step (and before application of the second step), the balance sheet can be illustrated thusly:

AB Partnership					
Assets			Liabilities		
	Adj. Basis	Book Value			
Blackacre	$20,000	$60,000			
			Capital Accounts		
				Adj. Basis	Book Value
			A	$10,000	$30,000
			B	$10,000	$30,000
Total	$20,000	$60,000	Total	$20,000	$60,000

It is worth examining the values of this balance sheet after step 1. The left-hand side shows the remaining portion of Blackacre, which is now two-thirds of the initial property (as one-third is considered to be transferred to C). As well, one-third of the initial built-in gain of $60,000 (i.e., $20,000) has been recognized, leaving two-thirds of the remaining built-in gain present (i.e., $40,000). On the right-hand side, some explanation is helpful to see the increases and decreases to the outside bases and capital account balances. Recall that A and B each started with an outside basis of $15,000 and capital account balance of $45,000. Two things happened: (1) the allocation of the built-in gain on the deemed transfer of Blackacre ($20,000) and (2) the compensation deduction ($30,000). Thus, it may be tempting to increase both their bases and capital accounts by their share of the $20,000 gain (i.e., $10,000 each) and then decrease basis and capital accounts by their share of the $30,000 deduction (i.e., $15,000) each, which would result in a net increase of $5,000. But that would be incorrect! The reason is that the capital account column already displays the built-in gain because it recorded Blackacre at its fair market value at the date of contribution. Thus, the capital accounts are not increased by the built-in gain; the capital accounts are, however, adjusted for the compensation deduction.

Stated more directly, A and B's outside bases are affected by both items (the built-in gain and compensation deduction), but the capital accounts are adjusted only for the compensation deduction. Therefore, A and B's outside basis are increased by $10,000 each (built-in gain allocation) then decreased by $15,000 (compensation deduction allocation), resulting in a net decrease of $5,000, which takes their outside bases from $15,000

9. Other Payments to Service Partners

to $10,000. A and B's capital accounts are decreased by the compensation deduction, i.e., $15,000 each, resulting in ending capital account balances of $30,000 each.

The second part of the transaction can be viewed as C now contributing his share of Blackacre, in which he has a basis of $30,000 with a value of $30,000 to the partnership. This step can be properly viewed as a § 721 contribution, in which C does not recognize gain or loss, and the partnership will take an inside basis of $30,000 under § 723. Similarly, C will have an outside basis in his partnership of $30,000 under § 722.[6] Consequently, after this second step, the partnership balance sheet can be depicted as follows:

AB Partnership					
Assets			*Liabilities*		
	Adj. Basis	Book Value			
Blackacre [A&B's 2/3]	$20,000	$60,000			
Blackacre [C's 1/3]	$30,000	$30,000			
			Capital Accounts		
				Adj. Basis	Book Value
			A	$10,000	$30,000
			B	$10,000	$30,000
			C	$30,000	$30,000
Total	$50,000	$90,000	Total	$50,000	$90,000

The above balance sheet has the single Blackacre asset broken into two lines to emphasize its two conceptual parts. The first part is the portion of Blackacre that A and B did not transfer to C. As you can see, it still has a built-in gain of $40,000 allocable to it, which is traceable to the portion of the gain that was not realized on the transfer to C. Second, you observe the portion that was essentially transferred to C, which has no built-in gain inherent in it. You also observe that A and B each still have a $20,000 difference between their capital accounts and outside basis, again traceable to the gain in Blackacre that has not been recognized yet.

For completeness, there is one more essential element to tackle in this simple example — and that is to ensure that the remaining built-in gain (the $40,000) eventually gets allocated to A and B. In other words, consistent with our general concerns about income shifting within a partnership,[7] that $40,000 built-in gain should not be shifted to C. There would be two steps to ensure this. The first step involves a revaluation of partnership property

---

6. This is like situation 2 in Rev. Rul. 99-5, 1999-1 C.B. 434. *See* Chapter 2.
7. *See, e.g.,* Chapter 5 (discussing § 704(c)).

9. Other Payments to Service Partners

for capital account purposes, and the second step involves ensuring a § 704(c)-like allocation of the then built-in gain to A and B. The first step is provided for in the § 704(b) regulations, which note that revaluations of property and corresponding capital account adjustments can be made if, among other things, the adjustments are "made principally for a substantial non-tax business purpose."[8] One such purpose is the grant of a partnership interest (after May 6, 2004) as consideration for services.[9] The second step is confirmed by the corresponding examples that the built-in gain needs to be allocated "in accordance with section 704(c) principles."[10] In the above case, then, the first $40,000 of gain needs to be shared equally between A and B (and not allocated to C).

PAYMENT WITH A PROFITS INTEREST IN THE PARTNERSHIP

Another way that a service partner can be compensated is with the grant of a profits interest. As discussed earlier, a profits interest simply means that the recipient is not entitled, immediately after the transfer, to any existing partnership capital. In other words, the partner's initial capital account is zero (and upon a liquidation, therefore, would be entitled to no capital). Conceptually, though, the partner has been given *something*—namely, an entitlement to *future* partnership profits (and resulting capital). Indeed, § 61 and its regulations clearly provide that, "if services are paid for in property, the fair market value of the property taken in payment must be included in income as compensation."[11] Because *something* has been *given* in exchange for *services*, one may argue that it seems like the § 83 framework should apply from a doctrinal perspective. Even if this is the case, the main rub, practically, is how to *value* the profits interest; this difficulty has been the focus of modern cases and administrative efforts in these situations. On the other hand, perhaps the receipt of a profits interest is not a taxable event because the partner will recognize the profits as they are earned by the partnership (and prior inclusion upon receipt of the profits interest would create a double tax or create other administration problems).

A critical case in the saga of the taxation of receiving a profits interest is *Diamond v. Commissioner*.[12] In *Diamond*, the Seventh Circuit agreed with the Tax Court and held that the receipt of a profits interest was compensation

---

8. Treas. Reg. § 1.704-1(b)(2)(iv)(f)(5)(iii).
9. Id.
10. Treas. Reg. §1.704-1(b)(5) Example 14.
11. Treas. Reg. § 1.61-2(d)(1).
12. 492 F.2d 286 (7th Cir. 1974).

9. Other Payments to Service Partners

for services and thus includible as ordinary income. Critical to this holding (and that of the Tax Court's opinion below) was that the profits interest had a "determinable market value."[13] Given the emphasis in *Diamond* that the value of the profits interest was readily determinable, the suggestion existed that a profits interest without such a determinable value may not be immediately taxable.[14]

That notwithstanding, the Tax Court in a later case, *Campbell v. Commissioner*, emphasized that, under the § 61 framework, "unless nonrecognition is provided for elsewhere," the value of received partnership interests must be included in income "immediately upon receipt."[15] This doubled down on the reasoning in *Diamond*. In *Campbell*, the petitioners argued that the § 721 regulations drew a distinction between receipt of a capital interest versus a receipt of a profits interest. In particular, the regulations provided that:

> Normally, under local law, each partner is entitled to be repaid his contributions of money or other property to the partnership. . . . To the extent that any of the partners gives up any part of his right to be repaid his contributions (*as distinguished from a share in partnership profits*) in favor of another partner as compensation for services (or in satisfaction of an obligation), section 721 does not apply.[16]

The argument went that the regulation excludes receipt of a capital interest from § 721's nonrecognition treatment, but that exclusion expressly carves out "a share in partnership profits," the negative implication of which is that the receipt of a profits interest qualifies for nonrecognition treatment.[17]

The Tax Court noted that it had rejected this line of reasoning in *Diamond*. It emphasized that "application of section 721 to a partnership interest which was received in exchange for a contribution of services would result in an impermissible distortion of the language of the statute."[18] The court also emphasized that, in *Diamond*, the taxpayer was able to sell his interest just a few weeks later, belied the argument that the partnership interest was worthless.[19] Thus, the court held that the general § 61 framework applied. On appeal, however, the Eighth Circuit reversed the Tax Court in *Campbell*, essentially on the grounds that the partnership interest's value was too speculative.[20]

---

13. Id. at 291.
14. *See, e.g.*, WILLIAM S. MCKEE ET AL., FEDERAL TAXATION OF PARTNERSHIPS ¶ 5.02[1] (2024).
15. Campbell v. Comm'r, T.C. Memo. 1990-162.
16. Treas. Reg. § 1.721-1(b)(1) (emphasis added).
17. *See, e.g.*, *Campbell*, T.C. Memo. 1990-162.
18. Id.
19. Id.
20. 943 F.2d 815, 823 (8th Cir. 1991).

9. Other Payments to Service Partners

After *Diamond* and *Campbell*, then, there was thus an aura of uncertainty surrounding the taxation of profits interest grants. Fortunately, the Service ameliorated these risks by issuing Revenue Procedure 93-27, which we discussed earlier in unpacking the differences between capital and profits interests.

As noted earlier, Revenue Procedure 93-27 starts with a definitions section that articulates the difference between capital and profits interests. Capital interests are those interests that "give the holder a share of the proceeds if the partnership's assets were sold at fair market value and then the proceeds were distributed in a complete liquidation of the partnership."[21] Profits interests, on the other hand, are interests other than capital interests.[22]

In addition to the definitions, the revenue procedure explains the tension in the case law (e.g., *Diamond* and *Campbell*) about the tax consequences of receiving a profits interest. It then proceeds to provide a taxpayer-friendly rule that "if a person receives a profits interest for the provision of services to or for the benefit of a partnership in a partner capacity or in anticipation of being a partner, the Internal Revenue Service will not treat the receipt of such an interest as a taxable event for the partner or the partnership."[23] There are three exceptions to this rule, which are:

> (1) If the profits interest relates to a substantially certain and predictable stream of income from partnership assets, such as income from high-quality debt securities or a high-quality net lease;
>
> (2) If within two years of receipt, the partner disposes of the profits interest; or
>
> (3) If the profits interest is a limited partnership interest in a "publicly traded partnership" within the meaning of section 7704(b) of the Internal Revenue Code.[24]

These exceptions make sense in light of the valuation concerns. Indeed, if the main rub is a valuation concern, then that concern does not apply in the provided exceptions. That is, each of the exceptions contemplate situations in which the partnership interest can be readily valued (e.g., if it's a publicly traded partnership).

Some additional gloss is needed to round out the discussion of Revenue Procedure 93-27. The Service clarified its application to nonvested partnership interests in Revenue Procedure 2001-43.[25] The Service explained that the determination of whether a partnership interest is a profits interest is made at the time of its grant, even if the interest is substantially nonvested

---

21. Rev. Proc. 93-27, § 2.01, 1993-2 C.B. 343.
22. Id. § 2.02.
23. Id. § 4.01.
24. Id. § 4.02.
25. 2001-34 I.R.B. 191, 2001-2 C.B. 191.

9. Other Payments to Service Partners

within the meaning of Treas. Reg. § 1.83-3(b).[26] Thus, both the initial grant and the event that vests the grant will not be considered a taxable event for the partner or the partnership.[27]

Despite the seeming clarity and détente that Revenue Procedure 93-27 ushered in, Treasury and the Service have issued proposed regulations[28] and a proposed revenue procedure.[29] The proposed regulations provide that a partnership interest is "property" for purposes of § 83; thus, a transfer of a partnership interest in exchange for services is governed by § 83. The proposed regulations apply § 83 principles to all partnership interests without making the historical capital versus profits interest distinction. In jettisoning that historical distinction, Treasury and the IRS explained that "[a]ll partnership interests constitute personal property under state law and give the holder the right to share in future earnings from partnership capital and labor."[30]

Under the proposed regulations, partnership interests granted for services are treated as guaranteed payments. Moreover, the § 83 timing rules will override the timing rules of §§ 706 and 707 to the extent they are inconsistent. In sum, § 83 will govern the timing issues incident to the inclusion and deduction. The proposed regulations will increase a service provider's capital account in the amount of the income inclusion under § 83 and the amount paid for the interest. The regulations also provide for "forfeiture allocations," which regard unwinding allocations attributable to a substantially nonvested partnership interest that had a § 83(b) election in place if later forfeited.[31]

A key issue in the proposed regulations—just like in the historic case law—is the valuation issues incident to the grant of a profits interest. Noting that some precedent concludes that profits interests have only speculative value, the Treasury and Service determined that, in certain situations, it is appropriate to allow the valuation to be based on the interest's "liquidation value." Liquidation value is defined by the proposed revenue procedure as "the amount of cash that the recipient of the [partnership interest] would receive if, immediately after the transfer, the partnership sold all of its assets (including goodwill, going concern value, and any other intangibles associated with the partnership's operations) for cash equal to the fair market value of those assets and then liquidated."[32] In essence, in a traditional profits interest, this amount would be zero. This election is allowed for a "safe

---

26. Id.
27. Id.
28. Partnership Equity for Services, 70 Fed. Reg. 29675-01 (proposed May 24, 2005).
29. Notice 2005-43, 2005-1 C.B. 1221.
30. Partnership Equity for Services, 70 Fed. Reg. 29675-01 (proposed May 24, 2005).
31. Id.
32. Notice 2005-43, 2005-1 C.B. 1221.

9. Other Payments to Service Partners

harbor partnership interest," which essentially borrows from the definition of a profits interest under Revenue Procedure 93-27.

Another issue that is important to discuss is the interaction of partnership allocations, potential forfeiture, and § 83(b) elections. Let's consider a prototypical partnership-interest-for-services transaction in which the incoming partner is receiving a one-third capital interest in exchange for services rendered; further, to mitigate various risks, the partnership interest is subject to a forfeiture provision, typically that the incoming service provider must continue those services for several years. As we've discussed, the presence of the forfeiture provision means that, under § 83(a), the service provider (and now putative partner) need not immediately include the partnership interest in income, and the partnership's compensation deduction is held in abeyance.

The service provider decides whether to make the § 83(b) election to presently include the value of the interest in income. An interesting collateral question, though, is how this election interacts with the service provider's status as a partner and concomitant partnership income allocations. Let's assume that in the above example that the service provider *does not* make the § 83(b) election. Under § 83 principles, then, she is *not* treated as the owner of the "property" (here, the nonvested capital interest in the partnership).[33] Well, that naturally gives rise to two questions of import. First, how does that non-owner status interact with allocations of partnership income? Second, how does that non-owner status interact with any distributions that may occur before the capital interest vests?

The § 83 regulations provide that "[u]ntil such property becomes substantially vested, the transferor shall be regarded as the owner of such property."[34] The Tax Court had occasion to explicate the first issue noted above in *Crescent Holdings, LLC v. Commissioner*.[35] There, the Tax Court held that an LLC, which was taxed as a partnership, was the "transferor" of membership interests that it granted in exchange for services rendered. It further held that the "transferor of a partnership capital interest must recognize in income the undistributed partnership profit or loss allocations attributable to a nonvested capital interest."[36] Based on that, the existing partners of the granting partnership must

---

33. Treas. Reg. § 1.83-1(a)(1) ("Until such property becomes substantially vested, the transferor shall be regarded as the owner of such property, and any income from such property received by the employee or independent contractor (or beneficiary thereof) or the right to the use of such property by the employee or independent contractor constitutes additional compensation and shall be included in the gross income of such employee or independent contractor for the taxable year in which such income is received or such use is made available.") (emphasis added).
34. Treas. Reg. § 1.83-1(a)(1).
35. 141 T.C. 477 (2013). Interestingly enough, despite the wide use of forfeiture provisions, it was only in 2013 that the Tax Court had to address this interaction effect between § 83, nonvested partnership interests, and partnership allocations.
36. 141 T.C. at 502.

9. Other Payments to Service Partners

be allocated the partnership profits and losses associated with the nonvested interest on a pro rata basis.[37]

The second issue—about actual distributions of property to the nonvested interest—appears to be handled directly by the § 83 regulations. They provide that "any income from such property received ... constitutes additional compensation and shall be included in the gross income of such employee or independent contractor for the taxable year in which such income is received or such use is made available."[38] Thus, if the service provider actually receives *distributions* of partnership property before vesting, that property must be included as compensation in the year it is received.

Now, what if the § 83(b) election is made? There are two possible scenarios to consider: (1) the partner keeps the interest, and (2) the interest is forfeited. There is nothing remarkable about the first scenario because the service provider is treated as a partner from the date of the § 83(b) election and there is no additional or collateral tax impact upon the forfeiture lapsing and the interest actually vesting as a partnership interest, as it had been treated since the § 83(b) election—that is, the tax consequences were incurred upon the making of the § 83(b) election. The second scenario, though, has collateral issues. It is important to emphasize that even if the interest is forfeited that does not change the earlier income inclusion upon the § 83(b) election—that is, the partner cannot retroactively change his or her mind; this is the quintessential § 83(b) gambit. The more interesting issue is how the § 83(b) election interacts with allocations of partnership income.

If a service provider makes the § 83(b) election for a nonvested compensatory partnership interest, he or she is now treated as the owner of the interest, meaning the service provider is a partner. Because the person is now a partner, he or she can receive allocations of partnership tax items. The rub, though, is that those tax allocations may be forfeited in the future! Because of this potential for forfeiture, the allocations of partnership items allocable to a nonvested interest *cannot* have substantial economic effect.[39]

The proposed regulations have a safe harbor rule to treat such allocations to be in accordance with the partners' interest in the partnership. This safe harbor has two requirements. First, the partnership agreement must provide for "forfeiture allocations" if the interest is later forfeited.[40] Second, all material allocations and capital account adjustments for the interests not subject to forfeiture are recognized under the § 704(b) rules.[41] The proposed regulations describe forfeiture allocations as allocations in the taxable

---

37. Id. at 506.
38. Treas. Reg. § 1.83-1(a)(1).
39. Partnership Equity for Services, 70 Fed. Reg. 29675-01 (proposed May 24, 2005).
40. See id.
41. See id.

9. Other Payments to Service Partners

year of forfeiture to the service provider of partnership tax items that offset prior distributions and allocations that relate to the forfeited interest.[42]

To summarize, the above discussed collateral impacts of receiving a nonvested capital interest in exchange for services (i.e., one that is subject to a forfeiture provision). If the § 83(b) election is not made, the service provider is *not* taxed upon receipt of the interest (because he or she is not treated as the owner of the interest). The service provider will be taxed when the interest later vests (at its then fair market value). Under the § 83 regulations, the service provider is not treated as the owner of the interest and therefore is not yet a "partner" for tax purposes. Consequently, the transferor of the interest (likely the partnership itself) is allocated the tax items relating to the interest; practically, this means the other partners will bear the tax consequences of the allocations. If the partner receives any distributions of property, those amounts are treated as compensation to the service provider under § 83.

What if, on the other hand, the service provider is provided a *vested* capital interest in the partnership? The consequences of that transaction were described earlier in the text—namely, that the partnership and partners are treated as transferring a proportionate interest in each asset of the partnership to the service provider. Although that was the historic understanding of how to understand and analyze a transfer of a vested capital interest, the proposed regulations change this treatment. The proposed regulations provide that "partnerships should not be required to recognize gain on the transfer of a compensatory partnership interest."[43] Despite the nonrecognition treatment advanced by the proposed regulations, they also provide that, under reverse § 704(c) principles, "historic partners generally will be required to recognize any income or loss attributable to the partnership's assets as those assets are sold, depreciated, or amortized."[44] There are exceptions to this nonrecognition treatment, namely that relating to an "eligible entity" that becomes a partnership—the paradigmatic example is that of a sole proprietorship that becomes a partnership upon the admission of a second owner.

Examples

1. April is a software developer. She has recently been asked to join a small software company that is taxed as a partnership, which presently has three partners. To entice her to join, the partnership is willing to make her a "full" one-fourth partner, including in existing partnership capital. The partnership interest is valued at $100,000. However, the existing

---

42. *See id.*
43. *Id.*
44. *Id.*

9. Other Payments to Service Partners

partners are unwilling to part with so much equity unless April is going to be a long-term, value-add to the team. Thus, the granted partnership interest is subject to a proviso that, if partnership gross profits don't increase at least 15% over the next two years and if April does not stay with the firm over the same period, her partnership interest is forfeited back to the partnership. Discuss the tax consequences of this arrangement to April.

2. Assume the same facts as Example 1, except that instead of granting April a partner in existing partnership capital, the deal is instead structured that she will be made a one-fourth partner in partnership profits after her admission date. She will forfeit this interest if she does not remain a partner for the next two years. Discuss the tax consequences of this arrangement to April.

3. How would the analyses and results change in Examples 1 and 2 if the proposed regulations and proposed revenue procedure applied?

4. Blaine is an orthodontist who graduated from dental school a few years ago. He has been working with a local dental practice. Recently, he has been elected to join the dental practice as a one-fourth partner. Even better, he is not being asked to "buy-in" to the partnership, and the partnership is granting him the interest in exchange for services he has provided to the partnership. Assume that that the dental practice's balance sheet looks as follows.

Dental Partnership						
Assets			Liabilities			
	Basis	Book Value				
Cash	$100,000	$100,000				
Accounts receivable	0	$200,000		Capital Accounts		
Real property	$500,000	$1,200,000			Basis	Book Value
				D1	$200,000	$500,000
				D2	$200,000	$500,000
				D3	$200,000	$500,000
Total	$600,000	$1,500,000		Total	$600,000	$1,500,000

For simplicity, assume that book values are equal to current fair market values. Blaine's interest is deemed to be worth $375,000. Evaluate the tax consequences to Blaine, the partnership, and the other partners (D1, D2, and D3) upon Blaine's admittance to the partnership.

5. How would your analysis change in Example 4 if the proposed regulations and revenue procedure applied?

9. Other Payments to Service Partners

Explanations

1. This problem presents three related issues. The first is the classification of the granted partnership interest. The second is the taxation to the service partner of that receiving that interest. The third is to evaluate the impact of § 83 to the service partner.

   To classify the partnership interest—either as a profits interest or a capital interest—we are guided by Revenue Procedure 93-27, which articulates the difference between capital and profits interests. Capital interests are those interests that "give the holder a share of the proceeds if the partnership's assets were sold at fair market value and then the proceeds were distributed in a complete liquidation of the partnership."[45] Profits interests are interests other than capital interests.[46] Here the facts provide that April is being offered a share of "existing partnership capital." This means that, if the partnership were to liquidate immediately after her admission, she would be entitled to partnership assets. Consequently, she is being offered a capital interest in the partnership.

   As we saw at the beginning of the chapter, if a service provider is paid with property (in-kind), the service provider must include the fair market value of that property as income under § 61. This does not change because the property being offered is a capital interest in a partnership, and this is confirmed in the § 721 regulations.[47] In the ordinary course, then, April would have to include $100,000 in income. As well, given the § 61 inclusion, she would take a tax-cost basis of $100,000 in her partnership interest.

   However, there is a complicating factor here, namely the risk of forfeiture of the partnership interest. The risk of forfeiture gives rise to potential application of § 83. Section 83 provides that, generally, if property is received in exchange for services, then the fair market value of the property received is included in income to the extent such amount exceeds the amount paid, if any, for such property.[48] The critical part of § 83(a) is that the timing of this inclusion happens "in the first taxable year in which the rights of the person having the beneficial interest in such property are transferable or are not subject to a substantial risk of

---

45. Rev. Proc. 93-27, § 2.01, 1993-2 C.B. 343.
46. Id. § 2.02.
47. Treas. Reg. § 1.721-1(b)(1) ("The value of an interest in such partnership capital so transferred to a partner as compensation for services constitutes income to the partner under section 61. The amount of such income is the fair market value of the interest in capital so transferred, either at the time the transfer is made for past services, or at the time the services have been rendered where the transfer is conditioned on the completion of the transferee's future services.").
48. I.R.C. § 83(a).

9. Other Payments to Service Partners

forfeiture."[49] Section 83 also provides that a substantial risk of forfeiture is present if "such person's rights to full enjoyment of such property are conditioned upon the future performance of substantial services by any individual."[50] The presence of a substantial risk of forfeiture, therefore, defers recognition until the substantial risk of forfeiture lapses.

An exception to this rule is the election provided by § 83(b). The election under § 83(b) provides that a person may elect to include the value of the property notwithstanding that a substantial risk of forfeiture exists. The main rub with the § 83(b) election is that it is not revocable. So, if a taxpayer decides to elect a current inclusion under § 83(b)—thus trigging an income inclusion for the received property—but then later forfeits that property, the prior inclusion is not unwound. In other words, there is no loss or other deduction for the service provider upon the forfeiture.

As applied here, § 83(a) would provide that, although the partnership interest (that is a capital interest) is worth $100,000, April need not include it presently in income because it is subject to a substantial risk of forfeiture. It is subject to a substantial risk of forfeiture because if April does not work for the partnership for the next two years and if the revenue targets are not satisfied, then the interest is forfeited back to the partnership. The lack of an inclusion, moreover, also pauses the expense deduction by the partnership under § 83(h). Although April need not presently include it, she needs to decide under § 83(b) whether she will elect to include it now. That decision depends on the likelihood that April thinks the interest will be forfeited. Let's consider the two alternatives.

In the first alternative, April sticks with the default treatment under § 83(a), meaning she need not include the capital interest's value now. The two years pass, and the forfeiture provision lapses. The inclusion is now triggered but at the interest's now fair market value, which may be substantially more! If the partnership interest is now worth, say, $175,000, she must include that amount (not the earlier value of $100,000). In the second alternative, April decides to make the § 83(b) election. By making the § 83(b) election, she has a current income inclusion of $100,000. Simultaneously, she now has a $100,000 basis in her partnership interest. She is now treated as a partner because she is treated as the owner of the property, despite the possibility of later forfeiture. If in two years the forfeiture lapses, there are no additional tax consequences. But, if on the other hand, she leaves the partnership and the interest is forfeited, she is unable to unwind the prior inclusion of $100,000.

---

49. Id.
50. I.R.C. § 83(c)(1).

9. Other Payments to Service Partners

2. The analysis for this problem is like that of Example 1, namely we must first classify the nature of the granted partnership interest; second, we must consider the taxation to the service partner of that receiving that interest; and third, we must evaluate the impact of § 83 to the service partner.

   Under Revenue Procedure 93-27, the nature of the interest granted to April would be a profits interest. It is classified as a profits interest because it is not a capital interest—a capital interest is defined as one that gives "the holder a share of the proceeds if the partnership's assets were sold at fair market value and then the proceeds were distributed in a complete liquidation of the partnership."[51] If the partnership were to liquidate immediately after April's admission, she would not be entitled to any current partnership capital—she is only entitled to future partnership profits (and, by extension, the capital from those profits).

   Given that the interest is a profits interest, its receipt is generally not currently taxable. Indeed, Revenue Procedure 93-27 provides that "if a person receives a profits interest for the provision of services to or for the benefit of a partnership in a partner capacity or in anticipation of being a partner, the Internal Revenue Service will not treat the receipt of such an interest as a taxable event for the partner or the partnership."[52] The revenue procedure provides three exceptions to this treatment: (1) the profits interest relates to a substantially certain and predictable stream of income, like that arising from a high-quality net let lease or high-quality debt securities; (2) if, within two years, she disposes of the interest; and (3) if the interest is that of a publicly traded partnership. None of these exceptions apply. Though, if she were to sell the interest within 2 years, that would trigger the second exception. As the facts exist now, the receipt of the profits interest does not trigger an inclusion.

3. This problem requires us to use the approach of the proposed regulation and revenue procedure instead of the capital- versus profits-interest distinction of Revenue Procedure 93-27.[53] The proposed regulations do a few things. The first is that it makes clear that § 83 applies to transfers of partnership interests, regardless of the type of interest. In other words, present law applies § 83 to transfers of *capital* interests,[54] but its application is unclear as applied to profits interests;[55] but the proposed

---

51. Rev. Proc. 93-27, § 2.01, 1993-2 C.B. 343.
52. Id. § 4.01.
53. The proposed regulations are found at 70 Fed. Reg. 29675. Partnership Equity for Services, 70 Fed. Reg. 29675-01 (proposed May 24, 2005).
54. *See* Schulman v. Comm'r, 93 T.C. 623 (1989); Kenroy, Inc. v. Comm'r, T.C. Memo. 1984-232.
55. *See* Campbell v. Comm'r, T.C. Memo. 1990-162, *aff'd in part, rev'd in part*, 943 F.2d 815, 821 n.7 (8th Cir. 1991) ("Arguably, the section 1.721–1(b)(1) distinction between capital and profits interests and the regulations under section 83 create the implication that a profits interest is not property subject to section 83.").

9. Other Payments to Service Partners

regulations would expressly apply it to any type of partnership interest. Thus, the preamble in the proposed regulations explains that "[a]ll partnership interests constitute personal property under state law and give the holder the right to share in future earnings from partnership capital and labor."[56] This stronger application of § 83 also has timing implications. Although the proposed regulations note that partnership interests issued in exchange for services rendered are to be treated as guaranteed payments, the guaranteed payment rules will yield to the § 83 rules. In short, § 83 will govern the timing of the income inclusion by the service partner and the expense deduction by the partnership.

Another salient issue advanced by the proposed regulation is the valuation of partnership interest. Section 83, of course, requires inclusion of the fair market value of the property interest transferred in exchange for rendered services. As we've discussed, though, the rub with the historic "profits interest" is, among other things, the speculative value of it.[57] The proposed regulations in conjunction with the proposed revenue procedure would, under certain circumstances, allow for the use of a liquidation value. Liquidation value would be the amount of cash the partner would be entitled to receive if, immediately after the transfer, the partnership was liquidated. A partner who has received a profits interest would naturally have a liquidation value of zero under this test.

As relevant here, the last critical change under the proposed regulation is that partnerships do not have to recognize gain on the transfer of a compensatory partnership interest. Unlike the examples provided in text that required the partnership to recognize built-in gain—because it was deemed to transfer a sliver of each asset to the service partner—the proposed regulations expressly obviate such gain. The one exception to this rule is for a transfer or substantial vesting of an "eligible entity"[58] that becomes a partnership due to the transfer or vesting,[59] which is not present here because the entity is already a partnership for tax purposes.

In sum, the proposed regulations and revenue procedure provide that (i) a compensatory partnership interest is property for purposes of § 83, (ii) it is to be treated like a guaranteed payment except to the extent inconsistent with § 83, (iii) it can be valued at liquidation value (with exceptions), and (iv) the partnership (and, by extension the historic partners) need not recognize any built-in gain upon the transfer.

Given that summarized framework of the proposed rule, let's now turn to Example 1. In Example 1, April was given a capital interest (using the traditional classification). That interest, though, was subject to a

---

56. Partnership Equity for Services, 70 Fed. Reg. 29675-01 (proposed May 24, 2005).
57. E.g., Campbell v. Comm'r, 943 F.2d 815 (8th Cir. 1991).
58. Treas. Reg. § 301.7701-3(a).
59. Partnership Equity for Services, 70 Fed. Reg. 29675-01 (proposed May 24, 2005).

9. Other Payments to Service Partners

substantial risk of forfeiture. Thus, the analysis does not really change. April does not need to include the value of the partnership in income until the forfeiture lapses or if she makes a § 83(b) election. When that event happens (the lapse or election), she will have an inclusion of the fair market value of the property interest and the partnership will have a concomitant deduction, both of which will be treated under the guaranteed payment rules.

In Example 2, April is now given a profits interest (again using the traditional classification). Historically, some argued that these types of interest were not property for § 83 purposes.[60] The proposed regulations plainly change that analysis. A critical issue then is the valuation of the compensatory interest for purposes of § 83. This requires an application of the proposed revenue procedure. Here, this interest would classify as a safe harbor partnership interest, which allows us to use the liquidation value. The liquidation value, of course, would be zero because April is not entitled to any cash upon a liquidation immediately after the transfer. Even though the interest is valued at zero, it is subject to a substantial risk of forfeiture and thus need not be included presently unless a § 83(b) election is made.

4. This problem is designed to allow a more robust application of the historic tax treatment of transferring a vested capital interest to a service provider who becomes a partner. Historically, some argued that it was understood that this effectuated a deemed transfer of a fraction of each of the partnership's assets to the service provider, which requires the partnership's recognition of built-in gain or loss and a concomitant allocation to the existing partners. Of course, the service provider has an inclusion under § 83 and § 61 in the amount of the transferred capital interest. Because there is no substantial risk of forfeiture, moreover, there is no need to consider § 83(b) elections.

In the facts as written, it is plain that Blaine has an income inclusion of $375,000, the current fair market value of the interest transferred to him. The partnership is deemed to transfer a one-fourth interest in each of the underlying assets, which Blaine is then deemed to contribute to the partnership under § 721. In the deemed asset transfer, then, the partnership transfers: (1) $25,000 of cash, (2) $50,000 of accounts receivable, and (3) $300,000 of real property. Consequently, the partnership recognizes no gain or loss on the cash, $50,000 of gain on the accounts receivable (it has a basis of zero), and a gain of $175,000 on the real property (the property's allocable one-fourth basis is $125,000). The gain on the accounts receivable and real property must be allocated to

---

60. That argument finds support in Treas. Reg. § 1.83-3(e), which excludes from "property" "an unfunded and unsecured promise to pay money or property in the future."

9. Other Payments to Service Partners

the existing partners. Assuming there are no § 704(c) issues, the gain on the accounts receivable will be allocated $16,667 to each existing partner, and the gain on the real property will be allocated $58,333 to each existing partner. The recognition of this gain allows the existing partners to upwardly adjust their basis accordingly by $75,000. This results in no change to their capital accounts.

Now that we've considered the built-in gain, we can now consider the impact of paying the service provider. The partnership is allowed a compensation deduction under § 162 in the amount of the property transferred, assuming that it need not be capitalized under § 263. Here the partnership paid Blaine $375,000 and can deduct that amount. The existing three partners, therefore, are allocated $125,000 of the compensation expense.

So far, we have handled the compensatory aspect of this transaction. The partnership has recognized the built-in gain on the deemed property disposition. Blaine has included the amount in his income. The existing partners have been allocated both their share of the built-in gain and the corresponding compensation deduction. We can now turn to the implied second step of this transaction, which is Blaine contributing the property that the partnership is deemed to have transferred to him. This is now a simple § 721 transaction and the normal rules apply. Blaine recognizes no additional gain or loss on the contribution, and he takes a basis in his partnership interest equal to that of the basis of the property contributed (here that is $375,000). As well, the partnership takes the same inside basis; so, it has a basis of $25,000 in the cash, $50,000 in the accounts receivable, and $300,000 in the real property. As you can now observe, there is no longer any built-in gain or loss on these fractional shares of property because it was all recognized on the deemed transfer to Blaine.

5. If the proposed regulation and proposed revenue procedure applied, the main difference would be regarding the need to recognize the built-in gain. The proposed regulations make clear that a transfer of a compensatory partnership interest—like the interest transferred to Blaine here—does not trigger the recognition of gain or loss by the partnership.[61] The proposed regulations provide that such transfer is to be treated as a guaranteed payment under § 707(c).

As applied to Blaine, then, he still must recognize income in the amount of the transferred vested compensatory interest, here $375,000.

---

61. The preamble notes that the proposed regulations are designed to provide that "a partnership generally recognizes no gain or loss on the transfer of an interest in the partnership in connection with the performance of services for that partnership." Partnership Equity for Services, 70 Fed. Reg. 29675-01 (proposed May 24, 2005).

9. Other Payments to Service Partners

Blaine would now have an outside basis in his one-fourth partnership interest of $375,000. For the partnership, it will not have to recognize any built-in gain and will treat the transferred interest like the payment of a guaranteed payment. Consequently, it will be able to deduct the payment, assuming it is not of a type or nature required to be capitalized, with the deduction being allocated to the historic partners.

Selling, Exiting, Terminating, and Other Partnership Exits

INTRODUCTION

In this chapter, we turn to the last part of the partnership's lifecycle: exits. There are several ways that a partner can leave or exit a partnership. The partner can sell his or her partnership interest to someone else. A partner may also receive a liquidating distribution, which operates to cease his or her interest in the partnership, which we discussed earlier in Chapter 7. Relatedly, a partner may retire and leave the partnership, or the partner may die, which also has tax consequences. In addition to partner-level events (such as a sale or liquidation), after which the partnership continues to operate later as an entity, there can also be entity-level events, such as a termination or merger. This chapter covers these partner-level and entity-level exit events.

SALE OF A PARTNERSHIP INTEREST

The first exit that we discuss is the sale of a partnership interest. At the outset, we are faced yet again with the philosophical question of *how* these transactions should be taxed — as an entity or as an aggregate of assets. For sales and transfers of partnership interests, the Code generally adopts the entity approach subject to a carveout to prevent character shifting between ordinary income and capital gain income. There are three parties to consider

10. Selling, Exiting, Terminating, and Other Partnership Exits

in these transactions: (1) the transferor-partner, (2) the transferee-partner, and (3) the remaining partners (and partnership as entity). All three parties will be considered in that order.

There are two main sections that operate for the transferor-partner, §§ 741 and 751. Section 741 implements the entity-approach to the taxation of selling the interest. The first part of § 741 is very simple and straightforward; it provides, "[i]n the case of a sale or exchange of an interest in a partnership, gain or loss shall be recognized to the transferor partner. Such gain or loss shall be considered as gain or loss from the sale or exchange of a capital asset. . . ."[1] The section continues, but let us first see if we can paint the problem that the rest of the section will be aimed at fixing.

First, let us consider the simplest example. Consider the ABC Partnership, in which there are three equal partners with the following balance sheet.

ABC Partnership					
Assets			Liabilities		
	Basis	Book Value			
Blackacre	$90,000	$120,000			
			Capital Accounts		
				Basis	Book Value
			A	$30,000	$40,000
			B	$30,000	$40,000
			C	$30,000	$40,000
Total	$90,000	$120,000	Total	$90,000	$120,000

Partner A sells his interest in the partnership to D for $40,000. Under the first part of § 741, A recognizes a $10,000 gain, that is, the excess of his amount realized ($40,000) over the outside basis in his partnership interest ($30,000). Section 741, moreover, instructs to consider this a gain or loss from a capital asset, and, if we assume that A has held his partnership interest for several years, A will therefore have $10,000 of long-term capital gain.

From a policy perspective, there is nothing awry with this outcome. That is, had A not been doing business in a partnership, and rather held the interest of Blackacre directly—and sold that real property interest to D—he would have still recognized a $10,000 long-term capital gain. There is parity between the entity and aggregate approach in this example.

Given where we are in this text (towards the end) and our prior explication of the policy aims of Subchapter K, you can likely readily anticipate the problem if this were the complete rule in § 741. Consider if the ABC Partnership balance sheet looked as follows:

---

1. I.R.C. § 741.

10. Selling, Exiting, Terminating, and Other Partnership Exits

ABC Partnership						
Assets			*Liabilities*			
	Adj. Basis	Book Value				
Inventory	$90,000	$120,000				
				Capital Accounts		
					Adj. Basis	Book Value
				A	$30,000	$40,000
				B	$30,000	$40,000
				C	$30,000	$40,000
Total	$90,000	$120,000		Total	$90,000	$120,000

Under the § 741 rule as we've unpacked it, A would still have $10,000 of gain, which would be characterized as long-term capital gain. This, now, is hugely problematic. Partner A has changed the character from ordinary income (gain from inventory) to capital gain; that is, he has accomplished a character shift by using the partnership form of business—a perennial concern for Subchapter K and thus evidences a breakdown in the entity versus aggregate parity.

Subchapter K generally does not allow character shift. It therefore must have a mechanism to prevent this. Consequently, consider now the full quote of § 741:

> In the case of a sale or exchange of an interest in a partnership, gain or loss shall be recognized to the transferor partner. Such gain or loss shall be considered as gain or loss from the sale or exchange of a capital asset, *except as otherwise provided in section 751 (relating to unrealized receivables and inventory items)*.[2]

The second part of § 741 therefore prevents the dreaded character shift of income relating to unrealized receivables and inventory items. This is the same mechanism that we unpacked in the context of partnership distributions.[3] Indeed, the concern was the same, namely that the net effect of the distribution would reallocate the balance of ordinary and capital income between the partners. The concern is similar here, namely by adopting a full entity approach, it would allow a character shift between the selling partner and the remaining partners. We thus carve out from the operation of § 741's entity treatment the amount of ordinary income that the transferor-partner would have recognized had an aggregate (asset) approach been used.

As with the sale of any asset—including an interest in a partnership—there are standard dimensions to consider, namely the tax consequences to

---

2. I.R.C. § 741 (emphasis added).
3. *See* Chapter 7.

The Transferor-Partner

We have already seen that, under § 741, the transferor-partner (i.e., the selling partner) generally recognizes gain or loss on the sale of the partnership interest like that of any other capital asset. This invokes the oft used § 1001 framework of calculating gain (defined as the amount realized over the adjusted basis) and calculating loss (defined as the adjusted basis over the amount realized).

As with any § 1001 analysis, the "amount realized" is equal to the amount of money received plus the fair market value of property received (other than money).[4] In essence, the amount realized is aimed at aggregating all the economic benefits that are flowing to the transferor. In the partnership context, we need to be mindful of how the partnership liabilities factor into this analysis. Recall the two types of partnership liabilities, namely recourse and nonrecourse liabilities. Two regulations inform this interaction. First, the § 1001 regulations provide that "the amount realized from a sale or other disposition of property includes the amount of liabilities from which the transferor is discharged as a result of the sale or disposition."[5] Relatedly, the same regulation provides that "[t]he liabilities from which a transferor is discharged as a result of the sale or disposition of a partnership interest include the transferor's share of the liabilities of the partnership."[6] Second, the § 752 regulations provide that "[i]f a partnership interest is sold or exchanged, the reduction in the transferor partner's share of partnership liabilities is treated as an amount realized under section 1001 and the regulations thereunder."[7] In sum, then, the amount realized includes the partner's share of the partnership liabilities as calculated under § 752.

The transferor-partner's adjusted basis is reflective of the initial basis as later adjusted under § 705. A partner's initial basis is determined under § 722 (for an interest acquired by contributions) or § 742 (for an interest acquired by transfer). The initial basis is then adjusted as determined under § 705. When we discussed basis earlier, we learned that a partner has a single (or unitary) basis in his partnership interest. This unitary basis concept informs the analysis for several dimensions—for example, if the partner has

---

4. I.R.C. § 1001(b).
5. Treas. Reg. § 1.1001-2(a)(1).
6. Treas. Reg. § 1.1001-2(a)(4)(v).
7. Treas. Reg. § 1.752-1(h).

10. Selling, Exiting, Terminating, and Other Partnership Exits

different types of interests (say, a general and limited partnership), transfers only a portion of the interest, or if the interest includes a share of partnership liabilities. These complexities were analyzed in Revenue Ruling 84-53.[8]

In Revenue Ruling 84-53, the Service reinforced several concepts. First, that "a partner has a single basis in a partnership interest, even if such partner is both a general partner and a limited partner of the same partnership."[9] Second, if a partner transfers only a portion of a partnership interest, then "the basis of the transferred portion of the interest generally equals an amount which bears the same relation to the partner's basis in the partner's entire interest as the fair market value of the transferred portion of the interest bears to the fair market value of the entire interest."[10] Third, if a partnership has liabilities, then "special adjustments" need to be made to take into account their effect on the partner's basis.[11] This third part requires additional unpacking and is related to the second point (about allocating basis).

There are two situations here to consider. The first is when the partner's share of partnership liabilities do not exceed the partner's adjusted basis. In this case, the basis is first determined without regard to the partnership liabilities. This liability-free basis is then allocated to the transferred portion based on the fair market value of the transferred portion relative to the entire interest. Then, the partner's share of liabilities considered to be discharged is added to the basis of the transferred portion.

Let's consider a quick example of this rule applied but focusing only on the basis rules. Assume Partner A is a general partner in the AB Partnership. A has an outside basis of $100 in his partnership interest, which is allocable to a $60 contribution and $40 in his share of recourse partnership liabilities. A intends to transfer 50% of his interest to C for its fair market value. A's basis is greater than his share of partnership liabilities. His basis determined without regard to the liabilities is $60. The allocated share of the basis is $30 because A is selling 50% of A's interest. We then need to add the share of liabilities considered to be discharged, which is $20 (half of the recourse liabilities). Thus, the basis for calculating gain or loss on this sale of 50% of the partnership interest is equal to $50.

The second situation is when the partner's outside basis is *less* than his share of the partnership liabilities. In this case, the basis of the transferred portion is "an amount that bears the same relation to the partner's adjusted basis in the entire interest as the partner's share of liabilities that is considered discharged on the disposition of the transferred portion of the interest bears to the partner's share of all partnership liabilities, as determined under

---

8. 1984-1 C.B. 159.
9. Id.
10. Id.
11. Id.

section 1.752-1(e)."[12] Revisiting the example, now assume that, although A's basis is still $100, his share of all partnership liabilities is $120. In this case, A's share of liabilities ($120) exceeds his adjusted basis ($100). The adjusted basis of the transferred portion, therefore, is the portion of the entire basis ($100) that bears the same relation of the share of liabilities considered discharged ($60, i.e., half of the liabilities) bears to the partner's share of all liabilities ($120), which is $50.

In addition, although we have seen how to adjust a partner's outside basis for items such as the distributive share of income, loss, and deduction, as well as partnership distributions, the more salient point is one of timing. The § 705 regulations provide that "[t]he determination of the adjusted basis of a partnership interest is ordinarily made as of the end of a partnership taxable year."[13] Sales of partnership interests, though, may not conveniently happen on the last day of the year. The regulations therefore provide that "where there has been a sale or exchange of all or a part of a partnership interest or a liquidation of a partner's entire interest in a partnership, the adjusted basis of the partner's interest should be determined as of the date of sale or exchange or liquidation."[14]

We have now unpacked the magnitude items: the amount realized and the adjusted basis for the transferor-partner. Let's now consider character and holding period items. We started the chapter noting that § 741 generally makes the gain capital in character, except for a carveout for § 751 items (i.e., "hot assets"). We will now drill deeper into this carveout for "hot assets."

Section 751(a) provides, in full:

> (a) Sale or exchange of interest in partnership.—The amount of any money, or the fair market value of any property, received by a transferor partner in exchange for all or a part of his interest in the partnership attributable to—
> (1) unrealized receivables of the partnership, or
> (2) inventory items of the partnership,
> shall be considered as an amount realized from the sale or exchange of property other than a capital asset.[15]

We have previously covered § 751 (see, for example, Chapter 7). The theme and purpose behind § 751 are to prevent character shift. We do not want partners to be able to turn certain ordinary income items into capital gain items, which may happen when we use an entity approach to partnership taxation (as exemplified in the motivating example at the beginning

---

12. Id.
13. Treas. Reg. § 1.705-1(a)(1).
14. Id.
15. I.R.C. § 751(a).

of this chapter). Thus, § 751 ensures that the ordinary income inherent in unrealized receivables and inventory items are still captured as such upon a transfer or sale of a partnership interest (just like it did, as we saw earlier, in partnership distributions). In other words, you cannot purge your ordinary income when you leave the partnership.

Section 751 targets "unrealized receivables" and "inventory items," which are known as "§ 751 property" or "hot assets." Each of these items are specifically defined in § 751. Unrealized receivables are defined as, to the extent not previously included in income, "rights (contractual or otherwise) to payment for . . . goods delivered, or to be delivered, to the extent the proceeds therefrom would be treated as amounts received from the sale or exchange of property other than a capital asset, or . . . services rendered, or to be rendered."[16] The quintessential unrealized receivable is an accounts receivable in the hands of a cash method taxpayer. For example, if a customer purchases a widget and promises to pay in the future, that promise is not currently includible in income for a cash method taxpayer.[17] That promise, though, now represents an asset for the partnership (the asset is the right to future payment).

In addition to its commonly understood accounting definition of unrealized receivable, § 751(c) also includes a litany of other items in this definition, which are found in its flush paragraph; the common denominator in the flush paragraph is that these items and properties would generate ordinary income if sold by the partnership. These items include mining property, § 1245 property, farm land, certain intellectual property rights, and other recapture property. These items are unrealized receivables to the extent of the ordinary income under the underlying provision. The flush paragraph, therefore, extends the character-shift protection of § 751 to other types of property that may be sold by a partnership.

Inventory items are defined in § 751(d). There are three ways to be an inventory item. The first is to be property as defined in § 1221(a)(1), which provides "stock in trade of the taxpayer or other property of a kind which would properly be included in the inventory of the taxpayer if on hand at the close of the taxable year, or property held by the taxpayer primarily for sale to customers in the ordinary course of his trade or business."[18] The second type of property—again more broad than the label of "inventory"—is any property sold by the partnership other than a capital asset or § 1231 property.[19] The third type of property is any other property which, if held by a selling or distributee partner, would be of the first two types.

---

16. I.R.C. § 751(c).
17. Note that this would not be the case for an accrual method taxpayer. An accrual method taxpayer would generally include the item in income upon the sale because of the "all events test." Treas. Reg. § 1.451-1(a).
18. I.R.C. § 1221(a)(1).
19. I.R.C. § 751(d)(2).

10. Selling, Exiting, Terminating, and Other Partnership Exits

One additional key point is needed here concerning inventory. In our earlier discussion of § 751, we covered how it operates to prevent a shifting of cold and hot assets in the case of a disproportionate distribution under § 751(b). Section 751(b), like subsection (a), includes unrealized receivables and inventory items. However, for § 751(b) purposes, inventory is considered only if it has "appreciated substantially in value,"[20] which occurs if its fair market value exceeds 120% of its adjusted basis.[21] The substantial appreciation requirement is not present for purposes of § 751(a) partnership interest transfers. This is a marked distinction between partnership distributions vis-à-vis partnership interest transfers.

Now with the hot assets defined, let's ascertain how their magnitude is calculated for purposes of §§ 741 and 751. Perhaps unsurprisingly, the regulations take another hypothetical sale transaction approach.[22] We calculate the amount of income or loss from § 751 property that would have been allocated to the partner if the partnership had sold all of its property for its fair market value in a fully taxable transaction for cash. The gain or loss allocated is ordinary in character. After the § 751 gain or loss has been calculated, the regulations then prescribe that "[t]he difference between the amount of capital gain or loss that the partner would realize in the absence of section 751 and the amount of ordinary income or loss determined under this paragraph (a)(2) is the transferor's capital gain or loss on the sale of its partnership interest."[23]

Let's proceed with an example of the operation of §§ 741 and 751. Consider the DEF Partnership with the following balance sheet. Assume that the partners contributed cash such that there are no § 704(c) issues.

DEF Partnership					
Assets			*Liabilities*		
	Basis	Book Value			
Cash	$300,000	$300,000			
Inventory	$90,000	$150,000	*Capital Accounts*		
Capital asset	$120,000	$300,000		Basis	Book Value
			D	$170,000	$250,000
			E	$170,000	$250,000
			F	$170,000	$250,000
Total	$510,000	$750,000	Total	$510,000	$750,000

---

20. I.R.C. § 751(b)(1)(A)(ii).
21. I.R.C. § 751(b)(3)(A).
22. Treas. Reg. § 1.751-1(a)(2).
23. Id.

10. Selling, Exiting, Terminating, and Other Partnership Exits

Partner D sells his entire partnership interest to G for $250,000 in cash on the first day of the taxable year. The first step is to calculate the total gain or loss using § 1001 principles. D's amount realized is the $250,000 in cash. D's adjusted basis is already provided on the balance sheet of $170,000; given that the sale happens on the first day, moreover, assume there is no need to allocate income items to D for the current year. Thus, the total gain is equal to $80,000 ($250,000 less the $170,000). Under § 741, this gain is capital in character, except to the extent it is displaced by § 751.

The second step, therefore, is to calculate the § 751 gain or loss, if any, to D. Under the regulations, we effectuate a hypothetical sale of all the assets. For completeness, let's unpack each asset. Upon a sale of the cash, there is, of course, no gain or loss to allocate to D. Upon a sale of the inventory—which is a § 751 asset—there is $60,000 of ordinary income, which would be allocated $20,000 to each partner (assuming no special allocations). Upon a sale of the capital asset, although there is a $180,000 gain, it is not § 751 property. Consequently, there is $20,000 of § 751 gain to D.

The third step is to calculate the "difference between the amount of capital gain or loss that the partner would realize in the absence of section 751 and the amount of ordinary income or loss determined under this paragraph (a)(2) is the transferor's capital gain or loss on the sale of its partnership interest."[24] The amount of capital gain that would be realized in the absence of § 751 is $80,000. The amount of ordinary income or loss under § 751 is $20,000 ordinary income. Therefore, the difference between those two amounts ($80,000 less $20,000) is the transferor's capital gain or loss, which here is $60,000 of capital gain. In sum, under §§ 741 and 751, D has to report a $60,000 capital gain (either short- or long-term depending on his holding period) and $20,000 in ordinary income. As we finish this example, take note of its purpose. There was $60,000 of ordinary income inherent in the partnership that D would eventually have to recognize had he remained a partner—his share would have been $20,000. By exiting the partnership, though, he essentially left that ordinary income to the remaining partners—that is, he would have effectuated a character shift (by turning some of his inherent ordinary income into capital gain income). Sections 741 and 751 work in tandem to prevent that character shift by forcing him to recognize the $20,000 in ordinary income upon the transfer of his partnership interest. As mentioned earlier—and that you can now see—you cannot purge the built-in ordinary income by exiting the partnership.

The above example was relatively straightforward. However, the interaction of §§ 741 and 751 isn't always obvious. Consider this following example, restating the DEF Partnership, which illustrates this point. Like

---

24. Id.

10. Selling, Exiting, Terminating, and Other Partnership Exits

before, the partners initially contributed cash to the partnership, and the transfer to G happens on the first day of the taxable year. The partnership has the following balance sheet.

DEF Partnership					
Assets			Liabilities		
	Basis	Book Value			
Cash	$300,000	$300,000			
Inventory	$90,000	$120,000	Capital Accounts		
Capital asset	$450,000	$300,000		Basis	Book Value
			D	$280,000	$240,000
			E	$280,000	$240,000
			F	$280,000	$240,000
Total	$840,000	$720,000	Total	$840,000	$720,000

Partner D sells his interest to G for $240,000 in cash. Like before, the first step is to calculate the total gain or loss. Here, D's adjusted basis ($280,000) exceeds the amount realized of $240,000, resulting in a total loss of $40,000. The second step is to calculate the § 751 gain or loss. The only hot asset is the inventory, which would generate $30,000 ordinary income, of which $10,000 would be allocated to D. The third step is to calculate the difference. In the absence of § 751, there would have been a capital loss of $40,000. The income or loss on § 751 property is $10,000. The difference between a loss of $40,000 and a gain of $10,000 is a $50,000 loss.[25]

At first blush, this may not make sense—that is, how can Partner D be assigned both a gain and loss, neither of which are the $40,000 amount from the § 1001 calculation. This is due to the nature of capital and ordinary losses, as well as our desire to prevent character shift. By making D recognize a $10,000 ordinary gain on the sale of his partnership interest, he cannot escape the ordinary income taint inherent in the economics of his partnership interest. Yet, economically, we know that he suffered an "economic loss" on the deal—that is, he had a $280,000 basis yet received only $240,000 in exchange for it. That is where the $50,000 in capital loss comes in; by netting the ordinary income and capital loss together, we arrive at the "$40,000" economic loss suffered. It is important to highlight that, although these items' magnitudes net out to $40,000, it does not follow that the tax consequences net out. Recall the rules for deducting long-term capital losses, for example, namely that they are annually limited to the extent of capital gains plus $3,000 for individual taxpayers.[26]

---

25. Another way to conceptualize this is that negative 40,000 minus 10,000 equals negative 50,000.
26. I.R.C. § 1211(b).

10. Selling, Exiting, Terminating, and Other Partnership Exits

Additional Look-Through and Collateral Impacts for Transferor-Partner

We have already seen how § 741 yields to the look-through requirements of § 751 to prevent the character shift (changing ordinary income into capital gain income). For those readers well versed in individual income taxation, you are likely familiar with the various rules surrounding capital gains taxation. In essence, under § 1(h), the Code affords preferential (i.e., lower) tax rates to long-term capital gains.[27] Things with tax, though, are rarely that straightforward, and § 1 actually applies various rates to capital gain property. Under § 1, net capital gain is taxed at a *maximum* rate of 20%. However, collectibles gain is subject to a maximum rate of 28% and unrecaptured § 1250 gain is subject to a maximum rate of 25%. Therefore, we must also consider how § 1 interacts with the transfer of a partnership interest.

Section 1 provides that, in the case of a sale of partnership interest, gain that is "attributable to unrealized appreciation in the value of collectibles shall be treated as gain from the sale or exchange of a collectible."[28] It further provides that "[r]ules similar to the rules of section 751 shall apply for purposes of the preceding sentence."[29] This makes conceptual sense given the purpose of § 751, which is to prevent character shift. Similarly, then, we need a mechanism to prevent the character shift *within* the capital gains rates. Just like being able to shift ordinary income into capital—which § 751 prevents—we need similar rules that prevent shifting of 28% rate gain into lower taxed gain rates.

The § 1(h) regulations set forth this framework; it provides that "[w]hen an interest in a partnership held for more than one year is sold or exchanged, the transferor may recognize ordinary income (e.g., under section 751(a)), collectibles gain, section 1250 capital gain, and residual long-term capital gain or loss."[30] It further defines "look-through capital gain" as the share of collectibles gain plus the share of § 1250 capital gain allocable to the share of sold partnership interest.[31]

Statutorily, "collectibles gain" is defined as the gain or loss from the sale or exchange of a collectible as defined in § 408(m).[32] Collectibles include items such as a work of art, rugs and antiques, metal or gems, and stamps or coins, as well as other items of tangible personal property specified by regulation.[33] For its part, § 1250 capital gain is defined as "the capital gain (not

---

27. Section 1(h) uses the phrase "net capital gain," which is defined in § 1222(11) and is defined as the excess of the net long-term capital gains over the net short-term capital loss for the year.
28. I.R.C. § 1(h)(5)(B).
29. Id.
30. Treas. Reg. § 1.1(h)-1(a).
31. Treas. Reg. § 1.1(h)-1(b)(1).
32. I.R.C. § 1(h)(5)(A).
33. I.R.C. § 408(m)(2).

otherwise treated as ordinary income) that would be treated as ordinary income if section 1250(b)(1) included all depreciation and the applicable percentage under section 1250(a) were 100 percent."[34]

A quick example will illustrate what § 1250 capital gain is targeting. Recall that § 1250 property is real property (other than § 1245 property) that is subject to depreciation. Quintessential § 1250 property items, therefore, are commercial buildings and residential rental property. Assume that you purchase a commercial building for $500,000, exclusive of the land.[35] Under § 168, the building would be depreciated over 39 years (its applicable recovery period is 39 years), using the straight-line method, and the mid-month convention.[36] For the sake of ease, we will ignore the depreciation conventions in this quick example, which means the annual depreciation is $500,000 divided by 39 = $12,821 per year,[37] and for further ease, let's round it to $13,000. Let's assume, moreover, that we are now three years into the property ownership, such that depreciation has been $39,000 over the three years. Thus, the property has an adjusted basis of $461,000.

Assume that, due to a booming real estate market, the firm can sell the property for $500,000. It would thus realize a gain of $39,000. But that gain is, in essence, a recapture of the previously allowed depreciation deduction. This is the type of gain that recapture provisions are designed for and how they operate generally — they treat the gain that is traceable to prior deprecation differently than other gains. However, this is not how § 1250 recapture works generally. Typically, § 1250 recaptures only the portion of depreciation that was in excess of straight-line depreciation. Although this is admittedly not clear from the face of the statutory text, this is the net effect of the operation of the "applicable percentage" and "additional depreciation" portions of § 1250(a) and (b).[38] In short, if the taxpayer used only straight-line depreciation on the property, then the "additional depreciation" would be zero, thus negating any § 1250 recapture.

But for this special § 1(h) look-through, we do not have normal § 1250 recapture. Rather, § 1(h)(6)(A) defines "unrecaptured section 1250 gain" as "the capital gain (not otherwise treated as ordinary income) that would

---

34. Treas. Reg. § 1.1(h)-1(b)(3)(i).
35. Recall that land (the actual dirt) is not depreciable, as it does not wear and tear, and therefore it does not satisfy the § 167 requirements. This example also ignores cost segregation and any application of § 1245.
36. See I.R.C. § 168 for these inputs. The applicable depreciation method is found in § 168(b), the applicable recovery period is in § 168(c), and the applicable convention in § 168(d).
37. Technically, the amount of depreciation for the first year depends on the month placed in service (due to the mid-month convention). For example, if the property was placed into service in the first month of the first year, the depreciation expense would be $500,000 × 2.461% = $12,305, and if placed into service in the sixth month, it would be $500,000 × 1.391% = $6,955. This uses Table A-7a provided in IRS Publication 946 ("How to Depreciate Property").
38. An unpacking of § 1250 is beyond this text.

be treated as ordinary income if section 1250(b)(1) included all depreciation and the applicable percentage under section 1250(a) were 100 percent." Thus, for this purpose, the "additional depreciation" here is $39,000, i.e., "all depreciation," and, given the applicable percentage of 100%, all the depreciation is unrecaptured §1250 gain, which is taxable at a maximum rate of 25%.[39]

For completeness, now assume that the firm can sell the same property for $525,000. Now there is a total gain of $64,000 ($525,000 less $461,000). Of that gain, $39,000 of it still constitutes unrecaptured § 1250 gain (the balance of the depreciation). The balance of the gain would depend on the operation of § 1231 to the firm. The gain would be a § 1231 gain in the amount of $25,000. Depending on the other § 1231 gains and losses, it may benefit from capital gains treatment.

Back to the application of the § 1(h) look-through to sales of partnership interests, we now need to ascertain the share of collectibles gain and § 1250 gain to the partnership interest. Again, the regulations spell this out. For collectibles gain, they provide that the transferor must recognize as collectibles gain the amount of net gain (but not loss) that he or she would have been allocated if the partnership sold all its collectibles at their fair market values for cash in a fully taxable transaction.[40] A similar hypothetical sales approach is used to determine the amount of the § 1250 gain.[41]

The regulations then further define the residual capital gain or loss under § 741 as the difference between the capital gain or loss without the look-through rules and with the look-through rules. Let's explore a simple example of an application of this rule and analysis to collectibles gain. Consider the ABC Partnership that has the following balance sheet.

ABC Partnership					
Assets				*Liabilities*	
	Adj. Basis	Book Value			
Cash	$300,000	$300,000			
Inventory	$60,000	$120,000		*Capital Accounts*	
Collectible	$120,000	$240,000		Adj. Basis	Book Value
Capital assets	$60,000	$90,000	A	$180,000	$250,000
			B	$180,000	$250,000
			C	$180,000	$250,000
Total	$540,000	$750,000	Total	$540,000	$750,000

---

39. That is, 100% of $39,000 = $39,000.
40. Treas. Reg. § 1.1(h)-1(b)(2)(ii).
41. Treas. Reg. § 1.1(h)-1(b)(3)(ii).

Assume that all partners contributed cash and have held their partnership interests for more than a year. Similarly, ABC has held its assets for more than one year. Partner A sells his interest to D for $250,000 in cash. We now proceed with our §§ 741 and 751 framework, as well as adding our new step to look-through for the § 1(h) gain.

First, we calculate the total gain or loss for A. A's amount realized is the $250,000 in cash, and his adjusted basis is $180,000, resulting in a total gain of $70,000. Second, we need to look for § 751 property, of which we have inventory, requiring a § 751 analysis. Here, if ABC sold its inventory for cash, it would realize $60,000 of ordinary income, of which $20,000 would be allocated to A. Third, we calculate the "difference between the amount of capital gain or loss that the partner would realize in the absence of section 751 and the amount of ordinary income or loss determined under this paragraph (a)(2) is the transferor's capital gain or loss on the sale of its partnership interest."[42] Here that is $70,000 capital gain less $20,000 ordinary income, which equals $50,000 as § 741 capital gain.

But now we need to drill-down even deeper into what that $50,000 constitutes for § 1(h) purposes; that is, it is not enough to tell A he has $50,000 of long-term capital gain, as that may distort and shift the type of capital gain he has. By examining the balance sheet, we readily observe that ABC has a collectible. If ABC sold that collectible for its fair market value, it would recognize a gain of $120,000 (the $240,000 amount realized less its $120,000 adjusted basis), of which $40,000 would be allocated to A. Thus, of the $50,000 of capital gain A recognizes on the sale, $40,000 of it constitutes collectibles gain, the remaining $10,000 is the "residual" long-term capital gain. To recap, A would recognize the following on this transaction: (1) $20,000 of ordinary income [traceable to the inventory], (2) a collectibles gain of $40,000 [traceable to his share of the collectibles gain inherent in the partnership], and (3) a $10,000 long-term capital gain [traceable to the residual amount of the § 741 capital gain less the portion that is collectibles gain].

The Transferee-Partner

We have seen that, for the transferor-partner, the tax considerations on the sale of a partnership interest consists of calculating the magnitude and character of the gain from such sale. For the transferee-partner, the core issues focus on basis and capital account balances. Section 742 provides that "[t]he basis of an interest in a partnership acquired other than by contribution shall

---

42. Treas. Reg. § 1.751-1(a)(2).

10. Selling, Exiting, Terminating, and Other Partnership Exits

be determined under part II of subchapter O (sec. 1011 and following)."[43] Therefore the general cost-basis rules apply, and if a transferee-partner purchases the interest in a taxable exchange, the initial outside basis will be its cost under § 1012. The purchasing partner then must factor in his or her share of any partnership liabilities under § 752.

In addition to calculating the transferee-partner's outside basis, we must also consider how the sale affects the inside basis of the partnership's assets. Section 743(a) provides that, unless a § 754 election is in place,[44] the inside basis of property is *not* adjusted as a result of the transfer of a partnership interest. In other words, the default rule is that the inside bases of assets remain static, even though the partner mix may change. This is another manifestation of the aggregate-entity distinction, namely that, for certain purposes, the partnership is an entity separate from its partners. The lack of a basis adjustment, however, may be unfortunate for the incoming partner, as the following example demonstrates.

Consider the GHI Partnership that has the following balance sheet.

GHI Partnership					
Assets			*Liabilities*		
	Basis	Book Value			
Cash	$120,000	$120,000			
Accounts receivable	$0	$120,000		*Capital Accounts*	
Capital asset	$90,000	$120,000		Basis	Book Value
			G	$70,000	$120,000
			H	$70,000	$120,000
			I	$70,000	$120,000
Total	$210,000	$360,000	Total	$210,000	$360,000

G sells his partnership interest to J for $120,000 in cash. Under § 742, J will have an outside basis of $120,000 in his partnership interest. Also, J will step into the capital account of G.[45] And, under § 743, the partnership does not adjust the basis of its assets. Consequently, after the transaction, the balance sheet looks thusly.

---

43. I.R.C. § 742.
44. We earlier saw the import of a § 754 election in the context of § 734 and adjusting the inside basis of partnership assets after a partnership distribution.
45. Treas. Reg. § 1.704-1(b)(2)(iv)(l). This regulation provides that the capital accounts will not be considered to be maintained in accordance with the § 704(b) regulations unless the transferor's capital account carries over to the transferee.

10. Selling, Exiting, Terminating, and Other Partnership Exits

JHI Partnership					
Assets			Liabilities		
	Basis	Book Value			
Cash	$120,000	$120,000			
Accounts receivable	$0	$120,000	Capital Accounts		
Capital asset	$90,000	$120,000		Basis	Book Value
			J	$120,000	$120,000
			H	$70,000	$120,000
			I	$70,000	$120,000
Total	$210,000	$360,000	Total	$260,000	$360,000

Observe how the bases columns no longer equal; the aggregate inside bases of $210,000 does not equal the aggregate outside bases. This is the result of § 743's "no adjustment rule." Moreover, the problem wrought by § 743 is made manifest when, for example, the partnership collects (or sells) the accounts receivables for $120,000. Here, the partnership will allocate the income $40,000 to each partner. For partners H and I, there is nothing awry with that; in other words, the $40,000 of income allocated to them represents, in part, the divergence between their bases and capital accounts (the remaining imbalance is due to the gain inherent in the capital asset). But, for partner J, this is somewhat nonsensical. When J is allocated his $40,000 as part of his distributive share, he must include that in income under §§ 702 and 704. For J, though, has not he already paid for that $40,000 of value when he purchased his interest for $120,000? In other words, ought not the $40,000 represent a return of capital (basis) instead of income (an accession to wealth)? This is the quintessential problem wrought by § 743's no adjustment rule.

Let's extend the example a tad further. Partner J, upon being allocated $40,000 in his distributive share, will be able to upwardly adjust his basis by the same, giving him an outside basis of $160,000. So now consider the consequences if, in this simplistic example, J sells his partnership interest for $120,000 (the same fair market value, assuming it's unchanged). Under § 741, he would have a $40,000 *capital* loss. This does *not* make him whole because the prior inclusion was *ordinary* and, at the individual level, he generally will not be able to use that capital loss to offset ordinary income. Plus, take note that this loss is only available when he *leaves* the partnership, which could be many (many) years into the future.

The practical effects of § 743's default no adjustment rule, then, do not seem very appealing for the entering transferee-partner. Fortunately, there is an escape hatch built in to avoid these results: the § 754 election.

10. Selling, Exiting, Terminating, and Other Partnership Exits

§ 754 Elections and § 743 Adjustments

As relevant here, § 754 provides that, if a partnership files an election, "the basis of partnership property shall be adjusted, . . . in the case of a transfer of a partnership interest, in the manner provided in section 743."[46] Before diving into the mechanics of the §§ 754/743 election, let's be sure we've crystalized the tension it is trying to resolve, as understanding the tension will help illustrate the mechanics.

Recall in the above example that when Partner J bought his partnership interest for $120,000, the partnership did not adjust any of its inside bases under the default rule of § 743. Thus, when the partnership sold or collected its receivables, that resulted in a gain allocable to J's interest, which was not treated as a return of basis. This was a pure entity approach to the transaction. Consider the result had we adopted an aggregate approach, instead, and J was considered to have purchased a proportionate sliver (interest) in each of the partnership's assets. Under this perspective, J would have, in essence, a basis of $40,000 in his share of the receivables. In other words, J's $120,000 bought him assets consisting of $40,000 of cash, $40,000 of accounts receivable (with a § 1012 cost basis of $40,000), and $40,000 of the capital asset (similarly with a $40,000 basis). So, if J were to sell his share of the accounts receivable for $40,000, he would not recognize any gain and the $40,000 would instead represent a return of capital (i.e., basis). The §§ 754/743 election is trying to replicate this aggregate approach.

The § 743 adjustment is required in two instances. The first instance was animated by the above example, namely when the partnership has a § 754 election in place. The second instance is when a partnership has a "substantial built-in loss" immediately after the transfer.[47] The § 743(b) adjustment can require either an increase or decrease to the inside bases of partnership property. The increase is defined as the "excess of the basis to the transferee partner of his interest in the partnership over his proportionate share of the adjusted basis of the partnership property,"[48] and the decrease is defined as "excess of the transferee partner's proportionate share of the adjusted basis of the partnership property over the basis of his interest in the partnership."[49] Both of these definitions include the partner's outside basis but also introduce a new concept, namely the transferee partner's

---

46. I.R.C. § 754.
47. When a partnership has built-in loss in its assets, it would not "elect" to reduce its inside basis. That is why the adjustment for substantial built-in loss is mandated.
48. I.R.C. § 743(b)(1).
49. I.R.C. § 743(b)(2).

10. Selling, Exiting, Terminating, and Other Partnership Exits

"proportionate share of the adjusted basis of partnership property." Thus, formulaically, the adjustments can be expressed as follows:

$$\S 743(b)\, Increase = Partner's\, Outside\, Basis - Prop.\, Share\, of\, AB\, of\, Partnership\, Property.$$

$$\S 743(b)\, Decrease = Prop.\, Share\, of\, AB\, of\, Partnership\, Property - Partner's\, Outside\, Basis$$

These formulas require us to define their two elements, namely (i) the transferee's basis in his partnership interest and (ii) his proportionate share of the adjusted basis of partnership property. Fortunately, the first element we've encountered regularly, namely the partner's outside basis. Under § 742, the transferee partner's outside basis is determined by "general basis rules for property."[50] Thus, if the transferee purchases his or her partnership interest, the basis is determined under § 1012 and will be its cost; this basis, of course, also needs to incorporate liabilities under § 752. Although this chapter is framed in terms of transferees who purchase their interests, transferees can also acquire their interest by other ways, such as lifetime gift or deathtime transfer; these basis rules are governed by §§ 1015 and 1014, respectively.

The new concept introduced by this formula is the partner's proportionate share of the adjusted basis of partnership property, which is defined in Treas. Reg. § 1.743-1(d), and it consists of two constituent parts. The first part is the transferee partner's share of the "partnership's previously taxed capital," and the second part is the transferee's share of partnership liabilities. The first part requires additional unpacking, and the second part has already been discussed in previous chapters.

A transferee partner's share of the partnership's previously taxed capital consists of three items. The first item is the amount of cash that the partner would receive on liquidation following a hypothetical transaction. The second additive item is the amount of tax loss allocated to the transferee partner in the hypothetical transaction. The third item, which is subtracted, is the amount of tax gain allocated to the transferee in the hypothetical transaction. Thus, the partner's share of partnership's previously taxed capital can be expressed as follows:

---

50. Treas. Reg. § 1.742-1(a).

10. Selling, Exiting, Terminating, and Other Partnership Exits

Transferee's Share of the Partnership's Previously Taxed Capital [§ 1.743-1(d)(1)]
Start with amount of cash the transferee would receive in liquidation following the hypothetical transaction
Increased by the amount of tax loss that would be allocated to the partner from the hypothetical transaction
Decreased by the amount of tax gain that would be allocated to the partner from the hypothetical transaction
Equals transferee's share of the partnership's previously taxed capital

We see that this "hypothetical transaction" is a critical element of this calculation. The hypothetical transaction is a deemed disposition of all the partnership assets for their fair market value in cash in a taxable transaction immediately after the transfer of the partnership interest.[51]

Let's revisit our earlier example and see how the § 743 calculations would work. Recall the GHI balance sheet, which looks as follows, and J is buying G's interest for $120,000 in cash.

GHI Partnership						
Assets				Liabilities		
	Adj. Basis	Book Value				
Cash	$120,000	$120,000				
Accounts receivable	$0	$120,000		*Capital Accounts*		
Capital asset	$90,000	$120,000			Adj. Basis	Book Value
			G		$70,000	$120,000
			H		$70,000	$120,000
			I		$70,000	$120,000
Total	$210,000	$360,000	Total		$210,000	$360,000

As explained earlier, the § 743 adjustment increase is expressed as:[52]

$$\S 743(b) \text{ Increase} = \text{Partner's Outside Basis} - \text{Prop. Share of AB of Partnership Property}$$

Given that J is buying his partnership interest, his initial outside basis is determined under § 1012 and is equal to his cost. Because there are no partnership liabilities, moreover, there are no basis adjustments for debt under § 752. Therefore, his outside basis is $120,000.

---

51. Treas. Reg. § 1.743-1(d)(2).
52. As a shortcut, this will be a § 743(b) *increase* because there is not a built-in loss. A *decrease* would be required when there is a built-in loss.

10. Selling, Exiting, Terminating, and Other Partnership Exits

Let's now calculate J's proportionate share of the adjusted basis of partnership property. This is calculated as J's share of the partnership's previously taxed capital and his share of the partnership liabilities. The latter is equal to zero because there are no liabilities. Thus, the focus here is on previously taxed capital. Partnership previously taxed capital is equal to the three items discussed earlier flowing from the hypothetical transaction; the hypothetical transaction requires us to "pretend" that the partnership sells all its assets for cash in a fully taxable transaction.

If the partnership sold all its assets for cash in a fully taxable transaction, it would yield $360,000, of which $120,000 would be payable to J (i.e., his one-third interest, with no liabilities to pay first). The second step is to determine the amount of tax loss that is allocated on the hypothetical transaction. Here, all the assets have built-in gains, so there is no tax loss to allocate. The third step is to determine the amount of tax gain that is allocated on the hypothetical transaction. Here, the accounts receivable and capital asset generate a total of $150,000 of gain ($120,000 from the accounts receivable and $30,000 from the capital asset); moreover, there are no § 704(c) or special allocations to consider in this example. Consequently, of the $150,000 of tax gain, $50,000 of it is allocated to J (i.e., his one-third share of the gain). The full previously tax capital result, therefore, is calculated as follows:

Transferee's Share of the Partnership's Previously Taxed Capital [§ 1.743-1(d)(1)]	
Start with amount of cash the transferee would receive in liquidation following the hypothetical transaction	$120,000
Increased by the amount of tax loss that would be allocated to the partner from the hypothetical transaction	+ $0
Decreased by the amount of tax gain that would be allocated to the partner from the hypothetical transaction	− $50,000
Equals transferee's share of the partnership's previously taxed capital	= $70,000

We can now plug the previously taxed capital into the § 743 adjustment formula for increases:

$$\S 743(b) \text{ Increase} = \text{Partner's Outside Basis} - \text{Prop. Share of AB of Partnership Property}$$

$$\S 743(b) \text{ Increase} = \$120,000 - \$70,000 = \$50,000$$

Thus, the § 743(b) adjustment is an increase of $50,000. Before continuing with what to do with this $50,000, let's consider how this comports with the

10. Selling, Exiting, Terminating, and Other Partnership Exits

why of the section. Recall the animating issue that we are trying to fix here is the default no-adjustment rule for the inside basis upon a transfer of a partnership interest. That is, when J purchased his partnership interest from G, he paid $120,000 but received no corresponding special inside basis for the assets; this, as we saw, would result in an allocable gain of $10,000 to J if the partnership immediately sold the capital asset and a similar $40,000 gain for the accounts receivable after his purchase of the partnership interest. What fixes this? The § 743(b) adjustment (by way of a § 754 election), which now gives J an *increase* in the *inside basis* of the partnership assets of $50,000—and note that this $50,000 is the aggregate of the two gain items he would have. In other words, if J had $50,000 more of inside basis, that $50,000 aggregate basis absorbs the built-in gain existing on his date of purchase!

Section 743 tells us how much *increase* (or *decrease*) to adjust for the transferee partner. It does not, however, directly tell us how to *pour* that increase or decrease—that is, what partnership assets are benefited or harmed by the adjustment. The job of allocating the increase or decrease goes to § 755.[53] The statutory text of § 755, however, does not do much lifting. We must turn to the § 755 regulations for the specific rules.

Treas. Reg. § 1.755-1 provides the rules for allocating basis adjustments for § 743(b) and § 734(b), and it provides a three-step process.[54] The first step is to determine the value of the assets under specific § 755 rules. The main wrinkle here is to ensure the use of the residual method under § 1060 for § 197 intangibles.[55] In addition to the § 197 intangibles, § 755 also requires that property secured by a nonrecourse debt be valued no less than such debt.[56] The second step is to allocate the basis adjustment between capital gain property and ordinary income property. The third step is to allocate the basis adjustment to property within each class. Relevant here, we will unpack the second and third steps in more detail in the context of § 743(b) adjustments.[57]

For § 743(b) adjustments, the § 755 regulations have two sets of rules, one for substituted basis transactions, and the other for all other transactions;[58] we focus on the latter. Like with determining the amount of the § 743(b) adjustment, the hypothetical transaction plays a central role. The first thing these rules are trying to do is to split the total § 743(b) adjustment into an ordinary income property amount and a capital gain property amount. The ordinary income property amount is the amount of ordinary income, gain, or loss that would be allocated to the transferee partner in

---

53. *See* I.R.C. § 743(c).
54. Treas. Reg. § 1.755-1(a)(1).
55. This is beyond the scope of this text.
56. Treas. Reg. § 1.755-1(a)(3) (incorporating I.R.C. § 7701(g)).
57. It is important to note that there are specific subsections for § 743(b) and § 734(b) adjustments.
58. Treas. Reg. § 1.755-1(b)(1)(i).

the hypothetical transaction.[59] The capital gain property amount is the total § 743(b) adjustment less that portion allocated to the ordinary income property portion.[60] However, in cases of decrease, the capital gain portion cannot exceed the partnership's basis in capital gain property.[61]

After we take the § 743(b) adjustment amount and bifurcate it into the two classes (ordinary income and capital gain amounts), we must then allocate each amount to the properties within each class. For ordinary income property, the basis adjustment is allocated based on the amount of income, gain, or loss that would be allocated to the transferee from the hypothetical sale of the item in the hypothetical transaction.[62] For capital gain property, it is a similar calculation, i.e., based on the amount generated by the hypothetical transaction. The exact calculations can be more complicated, which we will demonstrate later, but let's first continue with our above example.

Recall that, in the above example, we calculated a § 743(b) adjustment of $50,000. We can now allocate that special basis adjustment to specific partnership property using the rules of the § 755 regulation. First, we need to bifurcate the $50,000 into the two classes of property. Based on the hypothetical transaction, $40,000 of the adjustment emanates from the accounts receivable, which is ordinary income property. The capital gain portion is calculated as the entire adjustment ($50,000) less the ordinary income property portion ($40,000), which equals $10,000. Second, we then take those class amounts and pour them into the properties within each class. Given we have only one asset per class, that is relatively straightforward here. But, for completeness, let's follow the rule. The ordinary income property portion is allocated based on the hypothetical transaction. Here, all the ordinary income is traceable to the accounts receivable, so it receives the entire ordinary income basis adjustment. The same is true for the capital gain property portion. Thus, at the end of the § 743(b) adjustment as allocated by § 755, Partner J has a special inside basis of $40,000 in the accounts receivable (the $0 inside basis plus his $40,000 adjustment) and a special inside basis of $40,000 in the capital asset (his portion of the inside basis of $30,000 plus the basis adjustment of $10,000).

The above example, though it demonstrates the main operation of §§ 743(b) and 755, is relatively basic. Let's work through an example from the regulation that demonstrates a more rigorous application of these rules.[63] The AB Partnership has the following balance sheet, which depicts the assets' current fair market values. All the properties were purchased

---

59. Treas. Reg. § 1.755-1(b)(2)(i).
60. Id.
61. Treas. Reg. § 1.755-1(b)(2)(i)(B).
62. Treas. Reg. § 1.755-1(b)(3)(i)(A). This can be reduced if the limit of Treas. Reg. § 1.755-1(b)(2)(i)(B) is triggered.
63. Treas. Reg. § 1.755-1(b)(2)(ii) Example 1; Treas. Reg. § 1.755-1(b)(3)(iv) Example 2. This discussion in-text follows the noted examples.

10. Selling, Exiting, Terminating, and Other Partnership Exits

by the partnership, except for Capital Asset 1, which was contributed by A when its fair market value was $50,000.[64]

AB Partnership					
Assets			Liabilities		
	Basis	FMV			
Capital Asset 1	$25,000	$75,000			
Capital Asset 2	$100,000	$117,500		Capital Accounts	
Ordinary Property 1	$40,000	$45,000		Basis	Book Value
Ordinary Property 2	$10,000	$2,500	A	$75,000	–
			B	$100,000	–
Total	$175,000	$240,000	Total	$175,000	–

Assume that A and B are equal partners. The more complicated applications of § 755 occur when there is an "underpayment" for the partnership interest. Consequently, assume that A sells his interest to Transferee Partner (T) for $110,000.[65] The § 743 basis adjustment is calculated as follows.

$$\S 743(b) \text{ Increase} = \text{Partner's Outside Basis} - \text{Prop. Share of AB of Partnership Property}$$

T's outside basis is $110,000 under § 1012 principles. We need to calculate T's proportionate share of the adjusted basis of partnership property. This invokes the hypothetical transaction. In a hypothetical transaction, T would (i) receive $120,000 of cash, (ii) be allocated $1,250 of tax loss,[66] and (iii) be allocated $46,250 of tax gain.[67] Using the previously taxed capital formula, this results in a previously taxed capital calculated as follows.

---

64. The book values for the partners' capital accounts are not provided and are not necessary for these §§ 743 and 755 examples.
65. The underpayment here is $10,000. In other words, on an asset valuation, A's partnership interest is worth $120,000, i.e., one-half of the book value of the assets.
66. This comes from the sale of the ordinary income property: Ordinary Income Property 1 generates a $5,000 ordinary gain and Ordinary Income Property 2 generates a $7,500 loss, for a net loss of $2,500, which is borne equally between the partners.
67. The tax gain flows from the gain on Capital Asset 1, which has a total gain of $50,000, but $25,000 of it is § 704(c) gain which must be allocated exclusively to A; this leaves the remaining capital gain of $25,000 and the $17,500 of capital gain from Capital Asset, for a total of $42,500, which is borne equally between the partners.

10. Selling, Exiting, Terminating, and Other Partnership Exits

Transferee's Share of the Partnership's Previously Taxed Capital [§ 1.743-1(d)(1)]	
Start with amount of cash the transferee would receive in liquidation following the hypothetical transaction	$120,000
Increased by the amount of tax loss that would be allocated to the partner from the hypothetical transaction	+ $1,250
Decreased by the amount of tax gain that would be allocated to the partner from the hypothetical transaction	− $46,250
Equals transferee's share of the partnership's previously taxed capital	= $75,000

Given that there are no liabilities to allocate, the previously taxed capital amount is equal to the proportionate share of adjusted basis of partnership property. Consequently, the § 743 basis adjustment is equal to:

$$\S743(b) \text{ Increase} = \$110,000 - \$75,000 = \$35,000$$

Under § 755, we must now allocate the basis adjustment. Of the total basis adjustment, a loss of $1,250 is allocated to ordinary income property, which means $36,250 is allocated to capital gain property—recall the amount of adjustment to capital gain property is the total adjustment amount less the amount allocated to ordinary income property.[68] Here, that is expressed as $35,000 less a loss of $1,250, which equals $36,250. We first allocate to the ordinary income property. In the hypothetical sale, T would be allocated $2,500 in gain from the sale, so the amount of adjustment to Ordinary Income Property 1 is equal to $2,500. T would be allocated a loss of $3,750 from Ordinary Income Property 2, which is therefore equal to its adjustment. Now consider, though, the capital gain asset allocation. Under the § 755 formula, we have to allocate $46,250, but in the hypothetical sale, T would be allocated $37,500 from Capital Asset 1 and $8,750 from Capital Asset 2, which totals the $46,250, but this *exceeds* the amount of the § 743 basis adjustment (of $35,000)! We must therefore use the full calculation for allocating to capital gain property, which is reproduced below:

> (ii) Capital gain property. The amount of the basis adjustment to each item of property within the class of capital gain property is equal to—
> (A) The amount of income, gain, or loss (including any remedial allocations under § 1.704–3(d)) that would be allocated to the transferee (to the extent attributable to the acquired partnership interest) from the hypothetical sale of the item; minus

---

68. Treas. Reg. § 1.755-1(b)(2)(i).

10. Selling, Exiting, Terminating, and Other Partnership Exits

(B) The product of—
(1) The total amount of gain or loss (including any remedial allocations under § 1.704-3(d)) that would be allocated to the transferee (to the extent attributable to the acquired partnership interest) from the hypothetical sale of all items of capital gain property, minus the amount of the positive basis adjustment to all items of capital gain property or plus the amount of the negative basis adjustment to capital gain property; multiplied by
(2) A fraction, the numerator of which is the fair market value of the item of property to the partnership, and the denominator of which is the fair market value of all of the partnership's items of capital gain property.[69]

Let's walk through the two capital asset calculations given the full rule. For Capital Asset 1, the amount of income allocated to T would be $37,500, which is the subparagraph (A) amount, and for Capital Asset 2 that is $8,750. Let's unpack each subpart of (B). Subparagraph (B)(1) is the total amount of gain or loss from all items of capital gain items allocated to the transferee (here, that is $46,250) minus the amount of positive basis adjustments of capital gain property (here that is $36,250), plus the amount of negative basis adjustments to capital gain property (here that is $0). Thus, the subparagraph (B) amount is equal to $10,000. This is multiplied by subparagraph (2), which is a fraction, the numerator of which is the particular capital gain property being allocated, over a denominator of $192,500 (the value of the capital gain property). Expressing it fully, then, for the capital assets, the adjustment calculation is:

$$\text{Capital Asset 1 Adjustment} = \$37,500 - \left(\$10,000 \times \frac{\$75,000}{\$192,500}\right) = \$33,604$$

$$\text{Capital Asset 2 Adjustment} = \$8,750 - \left(\$10,000 \times \frac{\$117,500}{\$192,500}\right) = \$2,646$$

Let's take a step back and see if we can appreciate what the regulatory rule is trying to accomplish in this context. In this example, we have an underpayment for a proportionate share of the assets. Stated more simply, T paid $110,000 for $120,000 worth of partnership assets. Let us appreciate the impact of this underpayment. This is best demonstrated by considering what the § 743(b) adjustment would be in the absence of the underpayment, i.e.,

---

69. Treas. Reg. § 1.755-1(b)(3)(ii).

if T had paid $120,000 for the partnership interest. If T had paid $120,000, the § 743(b) adjustment would have been $45,000.[70] With a $45,000 adjustment, this could be borne fully by a $46,250 adjustment to capital gain property and a ($1,250) adjustment (a decrease) to the ordinary income property, which nets out to $45,000. With a $110,000 purchase price, however, the § 743(b) adjustment has to be something *less* than that. Given that, we are not able to allocate dollar-for-dollar the basis with the built-in gain or loss on the hypothetical transaction. Thus, we must decide which assets should bear that result, i.e., which assets should bear the reduced adjustment (traceable to the underpayment). The regulatory rule, although clunky, makes it such that the diminution in the adjustment traceable to the underpayment is borne by the capital assets in proportion to their relative fair market values.

Life After the § 743(b) Adjustment

Now that we have calculated the § 743(b) adjustment and allocated it to specific assets under § 755, we now must consider the downstream and collateral impacts of the special inside basis that the transferee partner now has in the partnership assets. The § 743 regulations provide the overarching principle that

> The basis adjustment constitutes an adjustment to the basis of partnership property with respect to the transferee only. No adjustment is made to the common basis of partnership property. Thus, for purposes of calculating income, deduction, gain, and loss, the transferee will have a special basis for those partnership properties the bases of which are adjusted under section 743(b) and this section. The adjustment to the basis of partnership property under section 743(b) has no effect on the partnership's computation of any item under section 703.[71]

Let's first consider the sale or exchange of a partnership asset for which a partner has a § 743(b) adjustment. The regulations provide that the amount of income, gain, or loss from the sale or exchange of the asset is "equal to the transferee's share of the partnership's gain or loss from the sale of the asset . . . minus the amount of the transferee's positive basis adjustment for the partnership asset . . . or plus the amount of the transferee's negative basis adjustment for the partnership asset."[72]

This can be illustrated by our earlier GHI example in which J purchased G's partnership interest and was benefitted by a § 743(b) adjustment of

---

70. This does not change the previously taxed capital calculation, but rather changes (increases) the transferee's outside basis by $10,000.
71. Treas. Reg. § 1.743-1(j)(1).
72. Treas. Reg. § 1.743-1(j)(3)(i).

10. Selling, Exiting, Terminating, and Other Partnership Exits

$50,000, which was $40,000 in the accounts receivable and $10,000 in the capital asset. If the partnership were to sell the capital asset for $150,000, it recognizes a tax gain of $60,000[73] and a book gain of $30,000. J is allocated a $20,000 tax gain and a $10,000 book gain from the sale. The tax gain is then reduced by the $10,000 basis adjustment, resulting in a recognized tax gain of $10,000; this makes sense because this gain represents J's share of the post-transfer asset appreciation. The basis adjustment does not affect the book gain.

In addition to a straight sale, we also must consider the impact of a basis adjustment on property if it is later distributed. This can manifest in three ways, each of which are provided for in the § 1.743-1(g) regulations. First, the partnership can distribute the property to the partner with the basis adjustment. In this case, the distributee partner is allowed to factor the basis adjustment in calculating his post-distribution basis of the distributed property under § 732.[74] Second, the partnership can distribute property subject to a basis adjustment to other partners (who do not have such a basis adjustment). Here, the distributee partner does not take the basis adjustment into account for § 732 purposes. The partner with the basis adjustment (who did not receive the distributed property) must allocate the basis adjustment to other partnership property.[75] Third, it can distribute the property to a partner in complete liquidation of a partner's interest. In this situation, the basis of the distributed property includes the liquidating partner's basis adjustments.[76]

Section 743(b) adjustments also have implications for cost recovery deductions. A positive basis adjustment results in additional depreciation for the transferee partner. The § 743 regulations treat the basis adjustment portion as a newly purchased asset that is placed into service when the transfer occurs.[77] As such, "any applicable recovery period and method may be used to determine the recovery allowance with respect to the increased portion of the basis,"[78] but no change can be made to the portion of the property that is not adjusted.[79] The partnership is allowed to elect additional first-year depreciation under § 168(k) for a basis increase of qualified property.[80] Relatedly, if the remedial method is used, the increased amount must be recovered over the remaining recovery period.[81]

---

73. Recall the partnership has an inside basis of $90,000 in the capital asset.
74. Treas. Reg. § 1.743-1(g)(1); Treas. Reg. § 1.732-2(b).
75. Treas. Reg. § 1.743-1(g)(2); Treas. Reg. § 1.755-1(c).
76. Treas. Reg. § 1.743-1(g)(3).
77. Treas. Reg. § 1.743-1(j)(4)(i)(B)(1).
78. Id.
79. Id.
80. Treas. Reg. § 1.743-1(j)(4)(i)(B)(1).
81. Treas. Reg. § 1.743-1(j)(4)(i)(B)(2).

10. Selling, Exiting, Terminating, and Other Partnership Exits

Some adjustments, though, result in decreases to basis. In those cases, a negative basis adjustment decreases the partner's share of depreciation from that item. If the basis adjustment exceeds the depreciation for the item, then the transferee's share of depreciation from other items must be reduced; if there is not enough other depreciation, the transferee recognizes ordinary income to such extent.[82] As to recovery period, the amount of decrease is recovered over the remaining useful life of the asset.

A final collateral point to make here. In these examples, there has been a singular transfer of a partnership interest. The real world, though, is often not so simple, and there may very well be later transfers of partnership interests. For example, in our earlier example, what happens if J (who has a § 743(b) basis adjustment) later sells his partnership interest to K? The regulations provide that "a transferee's basis adjustment is determined without regard to any prior transferee's basis adjustment."[83] Thus, any basis adjustment that would inure to K would be independent of any prior basis adjustment to J. Instead of selling the interest, J were to gift the partnership interest (or a portion thereof), the regulations provide that "the donor is treated as transferring, and the donee as receiving, that portion of the basis adjustment attributable to the gifted partnership interest."[84] So if J were to gift half of the partnership interest to K, K would receive half of the basis adjustment.

LIQUIDATING DISTRIBUTIONS

In Chapter 7, we discussed the tax implications of liquidating distributions in the context of analyzing the consequences of distributions. Here, we will add some additional contours of that analysis, which we did not unpack earlier. Section 736 is our starting point, and it has two main provisions, subsections (a) and (b). Note that the section uses the phrase "retiring or a deceased partner."[85] The regulations explain that "[a] partner retires when he ceases to be a partner under local law."[86] This is important because it encompasses situations other than the colloquial "retirement" concept that comes to mind — it applies to situations in which the partner becomes a non-partner (like leaving the partnership, even if not "retiring" in the colloquial sense). Section 736 does not provide any independent substantive rule; rather, it incorporates other substantive rules, depending on whether

---

82. Treas. Reg. § 1.743-1(j)(4)(ii)(A).
83. Treas. Reg. § 1.743-1(f).
84. Id.
85. I.R.C. § 736.
86. Treas. Reg. § 1.736-1(a)(1)(ii).

10. Selling, Exiting, Terminating, and Other Partnership Exits

the payment is classified under subsection (a) or (b). Payments under § 736(a) are treated as distributive shares of income or as guaranteed payments. Payments under § 736(b), on the other hand, are treated as a distribution, and they are thus governed by the rules that we covered in Chapter 7 (i.e., §§ 731 et seq.). In other words, then, § 736 is a traffic sign that directs payments to the (i) distributive share, (ii) guaranteed payment, or (iii) distribution rules.

The first question is whether we have a "retiring" (see above) or deceased partner. After that, we must naturally ask which path the § 736 traffic sign directs us to take. The main question here is "What is the payment for?" If the payment is for the partner's interest in partnership property, then the payment is a § 736(b) payment. If the payment is not for underlying partnership property, then § 736(a) essentially provides that it is either a payment of a distributive share or a guaranteed payment.

The valuation of the partner's interest in partnership property is thus critical. The regulations provide that "[g]enerally, the valuation placed by the partners upon a partner's interest in partnership property in an arm's length agreement will be regarded as correct."[87] Importantly, though, partnership property for this purpose does not include unrealized receivables and goodwill, both of which are treated as § 736(a) payments.[88] Payments for an interest in inventory can count as § 736(b) payments, but payments for *substantially appreciated* inventory have to abide by the § 751(b) rules.[89]

If a partner receives a § 736 payment, the partner needs to segregate and allocate the payment into the subsection (a) and (b) components.[90] If a fixed amount is to be received over a fixed number of years, the payments are prorated to § 736(b) payments and the balance is treated as a § 736(a) payment.[91] If the payments are not fixed, they are treated first as § 736(b) payments to the extent of the partner's interest in partnership property.[92]

Let's do an example based on the regulation that walks through these concepts.[93] Consider the DEF Partnership, which has the following balance sheet.

---

87. Treas. Reg. § 1.736-1(b)(1).
88. Treas. Reg. § 1.736-1(b)(2); Treas. Reg. § 1.736-1(b)(3).
89. Treas. Reg. § 1.736-1(b)(4).
90. Treas. Reg. § 1.736-1(b)(5).
91. Treas. Reg. § 1.736-1(b)(5)(i).
92. Treas. Reg. § 1.736-1(b)(5)(ii).
93. Adapted from Example 1 of Treas. Reg. § 1.736-1(b)(7).

10. Selling, Exiting, Terminating, and Other Partnership Exits

DEF Partnership					
Assets			Liabilities		
	Adj. Basis	FMV			$6,000
Cash	$26,000	$26,000			
Unrealized receivable	$0	$60,000	Capital Accounts		
Capital Asset 1	$40,000	$46,000		Adj. Basis	Book Value
			D	$22,000	$42,000
			E	$22,000	$42,000
			F	$22,000	$42,000
Total	$66,000	$132,000	Total	$66,000	$132,000

Partner D retires from the partnership. As part of his retirement, the partnership assumes his share of the partnership liability ($2,000). Also as part of his payout, he is paid $18,000 immediately in the year of withdrawal, plus $20,000 in each of the next two years.

The total amount that D receives for his partnership interest is $60,000, which consists of the liability assumption, the immediate payment, and the two successive-year payments. Assume further that the partners agree that D's interest in partnership property for § 736(b) purposes is equal to one-third of partnership assets; however, this does not include the unrealized receivable.[94] Consequently, his share of § 736(b) property is $24,000, which represents one-third of the value of the cash and capital asset. Thus, we have the § 736(b) and, by implication, the § 736(a) amount. Of the $60,000 received by D, $24,000 of it is a § 736(b) payment and the remainder ($36,000) constitutes a § 736(a) payment.

The § 736(b) payment is treated as a *distribution*, which incorporates the § 731 rules. Under these rules, a partner recognizes gain on a distribution only if the money distributed exceeds the partner's outside basis. Here, he received a deemed distribution of $24,000 and he has an outside basis of $22,000; therefore, he recognizes a $2,000 capital gain. The § 736(a) payment (here, $36,000) constitutes a § 736(a)(2) payment and is treated as a *guaranteed payment* because its amount is determined without regard to partnership income. Guaranteed payments, of course, are included in gross income under § 707(c).

Consider the sequence of the payments: $20,000 in Year 1 (consisting of the $18,000 in cash plus the $2,000 assumed liabilities), $20,000 in Year 2 (the first successive year payment), and $20,000 in Year 3 (the

---

94. Recall that unrealized receivables are carved out of § 736(b).

second successive year payment). Although we know the aggregate tax consequences of the § 736(a) and § 736(b) payments, we need to allocate them to *each* of the three payments. The allocation will be as follows.

$$\S 736(a) \text{ payment} = \$20,000 \times \left(\frac{\$36,000}{\$60,000}\right) = \$12,000$$

$$\S 736(b) \text{ payment} = \$20,000 \times \left(\frac{\$24,000}{\$60,000}\right) = \$8,000$$

Thus, 60% of each payment constitutes a § 736(a) payment (in particular, a guaranteed payment under § 707(c)) and 40% represents a § 736(b) payment, which is treated as a distribution.[95]

Although the above captures a lot of the main application § 736, let's change one fact to get an even more robust example. Assume the same facts as above, except now that the agreement between partners provides payments to D as a percentage of annual income (instead of a fixed amount).[96] Here, the payments that D receives up to $24,000 (the same amount calculated above) is treated as a § 736(b) payment, representing his interest in partnership property. Any payment amount in excess of that are treated as § 736(a) payments—in particular, § 736(a)(1) payments of distributive shares of partnership income.

DEATH OF A PARTNER

So far in this chapter we have covered partner-level exits (e.g., sale or retirement) and, in each of these situations, the partner has been *alive*. Sadly, individual partners can die. It is not uncommon for a well-drafted partnership agreement (or an LLC operating agreement) or even state law to provide that death dissociates the partner; dissociation means, among other things, that the partner can no longer participate in the management of the business. For state law purposes, this comports with one of the main drivers of partnership law, namely, to pick your partners. If a partner could pick their replacement (say, under a transfer in a will or other testamentary instrument), this would force the new partner into the existing partnership.[97]

---

95. The regulation also allows an additional way to allocate fixed payments as set forth in the second sentence of Treas. Reg. § 1.736-1(b)(6).
96. *See* Treas. Reg. § 1.736-1(b)(7) Example 2.
97. Thoughtfully planning for the admission of new partners (or members) is a critical aspect of formation documents.

It is therefore common for death to serve as a buyout trigger. Generally, buyouts can be structured as either *cross-purchases* or *redemptions*. A cross-purchase is when another partner purchases the deceased partner's interest. We have already implicitly covered how these would work—cross-purchase payments made to the decedent-partner's estate (to purchase the deceased members partnership interest) would be governed by the rules discussed in earlier in this chapter (concerning transfers of partnership interests).

On the other hand, *redemptions* occur when the partnership redeems (i.e., purchases) the deceased partner's interest. These payments are governed by § 736. Indeed, review the statutory language in § 736, which provides for payments to a *deceased partner*. Now, you cannot make payments to a *dead person*, but you can make payments to the decedent's *estate* or *successor in interest*, which are terms used in the § 736 regulations.[98]

Impact of Death or Retirement on the Taxable Year

A collateral issue to consider that is common to both the retirement and death of a partner is the impact on the partnership's tax year. Section 706(c) provides that the taxable year does not close because of "the death of a partner, the entry of a new partner, the liquidation of a partner's interest in the partnership, or the sale or exchange of a partner's interest in the partnership."[99] Although the tax year does not end for the partnership, the tax year does close with respect to "to a partner whose entire interest in the partnership terminates (whether by reason of death, liquidation, or otherwise)."[100] Consequently, as explained by the regulations, the "partner shall include in his taxable income for his taxable year within or with which the partner's interest in the partnership ends the partner's distributive share of items described in section 702(a) and any guaranteed payments under section 707(c) for the partnership taxable year ending with the date of such termination."[101] Additionally, if the partner's estate or successor sells the partnership interest (or if it is liquidated), the tax year for the estate or successor ends on the sale or completion of the liquidation.[102]

These rules are illustrated in the following basic example.[103] E, an individual, is a partner of a calendar-year partnership, the EFG Partnership. E dies on April 30, Year 1. In E's will, she leaves all her property to her husband (H). The administration of the estate is finalized on October 31, Year

---

98. E.g., Treas. Reg. § 1.736-1(a).
99. I.R.C. § 706(c)(1).
100. I.R.C. § 706(c)(2).
101. Treas. Reg. § 1.706-1(c)(2)(i).
102. Id.
103. See Treas. Reg. § 1.706-1(c)(2)(ii).

1, which includes the distribution of the partnership interest to H. The distribution of the interest to H does not count as a sale or exchange of a partnership interest. Under the § 706 rules, therefore, the taxable year of the partnership closes with respect to Partner E on April 30. Consequently, E must include in her final individual income tax return for Year 1 her distributive share of partnership items for January 1, Year 1 through April 30, Year 1. Husband will include on his Year 1 individual income tax return his share of partnership items for the period of May 1 through December 31, Year 1.

Death of a Partner and Income in Respect of a Decedent

An additional related item to consider in the context of the death of a partner is income in respect of a decedent, which we will briefly discuss here. Income in respect of a decedent (IRD) is a mechanism to ensure that income items are included in the income tax base. For income tax purposes, the tax year of an individual ends on his or her death,[104] and recall that individual taxpayers use the cash method of accounting, which includes an item of income when it is actually or constructively received. A quick example demonstrates the concept of IRD. Assume that A is an employee that receives a paycheck on the last day of each month. While he is alive, then, the paychecks are included in gross income when actually or constructively received. If A were to die on May 15, what happens when his last paycheck arrives in the mail on May 31? The check was received *after* his death, and therefore it is not *properly* included in the tax year that ended on his death. Thus, we need a mechanism to ensure that the paycheck is included in *someone's* income taxes. IRD fixes this problem.

Section 691 provides that "items of gross income in respect of a decedent which are not properly includible in respect of the taxable period in which falls the date of his death or a prior period" shall be in income by the (i) estate ("if the right to receive the amount is acquired by the decedent's estate from the decedent"), (ii) the person who acquires the right to receive the amount (if the amount is not acquired by the decedent's estate), or (iii) the person who acquires from the decedent the right to receive the amount by bequest, device, or inheritance (if the amount is received after a distribution by the decedent's estate of such right).[105] Continuing the example, if the employer pays the May paycheck to A's estate, the estate must include the amount in its income.[106]

Given that § 736 payments may be paid to a decedent's successor in interest, they give rise to IRD concerns. Indeed, § 753 provides that

---

104. Treas. Reg. § 1.451-1(d)(1).
105. I.R.C. § 691(a)(1).
106. *See* Treas. Reg. § 1.691(a)-2.

10. Selling, Exiting, Terminating, and Other Partnership Exits

"[t]he amount includible in the gross income of a successor in interest of a deceased partner under section 736(a) shall be considered income in respect of a decedent under section 691."[107] Given that the purpose of IRD is to ensure that the recipient of an IRD payment includes it in gross income, it is axiomatic that § 691(a)(3) provides that the character in the hands of the recipient is the same as it would have been in the hands of the decedent had he or she not died. As applied in the partnership context, therefore, the character of the § 736(a) payment is the same in the hands of the successor in interest. If the successor-in-interest later transfers the right to IRD payments, he or she must include in income the greater of its fair market value or the consideration received.[108]

TERMINATION OF A PARTNERSHIP

So far in this chapter, we covered a partner exiting from a partnership; in each situation, the partnership continued to operate as the same partnership (and just the partner mix was changing). Now we turn to the situation in which the partnership terminates, i.e., it ceases to be a partnership.[109]

Under § 708, a partnership continues until it is terminated.[110] A partnership is considered to terminate "only if no part of any business, financial operation, or venture of the partnership continues to be carried on by any of its partners in a partnership."[111] The regulations provide two examples of this rule. The first example is if two partners in a three-partner partnership sell their entire interest to the third partner. Here, the business is no longer carried on in a partnership (as there is just one owner now), the partnership terminates as of the date of sale.[112] The second example covers partnership dissolution. In this example, the partners agree on April 30 to dissolve the partnership, but carry on the business through a winding-up period ending September 30, when all the remaining assets are distributed. Here, the partnership does not terminate until September 30.[113] The import of this second example is that it is the distribution of assets that formally marks

---

107. I.R.C. § 753.
108. Treas. Reg. § 1.691(a)-4(a).
109. This text does not cover the historical rule of § 708(b)(1)(B), which was known as a "technical termination." A technical termination occurred when a sale or exchange of 50% or more of the total interest in partnership capital and profits occurred within 12-months. This provision was repealed as part of the law known as the Tax Cuts and Jobs Act; the repeal was effective for partnership taxable years beginning after December 31, 2017. See Pub. L. No. 115-97, § 13504, 131 Stat. 214 (Dec. 22, 2017).
110. I.R.C. § 708(a).
111. I.R.C. § 708(b)(1).
112. Treas. Reg. § 1.708-1(b)(1).
113. Id.

10. Selling, Exiting, Terminating, and Other Partnership Exits

the termination for tax purposes (even if the date is earlier for state-law purposes).

The first example warrants additional explication, particularly in its application to LLCs and disregarded entities, which was the focus of Revenue Ruling 99-6.[114] Revenue Ruling 99-6 discusses the federal income tax consequences if one person purchases all the ownership interest of a domestic LLC that is taxed as a partnership for federal income tax purposes. It advances two situations. In the first situation, A and B are equal partners in AB, LLC, and A sells A's entire interest in the LLC to B for cash, after which B continues the business of the LLC. In the second situation, C and D are equal partners in CD, LLC, and they both sell their full interest for cash to E, who is unrelated, after which E continues to operate the business.

In the first situation, the partnership terminates once B acquires A's entire interest under § 708(b)(1)(A). For A, this is treated as a sale of a partnership interest under § 741. For B, however, it is treated as an asset sale. In other words, because the AB partnership terminates, the AB partnership is deemed to make liquidating asset distributions to A and B, after which B is then treated as buying the assets that were distributed to A.[115] Consequently, B takes a § 1012 cost basis in the purchased assets from A, and B's holding period for these assets starts on the date following the sale.[116]

For B's part, upon the termination of AB, he is considered to have received a distribution of his assets from AB. B must therefore recognize gain, if any, under the rules of § 731. The basis of the assets B is deemed to receive in the liquidating distribution, moreover, are likewise governed by the distribution rules of § 732(b), and, under § 735(b), the holding period tacks (other than for § 735(a)(2) purposes).[117]

In the second situation, the partnership terminates once E purchases the entire interests of C and D. In this situation, C and D are treated as selling their partnership interests under § 741 and must report any gain or loss accordingly. For E, this is treated as an asset purchase; the CD partnership is treated as making a liquidating distribution of its assets to C and D, immediately after which the assets are acquired by E. E therefore has a cost basis in the assets under § 1012, and the holding period for the assets begins on the day following the date of sale.

---

114. 1999-6 I.R.B. 6, 1999-1 C.B. 432. The discussion that follows comes from the revenue ruling.
115. *See also* Rev. Rul. 67-65, 1967-1 C.B. 168.
116. *See* Rev. Rul. 66-7, 1966-1 C.B. 188.
117. *See* I.R.C. § 735(b).

VARYING AND SHIFTING PARTNERSHIP INTERESTS

The discussion of transfers of partnership interests naturally gives rise to an opportunity to analyze the impacts of varying partnership interests throughout the year. For example, if a partnership with three equal partners admits a new equal partner during the year, those once one-third partners are transformed into one-fourth partners. Changes in partnership interests can also arise due to gifts, contributions, and the death of a partner, among other ways. There are two main dimensions to consider here. First, whether a change (or "shift") in the partners' interest causes a close in the taxable year of the partnership. Second, the impact of the shift in calculating the partners' distributive shares. These two dimensions are governed by § 706(c) and (d), respectively.

Section 706(c) provides generally that a shift in a partner's interest does not cause a close of the partnership's taxable year. Indeed, we noted earlier that, "the taxable year of a partnership shall not close as the result of the death of a partner, the entry of a new partner, the liquidation of a partner's interest in the partnership, or the sale or exchange of a partner's interest in the partnership."[118] There are some exceptions, which are discussed elsewhere in this chapter—for example, if the partnership terminates under § 708(b). Although the taxable year of the partnership does not close because of an interest shift, the taxable year of a partnership closes with respect to a partner if the partner's entire interest terminates, regardless of reason (e.g., by death or liquidation).

If the partnership taxable year closes with respect to a partner under § 706(c), the partner must include in his income his distributive share of partnership tax items for the short tax year. For its part, § 706(d) provides that, if there is a change in a partner's interest in the partnership during the taxable year, then each item of the partner's distributive share must be determined in a way that "takes into account the varying interests of the partners in the partnership during such taxable year" as prescribed by regulations.[119] These regulations are prescribed in Treas. Reg. § 1.706-4.

As explained in more detail below, the regulations allow for two methods to take into account the variation of interests throughout the year: the interim closing method and the proration method. Unless the partners agree otherwise, the interim closing method must be used. The interim closing period, though, may be more expensive.[120] The regulations allow both methods to be used in the same taxable year and for different variations within the year.

---

118. I.R.C. § 706(c)(1).
119. I.R.C. § 706(d).
120. T.D. 9728, 2015-33 I.R.B. 169 (2015) (publishing final regulations under § 706).

10. Selling, Exiting, Terminating, and Other Partnership Exits

Under the interim closing method, the partnership essentially "closes" its books for each segment (i.e., portion of a year) and treats each segment as it were its own taxable year. However, limitations and special requirements are still based on their satisfaction as of the end of the taxable year. For example, the limits applicable to § 179 are still determined based on the full year and then apportioned among the segments.[121] Under the proration method, the partnership prorates partnership tax items on a daily basis.[122]

The regulation sets forth a ten-step process to allocate the distributive share items of § 702.[123] The first step is to determine whether any exceptions apply to allocation.[124] The regulation provides two exceptions. The first exception is for "contemporaneous partners."[125] The contemporaneous partner exception can apply so long as (i) the variation is not attributable to a contribution from or distribution to a partner and (ii) the allocations satisfy the § 704(b) regulations. The contemporaneous partner exception is rooted in § 761(c), which provides that the partnership agreement includes any modifications made prior to the filing of the partnership tax return for the taxable year. Thus, § 761(c)—coupled with § 704(a)—allows for, generally, retroactive allocations. The § 706(d) regulations, therefore, still preserve this flexibility, so long as the varying interests are not due to contributions or distributions. The second exception is for partnerships for whom "capital is not a material income-producing factor." For these partnerships and partners, they can use any reasonable method to account for the varying interests provided that the allocations still satisfy § 704(b).[126]

The second step is to determine if any of the items are subject to a special rule provided by the regulations.[127] These items are known as "extraordinary items." Extraordinary items are not allowed to be prorated; rather, these items must be allocated "among the partners in proportion to their interests in the partnership item at the time of day on which the extraordinary item occurred, regardless of the method."[128] Some of these items include those items arising from a change in accounting method, settlement of a tort claim, and certain tax credits.[129] There is also an exception to this rule for certain small items.[130]

The third step is to determine for each variation whether the partnership will use the "interim closing method" or the "proration method."[131]

---

121. Treas. Reg. § 1.706-4(a)(3)(vii).
122. See Treas. Reg. § 1.706-4(a)(3)(viii), (ix).
123. Treas. Reg. § 1.706-4(a)(3). This process applies for partnership taxable years that begin after August 3, 2015. Treas. Reg. § 1.706-4(g).
124. Treas. Reg. § 1.706-4(a)(3)(i).
125. Treas. Reg. § 1.706-4(b)(1).
126. Treas. Reg. § 1.706-4(b)(2).
127. Treas. Reg. § 1.706-4(a)(3)(ii).
128. Treas. Reg. § 1.706-4(e)(1).
129. Treas. Reg. § 1.706-4(e)(2).
130. Treas. Reg. § 1.706-4(e)(3).
131. Treas. Reg. § 1.706-4(a)(3)(iii).

10. Selling, Exiting, Terminating, and Other Partnership Exits

The default method is the interim closing method.[132] The fourth step is to determine when each variation is deemed to have occurred given the partner's selected convention.[133] The fifth step is to determine whether the partners have agreed to perform monthly or semi-monthly interim closings.[134] In the absence of an agreement, the interim closings will occur at each variation during the taxable year if using the interim closing method.[135]

The sixth step is to determine the partnership's "segments," which are defined as the "specific periods of the partnership's taxable year created by interim closings of the partnership's books."[136] The seventh step is to apportion the partnership's tax items among its segments.[137] Generally, each segment is treated as a separate distributive share period; for example, a segment may have a capital loss, even though the partnership has a net capital gain for the full year.[138]

The eighth step is to determine the partnership's proration periods.[139] These are "specific portions of a segment created by a variation for which the partnership chooses to apply the proration method."[140] The ninth step is to prorate each item in each segment among the proration periods within the segment.[141] The tenth step is to determine the partners' distributive share given the interests in the items for each segment and proration period.[142]

Another issue to consider here is the application of simplifying conventions that are contained in the regulation. The regulation allows for conventions to determine when each variation event is deemed to occur,[143] though extraordinary items cannot use a convention.[144] The regulation provides three conventions: (i) the calendar day convention, (ii) the semi-monthly convention, and (iii) the monthly convention. Under the calendar day convention, each variation event is deemed to happen at the end of the day on which the variation occurs.[145] Under the semi-monthly convention, events that occur during the 1st and 15th day of the month are deemed to occur on the last day of the immediately preceding calendar month, and events that happen on the 16th through the last day of the month are deemed to occur at the end of the 15th calendar day of the same month.[146] Under the

---

132. Id.
133. Treas. Reg. § 1.706-4(a)(3)(iv).
134. Treas. Reg. § 1.706-4(a)(3)(v).
135. Id.
136. Treas. Reg. § 1.706-4(a)(3)(vi).
137. Treas. Reg. § 1.706-4(a)(3)(vii).
138. Id.
139. Treas. Reg. § 1.706-4(a)(3)(viii).
140. Id.
141. Treas. Reg. § 1.706-4(a)(3)(ix).
142. Treas. Reg. § 1.706-4(a)(3)(x).
143. Treas. Reg. § 1.706-4(c)(1).
144. Id.
145. Treas. Reg. § 1.706-4(c)(1)(i).
146. Treas. Reg. § 1.706-4(c)(1)(ii).

monthly convention, events that occur during the 1st and 15th day of the month are deemed to occur on the last day of the immediately preceding calendar month, and events that happen on the 16th through the last day of the month are deemed to occur at the end of the last day of that calendar month.[147] The regulation provides that, generally, the calendar day convention should be used, but if the partnership uses the interim closing method, it can use the semi-monthly or monthly convention for the interim closing method variations.[148]

Although the regulations contemplate two methods generally, there are certain items that must be prorated, which are known as "allocable cash basis items" under § 706(d)(2). Allocable cash basis items are defined as interest, taxes, payments for services or for the use of property, or other items specified in regulations for which the partnership uses the cash receipts and disbursements method.[149] This rule applies regardless of the § 706 method used by the partnership. The reason for this rule is concern that partnerships may defer payment of certain expenses until near the close of the year and that delay coupled with the interim closing method may allow a new partner to be allowed full deduction for the delayed expense.[150]

The steps required by the regulation are illustrated in the following example. At the beginning of the current year, A, B, C, and D are equal partners in the ABCD Partnership. Partner A sells 50% of his interest to E on May 5th. For the entire tax year, ABCD earns $100,000 of ordinary income and incurs $40,000 of ordinary business expenses. The partnership has agreed to use the interim closing method with the calendar month convention. The partnership and its partners are cash basis, calendar year taxpayers. None of the partnership's items are allocable cash basis items. Let's now determine the distributive shares for the partners, focusing on A and E, whose interest vary during the year.

The first step is to determine whether any of the exceptions apply, such as the contemporaneous partner rule, which we will assume do not apply here. The second step is to determine whether any extraordinary items are present, which there are none in this example. The third step is to determine for each variation which method will apply. Here, there is one variation—the sale and admittance of E on May 5th. The fourth step is to determine when each variation is deemed to occur given the available conventions. Here, the partnership has properly agreed to use the calendar month convention. Under that convention, the sale of May 5th is deemed to occur on the last day of the preceding month (i.e., April 30th). The fifth step is to determine whether the partners have agreed to perform regular

---

147. Treas. Reg. § 1.706-4(c)(1)(iii).
148. Treas. Reg. § 1.706-4(c)(3)(i).
149. I.R.C. § 706(d)(2)(B).
150. See H.R. Rep. No. 98-432, at 1212-13 (1984), 1984 U.S.C.C.A.N. 697.

monthly or semi-monthly conventions. If the partners agree to this, then they will perform a monthly or semi-monthly closing of the books for each month, regardless of any variation. In the absence of an agreement to perform regular monthly or semi-monthly interim closings, the interim closings occur only upon an occurrence of a variation. Here, there is no such agreement, so the partners will have an interim closing on the occurrence of the variation, i.e., at the end of April (due to the calendar month convention).

The sixth step is to determine the partnership's segments, which are the specific portions of the year created by the interim closing of the books. The first segment starts with the beginning of the tax year and ends at the time of the first interim closing.[151] Any additional segment starts immediately after the closing of the prior segment and ends at the time of the next interim closing, but the last segment must end no later than the last day of the taxable year.[152] Here, there is one interim closing occurring on April 30. Thus, the partnership tax year has two segments: (i) the period from January 1 through April 30, and (ii) the period from May 1 through December 31.

The seventh step is to apportion the partnership's items for the year among its segments. The partnership determines that for its first segment it earned $20,000 of ordinary income and incurred $10,000 of expenses; the balance of the income and expenses were earned and incurred in the balance of the year. The eighth step is to determine proration periods, which is not applicable here because the partnership is not using the proration method. The ninth step is to prorate items of income in each segment among the proration period within each segment, which is not applicable here because the proration method is not being used.

The tenth step is to determine the partners' distributive share by taking into account each partner's interest in such items during each segment and proration period. Here, A, B, C, and D were equal partners in the first segment (Jan. 1 through April 30). They are therefore each allocated one-fourth of the partnership tax items attributable to this segment, which is $5,000 of ordinary income and $2,500 of ordinary expenses. For the second segment (May 1 through December 31), B, C, and D each still have one-fourth interests in the partnership, A and E have one-eighth interests. There is $80,000 of ordinary income and $30,000 of ordinary expenses in this segment. Therefore, B, C, and D are each allocated $20,000 of ordinary income and $7,500 of expenses;[153] A and E are each allocated $10,000 of ordinary income and $3,750 of ordinary expenses.[154]

---

151. Treas. Reg. § 1.706-4(a)(3)(vi).
152. Id.
153. These amounts represent 25% or one-fourth of the amounts.
154. These amounts represent 12.5% or one-eighth of the amounts.

PARTNERSHIP MERGERS

The last topic discussed in this chapter is that of partnership mergers. As a disclaimer, this treatment is not a comprehensive overview of deal structuring or the state-law considerations in effectuating a business merger. This section covers two main topics. First, how a partnership merger interacts with the § 708 termination rules. Second, how the form of the merger affects the tax consequences. Before we dive into these specifics, a brief overview of vocabulary and deal options is discussed for context.

Although not used in the Code, we will use the terms "Target Partnership" and "Bidder Partnership" to identify the parties to the transaction, in which Target Partnership refers to the partnership that is being "absorbed" by the Bidder (i.e., buying) Partnership. As we will see later, the Code refers to Bidder as the "resulting partnership," and Target as the "merg[ed] partnership." Also, let's distinguish the difference between a merger and a consolidation. Perhaps surprisingly, neither the Code nor the regulations define these terms for partnership tax purposes.[155] For corporate and business organizational law purposes, though, these words have specific meanings. In a merger transaction, two or more *existing* entities are *merged* into a single *existing* entity.[156] An example of a merger is Alpha Co. merges into Beta Co. and Beta survives and continues after the merger. A consolidation, on the other hand, is when two or more entities *consolidate* into a *new* entity. An example of a consolidation is Alpha Co. and Beta Co. consolidate into Gamma Co., which is a new resulting corporation formed by the consolidation.[157]

There are three ways to structure a merger or combination of a partnership.[158] In the first way, the Target Partnership sells its assets (and liabilities) to the Bidder Partnership in exchange for partnership interests in Bidder, which are then distributed to Target partners; this is known as an "assets-over" form transaction. In the second way, Target Partnership liquidates its assets to its partners, who then contribute those distributed assets to Bidder Partnership; this is known as an "assets-up" form transaction. In the third way, Target partners sell their partnership interests to Bidder Partnership in exchange for Bidder interests, and then Target liquidates into Bidder; this is known as an "interest-over" form transaction.

---

155. See T.D. 8925, 2001-1 C.B. 496.
156. See, e.g., Del. Code Ann. tit. 8, § 251(a).
157. See, e.g., id.
158. We will focus on mergers in this discussion. These forms are rooted in Rev. Rul. 84-111, which regards partnership incorporation, which the Service has used as an analogy. See 65 Fed. Reg. 1572-02, 2000-1 C.B. 455.

10. Selling, Exiting, Terminating, and Other Partnership Exits

With that context, let's first consider the termination rules. Section 708(b)(2)(A) provides a special rule for partnership mergers and consolidations. It provides that:

> In the case of the merger or consolidation of two or more partnerships, the resulting partnership shall, for purposes of this section, be considered the continuation of any merging or consolidating partnership whose members own an interest of more than 50 percent in the capital and profits of the resulting partnership.[159]

Here, the resulting partnership is Bidder Partnership, and the merged partnerships is Target Partnership. In other words, if the partners of the merged partnerships own more than 50% of the resulting (combined) partnership, the resulting partnership is considered a continuation of the merged partnership. The regulations provide that if the resulting partnership can be considered a continuation of more than one partnership, it will be considered to be a continuation of the partnership that contributed the greatest fair market value of assets to the resulting partnership.[160] Any merged partnership not considered to be continuing is terminated.[161] If none of the merged partnerships are considered to be continuing (i.e., the partners of the merged partnership do not own more than 50% of the resulting partnership), then the merged partnerships are terminated and a new partnership is created for tax purposes.[162]

Now that the termination rules have been set forth, we can now tackle how the form of the transaction affects its tax consequences. We will cover each form above in turn. The first is the assets-over merger. The regulations provide that when two or more partnerships merge or consolidate into one partnership, any merged partnership that is considered terminated is treated as taking an assets-over form if it is not deemed to be an assets-up form.[163] For tax purposes, this is treated as a two-step transaction. In the first step, the terminated partnership (Target) contributes its assets and liabilities to the resulting partnership (Bidder) in exchange for interests in the resulting partnership. Immediately thereafter, in the second step, the terminated partnership distributes its interests in the resulting partnership to its partners in liquidation.[164]

The second form is the assets-up form, and it similarly has two steps. In the first step, the terminated partnership distributes all its assets and liabilities in liquidation to its partners. Immediately thereafter, in the second step,

---

159. I.R.C. § 708(b)(2)(A).
160. Treas. Reg. § 1.708-1(c)(1).
161. Id.
162. Id.
163. Treas. Reg. § 1.708-1(c)(3)(i).
164. Id.

10. Selling, Exiting, Terminating, and Other Partnership Exits

those partners contribute the distributed assets and liabilities to the resulting partnership in exchange for interests in that resulting partnership.[165]

The third form is the interests-over form. Here, the partners of the terminating partnership simply transfer their partnership interest to the resulting partnership in exchange for partnership interests in resulting partnership. Although partners may structure a merger like this for *state law* purposes, the regulations reject this form for *tax* purposes.[166] If this structure is used for state law purposes, it is treated as the assets-over form for federal income tax purposes.[167] The reason for this rejection requires some historical unpacking and an examination of the partnership incorporation rulings, which are discussed briefly next.

In Revenue Ruling 84-111, the Service considered three situations of incorporating a partnership.[168] In the last situation, the partners contributed their interests to a newly formed corporation in exchange for stock. The Service noted that the partnership terminated upon the transfer of the partnership interests to the corporation — note that it can no longer be a partnership with just one owner (the corporation).[169] The ruling also treats the receipt of the interests by the corporation as a receipt of the partnership's assets, which follows the assets-up form.[170] The theory for this, as explained by the Service, is that "transferee corporation can only receive assets since it is not possible, as a sole member, for it to receive and hold interests in a partnership (i.e., a partnership cannot have only one member; so, the entity is never a partnership in the hands of the transferee corporation)."[171]

The Service continues to describe this as "hybrid treatment," that is, the transfers of the partnership interests by the partners are respected as such for them, but it is treated as a transfer of assets with respect to the corporation's tax treatment. The Service explained that "[a]dherence to the approach followed in Rev. Rul. 84-111 creates problems in the context of partnership mergers that are not present with respect to partnership incorporations."[172] The common denominator is that "the partnership rules impose certain tax results on partners based upon a concept that matches a contributed asset to the partner that contributed the asset."[173] When you have an asset mismatch, then, these rules breakdown — for example, application of §§ 704(c) and 737.

---

165. Treas. Reg. § 1.708-1(c)(3)(ii).
166. *See* 65 Fed. Reg. 1572-02, 2000-1 C.B. 455.
167. 65 Fed. Reg. 1572-02, 2000-1 C.B. 455 ("If partnerships use the Interest-Over Form to accomplish the result of a merger, the partnerships will be treated as following the Assets-Over Form for Federal income tax purposes.").
168. 1984-2 C.B. 88.
169. The ruling cites § 708(b)(1)(A), as it existed then, which is now the main rule in § 708(b)(1).
170. *See also* 65 Fed. Reg. 1572-02, 2000-1 C.B. 455.
171. *Id.* (citing McCaulsen v. Comm'r, 45 T.C. 588 (1966)).
172. *Id.*
173. *Id.*

10. Selling, Exiting, Terminating, and Other Partnership Exits

The interest-over form creates such an asset mismatch; "the partner is treated as contributing an asset that is different from the asset that the partnership is treated as receiving."[174] In particular, the partners have received corporate stock, but the corporation has received the underlying partnership assets (not partnership interests).

In sum, the regulations recognize two forms of partnership merger for federal income tax purposes: the assets-up form and the assets-over form.[175] If a merger is not structured expressly as one of these forms for state law purposes, the regulations require the assets-over form for tax purposes.[176] Moreover, there are fundamental differences between these forms for tax purposes. In an assets-up form, it is possible to recognize gain under §§ 704(c)(1)(B) and 737 because assets are first distributed to partners.[177] This is not the case with an assets-over form merger.[178] The differences also have basis equivalency issues. In an assets-over form, the inside basis of the assets of Target Partnership will carry-over to Bidder Partnership under § 723 (in the first step). In an assets-up form, on the other hand, the bases of Target Partnership's assets are first determined by § 732(b) and the partners' outside bases because the first step is a partnership liquidation. The § 732(c)-determined basis is therefore the basis for the second step, which is then governed by § 723. Consequently, "the adjusted basis of the assets contributed may not be the same as the adjusted basis of the assets in the terminating partnership," which would be the case "if the partners' aggregate adjusted basis of their interests in the terminating partnership does not equal the terminating partnership's adjusted basis in its assets."[179]

PARTNERSHIP DIVISIONS

The last item considered by this chapter is partnership divisions. A division occurs when a single partnership breaks (i.e., divides) into two or more partnerships. Section 708 provides that, in the case of a partnership division, the resulting partnerships are considered a continuation of the prior partnership, unless the members had an interest of 50% or less in the prior partnership.[180] Any resulting partnership not satisfying this rule is treated as a new partnership.[181] In addition, the partnership division rules recognize

---

174. Id.
175. Treas. Reg. § 1.708-1(c)(3).
176. Treas. Reg. § 1.708-1(c)(3)(i).
177. 65 Fed. Reg. 1572-02, 2000-1 C.B. 455.
178. Id.; see also Treas. Reg. § 1.704-4(c)(4); Treas. Reg. § 1.737-2(b).
179. 65 Fed. Reg. 1572-02, 2000-1 C.B. 455.
180. I.R.C. § 708(b)(2)(B).
181. Treas. Reg. § 1.708-1(d)(1).

10. Selling, Exiting, Terminating, and Other Partnership Exits

the assets-over and assets-up form of division.[182] Just like with mergers, the assets-over form is the tax treatment if the division does not follow the assets-up form.[183]

Examples

1. Ava and Brynn are equal partners in the AB Partnership. The partnership has the following balance sheet.

AB Partnership					
Assets			Liabilities		
	Adj. Basis	FMV			$40,000
Cash	$60,000	$60,000			
Loans receivable	$200,00	$200,000	Capital Accounts		
Capital assets	$140,000	$100,000		Adj. Basis	Book Value
Unrealized receivable	0	$280,000	Ava	$200,000	$300,000
			Brynn	$200,000	$300,000
Total	$400,000	$640,000	Total	$400,000	$640,000

Reflected in their individual bases of $200,000 is their share of the $40,000 of partnership liabilities, which they have shared equally (i.e., their outside bases without the debt is $180,000 each). None of the property recorded on the balance sheet was contributed by the partners. Assume further that the capital assets are not depreciable. The partnership does not have a § 754 election in place.

Brynn sells her partnership interest to Charlotte for $300,000. Calculate the tax consequences to Brynn on this transaction.

2. At the beginning of 2022, the Alpha Partnership had three equal partners: Alfred, Betty, and Charlotte. On April 16, 2022, Alfred sells 50% of his interest to Donald. On August 3, 2022, Betty sells 50% of her interest to Edward. During 2022, Alpha earned $225,000 of ordinary income, incurred $99,000 of ordinary expenses, and sustained a $27,000 capital loss. More specifically, for the period between January 1, 2022 and July 31, 2022, it (i) earned $180,000 of ordinary income, (ii) incurred $72,000 of ordinary expenses, and (iii) sustained $18,000 of capital loss. The remaining amounts were incurred during the balance of the

---

182. Treas. Reg. § 1.708-1(d)(3).
183. Treas. Reg. § 1.708-1(d)(3)(i).

year. None of Alpha's items are "extraordinary items" nor did it incur any "allocable cash basis" items. Finally, capital is a material income-producing factor for the partnership. The partnership and partners are cash basis, calendar year taxpayers. The partners agree to use the proration method only for the April-based variation and will abide default rules for any other variation. If possible, it desires to use the semi-monthly convention for any interim closing. Determine the distributive shares for the partners for tax year 2022.

3. Farah is a partner in the Beta Partnership, which has three equal partners. The partnership has a § 754 election in place. At the beginning of the year, Farah sells her partnership interest to Gail for $440,000. At the time of sale, the partnership has the following balance sheet, which also presents the assets' fair market values.

Beta Partnership					
Assets			*Liabilities*		
	Adj. Basis	FMV			$200,000
Cash	$100,000	$100,000			
Accounts receivable	$200,000	$200,000	*Capital Accounts*		
Inventory	$400,000	$420,000		Adj. Basis	Book Value
Depreciable assets	$400,000	$800,000	P1	$366,667	$440,000
			P2	$366,667	$440,000
			Farah	$366,667	$440,000
Total	$1,100,00	$1,520,000	Total	$1,100,000[184]	$1,520,000

Determine the amount of the basis adjustment under § 743(b) that arises due to the sale of Farah's partnership interest.

4. Hana and Ingrid form the HI Partnership, in which they are equal partners. Hana contributes $150,000 in cash and Blackacre, which is a nondepreciable capital asset that has a fair market value of $150,000 and a tax basis of $75,000. Ingrid contributes $300,000 in cash. After formation, the partnership uses its cash to buy four additional assets: (1) Greenacre, which it purchases for $300,000; (2) Blueacre, which it purchases for $60,000; (3) Redacre, which it also purchases for $60,000; and (4) Yellowacre, which it purchases for $30,000. Although Blackacre and Greenacre are capital assets, due to the nature of the partnership's business, Blueacre, Redacre and Yellowacre are not capital assets.

After a year, Hana sells her partnership interest to Janet for $360,000. The partnership's items of income and expense netted out for the first

---

184. Rounded down; the basis numbers reflect the one-third sharing of the $200,000 liability, which is $66,666.66 per partner.

10. Selling, Exiting, Terminating, and Other Partnership Exits

year of operations. The assets of the HI Partnership are presented with bases and fair market values below. The partnership has a § 754 election in place. Assume that any asset that is not a capital asset is not § 1231 property.

Assets of HI Partnership		
	Adj. Basis	FMV
Blackacre	$75,000	$225,000
Greenacre	$300,000	$352,500
Blueacre	$60,000	$67,500
Redacre	$60,000	$67,500
Yellowacre	$30,000	$7,500
Total	$525,000	$720,000

Calculate (1) the tax consequences to Hana on the sale, (2) the tax consequences to Janet on the sale, (3) the amount of any § 743(b) adjustment, and (4) the allocation of the § 743(b) adjustment.

5. Ken is a law partner in a three-partner law firm and has been so for most of his career. Given the nature of a law firm, its assets consist mainly of cash, future collectibles from clients, and the office building and underlying real property; the law firm has the following balance sheet, which also depicts fair market values.

Law Firm Partnership					
Assets			Liabilities		
	Adj. Basis	FMV			$150,000
Cash	$650,000	$650,000			
Accounts receivable	$0	$1,500,000	Capital Accounts		
Capital asset	$1,000,000	$1,150,000		Adj. Basis	Book Value
			P1	$550,000	$1,050,000
			P2	$550,000	$1,050,000
			Ken	$550,000	$1,050,000
Total	$1,650,00	$3,300,000	Total	$1,650,000	$3,300,000

Under the partnership agreement, there is a mandatory retirement once turning 70 years old—the birthday that Ken just recently celebrated. The retirement provision also provides that a partner who retires in good standing has his or her remaining partnership liabilities assumed by the partnership. The partners have calculated that Ken is owed $450,000 in

10. Selling, Exiting, Terminating, and Other Partnership Exits

the year of his retirement, plus $500,000 for the following two years. Calculate the tax consequences to Ken that occasion his retirement from the law firm.

Explanations

1. This example allows us to practice the interaction of §§ 741 and 751 on the sale or transfer of a partnership interest.[185] Section 741 provides that gain or loss on the sale of a partnership interest shall be capital in nature, except to the extent it is displaced by ordinary income under § 751. The first step is to calculate the gain or loss under § 1001 principles. Brynn's amount realized is $320,000, which represents the $300,000 in cash received from Charlotte, plus the $20,000 of partnership liabilities assumed by Charlotte. Brynn's basis is $200,000, which already includes her share of the partnership liabilities under § 752. Thus, in the absence of § 751, Brynn would recognize a capital gain of $120,000.

   The second step is to calculate the § 751 gain or loss, if any. This requires us to use the hypothetical sale of assets approach. AB has only one § 751 asset—the unrealized receivable. If AB sold the unrealized receivable for its fair market value, it would generate a $280,000 gain, of which $140,000 would be allocated to Brynn.

   The third step is to calculate the difference between the §§ 741 and 751 amounts. The difference between the capital gain that Brynn would realize in the absence of § 751 (here, $120,000) and the amount of ordinary income gain or loss under § 751 (here, $140,000), is a loss of $20,000. In sum, Brynn will recognize ordinary income of $140,000 and a capital loss of $20,000 from the transaction.

2. This example requires us to apply the varying interest rules of Treas. Reg. § 1.706-4(a).[186] Let's walk through the ten-step process required by the regulation. First, none of the exceptions apply, such as the contemporaneous partner rule or the safe harbor for partnerships for which capital is not a material income-producing factor. Second, the facts provide that none of the items are extraordinary items. Third, the partners have agreed to apply the proration method for the April variation and the default (interim closing) for the August variation. Fourth, we must determine the date of the deemed variation based on the partnership's selected convention. Because it elected to use the proration method for the April variation, it must use the calendar day convention for that variation. Consequently, the variation that results from Alfred's sale is deemed to occur at the end of the day on April 16, 2022. For the August variation,

---

185. This example is based on Example 1 of Treas. Reg. § 1.751-1(g).
186. This example is based on the example of Treas. Reg. § 1.706-4(a)(4).

10. Selling, Exiting, Terminating, and Other Partnership Exits

which uses the interim closing method, the partner has agreed to use the semi-monthly convention. Under this convention, the variation is deemed to occur on July 31, 2022 (the last day of the immediately prior month). Fifth, the partners have not elected to perform regular semi-monthly or monthly closing; thus, there is only one interim closing, which is deemed to occur on July 31, 2022.

Sixth, the partnership must determine its segments for the year, which are created by interim closing. Thus, there are two segments here, the first of which spans from January 1, 2022 through July 31, 2022, and the second of which spans from August 1, 2022 through December 31, 2022. Seventh, the partnership must apportion its tax items among its segments. As noted in the facts, in the first segment, the partnership generated (i) $180,000 of ordinary income, (ii) incurred $72,000 of ordinary expenses, and (iii) and sustained $18,000 of capital loss. For the second segment, the partnership generated (i) $45,000 of ordinary income, (ii) incurred $27,000 of ordinary expenses, and (iii) sustained a $9,000 capital loss.

Eighth, the partnership must determine its proration period. The first proration period begins at the beginning of the segment and ends at the first time of the first variation within the segment. The next proration period starts immediately after and ends at the next variation event or the end of the segment. Here, the first proration period starts on January 1, 2022 (the start of the segment that contains a proration variation, i.e., the April variation) and ends on April 16, 2022. The second proration period starts on April 17, 2022 and ends on July 31, 2022 (the end of the first segment).

Ninth, the partnership needs to prorate its tax items from the first segment among the proration periods within it. There are 106 calendar days between January 1, 2022 and April 16, 2022; similarly, there are 106 calendar days between April 17, 2022 and July 31, 2022. Because each allocation period is the same number of days, we can allocate 50% of each item to each proration period. Thus, each proration period contains, (i) $90,000 of ordinary income, (ii) $36,000 of ordinary expenses, and (iii) $9,000 of capital loss.

Tenth, the partnership calculates each partner's distributive share. Here, Alfred, Betty, and Charlotte were equal partners for the first proration period (January 1 to April 16), so they will each be allocated one-third of the items in the first proration period. They are therefore each allocated (i) $30,000 of ordinary income, (ii) $12,000 of ordinary expenses, and (iii) $3,000 of capital loss. For the second proration period, Alfred and Donald each had a one-sixth interest in the partnership; thus, they are each allocated (i) $15,000 of ordinary income, (ii) $6,000 of ordinary expenses, and (iii) $1,500 of capital loss. Betty and Charlotte, who are each still one-third partners in the second proration period, are each allocated (i) $30,000 of ordinary income, (ii) $12,000 of ordinary expenses, and (iii) $3,000 of capital loss. This has covered the first segment of the tax year, which contained two proration periods.

For the second segment of Alpha's tax year, Alfred, Betty, Donald, and Edward each have a one-sixth interest in the partnership. Consequently, they are each allocated (i) $7,500 of ordinary income, (ii) $4,500 of ordinary expenses, and (iii) $1,500 of capital loss. Charlotte, however, still has a one-third interest in the partnership, and she is therefore allocated (i) $15,000 of ordinary income, (ii) $9,000 of ordinary expenses, and (iii) a $3,000 capital loss.

The following table summarizes the allocation of income for the taxable year.

	1st Segment (Jan. 1 to July 31)		2nd Segment (Aug. 1 to Dec. 31)	Total
	1st Proration (Jan. 1 to Apr. 16)	2nd Proration (Apr. 17 to July 31)		
Alfred				
Ordinary income	$30,000	$15,000	$7,500	$52,500
Ordinary expense	$12,000	$6,000	$4,500	$22,500
Capital loss	$3,000	$1,500	$1,500	$6,000
Betty				
Ordinary income	$30,000	$30,000	$7,500	$67,500
Ordinary expense	$12,000	$12,000	$4,500	$28,500
Capital loss	$3,000	$3,000	$1,500	$7,500
Charlotte				
Ordinary income	$30,000	$30,000	$15,000	$75,000
Ordinary expense	$12,000	$12,000	$9,000	$33,000
Capital loss	$3,000	$3,000	$3,000	$9,000
Donald				
Ordinary income	–	$15,000	$7,500	$22,500
Ordinary expense	–	$6,000	$4,500	$10,500
Capital loss	–	$1,500	$1,500	$3,000
Edward	–			
Ordinary income	–	–	$7,500	$7,500
Ordinary expense	–	–	$4,500	$4,500
Capital loss	–	–	$1,500	$1,500

10. Selling, Exiting, Terminating, and Other Partnership Exits

3. The general rule of § 743 provides that the "basis of partnership property shall not be adjusted as the result of a transfer of an interest in a partnership by sale or exchange...."[187] An exception, of course, is if the partnership has an election under § 754 in place. A § 754 election allows a partnership to adjust the basis of partnership property in the manner provided in § 743 when there is a transfer of a partnership interest. Section 743(b) provides that, in the case of a transfer of a partnership interest, the partnership shall *increase* the inside basis of partnership property by the excess of the transferee's outside basis over his proportionate share of the adjusted basis of partnership property and shall *decrease* the inside basis of partnership property by the excess of the transferee's proportionate share of the adjusted basis of partnership property over his outside basis.

The transferee's proportionate share of the adjusted basis of partnership property is defined in Treas. Reg. § 1.743-1(d), and it consists of two items. The first is the transferee partner's share of the "partnership's previously taxed capital," and the second is the transferee's share of partnership liabilities. As unpacked in the chapter, the partnership's previously taxed capital is equal to the following items.

Transferee's Share of the Partnership's Previously Taxed Capital [§ 1.743-1(d)(1)]
Start with amount of cash the transferee would receive in liquidation following the hypothetical transaction
Increased by the amount of tax loss that would be allocated to the partner from the hypothetical transaction
Decreased by the amount of tax gain that would be allocated to the partner from the hypothetical transaction
Equals transferee's share of the partnership's previously taxed capital

In this problem, therefore, Gail's share of the partnership's previously taxed capital is calculated as follows. In the hypothetical transaction—which means that the partnership disposes of all its assets in a fully taxable transaction for cash—Gail would receive $440,000 of cash. This represents the liquidation of all the assets for their fair market values ($1,520,000) less the payment of the liabilities ($200,000), which leaves $1,320,000 to equally distribute to the partners ($440,000 each). For the second step, there is no tax loss to allocate in the hypothetical transaction. For the third step, there is a total of $420,000 of tax gain to allocate, arising from the gain inherent in the inventory ($20,000) and depreciable assets ($400,000); Gail's share is $140,000. Thus, her share of the partnership's previously taxed capital is equal to $300,000.

---

187. I.R.C. § 743(a). This example is based on Example 1 of Treas. Reg. § 1.743-1(d)(3).

10. Selling, Exiting, Terminating, and Other Partnership Exits

The second part of the partner's proportionate share of the adjusted basis of partnership property is her share of the partnership liabilities. Here, that amount is $66,667 (i.e., one-third of the $200,000). Gail's share of the adjusted basis of partnership property is $366,667.

Now that we have calculated Gail's share of the adjusted basis of partnership property, we can calculate the § 743(b) adjustment. Gail's outside basis (her basis in the partnership) is equal to $506,667, which represents the $440,000 that she paid, plus $66,667, which is her share of the partnership liabilities under § 752. With that, the § 743(b) adjustment is an *increase* of 140,000 (i.e., $506,667 less $366,667).

4. This problem requires us to consider the dimensions that accompany the sale of a partnership interest—namely, consequences to the transferor (gain/loss) and to the transferee (basis and the availability of a § 743(b) adjustment).[188] We will consider the items in order as requested in the problem. The first item is to calculate the tax consequences to Hana (the transferor). As we've discussed in this chapter, the sale of a partnership interest results in capital gain or loss (§ 741) except to the extent it is displaced under § 751. Here, the total gain using § 1001 on the sale is the amount realized ($360,000) less Hana's basis, which is $225,000 (recall the basis she would have immediately after formation (the sum of the bases of the transferred assets) and that because the items of income and expense netted out, there was no impact on her basis from operations). Thus, Hana's amount of total gain under § 741 is equal to $135,000. Now, we need to see if any of that gain gets displaced under § 751.

Although none of the assets are labeled as "inventory," § 751 nevertheless treats as "inventory" the sale of property that gives rise to ordinary income (unless if it is § 1231 property).[189] For § 751 purposes, therefore, all the property other than Blackacre and Greenacre is inventory for § 751. If the partnership were to sell the § 751 property, it would generate the following: (a) Blueacre, $7,500 ordinary income; (b) Redacre, $7,500 ordinary income; (c) Yellowacre, $22,500 ordinary loss. This sums to a total ordinary loss of $7,500, of which $3,750 would be allocated to Hana. We can then calculate the difference between the §§ 741 and 751 amounts; Hana must report $138,750 of long-term capital gain (under § 741) and $3,750 of ordinary loss (under § 751).

We can now turn to the tax consequences to the transferee, Janet. There are three main issues to consider here: (1) the basis that Janet takes, (2) the impact of the transfer on the inside basis, and (3) Janet's capital account balance. Janet's basis is determined under § 742, which provides that the basis of a partnership interest other than by contribution

---

188. This is loosely based on Example 1 of Treas. Reg. § 1.755-1(b)(2)(ii).
189. *See* I.R.C. § 751(d).

10. Selling, Exiting, Terminating, and Other Partnership Exits

is governed by the normal basis rules. Because Janet *purchased* her partnership interest, she will therefore take a cost basis of $360,000 under § 1012. Next, we need to consider the impact of the § 754 election.

As we've discussed elsewhere, generally the transfer of a partnership interest does not result in a change to the inside basis of partnership assets. One exception is if the partnership has an election in place under § 754, which allows an adjustment under § 743(b) — this is the case here. Under § 743(b), in the case of a transfer of a partnership interest, the partnership shall *increase* the inside basis of partnership property by the excess of the transferee's outside basis over his proportionate share of the adjusted basis of partnership property and shall *decrease* the inside basis of partnership property by the excess of the transferee's proportionate share of the adjusted basis of partnership property over his outside basis. We unpacked this process in the immediately prior example and explanation.

The transferee's proportionate share of the adjusted basis of partnership property is defined in Treas. Reg. § 1.743-1(d), and it consists of two items. The first is the transferee partner's share of the "partnership's previously taxed capital," and the second is the transferee's share of partnership liabilities. As unpacked in the chapter, the partnership's previously taxed capital is equal to the following items.

Transferee's Share of the Partnership's Previously Taxed Capital [§ 1.743-1(d)(1)]
Start with amount of cash the transferee would receive in liquidation following the hypothetical transaction
Increased by the amount of tax loss that would be allocated to the partner from the hypothetical transaction
Decreased by the amount of tax gain that would be allocated to the partner from the hypothetical transaction
Equals transferee's share of the partnership's previously taxed capital

Here, Janet would receive $360,000 in cash on the hypothetical transaction (the FMV of the assets with zero liabilities to satisfy, which will then be shared equally). Next, there is a $22,500 tax loss on Yellowacre, $11,250 of which would be allocated to Janet. Lastly, there is a total of $217,500 of tax gain remaining in the properties. However, some of that gain is § 704(c) gain attributable to Blackacre. The § 704(c) regulations provide that built-in gain or loss must be allocated to the transferee partner like it would have been to the transferor partner.[190]

---

190. Treas. Reg. § 1.704-3(a)(7).

10. Selling, Exiting, Terminating, and Other Partnership Exits

Blackacre had $75,000 of built-in gain at contribution that must therefore be allocated to Janet (its FMV at contribution of $150,000 less its basis at contribution of $75,000). The remaining gain in Blackacre is split equally between the partners ($75,000, which is then divided by two—$37,500 per partner). There is a total of $67,500 of gain in the remaining properties, which would be split $33,750 per partner. In total, then, Janet would be allocated $146,250 of tax gain ($75,000 + $37,500 + $33,750). Her share of partnership previously taxed capital, therefore, equals (a) $360,000, plus (b) $11,250, minus (c) $146,250, which equals $225,000. The § 743(b) basis adjustment is equal to her cost basis less her share of previously taxed capital: $360,000 less $225,000, which equals $135,000.

Now that we have determined the amount of the § 743(b) adjustment, we now must allocate among the partnership's assets, which is governed by § 755. The § 755 regulations provide that we must allocate income into classes,[191] and then we allocate the amounts within each class; there are two classes—ordinary income property and capital gain property.[192] The ordinary income class is determined by the total amount of ordinary income or loss that would be allocated to the transferee in the hypothetical transaction.[193] The capital gain class is equal to the total basis adjustment less the amount of the ordinary income class.[194]

Here, in the hypothetical transaction, Janet would be allocated an ordinary loss of $3,750, which is the amount of the ordinary income class. Consequently, the basis adjustment for capital gain property equals $138,750, which equals the total basis adjustment ($135,000) less the basis adjustment for ordinary income property (–$3,750). We must now allocate those amounts to each property within each class.

We must allocate $138,500 among the capital gain properties, which are Blackacre and Greenacre. Generally, we allocate the adjustment to each property based on the amount of income, gain, or loss that would be allocated to such property.[195] In the hypothetical transaction, Janet would be allocated $112,500 of capital gain from Blackacre, so we make an adjustment of $112,500 to Blackacre. Janet would be allocated $26,250 of capital gain from Greenacre, so we make an adjustment of the same to it. These two sums—$112,500 plus $26,250—equal the total adjustment for the capital gain class of $138,750.

---

191. Treas. Reg. § 1.755-1(b)(2).
192. Treas. Reg. § 1.755-1(b)(3).
193. Treas. Reg. § 1.755-1(b)(2)(i).
194. Id.
195. This is assuming we have enough adjustment; if not, we must apply the full rule provided in Treas. Reg. § 1.755-1(b)(3)(ii).

10. Selling, Exiting, Terminating, and Other Partnership Exits

Next, we can allocate within the ordinary income properties, which are the remaining properties. The allocation method is similar, namely if we have enough adjustment we allocate based on how much ordinary income or loss would be generated by the property in the hypothetical transaction.[196] Here, Janet would be allocated $3,750 of ordinary income from Blueacre, so we allocate that amount to it. Similarly, Janet would be allocated $3,750 from the sale of Redacre, so we allocate that amount to it. Lastly, Janet would be allocated a loss of $11,250 to Yellowacre, so we make a *decrease* to its basis by the that amount. These amounts—$3,750, plus $3,750, less $11,250—equal the amount of total amount of *decrease* allocated to the ordinary income property of $3,750.

The last part of the analysis requested is for how Janet's purchase affects her capital account. This is, fortunately, the simplest part of the analysis. The capital account regulations state that capital accounts will not be considered to be maintained in accordance with the § 704 regulations unless the capital account of the transferor carries over to the transferee.[197] Thus, Janet will step into Hana's capital account.

5. This problem requires us to consider § 736 and related sections.[198] Section 736 provides a roadmap that directs paths to § 736(a) or § 736(b), both of which include payments made to a "retiring partner." Payments under § 736(a) are treated as distributive shares of income or guaranteed payments; payments under § 736(b) are treated as a distribution. The critical query that separates § 736(a) and § 736(b) payments is the nature of the payment—if the payment represents a payment for the partner's interest in partnership property, it is considered a § 736(b) payment (and treated like a distribution).

The first thing to do is to determine how much Ken receives for his partnership interest. He receives (i) $450,000 paid in year of retirement, (ii) $50,000 of liabilities assumed, (iii) $500,000 in Year 2, and (iv) $500,000 in Year 3, which sums to $1,500,000. Let's now consider Ken's interest in partnership property for § 736(b) purposes. Importantly, § 736(b)(2)(A) provides that payments for partnership property shall not include amounts paid for unrealized receivables of the partnership. The law firm's account receivables, therefore, are not included in determining its § 736(b) property. The value of the § 736(b) property is $1,800,000 (the value of the cash and capital asset)—Ken's share is thus $600,000.

Payments made for partnership property is treated as a distribution under § 736(b). Of the $1,500,000 he receives in total, $600,000

---

196. Treas. Reg. § 1.755-1(b)(3)(i).
197. Treas. Reg. § 1.704-1(b)(2)(iv)(l).
198. This problem is based on Example 1 of Treas. Reg. §1.736-1(b)(7).

represents payment for his share of partnership property, which is governed by the distribution rules of § 731. Under § 731, a partner recognizes gain on a distribution to the extent the amount of money exceeds the partner's outside basis before the distribution. Ken's outside basis is $550,000 (which already reflects his share of liabilities under § 752). Ken therefore must recognize $50,000 in gain, which is treated as the gain from the sale of the partnership interest, and it is thus a long-term capital gain.

The remaining amount of the proceeds ($900,000) is treated as a § 736(a) payment; these must be treated as either a distributive share of partnership income or a guaranteed payment. Because the amounts are fixed and not based on the future income of the partnership, they are guaranteed payments under § 736(a)(2). Given that we have § 736(a) and § 736(b) payments, we must allocate each amount received between its § 736(a) and § 736(b) elements. The total amount of the § 736(a) payment is $900,000 and the total § 736(b) payment is $600,000. Thus we can allocate that ($900,000/$1,500,000) of each payment reflects the § 736(a) amount, and ($600,000/$1,500,000) of each payment reflects the § 736(b) amount.

The payment for the first year (the year of retirement) is $500,000, which represents the money ($450,000) and assumed liabilities ($50,000). Note as well that the next two years of payments are also $500,000 each, too. Thus, using the allocation fractions from the past paragraph, we can treat each annual payment of $500,000 to reflect a § 736(a)(2) payment of $300,000 and a § 736(b) payment of $200,000.[199]

---

199. The § 736(a)(2) payment is calculated as $500,000 × ($900,000/$1,500,000) = $300,000, and the § 736(b) payment is calculated as $500,000 × ($600,000/$1,500,000) = $200,000.

Table of Internal Revenue Code Sections

Section	Pages		Section	Pages
§ 1	297		§ 197	214, 307
§ 1(h)	37, 297, 298, 299, 300		§ 199A	14, 17, 18, 19
§ 1(h)(5)(A)	297		§ 199A(a)	19
§ 1(h)(5)(B)	297		§ 199A(b)	19
§ 1(h)(6)(A)	298		§ 212	53
§ 10	304		§ 213	53
§ 11	17		§ 214	53
§ 49(a)(1)(D)(iv)	77		§ 215	53
§ 55	54		§ 216	53
§ 61	11, 19, 21, 31, 208, 254, 264, 267, 271, 272, 279, 283		§ 263	248, 258, 260, 264, 284
			§ 263A(e)(4)	67
§ 61(a)	256, 258		§ 263(c)	53
§ 61(a)(11)	13		§ 267	31, 35, 145, 246, 260
§ 72	33		§ 267(e)	246
§ 83	21, 264, 271, 274, 275, 276, 277, 279, 281, 282, 283		§ 351	21, 28, 29, 264
			§ 351(e)	30
§ 83(a)	275, 279, 280		§ 368	21
§ 83(b)	274, 275, 276, 280, 283		§ 408	33
§ 83(c)(1)	280		§ 408(m)	297
§ 83(h)	280		§ 408(m)(2)	297
§ 108	13		§ 441	60
§ 111	53		§ 441(g)	60
§ 125	20		§ 446	8, 66
§ 151	50		§ 446(a)	67
§ 162	19, 258, 260, 261, 264, 268, 284		§ 446(b)	67
§ 162(a)	254, 256		§ 446(c)	64, 67
§ 163(d)(1)	90		§ 448	67, 68
§ 164	53		§ 448(a)	67
§ 165	123		§ 448(b)(1)	67
§ 165(d)	53		§ 448(b)(2)	67
§ 167	86, 248		§ 448(b)(3)	67
§ 168	86, 248, 298		§ 448(c)	67
§ 168(b)	298		§ 448(d)(2)	67
§ 168(c)	298		§ 461	68
§ 168(d)	298		§ 461(1)	81
§ 168(k)	160, 313		§ 461(i)(3)	68
§ 170	50, 53		§ 461(i)(3)(A)	68
§ 170(b)	53		§ 461(i)(3)(B)	68
§ 175	53		§ 461(i)(3)(C)	68
§ 179	89, 323		§ 465	68, 73, 74, 75, 76, 77, 81, 88, 94, 95, 109
§ 179(b)	89			
§ 179(b)(1)	89		§ 465(a)	94
§ 179(b)(2)	89		§ 465(a)(1)(A)	94

Table of Internal Revenue Code Sections

§ 465(a)(2)	95	§ 703(a)(2)(C)	72
§ 465(b)	94	§ 703(a)(2)(E)	50
§ 465(b)(1)	74, 76	§ 703(b)	8
§ 465(b)(2)	76	§ 703(d)	72
§ 465(b)(6)	77	§ 704	48, 54, 55, 56, 59, 75, 84, 86, 109, 179, 203, 204, 205, 206, 207, 209, 216, 257, 258, 259, 269, 302, 341
§ 465(b)(6)(A)	77		
§ 465(b)(6)(B)	77		
§ 465(b)(6)(D)(ii)	77	§ 704(a)	55, 97, 98, 143, 323
§ 465(c)	94	§ 704(b)	55, 97, 98, 99, 100, 103, 104, 106, 110, 133, 134, 143, 148, 178, 187, 188, 195, 244, 256, 271, 301, 323
§ 465(c)(1)	74		
§ 465(c)(2)	75		
§ 465(c)(2)(A)	76		
§ 465(c)(3)	74, 75	§ 704(c)	13, 35, 36, 144, 145, 146, 147, 148, 149, 150, 153, 154, 155, 158, 160, 162, 163, 164, 167, 169, 170, 178, 181, 182, 183, 185, 186, 187, 190, 199, 200, 201, 202, 222, 227, 235, 271, 277, 284, 294, 306, 329, 339
§ 465(c)(3)(B)	76		
§ 469	68, 77, 78, 80, 81		
§ 469(a)(1)(A)	78		
§ 469(a)(2)	78		
§ 469(b)	78, 80		
§ 469(c)	78		
§ 469(c)(2)	79	§ 704(c)(1)(A)	144, 145, 146
§ 469(c)(3)	78	§ 704(c)(1)(B)	330
§ 469(c)(6)	78	§ 704(d)	68, 69, 70, 71, 72, 73, 81, 88, 92, 93, 94
§ 469(c)(7)	79		
§ 469(d)	78	§ 704(d)(1)	69, 93
§ 469(g)	80	§ 704(d)(3)	72, 73
§ 469(g)(2)	80	§ 704(d)(3)(B)	73
§ 469(h)	78	§ 704(e)	110
§ 469(h)(2)	79	§ 704(e)(1)	110
§ 469(i)	79	§ 704(e)(2)	110
§ 469(i)(6)	80	§ 705	35, 71, 174, 205, 206, 207, 233, 290, 292
§ 613A	110		
§ 613A(c)(7)(D)	188	§ 705(a)	70
§ 615	53	§ 705(a)(1)	71, 93
§ 617	53	§ 705(a)(2)	71, 93
§ 691(a)(1)	319	§ 705(a)(2)(B)	71
§ 691(a)(3)	320	§ 706	8, 48, 49, 60, 62, 274, 319, 325
§ 701	48, 54, 57, 97	§ 706(a)	60, 61
§§ 701-704	48	§ 706(b)	60, 62
§§ 701-709	7	§ 706(b)(1)(3)	62
§ 702	48, 49, 50, 51, 52, 53, 54, 57, 58, 68, 70, 89, 97, 302, 323	§ 706(b)(1)(A)	62
		§ 706(b)(1)(B)	62, 91
§ 702(a)	48, 49, 50, 51, 53, 54, 57, 68, 72	§ 706(b)(1)(B)(ii)	63
		§ 706(b)(1)(B)(iii)	63
§ 702(a)(1)	51, 89	§ 706(b)(1)(C)	62, 64
§ 702(a)(1) to (7)	51, 54, 55, 56	§ 706(b)(2)(ii)	110
§ 702(a)(2)	51, 55, 89	§ 706(b)(3)	62, 91
§ 702(a)(7)	53, 54, 230	§ 706(b)(4)(A)(i)	62, 91
§ 702(a)(8)	55, 56, 57, 58, 59, 230	§ 706(b)(4)(A)(ii)	62, 91
§ 703	8, 48, 49, 50, 51, 57, 58, 89	§ 706(c)	322
§ 703(a)	49	§ 706(c)(1)	318, 322
§ 703(a)(2)	57	§ 706(c)(2)	318

Table of Internal Revenue Code Sections

§ 706(d)	110, 322, 323	§ 732(a)	219, 233
§ 706(d)(2)	325	§ 732(a)(1)	208, 210, 211
§ 706(d)(2)(B)	325	§ 732(a)(2)	208, 210, 211, 214
§ 707	8, 244, 247, 248, 250, 254, 259, 260, 263, 274	§ 732(b)	212, 214, 217, 220, 221, 232, 233, 238, 239, 240, 321, 330
§ 707(a)	203, 244, 245, 246, 247, 248, 254, 256, 257, 258, 259, 260, 264	§ 732(c)	210, 211, 221, 233, 239, 240, 330
§ 707(a)(1)	245, 249, 254	§ 732(c)(1)(A)(i)	211
§ 707(a)(2)	248, 249	§ 732(c)(1)(B)	211
§ 707(a)(2)(A)	249, 250, 260	§ 732(c)(3)	212
§ 707(a)(2)(B)	103, 252	§ 732(c)(3)(A)	212
§ 707(c)	203, 244, 245, 254, 256, 257, 258, 259, 260, 262, 264, 284, 316, 317	§ 732(c)(3)(B)	212
		§ 733	9, 71, 205, 209, 211, 216, 233
§ 708	320, 327	§ 734	213, 214, 215, 238, 239, 301
§ 708(a)	320	§ 734(a)	213, 240
§ 708(b)	322	§ 734(b)	240, 307
§ 708(b)(1)	320	§ 734(b)(1)	214
§ 708(b)(1)(A)	321	§ 734(b)(1)(A)	240
§ 708(b)(1)(B)	320	§ 734(b)(2)	214
§ 708(b)(2)(A)	328	§ 734(b)(2)(A)	240
§ 708(b)(2)(B)	330	§ 734(c)	214, 240
§ 721	7, 21, 28, 29, 30, 33, 34, 36, 37, 40, 41, 42, 43, 44, 45, 88, 144, 247, 252, 263, 264, 270, 272, 279, 283, 284	§ 735	39
		§ 735(a)(1)	222
		§ 735(a)(2)	222, 321
		§ 735(b)	222, 321
		§ 736	234, 314, 315, 317, 318, 319, 341
§§ 721-724	7	§ 736(a)	315, 316, 317, 320, 341, 342
§ 721(a)	28	§ 736(a)(1)	317
§ 721(b)	29, 30, 32, 43, 45	§ 736(a)(2)	316, 342
§ 721(c)	30	§ 736(b)	234, 235, 315, 316, 317, 341, 342
§ 722	7, 28, 31, 32, 33, 34, 36, 37, 44, 46, 88, 144, 174, 270, 290	§ 736(b)(2)(A)	341
§ 723	7, 28, 32, 33, 34, 36, 43, 45, 144, 270, 330	§ 737	216, 329, 330
		§ 741	9, 14, 21, 288, 289, 290, 292, 294, 295, 297, 299, 300, 302, 321, 334, 338
§ 724(a)	39	§§ 741-743	7
§ 724(b)	40	§ 742	290, 301, 304, 338
§ 724(c)	40	§ 743	9, 214, 301, 302, 303, 305, 306, 309, 310, 312, 313, 337
§ 724(d)(1)	39	§ 743(a)	301, 337
§ 724(d)(2)	39	§ 743(b)	303, 304, 305, 306, 307, 308, 311, 312, 314, 332, 333, 338, 339, 340
§ 731	9, 21, 30, 204, 205, 206, 208, 216, 217, 220, 232, 247, 248, 262, 315, 316, 321, 342		
§§ 731-736	238	§ 743(b)(1)	303
§§ 731-737	7	§ 743(b)(2)	303
§ 731(a)	205, 209, 216, 217, 218, 220, 221, 232, 233	§ 743(c)	307
§ 731(a)(1)	9, 205, 218	§ 751	6, 10, 14, 21, 209, 223, 224, 229, 230, 234, 235, 237, 288, 292, 293, 294, 295, 296, 297, 300, 334, 338
§ 731(a)(2)	205, 214, 220, 221, 233		
§ 731(b)	208, 209, 216, 217, 233, 238, 262		
§ 732	9, 205, 206, 208, 209, 212, 213, 216, 229, 313	§ 751(a)	292, 294

345

Table of Internal Revenue Code Sections

§ 751(a)(2)	235
§ 751(b)	53, 110, 212, 216, 222, 224, 225, 226, 227, 229, 230, 235, 236, 237, 238, 239, 294, 315
§ 751(b)(1)(A)	225
§ 751(b)(1)(A)(ii)	294
§ 751(b)(3)(A)	294
§ 751(b)(A)(ii)	235
§ 751(c)	225, 293
§ 751(c)(1)	225
§ 751(c)(2)	225
§ 751(d)	293, 338
§ 751(d)(1)	225
§ 751(d)(2)	225, 235, 293
§ 751(d)(3)	225
§ 752	30, 102, 107, 173, 174, 175, 183, 184, 190, 195, 196, 197, 198, 199, 236, 238, 290, 301, 304, 305, 334, 338, 342
§ 752(a)	174
§ 752(b)	174
§ 752(b)(3)	225
§ 752(c)	174
§ 752(d)	174
§ 753	319, 320
§ 754	213, 214, 232, 238, 239, 240, 301, 302, 303, 307, 331, 332, 333, 337, 339
§ 755	214, 240, 307, 308, 309, 310, 312, 340
§ 755(a)(1)	214
§ 755(a)(2)	214
§ 761	7, 127
§ 761(c)	127, 323
§ 871	247
§ 901	53, 73
§ 1001	11, 14, 21, 25, 28, 31, 41, 44, 219, 262, 290, 295, 296, 334, 338
§ 1001(b)	290
§ 1002	27
§ 1011	11, 31
§ 1012	11, 12, 31, 174, 301, 303, 305, 309, 321, 339
§ 1014	145, 304
§ 1015	31, 35, 304
§ 1016	86
§ 1031	27, 28, 30
§ 1060	214, 307
§ 1202	22
§ 1211	123
§ 1211(b)	296
§ 1212	123
§ 1221	37
§ 1221(a)(1)	45, 225, 293
§ 1221(a)(2)	38
§ 1222(2)	45
§ 1222(6)	51
§ 1222(7)	51
§ 1222(11)	51, 297
§ 1223	39, 42, 45
§ 1223(1)	37, 42, 44
§ 1223(2)	37, 39, 42, 43, 45
§ 1231	37, 38, 42, 43, 45, 53, 58, 89, 123, 124, 214, 293, 299, 333
§ 1231(a)	123, 124
§ 1231(a)(1)	89
§ 1231(a)(2)	89, 123
§ 1231(a)(3)(A)	37
§ 1231(a)(3)(B)	37
§ 1231(b)	37, 122, 240
§ 1231(b)(1)	45
§ 1231(b)(1)(A)	37
§ 1231(b)(1)(B)	37
§ 1231(b)(1)(C)	37
§ 1245	293, 298
§ 1250	297, 298, 299
§ 1250(a)	298
§ 1250(b)	298
§ 1256(e)(3)(B)	68
§ 1272	253
§ 1274	253
§ 1361	4
§§ 1361–1379	4
§ 1361(b)	4
§ 1361(c)	18
§ 1362	4
§ 1363	4, 18
§ 1363(b)	18
§ 1366	4, 55
§ 1368	21
§ 1372	21
§§ 1401–1403	20
§ 1402(a)	20
§§ 3101–3128	19
§§ 3301–3311	19
§ 6031	8, 49
§ 6662(d)(2)(C)(ii)	68
§ 7701(a)(1)	xvii
§ 7701(a)(43)	28
§ 7701(a)(44)	28
§ 7701(g)	307

Table of Treasury Regulations

§ 1.1(h)-1(a)	297	§ 1.704-1(b)(1)(i)	99
§ 1.1(h)-1(b)(1)	297	§ 1.704-1(b)(2)	99, 100
§ 1.1(h)-1(b)(2)(ii)	299	§ 1.704-1(b)(2)(i)	100, 118
§ 1.1(h)-1(b)(3)(i)	298	§ 1.704-1(b)(2)(ii)(a)	100
§ 1.1(h)-1(b)(3)(ii)	299	§ 1.704-1(b)(2)(ii)(b)	100, 101
§ 1.46-3	130	§ 1.704-1(b)(2)(ii)(b)(1)	100, 101
§ 1.58-2(b)	54	§ 1.704-1(b)(2)(ii)(b)(2)	100, 101, 105
§ 1.61-2(d)(1)	271	§ 1.704-1(b)(2)(ii)(b)(3)	100, 101, 106, 134
§ 1.83-1(a)(1)	275, 276	§ 1.704-1(b)(2)(ii)(c)	106
§ 1.83-3(b)	274	§ 1.704-1(b)(2)(ii)(c)(1)	135
§ 1.83-3(e)	283	§ 1.704-1(b)(2)(ii)(c)(1)(A)	106
§ 1.132-1(b)(1)	21	§ 1.704-1(b)(2)(ii)(c)(1)(B)	106
§ 1.132-1(b)(2)	21	§ 1.704-1(b)(2)(ii)(c)(2)	106, 135
§ 1.223-3(f)	39	§ 1.704-1(b)(2)(ii)(c)(4)	106, 107
§ 1.351-1(c)(1)	30	§ 1.704-1(b)(2)(ii)(c)(4)(B)	107
§ 1.446-1	66	§ 1.704-1(b)(2)(ii)(d)	108, 109, 110
§ 1.446-1(c)(1)(ii)	67	§ 1.704-1(b)(2)(ii)(d)(4)	110, 189
§ 1.446-1(c)(1)(ii)(A)	67	§ 1.704-1(b)(2)(ii)(d)(5)	110, 189
§ 1.446-1(c)(1)(ii)(B)	67	§ 1.704-1(b)(2)(ii)(d)(6)	110, 113, 114, 189
§ 1.446-1(c)(ii)(C)	67		
§ 1.451-1(a)	293	§ 1.704-1(b)(2)(ii)(e)	116
§ 1.451-1(d)(1)	319	§ 1.704-1(b)(2)(ii)(i)	118
§ 1.461-1(a)(1)	246	§ 1.704-1(b)(2)(iii)(a)	118, 119, 136
§ 1.461-1(a)(2)(i)	246	§ 1.704-1(b)(2)(iii)(a)(1)	119
§ 1.465-1T(a)	94	§ 1.704-1(b)(2)(iii)(a)(2)	119, 126
§ 1.469-1T(f)(2)	78	§ 1.704-1(b)(2)(iii)(b)	121, 127, 139
§ 1.469-2T(b)	78	§ 1.704-1(b)(2)(iii)(b)(1)	122
§ 1.469-2T(c)(3)	78	§ 1.704-1(b)(2)(iii)(b)(2)	122, 123
§ 1.469-2T(d)(6)(i)	80	§ 1.704-1(b)(2)(iii)(c)	111, 125, 127
§ 1.469-2T(d)(6)(iv)	81	§ 1.704-1(b)(2)(iii)(d)	111
§ 1.469-2T(e)	80	§ 1.704-1(b)(2)(iii)(d)(3)	111
§ 1.469-2T(e)(1)	80	§ 1.704-1(b)(2)(iv)	82, 101
§ 1.469-5T(a)	79	§ 1.704-1(b)(2)(iv)(b)	83, 89, 101, 102
§ 1.469-5T(e)	79	§ 1.704-1(b)(2)(iv)(c)	102
§ 1.469-5T(e)(3)(i)(B)	79	§ 1.704-1(b)(2)(iv)(d)	102
§ 1.691(a)-2	319	§ 1.704-1(b)(2)(iv)(d)(1)	102
§ 1.691(a)-4(a)	320	§ 1.704-1(b)(2)(iv)(d)(2)	102
§ 1.702-1	51	§ 1.704-1(b)(2)(iv)(e)	103
§ 1.702-1(a)(3)	89	§ 1.704-1(b)(2)(iv)(e)(1)	103
§ 1.702-1(a)(8)(i)	53, 54	§ 1.704-1(b)(2)(iv)(e)(2)	104
§ 1.702-1(a)(8)(ii)	54	§ 1.704-1(b)(2)(iv)(f)(5)(iii)	271
§ 1.704-1	118, 188	§ 1.704-1(b)(2)(iv)(h)	104
§ 1.704-1(b)	146, 188	§ 1.704-1(b)(2)(iv)(l)	301, 341

Table of Treasury Regulations

§ 1.704-1(b)(3)	99, 128
§ 1.704-1(b)(3)(i)	128, 135
§ 1.704-1(b)(3)(ii)	129
§ 1.704-1(b)(3)(iii)	129
§ 1.704-1(b)(4)	99, 130
§ 1.704-1(b)(4)(ii)	130
§ 1.704-1(b)(4)(iii)	130
§ 1.704-1(b)(4)(v)	188
§ 1.704-1(b)(5)	103, 117, 119, 122, 125, 129, 134, 136, 137, 139
§1.704-1(b)(5)	271
§ 1.704-1(d)	71
§ 1.704-1(d)(1)	69, 70
§ 1.704-1(d)(2)	70, 71, 93
§ 1.704-1(d)(4)	93
§ 1.704-2	130, 178, 185, 200
§ 1.704-2(b)(1)	179, 180, 187
§ 1.704-2(c)	180
§ 1.704-2(d)(1)	178, 179, 199
§ 1.704-2(e)	188, 192, 200
§ 1.704-2(e)(1)	188
§ 1.704-2(e)(2)	180, 188
§ 1.704-2(e)(3)	188
§ 1.704-2(e)(4)	188
§ 1.704-2(f)(1)	189, 193
§ 1.704-2(g)	181
§ 1.704-2(g)(1)	192, 199
§ 1.704-2(g)(2)	189, 193
§ 1.704-2(m)	189
§ 1.704-3(a)(1)	146
§ 1.704-3(a)(2)	146
§ 1.704-3(a)(3)(i)	146, 147
§ 1.704-3(a)(3)(ii)	147, 150
§ 1.704-3(a)(6)	181
§ 1.704-3(a)(7)	339
§ 1.704-3(b)(1)	147, 148, 149, 164
§ 1.704-3(b)(2)	148, 164
§ 1.704-3(c)(1)	154, 166, 167
§ 1.704-3(c)(2)	154
§ 1.704-3(c)(3)(i)	154
§ 1.704-3(c)(3)(iii)(A)	154, 167
§ 1.704-3(c)(3)(iii)(B)	154
§ 1.704-3(c)(4)	155, 166, 167
§ 1.704–3(d)	310
§ 1.704-3(d)(1)	157, 169
§ 1.704-3(d)(2)	159, 169
§ 1.704-3(d)(3)	157
§ 1.704-3(d)(4)(i)	158
§ 1.704-3(d)(4)(ii)	158
§ 1.704-3(d)(7)	158, 160, 169, 170, 171
§ 1.704-4(c)(4)	330
§ 1.705-1(a)(1)	292
§ 1.706-1(a)(1)	256
§ 1.706-1(a)(2)	256
§ 1.706-1(b)(2)(i)(C)	63, 91
§ 1.706-1(b)(3)(i)	64
§ 1.706-1(b)(3)(iv)	91
§ 1.706-1(c)(2)(i)	318
§ 1.706-1(c)(2)(ii)	318
§ 1.706-4	322
§ 1.706-4(a)	334
§ 1.706-4(a)(3)	323
§ 1.706-4(a)(3)(i)	323
§ 1.706-4(a)(3)(ii)	323
§ 1.706-4(a)(3)(iv)	324
§ 1.706-4(a)(3)(ix)	323, 324
§ 1.706-4(a)(3)(v)	324
§ 1.706-4(a)(3)(vi)	324, 326
§ 1.706-4(a)(3)(vii)	323, 324
§ 1.706-4(a)(3)(viii)	323, 324
§ 1.706-4(a)(3)(x)	324
§ 1.706-4(a)(4)	334
§ 1.706-4(b)(1)	323
§ 1.706-4(b)(2)	323
§ 1.706-4(c)(1)	324
§ 1.706-4(c)(1)(i)	324
§ 1.706-4(c)(1)(ii)	324
§ 1.706-4(c)(1)(iii)	325
§ 1.706-4(c)(3)(i)	325
§ 1.706-4(e)(1)	323
§ 1.706-4(e)(2)	323
§ 1.706-4(e)(3)	323
§ 1.706-4(e)(3)(iii)	323
§ 1.706-4(g)	323
§ 1.707-1	255
§ 1.707-1(a)	245, 247
§ 1.707-1(c)	254, 256, 260, 261, 262
§ 1.707-2(b)	250
§ 1.707-2(b)(2)	250
§ 1.707-2(c)	260
§ 1.707-2(c)(1)	249
§ 1.707-2(c)(1)(iii)	261
§ 1.707-2(c)(1)(iv)	261
§ 1.707-2(c)(2)	249
§ 1.707-2(c)(3)	249
§ 1.707-2(c)(4)	249
§ 1.707-2(c)(5)	249
§ 1.707-2(c)(6)	250
§ 1.707-2(d)	250, 260
§ 1.707-3(a)(1)	251
§ 1.707-3(a)(2)	252
§ 1.707-3(b)(1)	251

Table of Treasury Regulations

§ 1.707-3(b)(1)(i)	252	§ 1.743-1(j)(4)(i)(B)(2)	313
§ 1.707-3(b)(1)(ii)	252	§ 1.743-1(j)(4)(ii)(A)	314
§ 1.707-3(b)(2)	251	§ 1.751-1(a)(2)	294, 300
§ 1.707-3(c)	252	§ 1.751-1(b)(2)(ii)	230
§ 1.707-3(c)(1)	252	§ 1.751-1(b)(2)(iii)	229
§ 1.707-3(c)(2)	251	§ 1.751-1(b)(3)(ii)	230
§ 1.707-3(d)	251	§ 1.751-1(b)(3)(iii)	229
§ 1.707-3(f)	251, 253	§ 1.751-1(d)(1)	225
§ 1.708-1(b)(1)	320	§ 1.751-1(g)	234, 334
§ 1.708-1(c)(1)	328	§ 1.752-1	196
§ 1.708-1(c)(3)	330	§ 1.752-1(a)(1)	175
§ 1.708-1(c)(3)(i)	328, 330	§ 1.752-1(a)(2)	175
§ 1.708-1(c)(3)(ii)	329	§ 1.752-1(a)(4)	175
§ 1.708-1(d)(1)	330	§ 1.752-1(a)(4)(ii)	175
§ 1.708-1(d)(3)	331	§ 1.752-1(e)	196
§ 1.708-1(d)(3)(i)	331	§ 1.752-1(f)	196
§ 1.721-1(a)	28, 29, 264	§ 1.752-1(g)	196
§ 1.721-1(b)(1)	272, 279	§ 1.752-1(h)	290
§ 1.732-1(a)	232	§ 1.752-2	175
§ 1.732-1(b)	233	§ 1.752-2(a)	176, 197, 198
§ 1.732-1(c)	233	§ 1.752-2(b)(1)	176, 196
§ 1.732-1(c)(1)(ii)	234	§ 1.752-2(b)(3)	197
§ 1.732-1(c)(2)(ii)	234	§ 1.752-2(b)(3)(i)	176
§ 1.732-1(c)(4)	212, 233	§ 1.752-2(b)(3)(ii)(A)	197
§ 1.732-2(b)	313	§ 1.752-2(b)(3)(ii)(C)(1)(i)	197
§ 1.736-1(a)	318	§ 1.752-2(b)(3)(ii)(C)(2)	198
§ 1.736-1(a)(1)(ii)	314	§ 1.752-2(f)(1)	176, 196
§ 1.736-1(b)(1)	315	§ 1.752-2(f)(3)	177
§ 1.736-1(b)(2)	315	§ 1.752-2(f)(10)	197
§ 1.736-1(b)(3)	315	§ 1.752-3	196, 198, 199, 200
§ 1.736-1(b)(4)	315	§ 1.752-3(a)	178
§ 1.736-1(b)(5)	315	§ 1.752-3(a)(1)	178, 180
§ 1.736-1(b)(5)(i)	315	§ 1.752-3(a)(2)	178, 181
§ 1.736-1(b)(5)(ii)	315	§ 1.752-3(a)(3)	181, 200, 201
§ 1.736-1(b)(6)	317	§ 1.752-3(b)(1)	201
§ 1.736-1(b)(7)	315, 317	§ 1.752-3(c)	199, 200
§1.736-1(b)(7)	341	§ 1.752-7	175
§ 1.737-2(b)	330	§ 1.755-1	307
§ 1.742-1(a)	304	§ 1.755-1(a)(1)	307
§ 1.743-1(d)	304, 337, 339	§ 1.755-1(a)(3)	307
§ 1.743-1(d)(1)	305, 306, 310, 337, 339	§ 1.755-1(b)(1)(i)	307
§ 1.743-1(d)(2)	305	§ 1.755-1(b)(2)	340
§ 1.743-1(d)(3)	337	§ 1.755-1(b)(2)(i)	308, 310, 340
§ 1.743-1(f)	314	§ 1.755-1(b)(2)(i)(B)	308
§ 1.743-1(g)	313	§ 1.755-1(b)(2)(ii)	308, 338
§ 1.743-1(g)(1)	313	§ 1.755-1(b)(3)	340
§ 1.743-1(g)(2)	313	§ 1.755-1(b)(3)(i)	341
§ 1.743-1(g)(3)	313	§ 1.755-1(b)(3)(i)(A)	308
§ 1.743-1(j)(1)	312	§ 1.755-1(b)(3)(ii)	311, 340
§ 1.743-1(j)(3)(i)	312	§ 1.755-1(b)(3)(iv)	308
§ 1.743-1(j)(4)(i)(B)(1)	313	§ 1.755-1(c)	240, 313

Table of Treasury Regulations

§ 1.755-1(c)(1)(i)	215, 240	§ 1.1223-3(b)	42, 43
§ 1.755-1(c)(1)(ii)	215	§ 1.1223-3(f)(4)	46
§ 1.755-1(c)(2)(i)	215	§ 1.1361-1(l)	18
§ 1.755-1(c)(2)(ii)	215	§ 301.7701-2(a)(1)	22
§ 1.755-1(c)(6)	239	§ 301.7701-2(b)(1)	23
§ 1.761-1(d)	204	§ 301.7701-3	23
§ 1.1001-2(a)(1)	290	§ 301.7701-3(a)	23, 282
§ 1.1001-2(a)(4)(v)	290	§ 301.7701-3(b)(1)(i)	23
§ 1.1002-1(c)	27	§ 301.7701-3(b)(1)(ii)	23
§ 1.1223-3	38	§ 1469-5T(e)(3)(ii)	79

Table of Administrative Rulings and Materials

I.R.S. Priv. Ltr. Rul. 8405084, 72

Rev. Rul. 66-7, 1966-1 C.B. 188, 42, 43, 45, 321
Rev. Rul. 67-65, 1967-1 C.B. 168, 321
Rev. Rul. 69-124, 1969-1 C.B. 256, 20
Rev. Rul. 69-180, 1969-1 C.B. 183, 261
Rev. Rul. 74-71, 1974-1 C.B. 158, 90
Rev. Rul. 81-300, 1981-51 I.R.B. 11, 1981-2 C.B. 143, 257
Rev. Rul. 81-301, 1981-2 C.B. 144, 255, 257, 259
Rev. Rul. 84-53, 1984-1 C.B. 159, 38, 291
Rev. Rul. 84-111, 1984-2 C.B. 88, 321
Rev. Rul. 84-131, 1984-2 C.B. 37, 90
Rev. Rul. 87-57, 1987-2 C.B. 117, 65
Rev. Rul. 88-76, 1988-2 C.B. 360, 22
Rev. Rul. 89-7, 1989-1 C.B. 178, 89
Rev. Rul. 99-5, 1999-1 C.B. 434, 40, 42, 43, 270
Rev. Rul. 99-5, 1999-6 I.R.B. 8, 40
Rev. Rul. 99-6, 1999-1 C.B. 432, 321
Rev. Rul. 99-6, 1999-6 I.R.B. 6, 321
Rev. Rul. 99-43, 1999-4 C.B. 506, 127, 128
Rev. Rul. 2007-40, 2007-1 C.B. 1426, 262
Rev. Rul. 2008-12, 2008-1 C.B. 520, 90

Index

Accounting, partnership operations and, 47-95
  capital accounts, 81-86
    maintenance of, 82-86
    examples and explanations, 87-95
  losses, additional limits on, 68-81
    applying limitation, 80
    at-risk limitation, 73-77
    basis limitation, 69-73
    passive, 77-80
  methods, 66-68
  overview, 47-48
  partnership taxable income, 48-56
    computing, 49-50
    partners' distributive share, 54-56
    separately stated items, 51-54
    synthesis of, 56-59
  timing, importance of, 59-66
    partner's distributive share, taxable year of, 60
    partnership's taxable year, 59-66
Allocable cash basis items, 325
Allocations, partnership, 97-171
  alternate test, economic effect and, 108-111
    partial economic effect, 116-118
    qualified income offset provisions, 111-116
  economic effect, 100-101
    capital account requirement, 101-104
    deficit restoration obligation requirement, 105-107
    exceptions, 130
    liquidation requirement, 104-105
  economic equivalence, 118
  examples and explanations, 130-141, 162-171
  general matters and definitions, 146-147
  main test, synthesis of, 107-108
  overview, 97-99
  partner's interest, 128-130
  remedial allocation method, 157-162
  substantiality, 118-128
    general rule for, 119-121
    shifting tax consequences, 121-124
    strong likelihood, 126-128
    transitory allocations, 125-126
  traditional method, 147-153
    with curative allocations, 153-157
Alternate test, economic effect and, 108-111
  partial economic effect, 116-118
  qualified income offset provisions, 111-116
"Assets-over" transaction, 327
"Assets-up" transaction, 327
At-risk limitation, 73-77

Basis, 30-36
  inside, 32-36
  limitation, 69-73
  outside, 31-32
Built-in gain, 147
Built-in loss, 147

Capital accounts, 81-86
  maintenance of, 82-86
Capital interest, 264, 281
  payment with, 267-271
Ceiling rule, 148
Character, partnership formation and, 39-40
Check-the-box entity, 22-23
Choice of entity, partnership taxation and, 14-23
  check-the-box and, 22-23
  non-tax factors, 17-22
  tax factors, 17-22
Collectibles gain, 297
Curative allocation, 154, 166

Death of partner, 317-320
  impact in taxable year, 318-319
  income in respect of decedent, 319-320
Disguised payments
  for sales and services, 248-249
  for services, 249-250
Distributions and payments, partnership and, 203-241
  character issues and holding period, 222
  examples and explanations, 231-241

Index

Distributions and payments, partnership and (*continued*)
   "hot assets," distributions of, 222-230
   liquidating distributions, 216-221
   operating distributions, 204-208
   overview, 203-204
   property other than money, distributions of, 208-216

Economic effect, 100-101
   capital account requirement, 101-104
   deficit restoration obligation requirement, 105-107
   exceptions, 130
   liquidation requirement, 104-105
Economic equivalence, 118

Formation, partnership and, 25-46
   basis, 30-36
      inside, 32-36
      outside, 31-32
   character, importance of, 39-40
   examples and explanations, 44-46
   holding period, 37-39
   nonrecognition framework, 28-30
   overview, 25-27
   sole proprietorship, converting from, 40-43

Guaranteed payments, 254-256

Holding period, 37-39
"Hot assets," distributions of, 222-230

Inside basis, 32-36
"Interest-over" transaction, 327
Inventory items, 225, 293

Liabilities, partnership, 173-202
   determination of partner's share, 175
   examples and explanations, 194-202
   noncourse liabilities, 178-187
      excess, partner's share of, 181-187
      nonrecourse deductions, 179-180
      partnership minimum gain, 178-179
      partners' share of partnership minimum gain, 180-181
   nonrecourse deductions, allocating, 187-194
   overview, 173-175
   recourse liabilities, 176-178
Limited partnership, 3
Liquidating distributions, 84, 216-221, 314-317

Liquidation value, 274
Losses, additional limits on, 68-81
   applying limitation, 80
   at-risk limitation, 73-77
   basis limitation, 69-73
   passive, 77-80

Main test, synthesis of, 107-108
Medicare, 19

Net capital gain, 51
Noncourse liabilities, 178-187
   excess, partner's share of, 181-187
   nonrecourse deductions, 179-180
   partnership minimum gain, 178-179
   partners' share of partnership minimum gain, 180-181
Non-partner capacity, partner acting as, 245-254
   disguised sales, 250-254
   sales and services, disguised payments for, 248-249
   sales of property between partnership and partner, 247
   services, disguised payments for, 249-250
Nonrecourse deductions, 179-180

Old-Age and Survivors Insurance and Disability Insurance (OASDI), 19
Operating distributions, 204-208
Outside basis, 31-32

Partial economic effect, 116-118
Partners' distributive share, 54-56
   synthesis of, 56-59
   taxable year of, 60
Partnership
   allocations (*see* allocations, partnership)
   distributions and payments (*see* distributions and payments, partnership and)
   divisions, 330-331
   formation of (*see* formation, partnership and)
   liabilities (*see* liabilities, partnership)
   limited, 3
   mergers, 327-330
   nature of, 1-4
   partner's interest in, 128-130
   payments, between partners (*see* distributions and payments, partnership and; payments, partnership and its partner)
   state default rules, 2
   termination of, 320-321

Index

Partnership divisions, 330-331
Partnership interest, sale of, 287-314
   § 743 adjustments, 303-312
      life after, 312-314
   § 754 elections, 303-312
   transferee-partner, 300-302
   transferor-partner, 290-296
      collateral impacts of, 297-300
Partnership mergers, 327-330
Partnership minimum gain, 178, 189, 193
Partnership taxable income, 48-56
   computing, 49-50
   partners' distributive share, 54-56
   separately stated items, 51-54
   synthesis of, 56-59
Partnership taxation
   approaches, 4-6
   choice of entity, 14-23
      check-the-box and, 22-23
      nontax factors, 17-22
      tax factors, 17-22
   key themes, 10-14
   Subchapter K and, 6-10
Partner's interest, 128-130
Passive loss, 77-80
Payments, partnership and its partner, 243-262
   examples and explanations, 258-262
   guaranteed payments, 254-256
   non-partner capacity, partner acting as, 245-254
      disguised sales, 250-254
      sales and services, disguised payments for, 248-249
      sales of property between partnership and partner, 247
      services, disguised payments for, 249-250
   overview, 243-245
   section 707 synthesis, 256-258
Payments, service partners, 263-285
   capital interest, payment with, 267-271
   examples and explanations, 277-285
   overview, 263-267
   profits interest, payment with, 271-277
Phantom income, 56
Principal partner, 62
Profits interest, payment with, 271-277

Qualified income offset provisions, 111-116

Remedial allocation method, 157-162

§ 743 adjustments, sale of partnership interest and, 303-312
   life after, 312-314
§ 754 elections, sale of partnership interest and, 303-312
Service partners, payments to, 263-285
   capital interest, payment with, 267-271
   examples and explanations, 277-285
   overview, 263-267
   profits interest, payment with, 271-277
Sole proprietorship, partnership formation and, 40-43
Subchapter K, partnership taxation and, 6-10
Substantiality, partnership allocations and, 118-128
   general rule for, 119-121
   shifting tax consequences, 121-124
   strong likelihood, 126-128
   transitory allocations, 125-126
Syndicate, 68

Tax Cuts and Jobs Act (TCJA), 18
Tax shelter, 68
Termination of partnership, 320-321
Transferee-partner, sale of partnership interest and, 300-302
Transferor-partner, 290-296
   collateral impacts of, 297-300
   sale of partnership interest and, 290-296
      collateral impacts of, 297-300

Varying and shifting, partnership interests, 322-326